PEARSON　　　　　　　　　　ALWAYS LEARNING

Educational Psychology Reader

Compiled by Dr. Miranda D'Amico, Coordinator EDUC 210

D1364736

Cover Art: Courtesy of Digital Vision/Getty Images.

Copyright © 2013 by Pearson Learning Solutions
All rights reserved.

This copyright covers material written expressly for this volume by the editor/s as well as the compilation itself. It does not cover the individual selections herein that first appeared elsewhere. Permission to reprint these has been obtained by Pearson Learning Solutions for this edition only. Further reproduction by any means, electronic or mechanical, including photocopying and recording, or by any information storage or retrieval system, must be arranged with the individual copyright holders noted.

All trademarks, service marks, registered trademarks, and registered service marks are the property of their respective owners and are used herein for identification purposes only.

COPYRIGHT ACKNOWLEDGMENTS

"What Makes a Great Teacher?" by Erin Young, reprinted from *Phi Delta Kappan*, February 2009, by permission of Phi Delta Kappa.

"Reform: To What End?," by Mike Rose, reprinted from *Re-imagining School, Educational Leadership* 67, no.7, April 2010, by permission of the Association for Supervision and Curriculum Development (ASCD).

"Play and Social Interactions in Middle School," by Doris Bergen and Doris Pronin Fromberg, reprinted from *Phi Delta Kappan*, February 2009, by permission of Phi Delta Kappa.

"Why We Should Not Cut P.E.," by Stewart G. Trost and Hans Van der Mars, reprinted from *Health and Learning, Educational Leadership* 67, no.4, December 2009, by permission of the Association for Supervision and Curriculum Development (ASCD).

"Adolescent Decision Making: An Overview," by Bonnie Halpern-Felsher, reprinted from *The Prevention Researcher* 16, no.2, April 2009, by permission of The Prevention Researcher.

"What Educators Need to Know About Bullying Behaviors," by Sandra Graham, reprinted from *Phi Delta Kappan* 92, no.1, September 2010, by permission of Phi Delta Kappa.

"The Bridge to Character," by William Damon, reprinted from *Meeting Students Where They Are, Educational Leadership* 67, no.5, February 2010, by permission of the Association for Supervision and Curriculum Development (ASCD).

"Sam Comes to School: Including Students with Autism in Your Classroom," by Diana Friedlander, reprinted from *Clearing House: A Journal of Educational Strategies, Issues and Ideas*, 82, no.3, January 2009, by permission of Taylor & Francis.

"Universal Design In Elementary School and Middle School: Designing Classrooms and Instructional Practices to Ensure Access to Learning for All Students," by Margaret M. Flores, reprinted from *Childhood Education* 84, no.4 (summer 2008), by permission of Association for Childhood Education International.

"Social and Emotional Development of Gifted Children: Straight Talk," by Tracy L. Cross, reprinted from *Gifted Child Today* 32, no.2 (spring 2009), by permission of Sage Publications, Inc.

"Understanding Unconscious Bias and Unintentional Racism," by Jean Moule, reprinted from *Phi Delta Kappan*, January 2009, by permission of Phi Delta Kappa.

"Gender Matters in Elementary Education: Research Based Strategies to Meet the Distinctive Learning Needs of Boys and Girls," by Virginia Bonomo, reprinted from *Educational Horizons* (summer 2010), Pi Lambda Theta.

"Classroom Assessment and Grading to Assure Mastery," by John P. Lalley and J. Ronald Gentile, reprinted from *Theory Into Practice* 48, (2009), by permission of Taylor & Francis.

"To Find Yourself, Think for Yourself," by Barbara Fink Chorzempa and Laurie Lapidus, reprinted from *Teaching Exceptional Children*, Vol.41, no.3 (2009), by permission of the Council for Exceptional Children (CEC).

Copyright Acknowledgments

"What is Technology Education? A Review of the "Official Curriculum"," by Ryan A. Brown and Joshua W. Brown, reprinted from *The Clearing House* 83 no.2 (2010), by permission of Taylor & Francis.

"The Perils and Promises of Praise," by Carol S. Dweck, reprinted from *Early Intervention at Every Age* 65, no.2, October 2007, by permission of the Association for Supervision and Curriculum Development (ASCD).

"Should Learning Be Its Own Reward?" by Daniel T. Willingham, reprinted from *American Educator* (winter 2007-2008), by permission of the author.

"Beyond Content: How Teachers Manage Classrooms to Facilitate Intellectual Engagement for Disengaged Students," by Deborah L. Schussler, reprinted from *Theory Into Practice,* 48 (2009), by permission of Taylor & Francis.

"Classroom Management Strategies for Difficult Students: Promoting Change Through Relationships," by Mary Ellen Beaty-O'Ferrall et al., reprinted from the *Middle School Journal*, March 2010, by permission of National Middle School Association.

"Using Self Assessment to Chart Students' Paths," by Margaret Heritage, reprinted from the *Middle School Journal*, May 2009, by permission of National Middle School Association.

"Students' Reactions to a "No Failure" Grading System and How They Informed Teacher Practice," by Dick Corbett and Bruce Wilson, reprinted from *Theory Into Practice* 48 (2009), by permission of Taylor & Francis.

"Taking Play Seriously," by Robin Marantz Henig, reprinted by permission from the *New York Times Magazine*, February 17, 2008.

"The Moral Instinct," by Steven Pinker, reprinted by permission from the *New York Times Magazine*, January 13, 2008.

"What if the Secret to Success is Failure?" by Paul Tough, reprinted by permission from the *New York Times Magazine,* September 14, 2011.

"Beautiful Brains," by David Dobbs, reprinted by permission from *National Geographic Magazine*, October 2011.

"Students With Intellectual Disabilities Going to College? Absolutely!," by Harold L. Kleinert et al., reprinted from *Teaching Exceptional Children* 11 no.5, May 2012, by permission of the Council for Exceptional Children (CEC).

"Anatomy of a Scare," by Sharon Begley and Jeneen Interlandi, reprinted by permission from *Newsweek,* March 2, 2009.

"Helping Students with Disabilities Transition to College: 21 Tips for Students with LD and/or ADD/ADHD," by David J. Connor, reprinted from *Teaching Exceptional Children* 44, no.5 (2012), by permission of the Council for Exceptional Children (CEC).

"Addressing Test Anxiety," by Spencer J. Salend, reprinted from *Teaching Exceptional Children,* 44, no.2, November 2011, by permission of the Council for Exceptional Children (CEC).

"Prompting students to relax," reproduced from *Creating Inclusive Practices: Effective and Reflective Practices*, by Spencer J. Salend (2011), Pearson Education.

BRIEF TABLE OF CONTENTS

ARTICLE 1   *What Makes a Great Teacher?*   1

ARTICLE 2   *Reform: To What End?*   5

ARTICLE 3   *Play and Social Interaction in Middle Childhood*   11

ARTICLE 4   *Why We Should Not Cut P.E.*   17

ARTICLE 5   *Adolescent Decision Making*   23

ARTICLE 6   *What Educators Need to Know About Bullying
             Behaviors*   33

ARTICLE 7   *The Bridge to Character*   39

ARTICLE 8   *Sam Comes to School*   45

ARTICLE 9   *Universal Design in Elementary and Middle School*   51

ARTICLE 10   *Social and Emotional Development of Gifted Children:
             Straight Talk*   61

ARTICLE 11   *Understanding Unconscious Bias and
             Unintentional Racism*   65

ARTICLE 12   *Gender Matters in Elementary Education*   73

ARTICLE 13   *Classroom Assessment and Grading to Assure Mastery*   81

ARTICLE 14   *"To Find Yourself, Think for Yourself"*   91

ARTICLE 15   *What Is Technology Education? A Review of the
             "Official Curriculum"*   99

ARTICLE 16   *The Perils and Promises of Praise*   107

ARTICLE 17   *Should Learning Be Its Own Reward?*   113

ARTICLE 18 *Beyond Content: How Teachers Manage Classrooms to Facilitate Intellectual Engagement for Disengaged Students*   125

ARTICLE 19 *Classroom Management Strategies for Difficult Students: Promoting Change through Relationships*   135

ARTICLE 20 *Using Self-Assessment to Chart Students' Paths*   147

ARTICLE 21 *Students' Reactions to a "No Failure" Grading System and How They Informed Teacher Practice*   153

ARTICLE 22 *Taking Play Seriously*   161

ARTICLE 23 *The Moral Instinct*   173

ARTICLE 24 *What If the Secret to Success Is Failure?*   187

ARTICLE 25 *Teenage Brains*   199

ARTICLE 26 *Students with Intellectual Disabilities Going to College?* Absolutely!   207

ARTICLE 27 *Anatomy of a Scare*   221

ARTICLE 28 *Helping Students with Disabilities Transition to College*   229

ARTICLE 29 *Addressing Test Anxiety*   243

ARTICLE 1

What Makes a Great Teacher?

PDK Summit Offers Many Ideas

Great teachers do more than just advance student learning.
They also spread their own expertise to other teachers

ERIN YOUNG

In his office, Thomas Guskey has a poster of a photo from 1989. In the photo, one student is standing in front of four tanks in Tiananmen Square in Beijing. To Guskey, the photo symbolizes courage—the same courage that educators need to call upon.

Guskey, the keynote speaker at the 2008 Phi Delta Kappa Summit on High Performing Educators, urged attendees to become good leaders so they can lead the changes in education. But he warned that forging this path would take courage, similar to the courage displayed by the student in the photo as he stood before the tanks.

"Can you imagine the courage it took to do that?" Guskey asked. "That's the kind of stand you have to take. When you do that, it will instill courage in others."

Although educators may feel isolated when they try to create change in their organizations, they should remember that they have the knowledge base of the profession behind them, and they know what works and what doesn't, he said.

"We can't be satisfied with managing change; we have to lead change in our classrooms, schools, and districts," said Guskey, Distinguished Service Professor at Georgetown College in Georgetown, Kentucky. "We should use our knowledge base in good and

positive ways to help kids learn in new and positive ways."

The keynote address was part of last November's PDK summit in San Antonio, Texas, and began with a panel discussion about what makes a great teacher. Panelist Barnett Berry, president of the Center for Teaching Quality, argued that great teachers do more than just advance student learning—to be great, they must also spread their own expertise.

"It's not one, it's not the other," he said. "It's both."

Mary Clement, a panelist and associate professor of teacher education at Berry College in Georgia, said her list of what makes a great teacher has five elements: education, teacher preparation, hiring, quality induction, and ongoing support in a quality workplace.

"Who makes these things happen?" she asked. "We do. The people in this room. As one of my former professors always said, 'If not you, who? If not now, when?' We are professional educators. It's through our work, through our writing, our professionalism, and even our activism. This is how we can help to create and support the steps on my list that will make great teachers."

For panelist Sherie Williams, an assistant professor at Grand Valley State University in

1

Grand Rapids, Michigan, the definition of a great teacher is a teacher who creates a balance between curricular knowledge and the ability to build relationships with students. Research shows that students learn better when they have a relationship with the teacher.

"To make a wonderful, exemplary teacher, we have to help people learn skills to build relationships in the classroom," she said.

But great teachers are not all alike, Guskey said. He asked audience members to think of a great teacher in their lives. About half of the audience selected a teacher who was harsh, demanding, and authoritative, while the other half selected a teacher who was nurturing, warm, and endearing.

"In all of our research on effective teachers, it's been very difficult for us to come up with any set of personality characteristics that defines a highly effective teacher," he said.

To further complicate the issue, Guskey said, research in Tennessee has shown that a great teacher in one setting may be a poor teacher in another setting. Tennessee has a value-added accountability program that can show on average, for each teacher, how much the teacher's students have learned throughout the year.

"You would think we should be able to identify those teachers who are getting remarkable results, go and look at what they do, and just have everybody do the same," Guskey said. "But what they've discovered is it's not that easy."

Instead, he said, teachers who are effective in rural schools fail when they're put into urban schools, even though they're doing the same things they did in the rural schools, and vice versa.

"They've really called into question this notion of best practices," Guskey said. "Maybe best practices depend on where you are, the kind of students you're teaching, the kinds of communities in which they live, the cultural background they bring to school. Those things really need to be built in, because if what's effective depends on the kind of students who are in front of you, then we have to prepare our teacher candidates to really be familiar with those kids, what they're facing, and how they can be effective with them."

Participants at the 2008 Summit Said, A Great Teacher:

- Has the ability to be flexible, optimistic, self-reflective, progressive, and innovative;
- Must possess the ability to build relationships with students and teachers and have a passion for teaching;
- Excites a passion for learning in his or her students through skillful facilitation, using 21st-century tools;
- Goes beyond the classroom as a collaborator with colleagues;
- Wants to improve himself or herself by learning good instructional skills;
- Is someone who knows the curriculum and works well as part of a team;
- Builds relationships and facilitates lifelong learning;
- Collaborates with families, peers, and the community;
- Shows appreciation and enthusiasm for cultural differences;
- Inspires others to achieve their potential;
- Understands the complexity of the teaching and learning environment;
- Has consistently high expectations for all students;
- Recognizes and adapts when he or she isn't getting through to students;
- Addresses the needs of the whole child;
- Uses assessment to inform instructional decision making; and
- Gives back through mentoring.

He also reminded the audience that what students learn from great teachers often goes beyond what's in the lesson plan.

"We learn so much from teachers besides the things they set out to teach us," he said. "We carry forward those things for years and years afterward. How does that contribute to the effectiveness of teachers? More pressingly, how do we help young people entering teaching improve that and gather that so that when they become teachers, that can be a part of the quality they bring to their students?

"You really need to go home and become good leaders," Guskey said. "We have the knowledge base, but finding ways to put it into practice will take real courage at all levels."

ERIN YOUNG is managing editor of web and publications for *Phi Delta Kappa*.

ARTICLE 2

Reform: To What End?

We need a different orientation to school reform—
one that embodies a richer understanding of teaching and learning.

MIKE ROSE

This is an exciting time for education as the federal government, state houses, and private philanthropies are all focusing on school reform. A lot of good ideas are in the air—thoughtful proposals for ways to change things, to imagine a new kind of schooling in the United States.

The history of school reform has taught us, however, that good ideas can become one-dimensionalized as they move from conception through policy formation to implementation. Also, in the heat of reform, politics and polemics can become an end in themselves, a runaway train of reform for reform's sake. In addition, reforms can have unintended consequences. As a reform plays out in the complex, on-the-ground world of districts, school boards, and classrooms, it can lead to counterproductive practices. In the case of No Child Left Behind, for example, we saw the narrowing of the curriculum to prepare for high-stakes tests in math and language arts.

At this moment, when we're focusing so much attention on school reform and so much is possible, it would be good to step back and remind ourselves what we're ultimately trying to achieve. What is the goal of school reform? Most would agree it's to create rich learning environments, ones with greater scope and more equitable distribution than those we currently have.

As we reimagine school, some basic questions should serve as our touchstone for reform: What is the purpose of education in a democracy? What kind of people do we want to see emerge from U.S. schools? What is the experience of education when we do it well?

Happy as a Crab

One example of good teaching I saw comes from my book *Possible Lives: The Promise of Public Education in America* (Penguin, 1995/2006), an account of my travels across the United States to document effective public education. This 1st grade classroom in inner-city Baltimore has 30 students, all from modest to low-income households—the kinds of kids at the center of many school reforms.

As we enter the classroom, teacher Stephanie Terry is reading a book to her students, Eric Carle's *A House for Hermit Crab* (Simon and Schuster, 1991). Hermit crabs inhabit empty mollusk shells; as they grow, they leave their old shells to find bigger ones. In this story, a cheery hermit crab is searching for a more spacious home.

There's a glass case in the classroom with five hermit crabs—which Stephanie supplied—and 13 shells of various sizes. More than once during the year, students have noticed that a shell had been abandoned and that a larger one had suddenly become animated. As Stephanie reads the book, she pauses and raises broader questions about where the creatures live. This leads to an eager query from

Kenneth about where in nature you'd find her-mit crabs. "Well," says Stephanie, "let's see if we can figure that out."

She gets up and brings the case with the hermit crabs to the center of the room, takes the crabs out, and places them on the rug. One scuttles away from the group; another moves in a brief half circle; three stay put. While this is going on, Stephanie takes two plastic tubs from the cupboard above the sink and fills one with cold water from the tap and the other with warm water. Then she places both tubs side by side and asks five students, one by one, to put each of the crabs in the cold water. "What happens?" she asks. "They don't move," says Kenneth. "They stay inside their shells," adds Miko.

Stephanie then asks five other students to transfer the crabs to the tub of warm water. They do, and within seconds the crabs start to stir. Before long, the crabs are moving like crazy. "OK," says Stephanie. "What happens in the warmer water?" An excited chorus of students replies, "They're moving! They're walk-ing all over! They like it! They're happy like the crab in the book!" "So what does this sug-gest about where they like to live?" asks Stephanie.

That night, the students write about the experiment. Many are just learning to write, but Stephanie told them to write down their observations as best as they could, and that she would help them develop what they write. The next day, the students take turns standing in front of the class reading their reports.

Miko goes first: "I saw the hermit crab walking when it was in the warm water, but when it was in the cold water, it was not walking. It likes to live in warm water."

Then Romarise takes the floor, holding his paper way out in his right hand, his left hand in the pocket of his overalls: "(1) I observed two legs in the back of the shell; (2) I observed

that some of the crabs change [their] shell; (3) When the hermit crabs went into the cold water, they walked slow; (4) When the hermit crabs went into the warm water, they walked faster."

One by one, the rest of the students state their observations, halting at times as they try to figure out what they wrote, sometimes los-ing track and repeating themselves. But in a soft or loud voice, with a quiet sense of assurance or an unsteady eagerness, these 1st graders report on the behavior of the classroom's her-mit crabs, which have now become the focus of their attention.

There's a lot to say about Stephanie's mod-est but richly stocked classroom and the skill-ful way she interacts with the children in it. But I'll focus on two important points: what Stephanie demonstrates about the craft and art of teaching and the experience of learning that she generates for her class.

Growing Good Teachers

Everyone in the current reform environment acknowledges the importance of good teach-ing. But most characterizations of teaching miss the richness and complexity of the work. The teacher often becomes a knowledge-delivery mechanism preparing students for high-stakes tests.

Moreover, reform initiatives lack depth on how to develop more good teachers. There is encouragement of alternative pathways to qualification (and, often, animosity toward schools of education and traditional teacher training). There are calls for merit pay, with pay typically linked to test-score evidence of student achievement. There are general calls for additional professional development. And, of course, there is the widespread negative incentive: By holding teachers' "feet to the fire" of test scores, we will supposedly get more effort from teachers, although proponents of this point of view never articulate the social-psychological mechanisms by which the use of test scores will affect effort, motivation, and pedagogical skill.

But when you watch Stephanie, a very different image of the teacher emerges. She is knowledgeable and resourceful across multiple subject areas and is skillful at integrating them. She is spontaneous, alert for the teachable moment, and able to play out the fruits of that spontaneity and plan next steps incrementally as the activity unfolds. She believes that her students can handle a sophisticated assignment, and she asks questions and gives direction to guide them. Her students seem comfortable taking up the intellectual challenge.

What is interesting is that none of the current high-profile reform ideas would explain or significantly enhance Stephanie's expertise. Merit pay doesn't inspire her inventiveness; it doesn't exist in her district (although she would be happy to have the extra money, given that she furnished some classroom resources from her own pocket). Standardized test scores don't motivate her either. In fact, the typical test would be unable to capture some of the intellectual display I witnessed in her classroom. What motivates her is a complex mix of personal values and a drive for competence. These lead her to treat her students in certain ways and to continue to improve her skill.

A Human Capital Model

Some professional development programs are particularly good at capitalizing on such motivators. Several years earlier, Stephanie participated in a National Science Foundation workshop aimed at integrating science into the elementary school classroom. Teachers met for several weeks during the summer at the Baltimore campus of the University of Maryland, one of several regional training sites around the United States.

The teachers were, in Stephanie's words, "immersed in science"; they were reading, writing, observing presentations, and doing science themselves—all with an eye toward integrating science into their elementary school curriculums. The summer workshop extended through the year, as participating teachers observed one another's classrooms and came together on selected weekends to report on how they were incorporating science into teaching and give presentations themselves. "It gave us a different way," said Stephanie, "to think about science, teaching, and kids."

Because we are in the reimagining mode here, let me offer this: What if we could channel the financial and human resources spent on the vast machinery of high-stakes testing into a robust, widely distributed program of professional development? I don't mean the quick-hit, half-day events that so often pass for professional development, but serious, extended engagement of the kind that the National Science Foundation and the National Writing Project might offer—the sort of program that helped Stephanie conjure her rich lesson with the hermit crabs.

These programs typically take place in the summer (the National Writing Project runs for four weeks), although there are other options, including ones that extend through part of the school year. Teachers work with subject-matter experts; read, write, and think together; learn new material; hear from others who have successfully integrated the material into their classrooms; and try it out themselves.

Electronic media can be hugely helpful here, creating innovative ways for teachers to participate, bringing in people from remote areas, and further enabling all participants to regularly check in as they try new things. Such ongoing participation would be crucial in building on the intellectual community created during this kind of teacher enrichment program. All of this already exists, but we could expand it significantly if policymakers and reformers took into account this richer understanding of the teaching profession.

Although pragmatic lifestyle issues certainly come into play in choosing any profession, the majority of people who enter teaching do so for fairly altruistic reasons. They like working with kids. They like science, literature, or history and want to spark that appreciation in others. They see inequality and want to make a difference in young people's lives.

The kind of professional development I'm describing would appeal to those motives, revitalize them, and further realize them as a teacher's career progresses. Enriched, widely available professional development would substitute a human capital model of school reform for the current test-based technocratic one. And because such professional development would positively affect what teachers teach and how they teach it, it would have a more direct effect on student achievement.

Learning-Friendly Environments

For me, the bottom-line question is whether a particular reform will enable or restrict the kind of thing we see happening in Stephanie Terry's classroom. The hermit crab episode is, of course, drawn from a few days spent in just one classroom, but it represents some qualities I've seen again and again in good schools—K–12, urban or rural, affluent or poor. Let me delineate these qualities, and as you read them, ask yourself to what degree the reforms currently being proposed—from national standards to increased data collection to plans to turn around failing schools—would advance or impede their realization. Just as the representation of teaching is diminished in current education policy, so is the representation of learning. I have yet to see in policy initiatives a depiction of classroom life anywhere close to the one I just shared.

- *Safety.* The classrooms I visited created a sense of safety. There was physical safety, which for children in some locations is a serious consideration. But there was also safety from insult and diminishment. And there was safety to take risks, to push beyond what you can comfortably do at present—"coaxing our thinking along," as one student put it.
- *Respect.* Intimately related to safety is respect, a word I heard frequently during my travels. It means many things and operates on many levels: fair treatment, decency, an absence of intimidation, and beyond the realm of individual civility, a respect for the history, language, and culture of the people represented in the classroom. Respect also has an intellectual dimension. As one principal put it, "It's not just about being polite—even the curriculum has to convey respect. [It] has to be challenging enough that it's respectful."
- *Student responsibility for learning.* Even in classrooms that were run in a relatively traditional manner, students contributed to the flow of events, shaped the direction of discussion, and became authorities on their own experience and on the work they were doing. Think of Stephanie's students observing closely, recording what they saw, forming hypotheses, and reporting publically on their thinking. These classrooms were places of expectation and responsibility.
- *Intellectual rigor.* Teachers took students seriously as intellectual and social beings. Young people had to work hard, think things through, come to terms with one another—and there were times when such effort took students to their limits. "They looked at us in disbelief," said one New York principal, "when we told them they were intellectuals."

- *Ongoing support.* It is important to note that teachers realized such assumptions through a range of supports, guides, and structures: from the way they organized curriculum and invited and answered questions, to the means of assistance they and their aides provided (tutoring, conferences, written and oral feedback), to the various ways they encouraged peer support and assistance, to the atmosphere they created in the classroom—which takes us back to considerations of safety and respect.
- *Concern for students' welfare.* The students I talked to, from primary-grade children to graduating seniors, had the sense that these classrooms were salutary places—places that felt good to be in and that honored their best interests. They experienced this concern in various ways—as nurturance, social cohesion, the fostering of competence, recognition of growth, and a feeling of opportunity.

The foregoing characteristics made the rooms I visited feel alive. People were learning things, both cognitive and social; they were doing things, individually and collectively—making contributions, connecting ideas, and generating knowledge. To be sure, not everyone was engaged. And everyone, students and teachers, had bad days. But overall, these classrooms were exciting places to be—places of reflection and challenge, of deliberation and expression, of quiet work and public presentation. People were encouraged to be smart.

How directly do current reforms contribute to promoting such qualities?

The Most Important Question

In an important 18th-century essay on education, journalist Samuel Harrison Smith wrote that the free play of intelligence was central to a democracy and that individual intellectual growth was intimately connected to broad-scale intellectual development, to the "general diffusion of knowledge" across the republic.

As we consider what an altered school structure, increased technology, national standards, or other new reform initiatives might achieve, we should also ask the old, defining question, What is the purpose of education in a democracy? The formation of intellectually safe and respectful spaces, the distribution of authority and responsibility, the maintenance of high expectations and the means to attain them—all this is fundamentally democratic and prepares one for civic life. Teachers should regard students as capable and participatory beings, rich in both individual and social potential. The realization of that vision of the student is what finally should drive school reform in the United States.

MIKE ROSE is Professor of Social Research Methodology at the UCLA Graduate School of Education and Information Studies, Los Angeles, California. He is author of *Why School? Reclaiming Education for All of Us* (New Press, 2009).

ARTICLE 3

Play and Social Interaction in Middle Childhood

Play is vital for a child's emotional and cognitive development.
But social and technological forces threaten the kinds of play kids need most.

DORIS BERGEN AND DORIS PRONIN FROMBERG

Play is important to the optimum development of children during their middle childhood years. Unfortunately, though there is abundant research evidence showing that play supports young children's social, emotional, physical, and cognitive development, it has often been ignored or addressed only minimally (Fromberg and Bergen 2006). However, when young adults are asked to recall their most salient play experiences, they typically give elaborate and joyous accounts of their play during the ages of eight to 12 (Bergen and Williams 2008). Much of the play they report involves elaborate, pretense scripts conducted for a long duration at home, in their neighborhood, or in the school yard. The respondents report that they either personally played the roles or used small objects (action figures, cars, dolls) as the protagonists. They also report games with child-generated rules that they adapted during play. For example, they might have had bike-riding contests or played a baseball-like game that uses fence posts for bases and gives five-out turns to the youngest players. These young adults believed that their middle childhood play helped them learn "social skills," "hobbies," and often "career decisions" that influenced their later, adult experiences.

For many children, the opportunities for such freely chosen play are narrowing. Much of their play time at home has been lost to music, dance, or other lessons; participation on sport teams (using adult defined rules); and afterschool homework or test preparation sessions. At the same time, many schools, especially those considered to be poor performers, have reduced or eliminated recess (Pellegrini 2005). Often, the only outdoor time in the school day is the 10 to 15 minutes left from a lunch period, with rules such as "no running allowed." Thus, the importance of play during middle childhood must be reemphasized by educators who understand why it facilitates skilled social interaction, emotional regulation, higher cognitive processing, and creativity.

> **Many schools, especially those considered to be poor performers, have reduced or eliminated recess.**

Defining Middle Childhood Play

At any age, for an activity to count as play, it must be voluntary and self-organized. Children identify an activity as play when they choose it, but they define the same activity as work when an adult chooses it for them (King 1992). Play differs from exploring an object because such exploration answers the question: "What can it do?" In contrast, play answers the question: "What can I do with it?" (Hutt 1976).

Play in middle childhood continues to include practice play (repeating and elaborating on the same activities, often in the service of increasing skill levels), pretense (using symbolic means to envision characters and scenarios, using literary and other media experiences, as well as real-life experience sources), games with rules (revising existing games or making up elaborate games that have negotiated rules), and construction play (building and designing structures or artistic works). All of these types of play show increasing abilities to deal with cognitive, social, and emotional issues, as well as increases in physical skills.

The rules of play become apparent as children oscillate between negotiating the play scenarios and seamlessly entering into the activities, whether in selecting teams and rules for game play or borrowing media characters to "become" the pretend characters. Script theory, a kind of grammar of play (Fromberg 2002), outlines this oscillating collaborative process. The play process develops throughout the middle childhood years with 1) props becoming more miniaturized, 2) play episodes more extended, 3) language more complex, 4) themes more coherent, and 5) physical prowess more refined.

The Value of Middle Childhood Play

As the memories of young adults testify, play continues to be very valuable during the middle childhood years. Social and emotional competence, imagination, and cognitive development are fostered by many types of play.

- *Social and Emotional Competence.* Although adults may provide the space and objects with which their children play, during play children practice their power to self-direct, self-organize, exert self-control, and negotiate with others. Even when engaged in rough-and-tumble play, if it was a mutual decision, the children

involved demonstrate self-control (Reed and Brown 2000). Such experiences build confidence in deferring immediate gratification, persevering, and collaborating. Even when the play deals with hurtful themes, the children's intrinsic motivation ensures that the play serves a pleasurable, meaningful purpose for the players. For example, role playing threat, aggression, or death can help children deal with the reality of such issues.
- *Affiliation.* Children who negotiate their play together fulfill their need for affiliation. How to enter into play successfully is a negotiation skill, and it requires practice and the opportunity to be with peers. The loner child who stands on the outside of a group and observes may not have these skills; these children may meet their needs for affiliation by joining a gang or by resorting to bullying and violence.
- *Cognitive Development.* Middle childhood play fosters cognitive development. Children exercise their executive skills when planning pretense scripts, using symbols in games, designing constructions, and organizing games with rules. For example, in construction play with blocks, exploratory manipulation precedes the capacity to create new forms. These three dimensional constructions help older children develop the visual-spatial imagery that supports learning in mathematics, chemistry, and physics. Outdoor seasonal games that require eye-hand coordination and aiming—such as hopscotch, jump rope, tag, and baseball—also build the imagery that supports such concepts. Fantasy play can involve scripts that go on for days and become extremely elaborate. Sociodramatic play is a form of collaborative oral playwriting and editing, which contributes to the writer's sense of audience (Fromberg 2002). Thus, scripts often are written to guide the play.

Humor is very evident in middle childhood play, and although some is "nonsense" humor, most involves cognitive incongruity, which demonstrates what children know. That is, by using puns, jokes, exaggerations, and other word play, they show their knowledge of the world and gain power and delight in transforming that knowledge in incongruous ways. Much of this joking is designed to shock adults, but it also demonstrates children's increasing knowledge of the world. Playful use of language also shows up in "Pig Latin" and other code languages, which both include the play group and exclude others. Learning and performing "magic" tricks is also a delight and requires understanding the laws of objects and thus how to appear to bypass those laws.

Most humor involves cognitive incongruity, which demonstrates what children know

---

- *Imagination and Creativity*. Children dramatize roles and scenarios with miniature animals, toy soldiers, and media action figures, using themes from their experiences, including "playing school." Some urban children might dramatize cops and gangs. Children in both urban and rural areas engage in such pretense, trying on a sense of power and independence, by imagining "what if" there were no adult society. As they try roles and pretend possible careers, they seek privacy from adults during much of this play, preferring tree houses, vacant lots, basements, or other "private" spaces. Symbolic games, such as Monopoly (using a board or online forms), as well as other computer or board games, add to the development of social learning and competence as children

what about video-game?

increasingly become precise about following the rules of the game.

When children have had opportunities to practice pretense and use their imaginations, researchers have found that they're more able to be patient and perseverant, as well as to imagine the future (Singer and Singer 2006). Being able to imagine and role play a particular career, rent and furnish an apartment, and negotiate other aspects of daily living makes those actions seem less daunting later on.

Contemporary Middle Childhood Play

Play for children in this age group has changed. Today, there are virtual, technology-enhanced play materials, a constriction of play space from the neighborhood to one's own home and yard, and the actual loss of free time and school time to devote to active play.

- *Technology*. For children in the middle childhood years, virtual reality technology now provides three dimensional interactive games, such as Nintendo's Wii, which uses hand-held devices that can detect motion. These interactive games may be so engaging that children, mainly boys, abandon other activities that build negotiation skills and social competence with other children. Children also increasingly "instant message," creating abbreviation codes—a form of power—and demonstrate their deepening digital literacy. In addition, they listen to music on iPods, play virtual musical instruments, and make virtual friends with whom they interact. This period of childhood affords different opportunities for children in less affluent families, however, resulting in a widening gap in types of technology-enhanced play materials and experiences among children from different socioeconomic levels. For example, though children can initially access some web sites without cost, devices and software require purchases that are seductive, with consoles and accessories rising in cost.

Gender roles also are affected by technology. Virtual reality computer games for girls, such as Mattel's Barbie Girls, reinforce stereotypes. Boys are especially interested in virtual action games.

- *Spaces for Play.* Many parents are reluctant to allow their children to range far in their neighborhoods for the kinds of social experiences that were common for earlier generations. This could be caused by frequent media reports of potential dangers (Louv 2008). Parents may see city environments as too dangerous, and suburban parents may believe that homes are too far apart to allow children to walk to friends' houses or gather in neighborhood outdoor areas.

Suburban parents may believe that homes are too far apart to allow children to walk to friends' houses.

- *Time for Freely Chosen Play.* Administrators and teachers pressured to increase academic performance often reduce recess to a short period or omit it altogether because they believe this time is "wasted" or that it just will be a time for children to engage in bullying or other unacceptable behaviors. They also may fear lawsuits because of perceived dangers in freely chosen play, as indicated by prohibitions against running. In spite of research indicating that attention to school tasks may be greater if periods of recess are interspersed (Opie and Opie 1976), some adults don't seem to realize the potential of play as a means of supporting academic learning. Thus, time for play has

been reduced both in the home and school environments.

Adult Facilitation of Play

Because middle childhood play is so valuable for social, emotional, cognitive, and physical development and because some trends seem to prevent play's full elaboration and development during these years, adults must become advocates for play and facilitators of play in middle childhood. There are a number of ways they can do this.

- *Providing Play Resources.* When adults provide indoor and outdoor space and materials, children can adapt and use them creatively. The best kinds of materials have more than a single use but can be modified by interaction with others and elaborated with imagination.
- *Engaging in Play Interaction.* When adults provide real choices, children can build the trust they need to cope with solving physical problems and negotiating emerging interpersonal play. Adults should appreciate process and effort without judging outcomes. They might assist less play-competent children's interactions by offering relevant materials to help their children be invited into pretense games that other children have started.
- *Assessing Play Competence.* Educators, in particular, often find that most children comply with their suggestions about play activities, but there may be one or two who do not appear to be participating or, on closer observation, appear to comply, but in their own ways. Teachers, in particular, need to appreciate the multiple ways in which children may represent experiences and display a sense of playfulness. In addition, teachers' assessments should also include observations of children's play competence, especially as it relates to development of imaginative and creative idea generation.

14

- *Supporting Gender Equity.* Gender equity and children's aspirations are affected by sanctions and warrants. For example, boys have traditionally dominated play involving 3-D constructions, though some girls are now participating in Lego Robotics teams. To make girls more likely to participate, teachers should place themselves near 3-D construction areas or planned "borderwork" (Thorne 1993). Teachers should be sure to provide materials and equipment that do not have gender-suggestive advertising (Goldstein 1994). In this way, all children can be encouraged to have greater expectations for themselves.

Summary

Play has always been important in middle childhood, but its forms have changed with society and, in some cases, its very existence has been threatened. Parents and educators can facilitate aspects of play that support emotional, social, cognitive, and creative growth. To understand the importance of play for these children, they only have to recall the salience of their own play during this age period.

References

Bergen, Doris, and Elizabeth Williams. "Differing Childhood Play Experiences of Young Adults Compared to Earlier Young Adult Cohorts Have Implications for Physical, Social, and Academic Development." Poster presentation at the annual meeting of the Association for Psychological Science, Chicago, 2008.

Fromberg, Doris P. *Play and Meaning in Early Childhood Education*. Boston: Allyn & Bacon, 2002.

Fromberg, Doris P., and Doris Bergen. *Play from Birth to 12*. New York: Routledge, 2006.

Goldstein, Jeffrey H., ed. *Toys, Play, and Child Development*. New York: Cambridge University Press, 1994.

Hutt, Corinne. "Exploration and Play in Children." In *Play: Its Role in Development and Evolution*, ed. Jerome S. Bruner, Alison Jolly, and Kathy Sylva, 202–215. New York: Basic Books, 1976.

King, Nancy. "The Impact of Context on the Play of Young Children." In *Reconceptualizing the Early Childhood Curriculum*, ed. Shirley A. Kessler and Beth Blue Swadener, 42–81. New York: Teachers College Press, 1992.

Louv, Richard. *Last Child in the Woods: Saving Our Children from Nature-Deficit Disorder*. Chapel Hill, N.C.: Algonquin Books, 2008.

Opie, Iona A., and Peter M. Opie. "Street Games: Counting-Out and Chasing." In *Play: Its Role in Development and Evolution*, ed. Jerome S. Bruner, Alison Jolly, and Kathy Sylva, 394–412. New York: Basic Books, 1976.

Pellegrini, Anthony D. *Recess: Its Role in Education and Development*. Mahwah, N.J.: Lawrence Erlbaum Associates, 2005.

Reed, Tom, and Mac Brown. "The Expression of Care in Rough and Tumble Play of Boys." *Journal of Research in Childhood Education* 15 (Fall-Winter 2000): 104–116.

Singer, Dorothy G., and Jerome L. Singer. "Fantasy and Imagination." In *Play from Birth to 12: Contexts, Perspectives, and Meanings*, ed. Doris P. Fromberg and Doris Bergen, 371–378. New York: Routledge, 2006.

Thorne, Barrie. *Gender Play: Girls and Boys in School*. New Brunswick, N.J.: Rutgers University Press, 1993.

Doris Bergen is distinguished professor of educational psychology at Miami University, Oxford, Ohio, and co-director of the Center for Human Development, Learning, and Technology. With Doris Pronin Fromberg, she co-edited the book, *Play from Birth to Twelve,* 2nd ed. (Routledge, 2006).

Doris Pronin Fromberg is a professor of education and past chairperson of the Department of Curriculum and Teaching at Hofstra University, Hempstead, New York.

ARTICLE 4

Why We Should Not Cut P.E.

*Eliminate physical education to increase time for reading and math, the theory goes,
and achievement will rise. But the evidence says otherwise.*

Stewart G. Trost and Hans van der Mars

Thinking of cutting physical education? Think again. Even as we bemoan children's sedentary lifestyles, we often sacrifice school-based physical education in the name of providing more time for academics. In 2006, only 3.8 percent of elementary schools, 7.9 percent of middle schools, and 2.1 percent of high schools offered students daily physical education or its equivalent for the entire school year (Lee, Burgeson, Fulton, & Spain, 2007).

We believe this marked reduction in school-based physical activity risks students' health and can't be justified on educational or ethical grounds. We'll get to the educational grounds in a moment. As to ethical reasons for keeping physical activity part of our young people's school days, consider the fact that childhood obesity is now one of the most serious health issues facing U.S. children (Ogden et al., 2006).

School-based physical education programs engage students in regular physical activity and help them acquire skills and habits necessary to pursue an active lifestyle. Such programs are directly relevant to preventing obesity. Yet they are increasingly on the chopping block.

The Assumption: Time in the Gym Lowers Test Scores

No Child Left Behind (NCLB) has contributed to this trend. By linking federal funding to schools' adequate yearly progress in reading and mathematics, NCLB has created an environment in which such classes as physical education, music, and art are viewed as nonessential and secondary to the academic mission of the school.

According to a national study conducted by the Center on Education Policy in 2007, since the passing of NCLB in 2002, 62 percent of elementary schools and 20 percent of middle schools have significantly increased the instructional time they allocate to reading/language arts and math. To accommodate such increases, 44 percent of school districts reported cutting time in such areas as social studies, art, music, physical education, and recess. On average, schools reduced the time allotted to these subjects by more than 30 minutes per day.

But is the assumption that eliminating physical education improves academic performance sound? Not according to the evidence. A comprehensive review of the research shows that academic performance remains unaffected by variations in time allocated to physical education. In fact, in studies that did show physical activity had an effect, increasing instructional time for physical education resulted in *improvements* in academic performance.

The Evidence: P.E. Does Not Hurt— and May Help

In study after study, researchers have concluded that devoting more instructional time to physical education or another in-school physical activity program does not harm academics. Five prominent studies show that students' achievement levels remained unchanged when schools increased or reduced instructional time for physical education.

- Researchers in Australia studied 350 5th graders in seven schools throughout the country. They increased instructional time for physical education for some students by 210 minutes per week. After 14 weeks, there were no significant differences in math or reading skills between students who received additional physical education instruction and those who completed the standard three 30-minute periods of physical education per week (Dwyer, Coonan, Leitch, Hetzel, & Baghurst, 1983).
- A study in California investigated the effect on academic achievement of an intensive two-year program in seven schools that more than doubled the amount of time elementary students spent in physical education. Neither overall academic achievement nor achievement in language arts and reading were adversely affected (Sallis et al., 1999).
- A study of 214 6th graders in Michigan found that students enrolled in physical education had grades and standardized test scores similar to those of students who were not taking physical education, despite receiving nearly an hour less of daily instruction in core academic subjects (Coe, Pivarnik, Womack, Reeves, & Malina, 2006).
- A study involving 287 4th and 5th graders in British Columbia evaluated the effects of daily classroom physical activity sessions on academic performance. Ten elementary schools participated. Although students who attended schools implementing this program spent approximately 50 more minutes per week in physical activity, their standardized test scores in mathematics,

reading, and language arts were equivalent to those of students in control schools (Ahamed et al., 2007).
- A study involving more than 500 Virginia elementary schools examined the effect of *decreasing* time for physical education, music, and art on academic performance. Reducing or eliminating the time students spent in these content areas did not increase academic achievement (Wilkins et al., 2003).

In addition, three major studies indicate that when students participate in physical education, achievement is positively affected for some groups.

- A Canadian study examined the effects on 546 elementary students' academic performance of one additional hour per day of physical education. Students in grades 2 through 6 who received additional physical education earned better grades in French, mathematics, English, and science than did students who received the standard one period per week (Shephard, 1996).
- Studying 311 4th grade students in two schools, Tremarche, Robinson, and Graham (2007) found that students who received 56 or more hours of physical education per school year scored significantly higher on Massachusetts' standardized tests in English and language arts than did comparable students who received 28 hours of physical education per year. There were no significant differences on mathematics scores.
- A longitudinal study by the Centers for Disease Control and Prevention followed two national samples involving 5,316 students from kindergarten to 5th grade. Girls who participated in physical education for 70 or more minutes per week had significantly higher achievement scores in mathematics and reading than

did girls who were enrolled in physical education for 35 or fewer minutes per week. Among boys, greater exposure to physical education was neither positively nor negatively associated with academic achievement (Carlson et al., 2008).

The evidence is clear. Decreasing time for physical education does not significantly improve academic performance. Consequently, in an education climate that demands evidence-based instructional practices, the policy of reducing or eliminating school-based physical activity programs cannot be justified.

The Link Between Physical Fitness and Academic Performance

The case for sacrificing physical education is further eroded by studies reporting a significant positive relationship between physical fitness and academic performance. In a nutshell, physically active, fit youth are more likely to have better grades and test scores than their inactive counterparts.

National health surveys involving large representative samples of children and teens from the United States, Australia, Iceland, Hong Kong, and the United Kingdom have reported statistically significant positive correlations between physical activity and academic performance (Trost, 2007). One study analyzed data from nearly 12,000 U.S. high school students. Students who reported participating in school-based physical activities or playing sports with their parents were 20 percent more likely than their sedentary peers to earn an *A* in math or English (Nelson & Gordon-Larsen, 2006).

An analysis of fitness testing results from more than 800,000 students in California revealed a significant positive correlation between physical fitness achievement and performance on state achievement tests in

reading and mathematics (Grissom, 2005). And in a study conducted in Illinois, children who performed well on two measures of physical fitness tended to score higher on state reading and math exams than low physical performers, regardless of gender or socioeconomic status (Castelli, Hillman, Buck, & Erwin, 2007).

Although the relationship between physical activity and academic performance requires more research, available evidence suggests that the academic mission of schools may be better served by providing *more* opportunities for physical activity. In fact, controlled studies strongly suggest that engaging in physical activity throughout the school day makes students more focused and ready to learn.

Research has shown that aerobic exercise can improve memory and executive functioning in school-age youth, especially those who are overweight (Buck, Hillman, & Castelli, 2008; Davis et al., 2007). Drawing on a meta-analysis of more than 40 studies that looked at how engaging in regular physical training affects cognition, Sibley and Etnier (2003) concluded that regular physical activity significantly improves multiple categories of cognitive function in children and adolescents. Researchers found improvements in perceptual skills, IQ, scores on verbal and mathematics tests, concentration, memory, achievement (as measured by a combination of standardized test scores and grades), and academic readiness.

Giving students breaks for physical activity throughout the school day can significantly increase on-task behavior. A study conducted in North Carolina evaluated the effects of a classroom-based program that, for 12 weeks, gave students daily 10-minute breaks for organized physical activity. Researchers observed students in grades K through 5 for 30 minutes before and after each break. On average, the activity breaks increased on-task behavior by 8 percent. Among students who tended to be least focused in class, the breaks improved on-task behavior by 20 percent (Mahar et al., 2006).

Researchers don't understand well the physiological mechanisms responsible for enhancements in cognition related to physical activity. However, emerging evidence from neuroscience suggests that regular physical activity promotes the growth of new brain cells, stimulates formation of blood vessels in the brain, and enhances synaptic activity or communication among brain cells (Hillman, Erickson, & Kramer, 2008).

What We Can Safely Conclude

The research on the relationship between physical education and academic performance does have limitations. For one, the majority of studies have been conducted at the elementary school level; we need additional studies in middle and high schools. In addition, most studies use the *amount* of time spent in physical education as the key independent variable, without considering the *quality* of instruction. Studies of the effects of in-school physical activity on cognitive functioning also often lack what researchers call ecological validity (transferability of findings). For example, research findings may not transfer to school physical education settings if a study was conducted in a lab or if the type, amount, or intensity of physical activity in the study differed greatly from a typical session in a school gymnasium.

Perhaps most important, we know too little about the effect of in-school physical education on academic performance among students at the highest risk for obesity, including low-income children and those from black, Latino, American Indian, and Pacific Islander backgrounds.

Notwithstanding these limitations, we believe the evidence is sufficiently robust to enable us to draw the following conclusions:

- Decreasing (or eliminating) the time allotted for physical education in favor of traditional academic subjects does not lead to improved academic performance.
- Increasing the number of minutes students spend per week in physical education will not impede their academic achievement.
- Increasing the amount of time students spend in physical education may make small positive contributions to academic achievement, particularly for girls.
- Regular physical activity and physical fitness are associated with higher levels of academic performance.
- Physical activity is beneficial to general cognitive functioning.

Implications for Policymakers

Keeping in mind that overweight and obesity are compromising the health of one-third of U.S. students, we see three clear implications of these conclusions.

CONCLUSION 1: *Policymakers must stop trying to justify cuts to physical education on the grounds that such cuts will strengthen school achievement or, ultimately, the economy.*

To be sure, a strong academic education contributes to the future economic health of our society. However, the nation's economic and public health are linked in a delicate balance. It is indefensible to support an education system based primarily on promoting economic productivity in people who will likely be too unhealthy to enjoy whatever benefits come their way.

CONCLUSION 2: *Policymakers, school administrators, and teachers should stop arguing over whether physical education is essential.*

Physical education is now crucial for promoting and increasing physical activity for children and youth. Considering the amount of time students spend in school and the generally accepted mandate of schools to model wholesome life choices, the negative effect of keeping students sedentary all day seems obvious. Although school physical education programs cannot single-handedly reverse the trend of weight gain in youth, they can create conditions that help students learn the importance of leading physically active lives—and encourage them to lead such lives.

CONCLUSION 3: *School administrators must aggressively make room for physical education.*

Administrators may feel hamstrung because of the current climate, but they can promote healthier schools by recognizing the barriers to out-of-school physical activity that exist for many students, working with physical education staff to maximize opportunities for physical activity for all students, and monitoring what goes on in physical education classes.

Those who help shape the education of children can no longer ignore the evidence about physical activity and academics, as well as the serious negative health consequences of further reducing physical education. Physical activity is crucial to shaping future generations of healthy people. It has a legitimate claim to part of the school day.

References

Ahamed,Y., Macdonald, H., Reed, K., Naylor, P. J., Liu-Ambrose,T., & McKay, H. (2007). School-based physical activity does not compromise children's academic performance. *Medicine and Science in Sports and Exercise, 39*(2), 371–376.

Buck, S. M., Hillman, C. H., & Castelli, D. M. (2008).The relation of aerobic fitness to stroop task performance in preadolescent children. *Medicine and Science in Sports and Exercise, 40*(1), 166–172.

Carlson, S. A., Fulton, J. E., Lee, S. M., Maynard, M., Brown, D. R., Kohl, III, H. W., & Dietz, W. H. (2008). Physical education and academic achievement in elementary school: Data from the early childhood longitudinal study. *American Journal of Public Health, 98*(4), 721–727.

Castelli, D. M., Hillman, C. H., Buck, S. M., & Erwin, H. E. (2007). Physical fitness and academic achievement in third- and fifth-grade students. *Journal of Sport and Exercise Psychology, 29*(2), 239–252.

Center on Education Policy. (2007). *Choices, changes, and challenges: Curriculum and instruction in the NCLB era.* Washington, DC: Author.

Coe, D. P., Pivarnik, J. M., Womack, C. J., Reeves, M. J., & Malina, R. M. (2006). Effect of physical education and activity levels on academic achievement in children. *Medicine and Science in Sports and Exercise, 38*(8), 1515–1519.

Davis, C. L., Tomporowski, P. D., Boyle, C. A., Waller, J. L., Miller, P. H., Naglieri, J. A., & Gregoski, M. (2007). Effects of aerobic exercise on overweight children's cognitive functioning: A randomized controlled trial. *Research Quarterly for Exercise and Sport, 78*(5), 510–519.

Dwyer,T., Coonan, W. E., Leitch, D. R., Hetzel, B. S., & Baghurst, R. A. (1983). An investigation of the effects of daily physical activity on the health of primary school students in South Australia. *International Journal of Epidemiology, 12*(3), 308–313.

Grissom, J. B. (2005). Physical fitness and academic achievement. *Journal of Exercise Physiology Online, 8*(1), 11–25.

Hillman, C. H., Erickson, K. I., & Kramer, A. F. (2008). Be smart, exercise your heart: Exercise effects on brain and cognition. *National Review of Neuroscience, 9*(1), 58–65.

Lee, S. M., Burgeson, C. R., Fulton, J. E., & Spain, C. G. (2007). Physical education and physical activity: Results from the School Health Policies and Programs Study 2006. *Journal of School Health, 77*(8), 435–463.

Mahar, M. T., Murphy, S. K., Rowe, D. A., Golden, J., Shields, A. T., & Raedeke, T. D. (2006). Effects of a classroom-based program on physical activity and on-task behavior. *Medicine and Science in Sports and Exercise, 38,* 2086–2094.

Nelson, M. C., & Gordon-Larsen, P. (2006). Physical activity and sedentary behavior patterns are associated with selected adolescent health risk behaviors. *Pediatrics, 117,* 1281–1290.

Ogden, C. L., Carroll, M. D., Curtin, L. R., McDowell, M. A., Tabak, C. J., & Flegal, K. M. (2006). Prevalence of overweight and obesity in the United States, 1999–2004. *Journal of the American Medical Association, 295*(13), 1549–1555.

Sallis, J. F., McKenzie, T. L., Kolody, B., Lewis, M., Marshall, S., & Rosengard, P. (1999). Effects of health-related physical education on academic achievement: Project SPARK. *Research Quarterly for Exercise and Sport, 70*(2), 127–134.

Shephard, R. J. (1996). Habitual physical activity and academic performance. *Nutrition Reviews, 54*(4), S32–S36.

Sibley, B. A., & Etnier, J. L. (2003). The relationship between physical activity and cognition in children: A meta-analysis. *Pediatric Exercise Science, 15,* 243–256.

Tremarche, P., Robinson, E., & Graham, L. (2007). Physical education and its effects on elementary testing results. *Physical Educator, 64*(2), 58–64.

Trost, S. G. (2007). *Active education: Physical education, physical activity and academic performance* (Research Brief). San Diego, CA: Robert Wood Johnson Foundation Active Living Research. Available: www.activelivingresearch.com/alr/alr/files/Active_Ed.pdf

Wilkins, J. L., Graham, G., Parker, S., Westfall, S., Fraser, R. G., & Tembo, M. (2003). Time in the arts and physical education and school achievement. *Journal of Curriculum Studies, 35,* 721–734.

STEWART G. TROST is Associate Professor in the Department of Nutrition and Exercise Sciences at Oregon State University in Corvallis; stewart.trost@oregonstate.edu.

HANS VAN DER MARS is Professor in the College of Teacher Education and Leadership at Arizona State University in Mesa; hans.vandermars@asu.edu.

ARTICLE 5

Adolescent Decision Making:

An Overview

> "Adolescence is a time of great changes that result in desire for autonomy
> in decision making, and by mid to late adolescence, most individuals have the cognitive
> abilities to understand and judge risks. Nevertheless, adolescents may lack the
> psychosocial traits required to consistently make and act upon mature decisions."

BONNIE HALPERN-FELSHER, PH.D.

Adolescence is a time of great and rapid cognitive, psychological, social, emotional, and physical changes. These changes result in a more adult-like appearance, an increased ability to think abstractly, greater need for autonomy and independence, increased social and peer comparison, and greater peer affiliation. These changes typically translate into adolescents' desire to participate in, and eventually lead, their decision making. Learning to make decisions, experiencing related positive and negative consequences, and learning from these outcomes is an important developmental task.

In general, with some cultural variation, adolescents are afforded opportunities to make decisions in a wide range of areas such as friendship, academics, extracurricular involvement, and consumer choices. Simultaneously, their ability to make competent decisions is sometimes called into question because adolescence is also often a time of engagement in risky behaviors, such as using alcohol, tobacco and other drugs, or engaging in risky sexual activity. Often these behaviors represent simple adolescent experimentation; while for a few adolescents these early behaviors represent the first in a line of more harmful behaviors.

This article will provide an overview of adolescent decision making, including definitions of competent decision making, descriptions of decision-making models, and the physical, cognitive, social and emotional influences on adolescent decision making. This article will also discuss implications of adolescent decision making that are relevant to health educators, healthcare providers, policy makers, and adolescent researchers.

Definitions of Competent Decision Making

Definitions of what constitutes a competent decision vary widely. It is important to note that competent decision making refers to the *process* of *how* the decision was made. Competent decision making is *not* determined by the actual behavior or outcome. For example, while adults might disagree with an adolescent's decision to have sex, an adolescent can still demonstrate decision-making competence by showing that he or she has considered and weighed all of the options (e.g., have sex, not have sex, just kiss), risks (e.g., getting pregnant, feeling guilty), benefits (e.g., pleasure), and other key components involved in the decision-making process, as described next.

23

Since adults are generally considered competent in the eyes of the law, many have used adults as the gold standard against which to compare adolescents. Other definitions of decision-making competence employ a model against which to compare individuals. For example, the legal standards of informed consent stipulate that decisions must be made knowingly; that one must understand all procedures, related risks, and alternative courses of action; and that a person's choice must be made without substantial input or control from others (e.g., Gittler, Quigley-Rick, & Saks, 1990; Poythress, Lexcen, Grisso, & Steinberg, 2006).

Models of Decision Making

Normative models of decision making are commonly used in theory, empirical investigation, and policy to describe competent decision making. These models describe the most common steps that one should take in order to make the most rational decision for the individual. As noted above, competent decision making is defined as the process, not the ultimate decision. Normative models encompass elements similar to the legal definition, with the components articulated in terms of five general processes: 1) identifying all possible decision options; 2) identifying the possible consequences of each option, including all possible related risks and benefits; 3) evaluating the desirability of each consequence; 4) assessing the probability or likelihood that each particular consequence will actually occur, should that course of action be adopted; and 5) combining all information using a decision rule, resulting in the identification of the best option or action. It is important to note that in this decision-making process, it is expected that one not only consider engaging in a particular action, but that one also considers the consequences associ-

ated with *not* choosing an event or behavior. This is especially important for adolescents, for whom often the choice is between engaging or not engaging in a risky behavior, both of which have positive and negative outcomes for youth (Beyth-Marom, Austin, et al., 1993; Beyth-Marom & Fischhoff, 1997).

These models of decision making have been typically used to explain engagement in health-compromising or health-promoting behavior, such as tobacco use, alcohol use, sexual behavior, seatbelt use, and so on. Many theories of health behavior have incorporated elements of these normative decision-making models, including the Theory of Reasoned Action (Ajzen, 1985), Theory of Planned Behavior (e.g., Fishbein & Ajzen, 1975), and the Health Belief Model (e.g., Rosenstock, 1974). While specific model components vary across theories, in general these theories assume that adoption of health promoting and health compromising behaviors are the result of a deliberative, rational, and analytical process, with the outcome of this process leading to increased or decreased likelihood of performing the behavior. Specifically, as shown in Figure 1, intentions to engage and actual engagement in health-related behavior is determined by an individual's:

1. assessment concerning both the potential positive and negative consequences of their actions or inactions, such as feeling more relaxed after smoking a cigarette or getting into an accident if driving drunk;
2. perceptions of their vulnerability to those consequences, such as the perceived percent chance that one would get pregnant after having unprotected sex;
3. desire to engage in the behavior despite potential consequences (e.g., I know that I can get an STD from having sex, but it is more important to me to keep my relationship); and

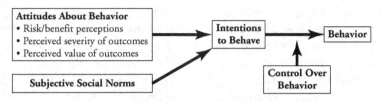

FIGURE 1   General Model of Health-Related Decision Making

4. perceptions of the extent to which similar others are engaging in the behavior (e.g., most of my friends are using marijuana, so why can't I?).

While these decision making models have been extremely useful in predicting a number of behaviors, the application of these models is limited when used to explain behaviors involving more irrational, impulsive, or socially undesirable behavior, such as tobacco use. Importantly, when placed within a developmental framework, decision making must be defined as much more than a series of complex cognitive, analytic, and rational processes. Instead, for an adolescent, the process of decision making must be immersed within the set of psychosocial, contextual, emotional, and experiential changes that define adolescence (e.g., Cauffman & Steinberg, 2000). These rational decision-making models are also less applicable to adolescents and some young adults for whom the ability to analytically process information is not yet fully formed (Gibbons et al., in press; Michels, Kropp, Eyre, & Halpern-Felsher, 2005; Reyna & Farley, 2006).

Dual-Process Models

To address the less deliberate and more social, emotional, and reactive process often employed by adolescents, it is useful to consider dual-process models that reflect multiple paths to decision making. One important path reflects the more analytic, rational processing discussed above. In this path, decision

making includes deliberate, cognitive processing such as consideration of consequences and perceptions of risks and benefits; attitudes about the behaviors and related outcomes; and injunctive social norms such as what one believes others expect them to do and not do. These factors are expected to predict intentions to behave, with intentions being the most immediate predictor of actual behavior. This path also includes additional decision-making criteria (e.g., Gibbons et al., in press; Reyna & Farley, 2006), such as:

- the willingness to make a decision;
- the capacity to make autonomous decisions;
- searching for, recognizing, and incorporating new information relevant to the decision;
- the ability to judge the value of advice from other sources;
- the willingness to change one's decisions;
- the ability to implement and carry out one's decisions;
- the ability to evaluate and learn from one's decisions;
- the ability to reach decisions one is satisfied with; and
- the ability to make decisions that are consistent with one's goals.

Their ability to make competent decisions is sometimes called into question because adolescence is also often a time of engagement in risky behaviors.

The second path represents the less planned and more experience-based, reactive, and affective path often employed by adolescents. This path includes descriptive social norms such as personal perceptions and misperceptions about the extent to which peers and other important groups are engaging in a behavior as well as images or perceptions regarding others who have engaged or are engaging in a behavior. For example, adolescents are less likely to smoke if they hold negative images that smokers are dirty, wrinkled, and have yellow teeth.

This path also includes variation in adolescents' psychosocial maturity to make decisions (Cauffman & Steinberg, 2000), including the following:

- acknowledgement that adolescents' decisions are often impulsive rather than planned;
- ability to recognize and acknowledge when advice is needed;
- social perspective taking, or the ability to recognize that other people may have a different point of view or set of knowledge from one's own;
- future perspective taking, including the ability to project into the future, to consider possible outcomes associated with various choices, and to plan for the future.

These variables are expected to predict willingness to consider a behavior. Willingness to engage is differentiated from the planful notion of intentions. While one may not have an active plan in mind to smoke or have unprotected sex, it is often the case that adolescents find themselves in situations in which they would consider engaging in the behavior even though they were originally committed to avoiding it. Figure 2 depicts these processes.

Adolescents' decisions are often impulsive rather than planned.

A particular focus within all of these models of decision making, especially as they pertain to adolescents, has been the notion of risk perceptions or risk judgments. Individuals' beliefs about the degree to which they are vulnerable to specific negative outcomes are viewed as crucial factors in individuals' decisions concerning health-damaging and health-promoting behaviors. More specifically, theory and research indicates that individuals take risks in part because they believe they are invulnerable to harm, or less likely to experience harm compared to others (e.g., Song et al., in press). More recently,

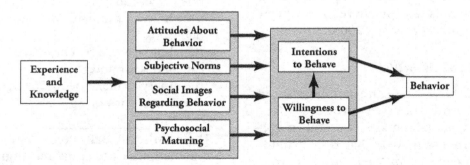

FIGURE 2   Dual-Process Model of Adolescent Decision Making: Cognitive, Psychosocial, and Experiential Factors

research suggests that in addition to health risks (e.g., lung cancer, pregnancy), adolescents view perceptions of and knowledge about social risks as critical in their decision making. This makes sense when one realizes that adolescence is a time when peers and other social factors play a large role in adolescent development, and therefore their decisions. It has also been recognized that an emphasis on perceived risk alone may be inadequate to predict or change behavior because risk is only part of the behavioral decision-making equation. Adolescents' perceptions of benefits have also been shown to factor into their decision-making equations, and may explain why adolescents engage in particular behaviors despite known risks (e.g., Goldberg, Halpern-Felsher, & Millstein, 2002; Millstein & Halpern-Felsher, 2002; Song et al., in press).

Factors Influencing Adolescent Decision Making

Gender Differences in Decision Making

Adolescent boys and girls do differ in their perceptions of and concerns over health-related risks and benefits. For example, girls are more likely to believe that they can get pregnant from having unprotected sex, get lung cancer from smoking, and have an accident while driving drunk. In contrast, boys perceive that they are more likely to experience positive outcomes, such as experiencing pleasure from sex. Despite these differences in perceptions, studies have not determined whether the actual decision-making process differs between adolescent boys and girls. The few studies that have examined gender differences in decision making have generally found that the process is remarkably similar (e.g., Michels et al., 2005).

Age Differences in Decision Making

Given the importance of understanding age differences in competent decision making, there are surprisingly few studies that have compared adolescents' and adults' decision making, or examined age differences in decision-making competence within the adolescent years. A review of the small literature base paints a mixed picture regarding adolescent decision-making competency, with some studies suggesting no or few age differences between adolescents and adults, and others showing significant age differences, with younger adolescents demonstrating less competence than older adolescents and/or adults. The age differences reported by these studies suggest that competence continues to increase throughout adolescence and into young adulthood. Furthermore, many of the attributes that are thought to be essential for competent decision making, such as resistance to peer pressure, self-reliance, perspective taking, future time perspective, and impulse control, also increase with age and over time (see, for example, Halpern-Felsher & Cauffman, 2001; Steinberg & Monahan, 2007).

Cultural Variation in Decision Making

Unfortunately, few studies have examined cultural variation in adolescent decision-making competence or decision-making processing.[1] However, there is racial, ethnic, and cultural variation in certain areas of psychosocial development known to influence

---

[1]Culture in this case encompasses a broad definition, including race, ethnicity, country of origin, acculturation, language use, economic status, and social status.

decision-making capacities, such as autonomy, orientation to the future, and values for academic achievement. Research has also documented that approaches to decision making itself vary. For example, in some cultures (such as some Native American or Asian cultures), decision making is a group dynamic, with much input and directive from the family or other adults. In these decisions, not only is the individual considered, but the impact that the decision and potential outcomes have on family members and others is put into the decision-making equation. In contrast, in other cultures such as in Northern Europe, decision making is more of an individual process, and the impact of the decision on the family is less likely to enter into the decision process. Clearly, in order to successfully understand and encourage competent adolescent decision making, one must have sufficient understanding of the relevant cultural systems that underlie decision making.

The Role of Experience and Knowledge

Adolescents simply have less experience with and knowledge about making decisions than do adults. Thus, adolescents have fewer opportunities to receive feedback, whether positive or negative, for the choices they have made. Experience with and knowledge about choices and obtaining feedback from decisions is especially important when one considers that perceptions of risks and benefits play a critical role in decision making. To the extent that adolescents have less experience with and less knowledge about making decisions, as well as less experience with decision outcomes, they might believe that they are less likely to experience harm and therefore discount harm in the future. Adolescents are also less aware of the cumulative nature of their behaviors as they have received so little feedback (Jacobs, 2004).

The Role of Social/Peer Affiliation

In addition to the vast number of individual-level physical, social, and emotional transformations occurring, adolescence is also defined as a time in which the social environment is also greatly changing. Compared to children, adolescents are less likely to be in structured and supervised settings, and they are more likely to affiliate with similar-aged peers rather than adults. Such environmental and social changes certainly lead to increased opportunities to make decisions and receive feedback. These decisions are also influenced by the normative behavior of adolescents' peers as well as by their perceived norms—that is, the extent to which they believe their peers are engaging in certain behaviors or making decisions. Simultaneous to adolescents' greater peer affiliation, they are also struggling with learning to make more autonomous decisions, which requires the ability to resist undue influence from others (e.g., Gibbons et al., in press).

In order to successfully understand and encourage competent adolescent decision making, one must have sufficient understanding of the relevant cultural systems that underlie decision making.

Brain Development

There are four lobes in the brain: parietal lobe, occipital lobe, temporal lobe, and the frontal lobe. The frontal lobe is the largest part of the brain, and contains the prefrontal cortex, which is located in front of the brain, behind the forehead. The prefrontal cortex is responsible for executive functions, including cognition, thought, imagination, abstract thinking, planning, and impulse control. In short, the prefrontal cortex oversees critical abilities for decision making. Research has shown that gray matter, or the tissue in the frontal lobe responsible for our ability to think, is reduced or "shed" during the adolescent and young adult years. Simultaneously, a process of myelination occurs, where the white matter in the brain matures to work more efficiently. These processes have been shown to continue through age 25. As such, the aspects of the brain responsible for decision making and impulse control are not fully developed until young adulthood, with males developing even slower than females (see for example, Giedd, 2008).

Adolescents' perceptions of benefits have also been shown to factor into their decision-making equations, and may explain why adolescents engage in particular behaviors despite known risks.

Implications and Importance of Adolescent Decision Making

The questions of how adolescents make decisions and the extent to which adolescents can and do make informed choices have been of great interest to researchers and practitioners in diverse areas including the behavioral sciences, medicine, social work, law, and social policy. A number of compelling forces have motivated this interest. The primary motivator has been the desire to understand and prevent adolescents' engagement in risky behavior. Adolescents' decisions to engage in risky behaviors have led many to conclude that adolescents take risks because they perceive low likelihood of experiencing negative consequences, perceive themselves to be invulnerable to harm, and have poorly developed decision-making skills. Others have interpreted adolescents' risky behavior as evidence of their impulsive nature and that they are easily persuaded by others. As such, intervention and prevention programs focus on enhancing decision-making competence through various knowledge and skill-building

efforts. For example, extensive efforts have been made to provide adolescents with information about risks, particularly health risks, to reduce their engagement in risky behavior. Program curricula have also focused on developing adolescents' skills, such as skills to resist peer pressure.

More recently, it has been recognized that rather than solely focusing efforts on disseminating information about the health implications of risky behavior, we need to broaden our discussions to include aspects of decision making most relevant and immediate to youth. For example, we need to acknowledge potential benefits of various risky behaviors, and provide youth with safer ways of obtaining similar benefits or learning how to delay the need or acknowledge and defer the desire for such benefits. We also need to include in the discussion social consequences that adolescents highly value in their decision-making process. For example, studies have shown that adolescents care greatly about whether they are popular or look more grown up, and such desires to gain positive social feedback and avoid negative social consequences influences their decisions (e.g., Ott, Millstein, Ofner, & Halpern-Felsher, 2006). Finally, we need to encourage youth to make conscious decisions and help them set meaningful boundaries for themselves that encompass their goals, relationship desires, and other developmental needs.

Concern over adolescents' decision-making competence is also relevant to adolescents' rights to make certain decisions, such as whether to participate in research studies, obtain medical treatment, or refuse medical treatment. Given results demonstrating adolescents' relative lack of maturity, many of these rights have been greatly restricted by federal, state, and local laws. Such presumptions about the inherent immaturity of adolescents are pervasive within the law. For example, the age of majority is 18 years in all but three states

(Alaska, Nebraska, and Wyoming, where the age is 19). Individuals below age 18 are neither expected nor permitted to be responsible for their own welfare. Similarly, research showing that adolescents' decision making is less competent compared to adults or compared to standards set forth in normative decision-making models has led to justifying raising the age at which adolescents accused of violent crimes may be tried as adults (Gittler et al., 1990; Grisso et al., 2003; Poythress et al., 2006).

Summary

In summary, there is great interest and importance in understanding the extent to which adolescents are able to make competent decisions. Adolescence is a time of great changes that result in desire for autonomy in decision making, and by mid to late adolescence, most individuals have the cognitive abilities to understand and judge risks. Nevertheless, adolescents may lack the psychosocial traits required to consistently make and act upon mature decisions. It is thus imperative that we protect adolescents from serious harm while simultaneously providing them with appropriately risky opportunities to practice and grow their decision-making skills.

References

Ajzen, I. (1985). From intentions to actions. In J. Kuhi & I. Beckman (Eds.), *Action Control from Cognition to Behavior*, New York: Springer-Verlag.

Beyth-Marom, R., Austin. L., Fischhoff, B., Palmgren, C., & Jacobs-Quadrel, M. (1993). Perceived consequences of risky behaviors: Adults and adolescents. *Developmental Psychology, 29,* 549–563.

Beyth-Marom, R., & Fischhoff, B. (1997). Adolescents' decisions about risks: A cognitive perspective. In J. Schulenberg, J.L. Maggs, & K. Hurrelmann (Eds.) *Health Risks and Developmental Transitions During Adolescence* (pp. 110–135). Cambridge University Press.

Caulfman, E., & Steinberg, L. (2000). (Im)maturity of Judgment in Adolescence: Why adolescents may be less culpable than adults. *Behavioral Sciences & the Law, 18,* 741–760.

Fishbein, M., & Ajzen, I. (1975). *Beliefs, Attitudes, Intention, and Behavior: An Introduction to Theory and Research.* Reading, MA: Addison-Wesley.

Gibbons, E.X., Houlihan A.E., & Gerrard, M. (In Press). Reason and reaction: The utility of a dual focus, dual processing perspective on promotion and prevention of adolescent health risk behavior. *British Journal of Health Psychology.*

Giedd, J.N. (2008). The teen brain. Insights from neuroimaging. *Journal of Adolescent Health, 42,* 335–343.

Gittler, J., Quigley Rick. M., & Saks. M.J. (1990). *Adolescent Health Care Decision Making: The Law and Public Policy.* Washington, DC. Carnegie Council on Adolescent Development.

Goldberg, J.H. Halpern-Felsher, B.L., & Millstein, S.G. (2002). Beyond invulnerability: The importance of benefits in adolescents' decision to drink alcohol. *Health Psychology, 21,* 477–484

Grisso, T., Steinberg, L., Woolard, J., Cauffman, F., Scott, F., Graham, S., et al. (2003). Juveniles' competence to stand trial: A companion of adolescents' and adults' capacities as trial defendants. *Law and Human Behavior, 27,* 333–63.

Halpern-Felsher, B.L., & Cauffman, F. (2001). Costs and benefits of a decision: Decision-making competence in adolescents and adults. *Journal of Applied Developmental Psychology, 22,* 257-273.

Jacobs, J. (2004). Perceptions of risk and social judgments: Biases and motivational factors. In R.J. Bonnie & M.E. O'Connell (Eds.), *Reducing Underage Drinking: A Collective Responsibility* (pp. 417-436). Washington, DC: The National Academies Press.

Michels, T.M., Kropp, R.Y., Eyre, S.L., & Halpern-Felsher, B.L. (2005). Initiating sexual experiences: How do young adolescents make decisions regarding early sexual activity? *Journal of Research on Adolescence, 15,* 583-607.

Millstein, S.G., & Halpern Felsher, B.L. (2002) Perceptions of risk and vulnerability. *Journal of Adolescent Health, 315,* 10-27.

Ott, M.A. Millstein. S.G., Ofner S., Halpern-Felsher, B.L. (2006). Greater expectations: Adolescents' positive motivations for sex. *Perspectives on Sexual and Reproductive Health, 38,* 84-89.

Poythress, N., Lexcen. F.J., Grisso, T., & Steinberg, L. (2006). The competence-related abilities of adolescent defendants in criminal court. *Law and Human Behavior, 30,* 75-92.

Reyna, V.F., & Farley, F. (2006). Risk and rationality in adolescent decision making. Implications for theory, practice, and public policy. *Psychological Science in the Public Interest, 7,* 1-44.

Rosenstock, I.M. (1974). Historical origins of the health belief model. In M.H. Becker (Ed.), *The Health Belief Model and Personal Health Behavior* (pp. 1-8). Thorofare, N.J: Charles B. Sclack.

Song, A.V., Morrell, H., Cornell, J.L., Ramos, M.E., Biehl, M., Kropp, R.Y., & Halpern Felsher, B.L., (in press). Perceptions of tobacco-related high risk and low benefit predict adolescent tobacco initiation. *American Journal of Public Health.*

Steinberg L., & Monahan, K.C. (2007). Age differences in resistance to peer influence. *Developmental Psychology, 43,* 1,531-1,543.

DR. BONNIE HALPERN-FELSHER (HalpernFelsherB@peds.ucsf.edu) is an Associate Professor in the Division of Adolescent Medicine, Department of Pediatrics, University of California, San Francisco. She is also the Associate Director of the General Pediatrics Fellowships, and is a faculty member at UCSF's Psychology and Medicine Postdoctoral Program, The Center for Health and Community, the Center for Tobacco Control Research and Education, the Comprehensive Cancer Center, and the Robert Wood Johnson Scholars Program. Dr. Halpern-Felsher is a developmental psychologist whose research has focused on cognitive and psychosocial factors involved in health-related decision making, perceptions of risk and vulnerability, health communication, and risk behavior; and she has published in each of these areas.

ARTICLE 6

What Educators Need to Know About Bullying Behaviors

SANDRA GRAHAM

Peer victimization—also commonly labeled *harassment* or *bullying*—is not a new problem in American schools, though it appears to have taken on more epic proportions in recent years. Survey data indicate that anywhere from 30% to 80% of school-age youth report that they have personally experienced victimization from peers, and 10% to 15% may be chronic victims (e.g., Card and Hodges 2008). A generation ago, if we had asked children what they worry most about at school, they probably would have said, "Passing exams and being promoted to the next grade." Today, students' school concerns often revolve around safety as much as achievement, as the perpetrators of peer harassment are perceived as more aggressive and the victims of their abuse report feeling more vulnerable.

In the past 10 years—perhaps in response to students' growing concerns—there has been a proliferation of new studies on school bullying. For example, a search of the psychology (PsycINFO) and Educational Resources Information Center (ERIC) databases using the key words *peer victimization*, *peer harassment,* and *school bullying* uncovered 10 times more studies from 2000 to 2010 than during the previous decade (about 800 versus 80).

Even though the empirical base has increased dramatically during these past 10 years, many widespread beliefs about school bullying are more myth than fact. I label these beliefs as myths because researchers who study bullies and victims of many different ages and in many different contexts have not found them to be true.

I define peer victimization as physical, verbal, or psychological abuse that occurs in and around school, especially where adult supervision is minimal. The critical features that distinguish victimization from simple conflict between peers are the intent to cause harm and an imbalance of power between perpetrator and victim. This intended harm can be either direct, entailing face-to-face confrontation; indirect, involving a third party and some form of social ostracism; or even "cyberbullying." Taunting, name-calling, racial slurs, hitting, spreading rumors, and social exclusion by powerful others are all examples of behaviors that constitute peer victimization. My definition doesn't include the more lethal types of peer hostility, such as those seen in the widely publicized school shootings; although some of those shootings may have been precipitated by a history of peer abuse, they remain rare events. My definition emphasizes more prevalent forms of harassment that affect the lives of many youth and that the American Medical Association has labeled a public health concern.

Six myths cloud our understanding of bullying behavior in schools and prevent us from addressing the issue effectively.

Myth #1: *Bullies have low self-esteem and are rejected by their peers.*

A portion of this myth has its roots in the widely and uncritically accepted view that people who bully others act that way because they think poorly of themselves. Recall the self-esteem movement of the 1980s whose advocates proposed that raising self-esteem was the key to improving the outcomes of children with academic and social problems. Yet there is little evidence in peer research to support the notion that bullies suffer from low self-esteem. To the contrary, many studies report that bullies perceive themselves in a positive light, often displaying inflated self-views (Baumeister et al. 2003).

Many people also believe that everybody dislikes the class bully. In truth, research shows that many bullies have high status in the classroom and have many friends. Some bullies are quite popular among classmates, which may in part account for their relatively high self-esteem. In our research with middle school students, we have found that others perceive bullies as especially "cool," where coolness implies both popularity and possession of desired traits (Juvonen, Graham, and Schuster 2003). As young teens test their need to be more independent, bullies sometimes enjoy a new kind of notoriety among classmates who admire their toughness and may even try to imitate them.

Myth #2: *Getting bullied is a natural part of growing up.*

One misconception about victims is that bullying is a normal part of childhood and that the experience builds character. In contrast, research quite clearly shows that bullying experiences increase the vulnerabilities of children, rather than making them more resilient. Victims are often disliked or rejected by their peers and feel depressed, anxious, and lonely (Card and Hodges 2008). Part of this psychological distress may revolve around how victims think about the reasons for their plight. For example, repeated encounters with peer hostility, or even an isolated yet especially painful experience, might lead that victim to ask, "Why me?" Such an individual might come to blame the predicament on personal shortcomings, concluding, "I'm someone who deserves to be picked on," which can increase depressive affect (Graham, Bellmore, and Mize 2006). Some victimized youth also have elevated levels of physical symptoms, leading to frequent visits to the nurse as well as school absenteeism. It is not difficult to imagine the chronic victim who becomes so anxious about going to school that she or he tries to avoid it at all costs. Nothing is character building about such experiences.

Myth #3: *Once a victim, always a victim.*

Although there is good reason to be concerned about the long-term consequences of bullying, research remains inconclusive about the stability of victim status. In fact, there is much more discontinuity than continuity in victim trajectories. In our research, only about a third of students who had reputations as victims in the fall of 6th grade maintained that reputation at the end of the school year and, by the end of 8th grade, the number of victims had dropped to less than 10% (Nylund, Nishina, Bellmore, and Graham 2007). Although certain personality characteristics, such as shyness, place children at higher risk for being bullied, there are also a host of changing situational factors, such as transitioning to a new school or delayed pubertal development, that affect the likelihood of a child continuing to get bullied. These situational factors explain why there are more temporary than chronic victims of bullying.

MYTH #4: *Boys are physical and girls are relational victims and bullies.*

The gender myth emerges in discussions that distinguish between physical and psychological victimization. The psychological type, often called "relational bullying," usually involves social ostracism or attempts to damage the reputation of the victim. Some research has suggested that girls are more likely to be both perpetrator and target of the relational type (for example, Crick and Grotpeter 1996). Because a whole popular culture has emerged around relationally aggressive girls (so-called *queen bees* or *alpha girls*) and their victims, putting these gender findings in proper perspective is important. In many studies, physical and relational victimization tend to be correlated, suggesting that the victim of relational harassment is also the victim of physical harassment. Moreover, if relational victimization is more prevalent in girls than boys (and the results are mixed), this gender difference is most likely confined to middle childhood and early adolescence (Archer and Coyne 2005). By middle adolescence, relational victimization becomes the norm for both genders as it becomes less socially accepted for individuals to be physically aggressive against peers. Relational victimization is a particularly insidious type of peer abuse because it inflicts psychological pain and is often difficult for others to detect. However, it's probably a less gendered subtype than previously thought.

Zero tolerance policies often don't work as intended and can sometimes backfire, leading to increases in antisocial behavior.

MYTH #5: *Zero tolerance policies reduce bullying.*

Zero tolerance approaches, which advocate suspending or expelling bullies, are sometimes preferred because they presumably send a message to the student body that bullying won't be tolerated. However, research suggests that these policies often don't work as intended and can sometimes backfire, leading to increases in antisocial behavior (APA Zero Tolerance Task Force 2008). Moreover, black youth are disproportionately the targets of suspension and expulsion, resulting in a racial discipline gap that mirrors the well-documented racial achievement gap (Gregory, Skiba, and Noguera 2010). Before deciding on a discipline

---

Resources

Teaching Tolerance, a project of the Southern Poverty Law Center

Dedicated to reducing prejudice, improving intergroup relations, and supporting equitable school experiences for children. Teaching Tolerance provides free educational materials to teachers. The organization's magazine, *Teaching Tolerance,* is also available free to educators.
www.tolerance.org

Office of Safe and Drug-Free Schools

Provides in-depth, online workshops focused on bullying prevention: "Exploring the Nature and Prevention of Bullying." Materials from that workshop are available online.
www2.ed.gov/admins/lead/safety/training/bullying/index.html

In addition, clicking on the link for "Resources and Links" will connect you with a lengthy list of relevant organizations, books, web sites, and videos.

Gay, Lesbian and Straight Education Network (GLSEN)

Provides resources and support for schools to implement effective and age-appropriate antibullying programs to improve school climate for all students.
www.glsen.org

strategy, school administrators must consider the scope of the problem, who will be affected, the fairness of the strategy, and what messages are communicated to students.

HOW CAN SCHOOLS AND TEACHERS RESPOND TO BULLYING?

Adults should intervene whenever they witness a bullying incident. Use bullying incidents as teachable moments to stimulate conversations, not merely as opportunities to punish the perpetrator. Teach tolerance for differences and an appreciation of diversity.

Myth #6: Bullying involves only a perpetrator and a victim.

Many parents, teachers, and students view bullying as a problem that's limited to bullies and victims. Yet, much research shows that bullying involves more than the bully-victim dyad (Salmivalli 2001). For example, bullying incidents are typically public events that have witnesses. Studies based on playground observations have found that in most bullying incidents, at least four other peers were present as either bystanders, assistants to bullies, reinforcers, or defenders of victims. Assistants take part in ridiculing or intimidating a schoolmate, and reinforcers encourage the bully by showing their approval. However, those who come to aid the victim are rare. Unfortunately, many bystanders believe victims of harassment are responsible for their plight and bring problems on themselves.

Thoughts on Interventions

Educators who want to better understand the dynamics of school bullying will need to learn that the problems of victims and bullies aren't the same. Interventions for bullies don't need to focus on self-esteem; rather,

bullies need to learn strategies to control their anger and their tendency to blame others for their problems. Victims, on the other hand, need interventions that help them develop more positive self-views, and that teach them not to blame themselves for the harassment. And peers need to learn that as witnesses to bullying, their responses aren't neutral and either support or oppose bullying behaviors.

Most bullying interventions are school-wide approaches that target all students, parents, and adults in the school. They operate under the belief that bullying is a systemic problem and that finding a solution is the collective responsibility of everyone in the school. Two recent meta-analyses of research on antibullying programs suggest that the effects are modest at best (Merrell et al. 2008; Smith et al. 2004). Only about a third of the school-based interventions included in the analyses showed any positive effects as measured by fewer reported incidents of bullying; a few even revealed increased bullying, suggesting interventions may have backfired. These findings don't mean schools should abandon whole-school interventions that have a research base. Instead, the modest results remind us that schools are complex systems and what works in one context may not be easily portable to other contexts with very different organizational structures, student demographics, and staff buy-in. Research on decision making about program adoption reveals that many teachers are reluctant to wholly embrace bullying interventions because they either believe the curriculum doesn't provide enough time and space to integrate such policies or that parents are responsible for developing antibullying attitudes (Cunningham et al. 2009).

Although obvious gains from systemwide interventions may be modest, teachers can take steps on an individual and daily basis to address bullying. First, teachers should never ignore a bullying incident. Because most bullying occurs in "un-owned spaces" like hallways and restrooms where adult supervision is minimal, teachers should respond to all bullying incidents that they witness. A response by a teacher communicates to perpetrators that their actions are not acceptable and helps victims feel less powerless about their predicament. This is especially important because students often perceive school staff as unresponsive to students' experiences of bullying.

Second, when possible, adults can use witnessed bullying incidents as "teachable moments," situations that open the door for conversations with students about difficult topics. For example, teachers may intervene to confront students directly about why many youth play bystander roles and are unwilling to come to the aid of victims, or how social ostracism can be a particularly painful form of peer abuse. At times, engaging in such difficult dialogues may be a more useful teacher response than quick and harsh punishment of perpetrators.

Bullying experiences make children more vulnerable, not more resilient.

Finally, one meaningful factor that consistently predicts victimization is an individual's differences from the larger peer group. Thus, having a physical or mental handicap or being highly gifted in a regular school setting, being a member of an ethnic or linguistic minority group, suffering from obesity, or being gay or lesbian are all risk factors for bullying because individuals who have these characteristics are often perceived to deviate from the normative standards of the larger peer group. Students also tend to favor the in-group (those who are similar to them) and to derogate the out-group (those who are different). A strong antidote to this tendency is to teach tolerance for

differences, an appreciation of diversity, and the value of multiple social norms and social identities co-habiting the same school environment. The effects of teaching tolerance may last a lifetime.

References

American Psychological Association Zero Tolerance Task Force. "Are Zero Tolerance Policies Effective in the Schools? Evidentiary Review and Recommendations." *American Psychologist* 63 (December 2008): 852–862.

Archer, John, and Sarah Coyne. "An Integrated Review of Indirect, Relational, and Social Aggression." *Personality and Social Psychology Review* 9, no. 3 (2005): 212–230.

Baumeister, Roy F., Jennifer D. Campbell, Joachim I. Krueger, and Kathleen D. Vohs. "Does High Self-Esteem Cause Better Performance, Interpersonal Success, Happiness, or Healthier Lifestyles?" *Psychological Science in the Public Interest* 4 (May 2003): 1–44.

Card, Noel, and Ernest V. Hodges. "Peer Victimization Among Schoolchildren: Correlates, Causes, Consequences, and Considerations in Assessment and Intervention." *School Psychology Quarterly* 23, no. 4 (December 2008): 451–461.

Crick, Nicki, and Jennifer Grotpeter. "Children's Treatment by Peers: Victims of Relational and Overt Aggression." *Development and Psychopathology* 8, no. 2 (1996): 367–380.

Cunningham, Charles E., Tracy Vaillancourt, Heather Rimas, Ken Deal, Lesley Cunningham, Kathy Short, and Yvonne Chen. "Modeling the Bullying Prevention Program Preferences of Educators: A Discrete Choice Conjoint Experiment." *Journal of Abnormal Child Psychology* 37, no. 7 (October 2009): 929–943.

Graham, Sandra, Amy Bellmore, and J. Mize. "Aggression, Victimization, and Their Co-Occurrence in Middle School." *Journal of Abnormal Child Psychology* 34 (2006): 363-378.

Gregory, Anne, Russell Skiba, and Pedro Noguera. "The Achievement Gap and the Discipline Gap: Two Sides of the Same Coin?" *Educational Researcher* 39, no. 1 (January 2010): 59-68.

Juvonen, Jaana, Sandra Graham, and Mark A. Schuster. "Bullying Among Young Adolescents: The Strong, the Weak, and the Troubled." *Pediatrics* 112 (December 2003): 1231-1237.

Merrell, Kenneth W., Barbara Gueldner, Scott Ross, and Duane Isava. "How Effective Are School Bullying Intervention Programs? A Meta-Analysis of Intervention Research." *School Psychology Quarterly* 23, no. 1 (March 2008): 26-42.

Nylund, Karen, Adrienne Nishina, Amy Bellmore, and Sandra Graham. "Subtypes, Severity, and Structural Stability of Peer Victimization: What Does Latent Class Analysis Say?" *Child Development* 78, no. 6 (2007): 1706-1722.

Salmivalli, Christina. "Group View on Victimization: Empirical Findings and Their Implications." In *Peer Harassment in School: The Plight of the Vulnerable and Victimized*, ed. Jaana Juvonen and Sandra Graham: 39-420. New York: Guilford, 2001.

Smith, J. David, Barry Schneider, Peter Smith, and Katerina Ananiadou. "The Effectiveness of Whole-School Anti-Bullying Programs: A Synthesis of Evaluation Research." *School Psychology Review* 33, no. 4 (2004): 547-560.

SANDRA GRAHAM is a professor of education in the Graduate School of Education and Information Studies, University of California Los Angeles.

ARTICLE 7

The Bridge to Character

To help students become ethical, responsible citizens,
schools need to cultivate students' natural moral sense.

WILLIAM DAMON

Once when I was a guest on a radio talk show, a parent phoned in to tell us about a school incident that frustrated and disturbed her. A few weeks earlier, the parent had received a curt note from her son's 5th grade teacher informing her that her son had been caught taking lunch money out of his classmates' backpacks. Students in the class had been reporting missing lunch money for some time, and the school finally identified this woman's son as the culprit.

The woman requested a meeting at the school, and the next day she found herself in a room with the 5th grade teacher and an assistant principal who was there in the role of guidance counselor. The woman expressed her dismay at her son's behavior and said that she was determined to see that it never happened again. She then asked how they could work together to give him the message that stealing is wrong.

The teacher and counselor greeted this question with a moment of awkward silence. Then the counselor said something along the lines of, "Well, it's important for you to know that we are speaking with your son about this incident, and we are not referring to it as 'stealing.' We don't want to give your child a self-image as a thief, which could only stigmatize him. Instead, we are calling it 'uncooperative behavior,' and we have explained to him that he will never be popular if he continues to act this

way. This approach reflects our professional judgment, and we recommend that you take the same approach and support our efforts."

The mother said that when she tried to discuss the matter with her son, he "just blew it off" by saying, "Don't worry, Mom, the school is handling this." She had no confidence that the boy had learned any kind of indelible lesson from his misconduct.

Now the school, in its well-intended but clumsy way, certainly tried to meet this student where he was, playing on his desire for popularity and social acceptance. But by consciously avoiding terms like *right, wrong*, and *stealing* (the literal description of the student's deed), the school rejected moral language that could guide the student throughout his life. The message the school offered the boy was instrumental and amoral: You should avoid actions that will make you unpopular. This is hardly a charter for a life of ethical integrity.

The Building Blocks

Morality is a natural part of the human system. Every child begins life with the rudimentary building blocks of character. Four such blocks identified in recent scientific studies are empathy, fairness, self-control, and obligation (Damon, 1992, 1999; Kochanska, Murray, & Harlan, 2000; Thompson, 1998; Wilson, 1993).

Empathy, the capacity to experience another's pleasure or pain, provides the foundation for caring and compassion. Even newborns cry when they hear sounds of crying and show signs of pleasure at happy sounds; by the second year of life, it is common for children to comfort a peer or a parent in distress.

A concern for fairness emerges as soon as children begin playing with friends. When a playmate grabs all the cookies or refuses to relinquish a spot on a swing set, the protest "That's not fair!" is a predictable response, because even very young children understand that they have an obligation to share with others. The child's desire for self-control can be seen in an infant's eagerness to regularize behavior through repetition, rituals, and rules. Obligation expresses itself in children's wishes to follow the directives and expectations of their caregivers.

Yet despite these robust early beginnings, the child's natural moral sense requires nurturing if it is to develop into a mature and reliable commitment to act in a caring and ethical manner. For one thing, the child's initial moral inclinations rely entirely on transient mood states. A flash of anger in a 3-year-old quickly extinguishes any empathy for the playmate who provoked the anger. In addition, the child's early leanings do not come with any program for moral action. We would not want to count on children to create a just social world, as *The Lord of the Flies* by William Golding (Coward-McGann, 1954) illustrated in a chilling way.

The Need for Guidance

In order for children's natural moral capacities to become fully formed character dispositions, their natural empathy must develop into a sustained concern for others, their sense of fairness must grow into a commit-ment to justice, their desire for self-control must grow into a sense of personal responsibility, and their feeling of obligation must become a determination to contribute to noble purposes beyond the self. Without this kind of growth, the child's early capacities may atrophy or take on grotesque forms.

For example, a counselor working with delinquent youth recalled one homicidal 14-year-old saying that he felt broken-hearted whenever he thought about people cutting down trees for Christmas (Samenow, 1984). This boy had wreaked violence on numerous people without regret, yet he felt sadness for fallen pine trees. The annals of criminal justice are full of such cases, psychopaths who have feelings for a pet or a younger sister but who treat nearly everyone else with absolute callousness.

Adult guidance is an essential ingredient in transforming children's natural moral inclinations into dependable and effective character traits. Education provides the bridge from the natural virtues to lives of ethical integrity and compassion.

All students enter school with a rich and lively morality, stemming from the moral inclinations they were born with and enhanced by their experiences since birth. They care about their family and friends and want to do the right thing. At the same time, they don't always know what the right thing is, and they (like all of us) are capable of selfish, destructive, and dishonorable behavior.

It is the vital responsibility of every school to work with the vigorous moral sense that students bring with them in a way that turns these inclinations into solutions for the ethical challenges students will confront. In a world where parents are not always on the scene and many communities have disintegrated, the bridge from a student's natural moral sense to the student's established moral character runs through the school.

Making the Most of Opportunities

The boy who stole lunch money no doubt had a moral sense. He very likely cared about other people in his life, including at least some of his classmates, and he almost certainly understood that losing valued property is painful. When he stole the money, he probably did not think about how his actions caused pain for others. Nor did he take seriously the social laws against stealing. These are insights that any school should be prepared to teach. The boy's behavior provided the school with an opportunity for education about the moral implications of stealing and other antisocial behavior, as well as about the purpose of societal laws. On this chance to score valuable points toward its moral education aims, the school dropped the ball.

In my travels to schools, I have witnessed many similar missed opportunities. The most common of these revolve around cheating and other breaches of academic integrity. Cheating and plagiarism on homework assignments occur with astonishing frequency—I have heard rates as high as 80 percent of students who have done this at least once during high school—yet relatively few schools use such incidents to teach moral awareness.

How can schools teach such awareness? I suggest that they emphasize the following four messages:

1. Cheating is unfair because it gives the cheater an unfair advantage over students who do not cheat.
2. Cheating breaks the trust between student and teacher.
3. Cheating violates the school rules, and rules are necessary for preserving social order and individual rights.
4. Cheating is dishonest behavior, and no one wants to become a person who is known (by self and others) as dishonest.

These four points all connect with students' natural moral capacities: fairness, empathy, social regulation, and self-control. But they also show students how their natural inclinations apply to real-world challenges, such as living up to the code of academic integrity, despite temptations to do otherwise.

In the stealing example that I presented at the outset of this article, the school could have emphasized the *moral*—not just instrumental—reasons why people shouldn't steal. Such moral reasons include respecting the rights of others in the same way that you expect them to respect your rights (the Golden Rule); refraining from disreputable behavior so you will be known as a person of integrity; upholding rules that are necessary for social harmony and justice; and having compassion for peers who need the goods you might steal from them. When a teacher conveys such principles to a student, the teacher conveys both an understanding of how decent societies work and a program for a life of good character.

Considering Student Concerns

The example of the lunch-money thief was a case of a school's stooping to a student's level rather than attempting to elevate it. Rather than show the student how his deed violated important moral norms, the school did little more than validate the idea—already familiar enough in early adolescence—that popularity is desirable.

But at least as common as such mistakes are examples of the opposite sort—that is, schools that pay too little attention to what students know or care about. These schools try to reach students with language that is too removed from their own motives and experiences. In such cases, no bridges at all are built, and the students ignore or misunderstand the schools' messages.

Recently a friend who works with a major state education department showed me the standards that the state currently uses to guide instruction in 8th grade civics. As we read through the document, we both felt abashed at our ignorance of many of the concepts that the standards required. Students were expected to be able to "describe the nation's blend of civic republicanism, classical liberal principles, and English parliamentary traditions" and to "analyze the principles and concepts codified in state constitutions between 1777 and 1781 that created the context out of which American political institutions and ideas developed." We looked at each other in amazement: This is meant for 8th graders, not political science doctoral students!

In all the nuanced treatments of political process and constitutional democracy, it was hard to see what any 13-year-old could connect with. Missing entirely were insights about the kinds of issues that children have experienced: governing play and games through social rules; establishing just solutions when peers disagree; respecting authority (including determining whether authority is legitimate); and obtaining redress for legitimate grievances.

When civics is taught through the lens of a student's own concerns and experiences, it comes to life. For example, the civil rights movement of the 1960s taught thousands of young people—many of whom had experienced discrimination in their own lives—valuable lessons about constructive civic participation and democracy that have lasted them a lifetime (see MacAdam, 1988).

Moral and character education must consist of more than skin-deep efforts that ask students to merely recite virtuous words such as honesty, tolerance, respect, courage, and so on. Moral and character education need to engage students in activities that help them acquire regular habits of virtuous behavior. Such active engagement nurtures students' capacity to make moral choices freely.

Toward an Enduring Moral Sense

Teachers should make the effort to present admirable examples to the young, and they should regularly discuss with students the deep questions of meaning, purpose, and what really matters in life. Our research shows that youngsters learn moral truths by seeing them enacted in the lives of real people and by reflecting on how this informs their own search for direction (Damon, 2009). At the same time, it is essential that teachers help build bridges from students' own lived experiences to their development of a mature moral character.

To accomplish this, teachers must be careful not to lose their students in a barrage of negativity. Character education, in addition to teaching children what not to do (don't lie, don't cheat, don't act disrespectfully, and so on) also must have a positive side, inspiring young people to dedicate themselves to higher purposes. In the long run, it is a sense of positive inspiration that captures students' imaginations.

Charitable work is one way to introduce students to a larger purpose. Research has found that community service programs, especially when combined with reflection about the significance of serving others, are powerful supports for character development (Hart, Atkins, & Donnelly, 2006; Youniss & Yates, 1997).

Another source of inspiration that students are eager to speak about is vocation, which goes beyond working to earn a living (as important as that is). The idea that work can be a calling—a means of using one's skills and talents to contribute to the betterment of the world—is a powerful source of purpose for any student. As a discussion topic, the meaning of work fits naturally into many parts of the school day. Teachers, guidance counselors, and coaches can all take part in helping students develop a sense of vocation.

To fulfill their character education missions, schools should make special efforts to provide students with these sources of inspiration, enabling young people to discover their own admirable purposes. Once young people are committed to truly noble aims, they won't need external injunctions to walk the straight and narrow path.

References

Damon, W. (1992). *The moral child.* New York: The Free Press.

Damon, W. (1999). The moral development of children. *Scientific American, 281*, 72-88.

Damon, W. (2009). *The path to purpose: How young people find their calling in life.* New York: Free Press.

Hart, D., Atkins, R., & Donnelly, T. M. (2006). Community service and moral development. In M. Killen & J. Smetana (Eds.), *Handbook of moral development* (pp. 633-656). Mahwah, NJ: Erlbaum.

Kochanska, G., Murray, K. T., & Harlan, E. T. (2000). Effortful control in early childhood: Continuity and change, antecedents, and implications for social development. *Developmental Psychology, 36*, 220-232.

MacAdam, D. (1988). *Freedom summer.* New York: Oxford University Press.

Samenow, S. E. (1984). *Inside the criminal mind.* New York: Random House.

Thompson, R. A. (1998). Empathy and its origins in early development. In S. Braten (Ed.), *Intersubjective communication and emotion in early ontogeny* (pp. 144-157). Cambridge, UK, and New York: Cambridge University Press.

Wilson, J. Q. (1993). *The moral sense.* New York: Free Press.

Youniss, J., & Yates, M. (1997). *Community service and social responsibility in youth.* Chicago: University of Chicago Press.

WILLIAM DAMON is Professor of Education at Stanford University and Director of the Stanford Center on Adolescence, Stanford, California; wdamon@stanford.edu.

ARTICLE 8

Sam Comes to School: Including Students with Autism in Your Classroom

DIANA FRIEDLANDER

Sam's first day of school was different from everyone else's. He walked into the brightly lit, cheerful classroom and quickly became engrossed in the faint whirring of an overhead fan. Chewing on his shirtsleeve, he began rocking and humming. His eyes darted from the welcome message the teacher had printed on the board to posters of color words and days of the week and names printed above each cubby, avidly reading each word and trying to make sense of this new world. Whereas most of the children were eager to meet their teacher and classmates, Sam did not notice them or the other adults in the classroom. Sam's autism created an invisible barrier around him, protecting him from the social world of the classroom and allowing him to find comfort in familiar sounds, symbols, and patterns. At times, however, the barrier was not enough and other stimuli sent him into a panicky terror.

Autism: A Social Disorder

Autism is one of a group of developmental disorders called Autism Spectrum Disorders (ASDs). ASDs include a wide continuum: Autism, Pervasive Development Disorder, Asperger's Syndrome, Fragile X Syndrome, and Obsessive Compulsive Disorder (Cohen and Volkmar 1997). Researchers are beginning to understand the genetic components of autism, which affects about 1 in 166 children born in the United States (Frombonne 2007). This frequency is put in perspective by the statistical knowledge that only 1 in 800 babies is born with Down Syndrome (Centers for Disease Control and Prevention 2006).

Most children diagnosed with an ASD have difficulty in social areas, such as picking up cues from their environment and the ability to form typical relationships. Language is another area of difficulty. Although children with an ASD may have adequate expressive language, sometimes beyond their years, receptive language may be compromised. Sensory integration is another troublesome spot. Students with an ASD can have difficulty regulating input into their central nervous system, resulting in sensitivity to touch, sound, taste, or smell. Sam once told a story of how he caught a snake after hearing it slither.

When a child is diagnosed with autism, a lack of social or emotional reciprocity in his or her classroom experience causes the most impact. The social aspects of childhood and school come easily to most children, but not to children with autism. Children learn to thrive and grow in their environment by watching and copying others; however, those who have autism often fail to make these social connections. Their isolation causes them to remain inexperienced in a world of comparably savvy children and can make adolescence an unnavigable maze.

Help with Getting It

Teachers slowly come to know their students. In the first few days of class they find out who is an avid reader or a social butterfly, who has the book out and is on the correct page, and who needs their hand held on the way to and from the lunchroom. Find out all you can about your student with autism before he or she arrives in your classroom; this will ease the transition for the student, for you, and for the class. Parents are the most important resource because they know their child best. As with all children, those who have autism are unique. Although they may share some common strengths and weaknesses, each child's individual needs must be evaluated.

Teachers should consider that children with autism are generally rigid in their thinking and behaviors. Typically, once they gain an understanding of a specific concept, they tend to access related information in the confines of that concept. For example, one child learned that a specific pet was called a *dog;* therefore, all pets became known to that child as dogs. This concrete analysis of the world helps them to maintain an orderly and comfortable life with few surprises. Routinization and rituals are common behaviors among some students with autism, as the familiar bears less uncertainty. Often behaviors that are troublesome in school are actually manifestations of uncertainty and lack of order or ritual, which can be frightening to children with autism. Sometimes a child's controlled world may not blend well with the organization you had planned to make your classroom work. A meeting with parents and their child before school begins will give you and the family time to plan for and avoid pitfalls. Parents have a good sense of how their child will react in a given setting. They have developed strategies to make life at home and school work for their child. Brainstorming with them on how to make this transition easy will pay off.

In some cases, easing the transition can be as simple as allowing the child to visit his or her classroom a few times in late summer or setting up a buddy system with a familiar child. Often, you will need to take further steps. For example, a clearly delineated visual schedule, often written out or using drawings or photographs, can help ease the uncertainty of time and transitions by providing advance notice and giving the child with autism a visual cue as to what comes next, thereby increasing his or her comfort level and allowing him or her to internalize the change and respond better. Seeing the chart change or participating in changing the icons helps the child understand and accept change (Quill 1995). Students who have relied on this type of system to help structure their early school years can progress to the more sophisticated support of a highly organized day planner or an electronic personal organizer. Parents can provide assistance by predetermining where their child might encounter difficulty throughout the school day and sharing various techniques for addressing these difficulties. Together, you can formulate an environmental support plan to help the child meet daily expectations.

Implementation of this plan must be consistent or it will add to the child's anxiety level. It must be appropriately designed to meet each child's unique needs; if Sam needs to adapt to a busy cafeteria, he should be taught supportive strategies. This may include bringing comfort foods from home, having a designated seat, being told exactly how much time he has to eat before he is expected to clean up his place, or being assigned a buddy who understands his discomfort and who will model appropriate lunchroom protocol for him until he understands it.

I Did Not Teach Him to Read

Parents often report to teachers that their child possesses precocious reading decoding ability with little to no instruction. Hyperlexia (precocious reading ability accompanied by difficulty acquiring language or social skills) is not a rare phenomenon in these children. Decoding symbols, a visual and spatial task, is a unique strength for some children with autism. Armed with advance awareness of these highly developed visual learning abilities, you can begin to think of ways to use this strength in your classroom.

Gray (1994) developed the Social Stories method to help children with autism capitalize on their visual learning abilities. In this method, an educator, parent, or individual close to the child creates a captioned picture book to improve the social understanding of people on both sides of a social equation. This technique can be extremely helpful in new settings in which expectations for your class may seem clear to you but may not be for your student with autism. Teachers can also use it to encourage or change behaviors by explaining with visual support just what it is you want your student to do and how. For example, a visit to the school library was a difficult time for Sam. The librarian told him he could borrow two books on each weekly visit. When Sam chose to borrow magazines, he was only allowed one because a different rule applied and he became loud and anxious. The teacher drew a Social Story to show him taking one magazine home. This visual explanation helped Sam to understand the change in procedure and calm his behavior. Social Stories can be helpful to students with autism in all aspects of their lives because they teach social expectations to students who may otherwise have difficulty attaining them. They are tools that can be used to lessen the anxiety a student's misreading of social cues creates.

Written on an individual basis, they address any situation that may arise, such as a simple procedure like using the library or a more complex dynamic like asking for a date.

The Squeezing Machine

A lack of understanding of one's social world along with an unregulated sensory integration system can be anxiety producing. As students grow and mature, they face uncharted territory. These challenges are often met with heightened anxiety and overt behaviors. Temple Grandin (1995), a professor who writes simply and honestly about her own autism, describes an anxiety reducing machine she built at age eighteen that consisted of two heavily padded boards that squeezed along the sides of her body. This machine produced the sensory input she craved and desensitized her overworked nervous system, thus reducing her anxiety.

Children with autism sometimes feel sensory overload in environments in which most people feel comfortable. Overhead lighting, especially fluorescent lights that buzz or flash; noise from fans or air conditioners; the clinking of dishes in the cafeteria down the hall; or a line tapping against a metal flagpole outside can send them into a tailspin. Sensory issues in which the central nervous system craves input may also appear. These children need constant sensory stimulation and may benefit from wearing a weighted vest, having a fidget toy, sitting on an inflated or rice-filled chair cushion, or using an exercise band strung between the front legs of their chair that they can push with their foot or leg. These sensitivities and the strategies for coping with them can influence learning, attention, behavior, and social interaction.

Support from parents and a knowledgeable occupational therapist are crucial in developing a sensory diet. Classroom teachers have the responsibility of observation and intervention and of providing reliable feedback to support staff. Creating opportunities for students to move about freely and to have some decision making in determining their sensory levels is essential.

What Teachers Need to Do

The inclusion of children with autism into the general education classroom affords teachers gifts and responsibilities; like all students, however, instruction and environmental considerations must be differentiated for them to reach their potential as learners. Here are some simple strategies teachers can use to help all students succeed:

- Order the classroom in almost every way. Maintain a posted schedule and encourage older students to use the strategies they have learned to organize their school lives. Always give students notice of expected due dates and upcoming tests. When possible, give advance reminders of half days, schedule and class changes, and fire drills.
- Use consistent visual cues and supports to navigate the school day and to complete academic tasks. This may include different-color desk folders for each subject, specific bins for turning in completed work, or a hands-on system for ordering lunch choices (i.e., one that uses visual supports such as picture cards of available food choices placed in appropriate baskets). Students who change classes may find it easier to leave materials behind in a designated place so they do not have the added responsibility of organizing them each class period.
- Be aware of sensory issues and consult professional staff and parents when developing strategies.
- Provide social supports and models to help students with autism learn socially appropriate behaviors from peers.
- Develop a behavioral plan that supports classroom expectations and promotes learning in a general education program.

Pay attention to your verbal directions. Fewer words are always better and a clearly defined message that is consistent works best. Students like Sam can and do learn and grow in the general education classroom. The daily opportunities for interaction with other students are vital to their social, communication, and academic progress. When a student with autism is given the opportunity to observe and interact, peers and others in the greater

---

Appendix

Support Organizations for Families, Teachers, and Practitioners Working with Students Who Have Autism Spectrum Disorder

The Autism Society of America is a voice and resource in education, advocacy, services, research, and support for the autism community. http://www.autism-society.org/ *Autism Collaboration* raises millions of dollars each year for research in autism with an eye toward parent driven decisions. http://www.autism.org/

Autism Speaks provides autism information, resources, and news on research and treatments. http://www.cureautismnow.org
Centers for Disease Control and Prevention Autism Information Center is the official information site on autism and provides general information, screening procedures, treatments, and research updates. http://www.cdc.gov/ncbddd/dd/ddautism.htm

world of school teach targeted and nontargeted information by example. Providing all students with a rich, inclusive classroom environment that includes individual goals will foster mutual respect and understanding for all.

References

Centers for Disease Control and Prevention, National Center for Health Statistics. 2006. Health, United States, 2006. http://www.cdc.gov/nchs/hus.html (accessed December 18, 2006).

Cohen, D., and F. Volkmar. 1997. *Handbook of autism and pervasive developmental disorders.* New York: Wiley.

Frombonne, E. 2007. *Autism Spectrum Disorders; Rates, trends and links with immunizations.* Lecture presented at Advances in Autism Conference: New Insights in the Diagnosis, Neurobiology, Genetics, and Treatment of Autism, New York.

Grandin, T. 1995. *Thinking in pictures.* New York: Doubleday.

Gray, C. 1994. *The new social story book.* Arlington, Texas: Future Horizons.

Quill, K.A., ed. 1995. *Teaching children with autism.* New York: Delmar.

DIANA FRIEDLANDER is a special education inclusion teacher in elementary education in Ridgefield, CT, and a doctoral candidate at Western Connecticut State University.

ARTICLE 9

Universal Design in Elementary and Middle School

Designing Classrooms and Instructional Practices to Ensure Access to Learning for All Students

MARGARET M. FLORES

The Association for Childhood Education International's (ACEI) mission includes helping educators meet the needs of students in a climate of societal change. One such change is the increasing diversity of learning needs within elementary and middle school classrooms. Increased numbers of students with disabilities served within the general education classroom have contributed to this diversity (U.S. Department of Education, 2005). Students with diverse needs present a challenge for elementary and middle school teachers because it may be difficult to ensure that all students meet expectations. Under current legislation, such as the No Child Left Behind Act (2002), all students, including those with disabilities, are expected to be proficient at grade level by 2013. Similarly, the Individuals With Disabilities Education Improvement Act (2004) states that students with disabilities should have increased access to the general education curriculum and that accommodations should be designed according to the students' needs.

In carrying out the mission of ACEI and complying with federal legislation, it is important that students with disabilities have accommodations written into their individualized educational programs (IEPs) and that these students receive accessible instruction. General education teachers play a critical role in both IEP development and implementation of accessible instruction. As members of the multidisciplinary IEP team, general education teachers have a unique understanding of curricular materials, texts, equipment, and technology within the general education setting that is critical in designing appropriate accommodations. These accommodations should support teachers' other role, that of implementing instruction that is assessible to all students. While this role may seem daunting, tools are available for designing classroom environments and instruction that are conducive to the learning of all students.

Universal Design for Instruction (UDI) is a set of principles helpful in guiding this process. UDI, designed by the Center for Applied Special Technology, is a framework that has been successful for all students, including those with disabilities in general education settings (Cawley, Foley, & Miller, 2003; McGuire, Scott, & Shaw, 2006; Pisha & Coyne, 2001; Pisha & Stahl, 2005). UDI ensures that all students have access to instruction through the following principles: 1) equitable use, 2) flexibility in use, 3) simple and intuitive, 4) perceptible information, 5) tolerance for error, 6) low physical effort, and 7) size and space for approach and use. The purpose of this article is to provide an overview of UDI, as well as practical classroom applications for elementary and middle school teachers.

Equitable Use

Equitable use means that all students can use materials, equipment, and technology in the classroom. The most common materials that can be inaccessible to students with disabilities are textbooks. As students advance in school, the emphasis on reading to learn increases and accessibility of textbooks becomes increasingly important in the content areas as students move through to middle school. Textbooks are inaccessible if students' reading levels are several levels below their grade placement, students cannot read the print due to its small size, and/or students have difficulty holding a book due to its size and weight. However, textbooks can be made accessible to students through the use of books on tape and through digital texts (Boyle et al., 2003; Twyman & Tindal, 2006). Books on tape are available through such nonprofit organizations as Readings for the Blind and Dyslexic, a free service for school districts and individuals with reading and visual disabilities. Digital texts allow for physical access, magnification of print, changes in contrast (i.e., increased color contrast between the print and page background), as well as audio output.

Technology, classroom equipment, and materials may not be accessible to all students, due to various student characteristics. Equipment and materials may be difficult to grasp or manipulate and/or visually perceive. Fortunately, equipment and materials used for instruction can be made accessible to all students through the use of grips, changes in size and dimension, and high-contrast materials. For lower and intermediate elementary students, these materials might include: special grips for pencils or other writing utensils; adaptive scissors; use of high contrast and/or large print, pictorial directions, and/or audio directions within learning centers; use of paper with raised lines; and manipulatives that are made easier to grip through size and texture (D'Angiulli, 2007; Judge, 2006; Russell et al., 2007). Although these materials will continue to be helpful for students at the late elementary and middle school level, additional items might include high-contrast print materials and graphic organizers or diagrams, and the use of graphic organizers and diagrams with raised lines (D'Angiulli, 2007; Russell et al., 2007).

Technology difficulties include becoming "lost" when searching the Internet for research, the computer font being too small or lacking color contrast, motor difficulties interfering with mouse manipulation, keyboard keys being too small, or the keyboard's lack of color contrast. As students progress through elementary and middle school, they will use technology more independently for research. Technology solutions for these students include the creation of web quests, in which the necessary websites are linked and/or the sites are contained within a single main site (Skylar, Higgins, & Boone, 2007). For all students, regardless of their grade level, computer equipment can be modified through the use of mouse balls that accommodate for fine motor difficulty, high contrast, and/or large-print stickers placed on top of keyboard keys. Keyboards are also available with large keys. Computer software is available to provide audio output so that print can be read to the student. The contrast of the screen and print can be adjusted to provide appropriate color contrast.

Flexibility in Use

Flexible use means that instruction and accompanying activities accommodate a wide range of individual preferences and abilities. Instruction can be designed in a variety of ways to accommodate a variety of learning strengths. It is helpful to design instruction using several different modes in order to make learning accessible for students with diverse learning needs.

Visual Representation. Adding visual representations in the form of graphic organizers or schematic maps helps students organize concepts and information (Boulineau, Fore, & Hagan-Burke, 2004; Ives, 2007; Lovitt, & Horton, 1994; McCoy & Ketterlin-Geller, 2004; Williams et al., 2007). These tools also help students recognize relationships between ideas and concepts. Students who have difficulties processing information, and students who lack background knowledge, may have difficulty connecting ideas and understanding how ideas come together to form overall concepts. Emphasis on pictures and symbols may be more appropriate when designing graphic organizers for elementary students. For middle school students, the use of graphic organizers or schematic maps may be helpful as instructional advance organizers and as instructional guides throughout units. The use of color, size, and shape also can be helpful in emphasizing relationships and hierarchies within graphic organizers. Other ways to appeal to visual learners at all grade levels is through pictures and videos. Visual depictions of information and relationships also may be helpful for memory or retention by providing students with an avenue for "picturing information in their mind."

Hands-on Activities. Hands-on activities can be helpful for students, at all grade levels, who have difficulty acquiring information by more traditional means (Butler, Miller, Crehan, & Babbitt, 2003; Cass, Cares, Smith, & Jackson, 2003; Kerry-Moran, 2006; Kinniburgh & Shaw, 2007; Mastropieri et al., 2006; Witzel, Mercer, & Miller, 2003). Although these types of activities may be associated with science in the form of experiments and demonstrations, they provide opportunities throughout content areas. In mathematics, the use of manipulatives is a way to increase understanding of concepts and procedures, regardless of grade level. Although using and managing the use of manipulatives may be challenging, research has shown that students with learning disabilities need an average of three experiences with manipulatives in order to understand mathematical concepts (Mercer & Miller, 1992). In addition to building understanding, hands-on and participatory activities provide students who have difficulty expressing themselves through oral and written language with an opportunity to demonstrate their understanding.

Assignment Completion. It is important to assess students' understanding of concepts and ideas; however, providing one avenue for expression of one's understanding may lead to inaccurate results. For example, students with learning disabilities in writing may not be able to fully express their ideas in writing, but they could discuss them in detail. Offering assignment or project menus could provide a variety of ways in which students can demonstrate their understanding. A menu allows all students to choose their preferred format without singling out particular students. For example, students might be given the option of writing a paragraph (for younger students) or an essay (for older students), an oral report to a group or through audio recording, or a multimedia presentation. The choices offered should each allow for appropriate assessment of students' understanding of the target objective or concept.

Another way to be flexible about assignment completion throughout elementary and middle levels is through cooperative grouping. Cooperative groups should be structured so that all members of the group have roles and responsibilities. These roles should be tailored to students' strengths and weaknesses and lead to active participation for all students. Each student should be accountable for his or her contribution to the group, as well as for the overall group's performance. The provision of individual roles ensures that all students actively learn and contribute, rather than only a few members of the group completing the work.

Simple and Intuitive

Simple and intuitive means that instruction is easily understood, regardless of students' experience, knowledge, or language skills. This includes priming students' background knowledge prior to beginning instruction. Priming background knowledge involves explaining how new information is connected to prior knowledge and experience. For example, an instructional unit about the American Civil War might include discussions about instances when students might have felt that another person or group did not attend to their point of view or needs. The experiences of students and how this discussion is moderated will differ depending on the grade level. Another way to make instruction simple and intuitive for elementary and middle school students is through analogies between new concepts and well-known concepts. It is important to be aware of students' diverse experiences while creating or designing these analogies, so that all students easily connect the two concepts.

Using consistent language is another way of making instruction simple and intuitive for elementary and middle school students. Students with language processing deficits and/or students who are second language learners have difficulty understanding instruction when each explanation involves different vocabulary and terminology. Therefore, using similar language each time an explanation is provided will lead to more efficient learning and understanding. In addition, language should be not only appropriate for a given skill, task, or concept, but also easily understood by students. Keep explanations as simple as possible, adding vocabulary instruction, if needed.

Perceptible Information

Perceptible information refers to that information that can be perceived regardless of skill and ability. This includes the use of instructional materials with appropriate color contrast for students with visual impairments. Black and yellow provide the highest color contrast, and computer screens, PowerPoint presentations, keys on computer keyboards, and handouts can be adjusted to allow for increased visual perception. Seating within the classroom also can provide for increased perception. Placing students near the instructor and away from windows and hallways will increase students' ability to hear, see, and attend to instructional activities. Assignments and instructional materials also can be made more perceptible by changing their format. This begins with directions that are written clearly and at a level that students with various reading abilities can understand. Format also includes the amount of space between activities or problems, the use of lines for written responses, the layout, and the order of questions. Activities and assignments that involve written problems or scenarios can be adjusted for readability. Tests and quizzes that accompany textbooks may not be written at a level that all students understand. The wording of questions can be changed so that students are assessed based on their level of subject matter knowledge, rather than on their reading ability.

Tolerance for Error

Tolerance for error means that students have the opportunity to engage in ongoing assignments and projects. This allows for revision and editing over time, and students receive credit for correcting their errors. Students have the opportunity for feedback and ongoing learning. Over time, students learn from their mistakes and practice the appropriate skill, an opportunity that is lost with one-time assignments. These ongoing assignments and projects would be appropriate, regardless of students' grade placement.

Low Physical Effort

Low physical effort means that all students have access to materials and activities without great physical effort. The use of technology can decrease the amount of physical effort (Bahr & Nelson, 1996; Strassman & D'Amore, 2002; Tumlin & Heller, 2004). For example, if writing is physically taxing for students with fine motor difficulties, then the use of a keyboard can be of assistance. Hardware, software, and accessories are available to make computers accessible to students with more significant motor difficulties. Classroom materials, such as scissors, writing utensils, lab equipment, and desks, are all available in versions that are easily accessible for students with physical disabilities (Judge, 2006). These accommodations allow students to focus their attention and energy on learning rather than on manipulating materials.

Size and Space for Approach and Use

Size and space for approach and use means enough space is available so that all students can participate. The classroom is set up so that all students can maneuver throughout the room and participate in a variety of activities without excess physical effort. Students with physical disabilities have enough space to engage in the same types of activities as students without disabilities. Movement throughout the room and transition to activities is facilitated by its layout and design. Enough space is available between learning

centers within elementary classrooms and middle school classrooms. Students should be able to move easily from small-group instruction to other areas within the room. As students begin to change classrooms, backpacks and other student materials can create clutter and hazards for students with visual impairments, physical disabilities, and/or students who use wheelchairs. Providing a special area within the room for these materials or using individual storage crates under chairs or tables can alleviate this problem.

Conclusion

The scenarios in Figures 1 and 2 are from elementary and middle level classrooms that exemplify different UDI principles in action. Figure 1 describes a 3rd-grade classroom in which the following principles are emphasized: equitable use, flexibility in use, perceptible information, low physical effort, and size and space for approach. Figure 2 describes a 7th-grade classroom in which the following principles are emphasized: equitable use, flexibility in use, simple and intuitive, perceptible information, tolerance for error, and size and space for approach.

Students with disabilities have IEPs that are written each year by a multidisciplinary team, including, but not limited to, general education teachers, special education teachers, parents, and administrators. The general education teacher has the most experience and information about the curriculum, activities, and materials used within the general education setting. In order to ensure that instruction is accessible to all students, appropriate modifications and accommodations need to be planned and implemented. The general education teacher is a critical participant in this process because of his or her knowledge of the general education setting. Parents, special education teachers, and administrators might not be as knowledgeable

Mr. Jackson teaches 3rd grade at North Hills Elementary School and utilizes UDI in order to make his classroom accessible to a diverse group of learners. Mr. Jackson's room includes three types of learning centers (mathematics, writing, and reading), a classroom library (which includes audio books), an area for small-group instruction, and an area for whole-group instruction. Therefore, he has flexibility in his grouping, allowing him to individualize instruction for a small group while others are engaged in alternate learning activities. He places the learning centers along one side of the room, far enough apart so that students in one center will not be distracted by students in another, but still allowing easy movement from one to another. The large group area consists of grouped desks (conducive for cooperating group work) placed in a semicircle formation in front of the classroom's whiteboard. The classroom library (close to the reading center) and the small-group area are situated on each end of the room. Mr. Jackson has instituted a class book club in which students chose books based on the groups' interests. Mr. Jackson has acquired audio-books from the Association for the Blind and Dyslexic so that all students can participate fully in the experience. Each learning center includes written (large print, high contrast) directions, pictorial directions, and audio directions through headsets. Menus of activities also are included for each center in order to differentiate them based on students' strengths. The materials for the centers are modified according to students' needs. For example, the math center's manipulatives are large, with high-contrast coloring. The keyboards are portable and can be moved throughout learning areas. The students' written work can be saved on the classroom computer so it can be downloaded for editing and printing later.

FIGURE 1   Mr. Jackson's 3rd-grade Classroom: UDI Example for Elementary Level Classroom

Ms. Vargas is a member of a four-person team and teaches 7th-grade science at Green Oaks Middle School. She utilizes the principles of UDI to make her science class accessible to diverse groups of learners. Ms. Vargas' science textbook package includes audio versions of the text that she makes available to students with visual and learning disabilities. Ms. Vargas has acquired software and hardware that allows students to scan print materials into the classroom computer, which then converts the print into an audio format. Prior to beginning an instructional unit, Ms. Vargas provides all students with a schematic map for the unit. She refers to the map often and highlights important connections between concepts learned previously and those in the current lesson. When instruction involves lecture and note taking, Ms. Vargas provides all students with an outline that includes key words and a hierarchical structure to ensure that students have useful study notes. Students also may audio-record classroom instruction. During these lectures, Ms. Vargas uses PowerPoint presentations with a large, high-contrast font. During laboratory activities, students work in pairs, with each person responsible for specific duties. Plastic (rather than glass) containers and equipment are used and materials are kept on a series of lazy Susans so that they may be accessed easily. When needed, Ms. Vargas modifies the procedures so that larger weights and volumes can be used, allowing students with fine motor problems to grip and move containers and objects more easily. Laboratory reports can be produced either in writing (handwritten or word processed) or as an audio recording. More complicated lab reports and projects are ongoing assignments in which students complete the product in stages and receive feedback.

FIGURE 2   Ms. Vargas' 7th-grade Classroom: UDI Example for a Middle Level Classroom

about what might be needed within this setting. The general education teacher could add valuable suggestions about modifications and accommodations that might be otherwise overlooked. The principles of universal design should guide this planning process. The general education classroom should be thought of with regard to the students' accessibility, specifically in terms of equitable use, flexibility in use, simple and intuitive, perceptive in formation, perceptible in formation, tolerance for error, low physical effort, and size and space for approach and use.

The No Child Left Behind Act (2002) requires that students with disabilities perform proficiently on grade level in all areas by 2013. These are high expectations to meet. Therefore, it is critical that all students have access to instruction within the general education classroom. Students' IEPs provide for the necessary accommodations and modifications for access to instruction. The multidisciplinary team who creates a student's IEP is responsible for assessing the student's needs and designing the necessary modifications. The general education teacher has unique knowledge of the curricular standards, instructional activities, materials, and physical design of the classroom. The awareness of these factors, as well as the knowledge of the principles of universal design, provides teachers with the tools necessary to fully participate in this process of meeting students' needs and ensuring that all students have access to instruction.

Rose, D. H., Meyer, A., & Hichcock, C. (2005). The universally designed classroom. Cambridge, MA: Harvard University Press.
This book provides an introduction to Universal Design and is useful for teachers, administrators, and parents. It includes strategies and resources for creating a classroom that provides access to the general education curriculum for all students.

Rose, D. H., & Meyer, A. (2002). Teaching every student in the digital age: Universal design for learning. Alexandria, VA: Association for Supervision and Curriculum Development.
This book provides an overview of Universal Design for Learning, as well as real-world strategies for implementing Universal Design in the classroom. The authors explicitly connect ideas and concepts, using graphic organizers and examples throughout the book.

Council for Exceptional Children. (2005). Universal design for learning. Upper Saddle River, NJ: Prentice Hall.
This book serves as a practical guide to implementing Universal Design in the classroom. It includes a case-based scenario about teachers, experiences with Universal Design. Discussion questions throughout the book offer opportunities for application and reflection upon the content.

TABLE 1 Books That Provide Resources and Additional Information about Implementation of Universal Design for Instruction

Websites

Lesson Builder: http://lessonbuilder.cast.org
This site provides models and tools to create and adapt lessons in order to increase accessibility for all students. Model lesson plans across content areas and grade levels are included.

Book Builder: http://bookbuilder.cast.org
This site provides information and the tools to create engaging digital books for students. Universally designed books will engage, and provide access for, diverse groups of students.

Creating Accessible WebQuests and Web-based Student Activities: www.4teachers.org
This site offers tools and resources to integrate technology into the classroom. These include Web lessons, quizzes, rubrics, classroom calendars, and other tools for student use.

TABLE 2 Interactive Websites That Provide Tools for the Implementation of Universal Design for Instruction Principles

References

Bahr, C. M., & Nelson, N. W. (1996). The effects of text-based and graphics-based software tools on planning and organizing of stories. *Journal of Learning Disabilities, 22,* 355-270.

Boulineau, T., Fore, C., & Hagan-Burke, S. (2004). Using story mapping to increase the story grammar of elementary students with learning disabilities. *Learning Disability Quarterly, 27*(2), 105-114.

Boyle, E. A., Rosenberg, M. S., Connelly, V. J., Gallin-Washburg, S., Brinckerhoff, L. C., & Banerjee, M. (2003). Effects of audio-texts on the acquisition of secondary level content by students with mild disabilities. *Learning, Disability Quarterly, 26,* 204-214.

Butler, F. M., Miller, S. P., Crehan, K., & Babbitt, B. P. (2003). Fraction instruction for students with mathematics disabilities: Comparing two teaching sequences. *Learning Disabilities Research and Practice, 18*(2), 99-111.

Cass, M., Cares, D., Smith, M., & Jackson, C. (2003). Effects of manipulative instruction on solving area and perimeter problems by students with learning disabilities. *Learning Disabilities Research and Practice, 18*(2), 112-120.

Cawley, J. F., Foley, T. E., & Miller, J. (2003). Science and students with mild disabilities. *Intervention in School and Clinic 38,* 160-171.

D'Angiulli, A. (2007). Raised-line pictures, blindness, and tactile beliefs: An observational case study. *Journal of Visual Impairment and Blindness, 101,* 172-178.

Individuals with Disabilities Education Improvement Acts of 2004, Pub. L. No. 108-446, 118 Stat. 2647 (2004) (amending 20 U.S.C. §§ 1440 et seq.).

Ives, B. (2007). Graphic organizers applied to secondary algebra instruction for students with learning disorders. *Learning Disabilities Research and Practice, 22*(2), 110-118.

Judge, S. (2006). Constructing an assistive technology toolkit for young children: Views from the field. *Journal of Special Education Technology, 21*(4), 17-24.

Kerry-Moran, K. J. (2006). Nurturing emergent readers through readers' theater. *Early Childhood Education Journal, 33,* 317-323.

Kinniburgh, L., & Shaw, E. (2007). Building reading fluency in elementary science through readers' theater. *Science Activities, 44*(1), 16-20.

Lovitt, T. C, & Horton, S. V. (1994). Strategies for adapting textbooks for youth with learning disabilities. *Remedial and Special Education, 15,* 105-116.

Mastropieri, M. A., Scruggs, T. E., Norland, J. J., Berkley, S., McDuffie, K., Tornquist, E. H., & Connors, N. (2006). Differentiated curriculum enhancement in inclusive middle school science: Effects on classroom and high stakes tests. *Journal of Special Education, 40*(3), 130-137.

McCoy, J. D., & Ketterlin-Geller, R. (2004). Rethinking instructional delivery for diverse student populations: Serving all learners with concept-based instruction. *Intervention in School and Clinic, 40*(2), 88-95.

McGuire, J. M., Scott, S. S., Shaw, S. F. (2006). Universal design and its application in educational environments. *Remedial and Special Education, 27,* 166-175.

Mercer, C. D., & Miller, S. P. (1992). Teaching students with learning problems in math to acquire, understand, and apply basic math facts. *Remedial and Special Education, 13*(3), 19-35.

Pisha, B., & Coyne, P. (2001). Smart from the start. *Remedial and Special Education, 22,* 197-203.

Pisha, B., & Stahl, S. (2005). The promise of new learning environments for students with disabilities. *Intervention in School and Clinic, 41,* 67-75.

Russell M. E., Jutai, J.W., Strong, J. G., Campbell, K.A., Gold, D., Pretty, L., & Wilmot, L. (2007). The legibility of typefaces for readers with low vision: A research review. *Journal of Visual Impairments and Blindness, 101,* 402-415.

Skylar, A.A., Higgins, K., & Boone, R. (2007). Strategies for adapting webquests for students with learning disabilities. *Intervention in School and Clinic, 43*(1), 20-28.

Strassman, B. K., & D'Amore, M. (2002). The write technology. *Teaching Exceptional Children, 34*(6), 28-31.

Tumlin, J., & Heller, K.W. (2004). Using word prediction software to increase fluency with students with physical disabilities. *Journal of Special Education Technology, 19*(3), 5-14.

Twyman, T., & Tindal, G. (2006). Using computer-adapted, conceptually based history text to increase comprehension and problem-solving skills of students with disabilities. *Journal of Special Education Technology, 21*(2), 5-16.

U.S. Department of Education. (2002). *No Child Left Behind: A desktop reference.* Washington, DC: Author.

U.S. Department of Education, National Center for Education Statistics. (2005). *The condition of education 2005* (NCES 2005-094).

Williams, J. P., Nubla-Kung, A. M., Pollini, S., Stafford, K. B., Garcia, A., & Snyder, A. E. (2007). Teaching cause and effect text structure through social studies content to at-risk second graders. *Journal of Learning Disabilities, 40*(2), 111-120.

Witzel, B. S., Mercer, C. D., & Miller, S. P. (2003). Teaching algebra to students with learning difficulties: An investigation of an explicit instruction approach. *Learning Disabilities Research and Practice, 18*(2), 121-131.

MARGARET M. FLORES is Assistant Professor, Special Education, Department of Interdisciplinary Learning and Teaching, University of Texas at San Antonio.

ARTICLE 10

Social and Emotional Development of Gifted Children: Straight Talk

Tracy L. Cross, Ph.D.

In the past year I have been asked during interviews on two different occasions what message I would like to convey directly to parents, teachers, and counselors of gifted children. Consequently, I have had a fair amount of time to think about this and have developed a list of eight topics I think are important enough to speak to quite directly.

1. The first topic that I would like to address is the question "Are all students gifted?" The answer to this question is no. As Jim Gallagher has said on many occasions, "gifted in what?" To be gifted one must ultimately be gifted in something. All children are wonderful. They are considered in many cultures as the most valuable beings in the world. Even so, they are not gifted by the profession's definitions. Giftedness is a scientific construct that has a relatively circumscribed definition. Therefore, only a small portion of children would actually be identified as gifted.

2. Students with gifts and talents are as equally mentally and physically healthy (if not more so) as the general population of students. Studies in the United States going back 80 or more years, along with multiple more recent studies, have illustrated this fact again and again. Even in very specific areas such as suicidal behavior, recent research has shown that suicide ideation among the gifted is at the same level or less than that of the general population. And, while we do not know for sure in terms of prevalence rates of completed suicide, significant differences between the general population and students with gifts and talents have not been shown.

3. This third issue is difficult to describe as it deals with how we come to know about gifted children. Who are the gifted, and how do we come to find them? We tend to define giftedness as children who require a special education. We tend to identify them on the basis of the potential or abilities for outstanding performance in the future. Then, over time, we anoint them gifted or talented on the basis of their achievement in a specific domain.

Although these three emphases of definition, identification, and recognition seem quite similar, in fact they are different. With young students who have verbal skills, we typically find them with some indication on a standardized test or a hint a teacher picks up on. This is really an effort to predict the future by determining that a child has a need warranting a special education. Then we bring to bear what we can in terms of teaching, curriculum, and other opportunities to develop these potentialities into talent areas such as mathematics, language arts, and the like. The primary problem is that we know there are influences on each of these three areas, including social class. So, economic status tends to end up being a very important variable that prevents us from identifying and providing the services these children need to be successful. This is very important given the increasing diversity in our country. This is, in my opinion, the most important issue of our day—finding and servicing all of the children with gifts and talents.

4. Another very important issue is the fact that many of us have changed our views about what giftedness is, from that of an entity, meaning something that one is born with, to a phenomenon that is incremental in its development. Professionals including Carol Dweck have written about this way of thinking. The incremental model is much more representative of what actually takes place in a person's life from birth until death relative to developing specific skills. Across the lifespan, people receive instruction, struggle with some failure and develop knowledge and skills. This is a much healthier notion to guide the efforts of a parent, teacher, or counselor in terms of the work we do on behalf of our children. We should not think of them as fully formed because someone has anointed them as gifted (entity model). But, rather, we should think of them as requiring a special education now and over time. With our expertise being brought to bear, the child will hopefully reach his or her full potential.

5. The fifth topic is parenting and the development of students with gifts and talents. The research base here over the years has been rather meager but it is growing. We know from research on the development of children in general that there are predictable outcomes of parenting styles and approaches. As we continue to pursue the development of students with gifts and talents, we need to conduct considerable research in this area

so we can better guide and prepare parents to work with children. Engaging children in dialogue that accentuates communication, while at the same time helping them individuate, can lead to high levels of agency and greater life successes. Until the research base in this area expands, however, we would be wise to draw on the best practices of parenting research in general. We also can draw from research investigating the lived experiences of gifted students and how they cope with their lives in school. These two databases will shed light on parenting issues. With gifted studies research, we should carefully monitor the growing research bases on perfectionism and resiliency and gifted students. Insights about parenting students with gifts and talents, while in its early stages, are being revealed, holding great promise for guiding parenting practices in the future.

6. The next issue is diversity and giftedness. There is so much yet to know about diversity and gifted students that we are just scratching the service. All groups of people have samples within them who have outstanding potential to develop into great talents within and outside of the traditional culture they represent. Moreover, as we become more diverse as a country, this fact has become increasingly obvious in some areas such as the visual arts, where there is a physical manifestation of emerging talent that most adults can recognize. It is easy to garner the resources to support these students while other talent domains such as early mathematic potential or logic takes awhile to reveal itself in a manner that the general population can understand. So much work needs to be done in the area of diversity and giftedness to maximize the potential of all the students.

An interesting corollary to the diversification of America intersecting with the technology evolution is playing out socially among our students. We have been living through fascinating changes in American culture over the past 20 years or so as an evolution of technologies in terms of laptop computers, desktop computers, and, more recently, gaming in the extent to which people from all walks of life participate in these activities. One of the manifestations of this evolution has been the change of the language associated historically with gifted children such as being called a *nerd*, a *geek*, a *brainiac*, or any number of other things. This evolution where gifted children often are top competitors in games, in fixing computers, or in setting up things has raised their status in the general population. Stores have Geek Squads and adults will use the term *geek* or *nerd* as an adjective rather than a noun. I think it is showing that as our country becomes more diverse, being an academically or intellectually gifted person gets defined in the broad context and over time is becoming less as a problem for gifted people as compared to what it was 50 or even 20 years ago.

7. True for the general population of adolescents, and especially true for some gifted adolescents, is the desire for authenticity among the adults they deal with. In my work at the Indiana Academy, I observed that many intellectually gifted adolescents desired interactions to be absolutely authentic and when they assess that an adult person is not being authentic—genuine—not only do they devalue that person but it causes them conflict in trying to make sense out of the importance they describe to adults and the authentic behavior. For some of these gifted young people, they conclude that most people are inauthentic most of the time and that the only true feeling is that of pain, and that every other feeling state is more manufactured than authentic. There are all sorts of negative ramifications to the belief that this feeling state of pain is the only genuine one. One of the results is students will find ways to feel pain so they feel themselves to be authentic, so they have feelings they can identify, and so they can gain a sense of relief. We know from our research that cutting behavior among our youth, adolescents, and young adults has increased quite a bit in the last 20 years and in my opinion is quite likely associated in some cases with this desire for authenticity.

8. The last important issue is that it is incumbent upon us as adults to act proactively on behalf of students with gifts and talents. The important point here is that we should all feel morally obligated to act on behalf of students with gifts and talents because not to do so is, in fact, choosing not to act. Inaction has all sorts of consequences for gifted students in terms of their not being challenged in school, feeling frustrated, feeling unvalued, feeling like there is something wrong with them, and so forth. We cannot be guilty of turning a blind eye to the social and emotional issues and needs of students with gifts and talents. If we do nothing, we become complicit in the decline of their psychological well-being.

One approach to engaging others is for us use language that does not pit us against our colleagues. For example, when we talk about students with gifts and talents, we should frame our conversation within the goal set that our schools should aspire to all students maximizing their potential, including gifted children. This will allow a different kind of conversation to be held than often occurs. This goal for students runs counter to minimum competency testing common to the U.S. Changing the conversation from minimum competency to maximizing the potential of all students will dramatically affect the opportunities for all students, including students with gifts and talents.

The social and emotional development of students with gifts and talents lasts a lifetime. We have learned many important lessons about how to help them develop during their school-age years and with this newfound knowledge have corresponding responsibility to act. The eight issues discussed in this column bring to light some of the current thinking that can be helpful to those of us (parents, teachers, counselors) who are in important positions to help them develop. Understanding what giftedness actually is and is not, how to identify it, moving from an entity model of giftedness to an incremental model, continuing to strive to be as effective a parent as one can be, and understanding the needs of authenticity enable adults to assist in the social and emotional development of students with gifts and talents.

ARTICLE 11

Understanding Unconscious Bias and Unintentional Racism

Acknowledging Our Possible Biases and Working Together Openly Is Essential for Developing Community in Our Schools

JEAN MOULE

In the blink of an eye, unconscious bias was visible to me, an African American. A man saw my face as I walked into the store and unconsciously checked his wallet. On the street, a woman catches my eye a half block away and moves her purse from the handle of her baby's stroller to her side as she arranges the baby's blanket. In the airport, a man signals to his wife to move her purse so it is not over the back of her chair, which is adjacent to the one I am moving toward. What is happening in these instances? Were these actions general safety precautions? If so, why did the sight only of my brown face, not the others who moved among these individuals, elicit these actions?

I believe these are examples of "blink of the eye" racism. Such unconscious biases lead to unintentional racism: racism that is usually invisible even *and especially* to those who perpetrate it. Yet, most people do not want to be considered racist or capable of racist acts because the spoken and unspoken norm is that "good people do not discriminate or in any way participate in racism" (Dovidio and Gaertner 2005, p. 2).

Such unconscious biases affect all of our relationships, whether they are fleeting relationships in airports or longer term relationships between teachers and students, teachers and parents, teachers and other educators.

Understanding our own biases is a first step toward improving the interactions that we have with all people and is essential if we hope to build deep community within our schools.

Biases are rooted in stereotypes and prejudices. A stereotype is a simplistic image or distorted truth about a person or group based on a prejudgment of habits, traits, abilities, or expectations (Weinstein and Mellen 1997). Ethnic and racial stereotypes are learned as part of normal socialization and are consistent among many populations and across time. An excellent illustration of this phenomenon is a recent exchange that repeated Clark's classic 1954 doll study. In a video, completed by a 17-year-old film student and disseminated through the media, a young black child clearly reflects society's prejudice: The child describes the black doll as looking "bad" and the white doll as "nice" (Edney 2006). Children internalize our society's biases and prejudices, as have all of us; they are just a little less able to hide it. I am reminded of the story of a 4-year-old in an affluent suburb who remarked to her mother upon seeing a young Latina while in line at the grocery store, "Look, mommy, a baby maid."

And when we receive evidence that confronts our deeply held and usually unrecognized biases, the human brain usually finds ways to return to stereotypes. The human brain uses a mechanism called "re-fencing" when confronted with evidence contrary to the stereotype. Allport coined the term: "When a fact cannot fit into a mental field, the exception is acknowledged, but the field is hastily fenced in again and not allowed to remain dangerously open" (Allport 1954, p. 23). This is illustrated by such statements as "some of my best friends are black." That statement, while used to deny bias, has within it the seeds of a defense of negative feelings toward blacks. The context of the statement usually means that "my best friend" is an exception to stereotypes and, therefore, that other blacks would *not* be my friends. Thompson (2003) refers to this as *absolution* through a connected relationship (i.e., I am absolved from racism because my best friend is black). Dovidio and Gaertner describe this inability to connect stated beliefs and unconscious bias as *aversive racism,* "the inherent contradiction that exists when the denial of personal prejudice co-exists with underlying unconscious negative feelings and beliefs" (2005, p. 2).

In many situations, from either the dominant or the oppressed, simple unconscious associations may drastically change outcomes. An example is Steele and Aaronson's (1995) work on *stereotype threat,* in which the performance of African-American students in a testing situation was cut in half by asking them to identify their race at the start of the test. This simple act unconsciously reminded students of the stereotypes connected with their race. Moreover, when asked at the end of the test, the students who were primed to remember their race were unable to identify the reminder as a factor in their poorer test score (Steele 1997).

In ambiguous situations, people's minds may also *reconstruct* a situation in order to conform to their stereotypes. An example is a study of people who harbor negative attitudes about African Americans: In a quickly seen image in which a white man with a weapon chases a black man, some people reverse the race of the perpetrator of the violence in order to make it conform with their preconceived notions (Diller and Moule 2005). Such unconscious biases have a role in determining the length of jail sentences (Vedantam 2005) and the fact that, regardless of explicit racial prejudices, police officers are more likely to shoot an unarmed black target than an unarmed white target (Correll et al. 2002).

Regarding violence, it is important to remember that we are programmed to quickly discern who is enemy and who is friend, for in the past—and certainly in many places in the world today—the ability to quickly identify friend or foe may be a matter of life or death (Begley 2004).

Uncovering Biases

Because people are more likely to act out of unconscious or hidden bias, knowing that you have a bias for or against a group may cause you to compensate and more carefully consider your possible responses or actions. Acknowledging biases often opens doors for learning and allows people to consciously work for harmony in classrooms and communities (Polite and Saenger 2003). How do we find a key to unlock this door to the mind? The Implicit Association Test (IAT) has helped millions of people—those who accept the often startling results—reveal their unconscious biases to themselves (https://implicit.harvard.edu/implicit/).

Anthony Greenwald and Mahzarin Banaji developed the test in the mid-1990s because "it is well known that people don't always 'speak their minds,' and it is suspected that people don't always 'know their minds'" (Greenwald, McGhee, and Schwartz 1998). The IAT "presents a method that convincingly demonstrates the divergences of our conscious thoughts and our unconscious biases," according to the Harvard web site on Project Implicit.

Strangely enough, the first evidence of this unconscious bias came from insects and flowers. Greenwald made a list of 25 insect names and 25 flower names and found that it was far easier to place the flowers in groups with pleasant words and insects in groups with unpleasant words than the reverse. It was just difficult to "hold a mental association of insects with words such as 'dream,' 'candy,' and 'heaven,' and flowers with words such as 'evil,' 'poison' and 'devil'" (Vedantam 2005, p. 3).

Greenwald then took the next step and used stereotypically white-sounding names, such as Adam and Emily, and black-sounding names, such as Jamal and Lakisha, and grouped them with pleasant and unpleasant words. According to Vedantam, Greenwald himself was surprised: "I had as much trouble pairing African-American names with pleasant words as I did insect names with pleasant words" (Vedantam 2005, p. 3). His collaborator, Banaji, was even more self-reflective, "'I was deeply embarrassed,' she recalls. 'I was humbled in a way that few experiences in my life have humbled me'" (p. 3).

This unconscious pairing has direct real-world consequences. Unconscious bias allows people who consciously said they wanted qualified minority employees to then unconsciously rate resumes with black-sounding names as less qualified. With other factors held constant, white-sounding names at the top of resumes triggered 50% more callbacks than African-American names. Human resources managers were stunned by the results. Explicit bias can occur not only without the intent to discriminate, but despite explicit desires to recruit minorities (Bertrand and Mullainathan 2004).

In *See No Bias,* Vedantam (2005) shares the disappointment and surprise that two recent test takers experienced when they found that their results on the Implicit Association Test did not mesh with their perceived views of themselves. To the dismay of these individuals, the test results were also in conflict with their life and career goals. Vedantam describes in detail a woman, an activist, taking a recent version of the test:

> The woman brought up a test on her computer from a Harvard University web site. It was really very simple: All it asked her to do was distinguish between a series of black and white faces. When she saw a black face, she was to hit a key on the left; when she saw a white face, she was to hit a key on the right. Next, she was asked to distinguish between a series of positive and negative words. Words such as "glorious" and "wonderful" required a left key, words such as "nasty" and "awful" required a right key. The test remained simple when two categories were combined: The activist hit the left key if she saw either a white face or a positive word, and hit the right key if she saw either a black face or a negative word.
>
> Then the groupings were reversed. The woman's index fingers hovered over her keyboard. The test now required her to group black faces with positive words, and white faces with negative words. She leaned forward intently. She made no mistakes, but it took her longer to correctly sort the words and images.
>
> Her result appeared on the screen, and the activist became very silent. The test found she had a bias for whites over blacks.
>
> "It surprises me I have any preferences at all," she said. "By the work I do, by my education, my background. I'm progressive, and I think I have no bias. Being a minority myself, I don't feel I should or would have biases."
>
> "I'm surprised," the woman said. She bit her lip. "And disappointed." (p. 2)

Such reactions should not really be a surprise according to the writings of many white anti-racist activists, including Tim Wise, who acknowledge residual racism still inside them. Wise notes how unconscious bias relegates the role of whiteness or race "to a nonfactor in the minds of whites" (2005, p. 18). When the role of whiteness or race becomes clear to a person, such as the activist described above, surprise and disappointment are likely results.

While I started this piece with evidence of people who responded to their gut reactions to my brown skin in surprising nonverbal ways, many of the same people would be quite gracious if given another second or two. Recent research shows that while most people have an instant activity in the "fight or flight" amygdala part of their brains upon encountering an *unexpected* person or situation, that first reaction is often consciously overridden in a nanosecond by many people in order to overcome built-in biases and respond as their better, undiscriminating selves. This ability to overcome embedded biases is particularly important when we consider that, "although many white Americans consider themselves unbiased, when unconscious stereotypes are measured, some 90% implicitly link blacks with negative traits (evil, failure)" (Begley 2004, p. 1).

I pick up subtle clues, either consciously or unconsciously, as to who is a good, open contact for me versus someone who may have difficulty engaging with me easily based on my race.

Changing Attitudes

Do we have the ability to change our attitudes and behaviors? Gladwell explains the two levels of consciousness in a manner that gives us hope. He says that in many situations, we are able to direct our behavior using our conscious attitudes—what we choose to believe or our stated values—rather than our "racial attitude on an *unconscious* level—the immediate, automatic associations that tumble out before we've even had time to think" (2005, p. 84). He continues, "We don't deliberately choose our unconscious attitudes . . . we may not even be aware of them" (p. 85). Because our unconscious attitudes may be completely incompatible with our stated values, we must know just what those unconscious attitudes

are, for they are, as Gladwell states, a powerful predictor of how we may act in some spontaneous situations.

Gladwell describes the type of circumstances where blacks and whites will both engage and disengage around climate and personal relation issues:

> If you have a strongly pro-white pattern of associations . . . there is evidence that that will affect the way you behave in the presence of a black person. . . . In all likelihood, you won't be aware that you are behaving any differently than you would around a white person. But chances are you'll lean forward a little less, turn away slightly from him or her, close your body a bit, be a bit less expressive, maintain less eye contact, stand a little farther away, smile a lot less, hesitate and stumble over your words a bit more, laugh at jokes a bit less. Does that matter? Of course it does. (pp. 85–86)

Gladwell goes on to describe the possible repercussions of these unconscious biases at a job interview. The same factors may affect behaviors in parent-teacher conferences or affect student outcomes in classrooms.

Another study describes matching whites with blacks for the completion of a task (Dovidio and Gaertner 2005). Whites were first divided into two groups: those who expressed egalitarian views and those who expressed their biases openly. These individuals were then observed to see if their actions, such as those described by Gladwell, showed unconscious biases. Each white person then engaged in a problem-solving task with a black person. The time it took to complete the joint task was recorded (see Table 1).

Two important points bear emphasis here. First, the African-American individuals, either consciously or unconsciously, were aware of the behavior that showed bias. In this study, "blacks' impressions of whites were related

White Member of Pair	Time to Complete Task with a Black Person
Unbiased in word and behavior	4 minutes
Biased in word and behavior	5 minutes
Unbiased by self-report, behavior shows bias	6 minutes

TABLE 1 Biased and Unbiased White Individuals' Time to Complete Paired Task

mainly to whites' unconscious attitudes ... the uncomfortable and discriminatory behavior associated with aversive racism is very obvious to blacks, even while whites either don't recognize it or consider it hidden" (Dovidio and Gaertner 2005, pp. 3–4). I know that as an African American, when I enter a room of white people, I pick up subtle clues, either consciously or unconsciously, as to who is a good, open contact for me versus someone who may have difficulty engaging with me easily based on my race.

Second, white individuals who said they were unbiased, yet showed nonverbal biased behavior, reported their impressions of their behavior related to their *publicly expressed* attitudes and were likely to maintain their stated level of biases when questioned. Therefore, they are likely to blame *the victim,* the black individual, for their slowness in completing the task (and incidentally, possibly reinforce their stereotypes). Sleeter contends, "We cling to filters that screen out what people of color try to tell us because we fear losing material and psychological advantages that we enjoy" (1994, p. 6).

> **We are far better off to acknowledge our possible biases and to try to work together openly with that knowledge.**

It is important to note that the *well-intentioned* are still racist:

> Because aversive racists may not be aware of their unconscious negative attitudes and only discriminate against blacks when they can justify their behavior on the basis of some factor other than race, they will commonly deny any intentional wrongdoing when confronted with evidence of their biases. Indeed, they do not discriminate intentionally. (Dovidio and Gaertner 2005, p. 5)

For example, if white individuals who are self-deceived about their own biases were sitting in a position to influence a promotion decision, they might not support the advancement of a "difficult" black individual and would select another factor as a reason for their action, rather than see or acknowledge their own conflicted perceptions.

This study on task completion strongly suggests that we are far better off to acknowledge our possible biases and to try to work together openly with that knowledge. If we mask our true attitudes, sometimes invisible to our own selves, we will continue to work slowly or unproductively. Consider the white individuals whose conflict over their true or hidden selves and their outward statements made a simple task both time-consuming and psychologically difficult for both the black individuals and themselves (Dovidio and Gaertner 2005).

Unintentional racism is not always determined by whether an individual possesses prejudiced beliefs or attitudes, and it can take many different forms. These forms include the unconscious gestures mentioned before or "the dominant norms and standards."

> Because many people believe these norms and standards are culturally neutral and universally right, true, and good, they do not understand how these norms and standards oppress others. They are

---

When Race Becomes an Issue

Dovidio and Gaertner Offer Some Suggestions for Action:

- When a person of color brings up race as an issue—listen deeply!
- If the person indicates that he or she is offended, don't be defensive.
- Do not begin talking quickly.
- Do not explain why they are misinterpreting the situation.
- Do not begin crying. (These are some of the most infuriating responses people of color encounter when they challenge a situation that feels wrong.)
- If you hear about something third-hand, don't get angry. Remember that it is almost never completely safe for a person of color to challenge a dominant perception.

Source: Dovidio, Jack F., and Sam L. Gaertner. "Color Blind or Just Plain Blind." Nonprofit Quarterly (Winter 2005): 5.

---

not even aware of this possibility—and, in this sense, such racism is unintentional. (Applebaum 1997, p. 409)

Hard Work of Honesty

Unpacking our levels of consciousness and intent requires hard work. First, there needs to be unswerving, unnerving, scrupulous honesty. Individuals need to become less focused on feeling very tolerant and good about themselves and more focused on examining their own biases. One must realize and accept that the foundation and continuation of a bias may have, at its root, personal and group gain.

I recall sharing with my graduate and undergraduate students that true equity will be reached when 40% of all service people . . . meaning hotel housekeepers, groundskeepers, etc., are white men. The loss from 80% of the managerial jobs in this country to 40%, their proportion of the population, would be an actual loss in the number of jobs currently *allotted* to them based on race and gender. That is, they would not have the jobs they may perceive as expected and modeled as their right in the workplace. Can we all embrace such a future? Delpit maintains, "Liberal educators believe themselves to be operating with good intentions, but these good intentions are only conscious delusions about their unconscious true motives" (Delpit 1988, p. 285). I am not quite that cynical. I believe in change, slow as it may be.

Individuals need to become less focused on feeling very tolerant and good about themselves and more focused on examining their own biases.

Finally, Teaching Tolerance, a group dedicated to reducing prejudice, improving intergroup relations, and supporting equitable school experiences for our nation's children, says, "We would like to believe that when a person has a conscious commitment to change, the very act of discovering one's hidden biases can propel one to act to correct for it. It may not be possible to avoid the automatic stereotype or prejudice, but it is certainly possible to consciously rectify it" (2001, p. 4). Otherwise, we are all at the mercy of a blink of the eye.

References

Allport, Gordon. *The Nature of Prejudice.* Cambridge, Mass.: Addison-Wesley, 1954.

Applebaum, Barbara. "Good, Liberal Intentions Are Not Enough: Racism, Intentions, and Moral Responsibility." *Journal of Moral Education 26* (December 1997): 409-421.

Begley, Sharon. "Racism Studies Find Rational Part of Brain Can Override Prejudice." *Wall Street Journal,* November 19, 2004, p. B1.

Bertrand, Marianne, and Sendhil Mullainathan. "Are Emily and Greg More Employable Than Lakisha and Jamal?" *American Economic Review 94* (2004): 991-1013.

Correll, Joshua, Bernadette Park, Charles. M. Judd, and Bernd Wittenbrink. "The Police Officer's Dilemma: Using Ethnicity to Disambiguate Potentially Threatening Individuals." *Journal of Personality and Social Psychology 83* (December 2002): 1314-1329.

Delpit, Lisa. "The Silenced Dialogue: Power and Pedagogy in Educating Other People's Children." *Harvard Educational Review 58* (August 1988): 280-298.

Diller, Jerry V., and Jean Moule. *Cultural Competence: A Primer for Educators.* Belmont, Calif.: Wadsworth, 2004.

Dovidio, Jack F., and Sam L. Gaertner. "Color Blind or Just Plain Blind." *Nonprofit Quarterly* (Winter 2005).

Edney, Hazel Trice. "New 'Doll Test' Produces Ugly Results." *Portland Medium,* August 18, 2006, pp. 1, 7.

Gladwell, Malcolm. *Blink: The Power of Thinking Without Thinking.* New York: Little, Brown, 2005.

Greenwald, Anthony, Debbie E. McGhee, and Jordan L. K. Schwartz. "Measuring Individual Differences in Implicit Cognition: The Implicit Association Test." *Journal of Personality and Social Psychology 74* (June 1998): 1464-1480.

Harvard University. "Project Implicit." 2007. https://implicit.harvard.edu/implicit.

Polite, Lillian, and Elizabeth B. Saenger. "A Pernicious Silence: Confronting Race in the Elementary Classroom." *Phi Delta Kappan 85* (December 2003): 274-278.

Sleeter, Christine E. "White Racism." *Multicultural Education 1* (Summer 1994): 1, 5-8.

Steele, Claude. "A Threat in the Air: How Stereotypes Shape Intellectual Identity and Performance." *American Psychologist 52* (June 1997): 613-629.

Steele, Claude M., and Joshua Aaronson. "Stereotype Threat and Intellectual Test Performance of African Americans." *Journal of Personality and Social Psychology 69* (November 1995): 797-811.

Teaching Tolerance. "Hidden Bias: A Primer." 2001. www.tolerance.org/hidden_bias/tutorials/04.html.

Thompson, Audrey. "Tiffany, Friend of People of Color: White Investments in Antiracism." *International Journal of Qualitative Studies in Education 16* (January 2003): 7-29.

Vedantam, Shankar. "See No Bias." *Washington Post,* January 23, 2005, p. 3. www.vedantam.com/bias01-2005.html.

Weinstein, Gerald, and Donna Mellen,. "Anti-Semitism Curriculum Design." *In*

Teaching for Diversity and Social Justice, ed. Maurine Adams, Lee Anne Bell, and Pat Griffin. New York: Routledge, 1997.

Wise, Tim. *White Like Me: Reflections on Race from a Privileged Son.* Brooklyn, N.Y.: Soft Skull, 2005.

JEAN MOULE is an associate professor at Oregon State University, Corvallis, Oregon, and president of the Oregon Chapter of the National Association for Multicultural Education. She is co-author of the book, *Cultural Competence: A Primer for Educators (Wadsworth, 2004),* and writes the "Ask Nana" column for *Skipping Stones,* a multicultural magazine for children.

ARTICLE 12

Gender Matters in Elementary Education

Research-based Strategies to Meet the Distinctive Learning Needs of Boys and Girls

VIRGINIA BONOMO

Research indicates that gender influences how children learn. Those findings do not necessarily mean that boys learn one way and girls another. Still, there are significant differences with respect to gender and how our brains develop. Researchers have found that no single area of development influences those gender differences: rather, a combination of developmental differences affects the brain, sensory motor, and physical development. In order to teach to gender differences, educators need to be aware of them and have knowledge of effective gender-based teaching strategies.

Brain-based Gender Differences

The research has established that the male brain is on average 10 to 15 percent larger and heavier than the female brain. However, in addition to size, differences in the autonomy of the brain are present across genders. Using brain mapping, research has established that men possess on average more than six times the amount of gray matter related to general intelligence than women, while women have nearly ten times the amount of white matter related to intelligence than do men. One study also indicates that differences in the brain areas correlate with IQ between the sexes (Kaufmann and Elbel 2001). That

study and an ongoing series of other studies make it evident that one part of males' brains, the inferior parietal lobe, is generally larger. That lobe is involved in spatial and mathematical reasoning, skills that boys tend to perform better than girls. The left side of the brain, which is responsible for the ability to use language and connected to verbal and written ability, develops sooner in girls, and girls therefore tend to perform better than boys in those areas (Gabriel and Schmitz 2007).

Although those differences are significant, it is important to examine how that information relates to developmental gender differences. More-recent research indicates that the significant difference between girls and boys is not the brain's structure but the size and sequence of development in the different regions of the brain. In 2007 a longitudinal study conducted by the National Institutes of Health demonstrated consistent sex differences in the speed of the brain's maturation (Lenroot et al. 2007). It also showed that boys' brains develop differently than girls' brains. Rather than develop along the same lines as girls' brains, only slower, boys' brains develop at a different order, time, and rate than girls' in the areas of the brain that affect language, spatial memory, and motor coordination. While the areas involved in language and fine motor skills mature about six years earlier in girls

Girls	Boys
Girls can multitask better than boys because the female corpus callosum is 26 percent larger than the male. The corpus callosum is the nervous tissue that sends signals between the two halves of the brain.	In the male brain, a larger area is devoted to spatial mechanical functioning and half as much to verbal emotive functioning.
Girls have the ability to transition between lessons more quickly and are less apt to have attention span issues.	Boys utilize the cerebral cortex less often than girls and they access the primitive areas of the brain more often while performing the same types of activities or tasks.
The neural connectors that create listening skills are more developed in the female brain and therefore enhance listening skills, memory storage, and tone of voice discrimination in girls.	For the male brain to renew or recharge it will go into rest states, while the female brain does so without rest states or sleep.
Girls make fewer impulsive decisions than boys due to a higher serotonin level.	Boys have less serotonin and less oxytocin, which makes them more impulsive and less likely to sit still to talk to someone.
The female brain has 15 percent more blood flow than the male brain, allowing for enhanced integrated learning.	Boys structure or compartmentalize learning due to the fact that they have less blood flow to the brain.
Because girls have more cortical areas devoted to verbal functioning, they are better at sensory memory, sitting still, listening, tonality, and the complexities of reading and writing (the skills and behaviors that tend to be rewarded in school).	Boys' brains are better suited to symbols, abstractions, and pictures. Boys in general learn higher math and physics better than girls. Boys prefer video games for the physical movement and destruction. Boys get into more trouble for not listening, moving around, sleeping in class, and incomplete assignments.

Adapted from Sax 2006, 192

TABLE 1   Gender-based Differences between Girls and Boys

than in boys, the areas involved in targeting and spatial memory mature some four years earlier in boys than they do in girls (Hamlon, Thatcher, and Cline 1999).

Sensory-Perception-based Differences

Sex differences are prevalent not only in brain-based research but in sensory-perception research as well. Studies have found significant differences in the ways boys and girls hear, see, and smell. Only recently have researchers begun examining sensory perception and sex differences in education.

In 2001, Dr. Edwin Lephart, the director of neuroscience at Brigham Young University, became the first to search for sex differences by examining dead animals' eyeballs. He found dramatic differences in how the eye is constructed in the male versus in the female: for instance, the visual cortices are fundamentally different.

In addition to such contrasts in construction, the male eye is drawn to cooler colors such as silver, black, blue, and gray, and boys tend to draw pictures of moving objects. In contrast, the female eye is drawn to textures and colors. It is also oriented toward warmer colors—reds, yellow, and oranges. Girls tend to draw more-detailed visuals with faces and people; boys draw more object-based pictures (Sax 2006). In addition, a comprehensive study of newborn infants demonstrated that female infants responded to faces and male infants responded favorably to moving objects, such as mobiles placed above the cribs (Killgore, Oki, and Yurgelun-Todd 2001).

Although consideration of sensory perception is relatively new, the first evaluation of hearing in girls versus boys was conducted in the 1960s. The study found that girls hear better than boys, especially in higher ranges—frequencies above 2 kHz (Corso 1963). A later study found that among 350 newborn babies, the girls' hearing was more sensitive than boys', especially in the 1000–1400 Hz range, which is critical for speech discrimination (Cassidy and Ditty 2001). In addition, more-recent studies have confirmed girls' superior hearing at higher frequencies. That may be due to girls' shorter, stiffer cochleae, which provide a more-sensitive response to frequency (Corso 1963). The research also concludes that such differences increase as children get older. Girls interpret a loud speaking tone as yelling: thinking the speaker is angry, they may tune out. Girls' more-finely tuned aural structure makes them more sensitive to sounds than boys are (Kaufmann 2009).

In addition to hearing and sight, a female's sense of smell under certain conditions is at least one hundred thousand times more sensitive than a male's. Such differences can prove significant in determining interest and success in the classroom environment (Dalton 2006, cited in Sax 2006).

Physical Differences

The autonomic nervous system maintains blood pressure, body temperature, and internal homeostasis. It is divided into two parts: 1) the sympathetic nervous system, which is responsible for the "fight or flight" response (the adrenalin-mediated cascade of accelerated heart rate, vasoconstriction, dilated pupils, etc., triggered by violence or confrontation, which prepares the organism to fight or to run away), and 2) the parasympathetic nervous system, responsible for "rest and digest," i.e., mediating digestion and underlying the slower heart rate, vasodilatation, and increased continuous blood flow (flushing) that in turn affect the response to higher ambient temperatures (Sax 2006).

Studies are demonstrating a gender-related difference in the organization of the two systems. Apparently, the female autonomic system is influenced more by the parasympathetic nervous system; in contrast, the male sympathetic nervous system has a greater influence on the control of autonomic responses. The greatest probable effect of those divisions pertaining to gender is that exposure to threats or confrontations sharpens males' senses and exhilarates them. Most females exposed to such stimuli feel dizzy and may have trouble expressing themselves or reacting.

Consider a situation in which a teacher calls upon a child and expects a quick answer: how differently will the boys and girls react? Knowledge of those differences can sway teaching strategies to enhance student success.

Biological Differences

Research conducted on ambient temperature in the classroom has reached some surprising conclusions. A professor was shocked to visit a prominent all-boys school and find it uncomfortably chilly. Appalled to find such conditions in an expensive school, she asked the headmaster about the temperature. He replied, "If you turn up the heat, the boys go to sleep. Not literally asleep, but they might as well be. If it's too warm in the classroom, the

	Girls	Boys
The response to a stressful situation is activated by different parts of the nervous system depending upon gender.	Girls' responses derive from the parasympathetic part of the autonomic nervous system.	Boys' responses derive from the sympathetic part of the autonomic nervous system.
What is the primary humoral difference between the two genders?	Acetylcholine	Adrenalin
What is the reaction when the system is activated?	The female will react by freezing or feel unable to move or react physically to the situation.	The male tends to feel a sense of excitement and the senses are enhanced.
How will the students feel?	The female tends to feel sick or nauseated and feel stress.	The male will enjoy the experience.

Adapted from Sax 2006, 190–200

TABLE 2   Autonomic Differences between Girls and Boys

boys get sluggish and their eyelids get heavy. If you keep it just a little chilly, the boys learn better" (Sax 2006). Ergonomic specialists have found that the ideal ambient temperature is about 71 F for young men, as opposed to 77 for women. Because the study group wore bathing suits, the ideal temperature in school clothes would most likely be about 2 F lower, or 69 for boys and 75 for girls. Keep in mind that the researchers excluded students who might have been overweight or underweight, because the conditions would have skewed their ambient temperatures (Beshir and Ramsey 1981). Given that temperature is a factor in attentiveness, an educator should consider how that might impact late-spring or early-fall afternoon lessons.

How Is This Relevant to Education? Strategies for Teaching with Respect to Gender Differences

Although dozens of studies published in the past five years have demonstrated dramatic sex differences in brain-based, sensory-perception-based, and autonomic function, the educational literature has not emphasized the studies and their potential significance for education. Dr. Bruce Perry, a Houston neurologist, believes that our current educational system creates an environment that is biologically disrespectful, even if well intended (Gurian and Stevens 2005).

What, then, will encourage the educational system to respect gender differences? Educators should be educating themselves about gender differences in all areas of development and then building upon that knowledge with sound instructional design and implementation strategies for teaching with respect to gender differences. As they apply their knowledge of the brain, sensory perception, and physically based differences to an action classroom plan, they need to realize how those differences develop in children. The following table shares some actions educators could witness in girls and boys. Keep in mind that there can be many variations among the sexes as well: some boys may tend to have the usual girls' traits and vice versa.

Girls Usually	Boys Usually
Hear better than boys.	Have 35 percent less hearing than girls due to the cochlea length in the ear.
Can discriminate between objects better than boys.	Locate objects better than girls.
Focus on faces and warm colors.	Focus on movement and cold colors.
Use the advanced portion of the brain.	Use more of the primitive parts of their brains.
Can explain and describe their feelings.	Find it difficult to talk about feelings.
Develop language and fine motor skills about six years earlier than boys.	Develop targeting and spatial memory about four years earlier than girls.
Multitask well and make easy transitions.	Focus on a task and transition more slowly.
Friendships are focused on other girls.	Friendships are focused on a shared activity.
Find conversation important.	Find conversation unnecessary.
Self-revelation and sharing are precious parts of a friendship.	Self-revelation is to be avoided if possible.
Enjoy a close relationship with a teacher.	May not ask for help to avoid being perceived as "sucking up" to a teacher.
Like to be faced, looked in the eye, and smiled at.	Avoid eye contact and prefer you sit beside them.
Retain sensory memory details well.	Don't retain sensory details.
Do not deal with moderate stress well.	Deal with moderate stress well.
Want to be with friends when under stress.	Want to be alone when under stress.
Feel sick or nauseated when faced with threat and confrontation.	Feel excited when faced with threat and confrontation.
Prefer to read fiction.	Prefer nonfiction.

Adapted from Gurian 2003

TABLE 3   Brain-based Genetic Differences in Girls and Boys

Based on the research conducted and reviewed on gender differences, educators need to consider implementing strategies that will successfully engage both boys and girls in the classroom. Here are some suggested strategies:

BOYS

- Be brief and involve them actively in the lesson. Encourage them with quick praise, cut down on written tasks, and use models and rubrics they can follow. Challenge them—boys thrive on competition.

- Keep a close eye on boys, but let them play. Without a physical outlet, their aggressiveness will show up elsewhere inappropriately. Thus, provide large spaces for boys when possible.

- Lessons should be kinesthetic and experiential. Use a variety of manipulatives. Be aware of ambient temperature—try to keep the boys from warmer areas in the classroom. Males do not hear as well as girls, so move them closer to the instruction.

GIRLS
- Girls work well in groups when they are facing one another or the teacher. Find activities that allow them to help the teacher. Don't protect girls from activities that may cause them to get dirty or skin their knees a bit, which could promote "learned helplessness." Safe-risk activities provide opportunities for girls to take calculated risks.
- Girls do not respond well to loud, sharp, short tones. They prefer softer voices. Girls enjoy tying lessons into emotions. They respond to descriptive phrases. Loud, repetitive noise can be distracting and disturbing to girls.
- Make it bold: girls prefer a lot of colors. Use puzzles to promote perceptual and symbolic learning. Girls' attention will focus on overheads or writing on the chalkboard. (West 2002)

Conclusion

We can conclude from the research that there are significant differences in how boys and girls learn. The cognitive differences are brain based; behavioral differences can be brain based or a result of responses from brain-based differences. The very architecture of the brain and the resultant differences in sensory perception and physical skills differ markedly between the sexes in the classroom and in society. Understanding those differences will help educators provide a positive and encouraging environment for their students and promote teaching with respect to gender differences.

References

Beshir, M., and J. Ramsey. 1981. "Comparison between Male and Female Subjective Estimates of Thermal Effects and Sensations." *Applied Ergonomics* 12: 29–33.

Cassidy, J., and D. Ditty. 2001. "Gender Differences among Newborns on a Transient Otoacoustic Emissions Test for Hearing." *Journal of Music Therapy* 37: 28–35.

Corso, J. 1963. "Aging and Auditory Thresholds in Men and Women." *Archives of Environmental Health* 61: 350–356.

Gabriel, P., and S. Schmitz. 2007. "Gender Differences in Occupational Distributions among Workers." *Monthly Labor Review* (June).

Gurian, M. 2003. *The Boys and Girls Learn Differently Action Guide for Teachers*. San Francisco: Jossey-Bass.

Gurian, M., and K. Stevens. 2005. "With Boys in Mind." *Educational Leadership* (November).

Hamlon, H., R. Thatcher, and M. Cline. 1999. "Gender Differences in the Development of EEG Coherence in Normal Children." *Developmental Neuropsychology* 16 (3): 479–506.

Kaufmann, C. 2009. "How Boys and Girls Learn Differently." Retrieved May 21, 2010, from <http://www.rd.com/content/printContent.do?contentID=103575>.

Kaufmann, C., and G. Elbel. 2001. "Frequency Dependence and Gender Effects in Visual Cortical Regions Involved in Temporal Frequency Dependent Pattern Processing." *Human Brain Mapping* 14 (1): 28–38.

Killgore, W., M. Oki, and D. Yurgelun-Todd. 2001. "Sex-specific Developmental Changes in Amygdale Response to Affective Faces." *Neuroreport* 12: 427–433.

Lenroot, R., N. Gogtay, D. Greenstein, E. Wells, G. Wallace, L. Clasen, J. Blumental, J. Lerch, A. Zijdenbos, A. Evans, P. Thompson, and J. Geidd. 2007. "Sexual Dimorphism of Brain Developmental Trajectories during Childhood and Adolescence." *NeuroImage* 36: 1065–1073.

Sax, L. 2006. "Six Degrees of Separation: What Teachers Need to Know About the Emerging Science of Sex Differences." *Educational Horizons* 84 (Spring): 190–212.

West, P. 2002. *What Is the Matter with Boys?* Sydney: Choice Books.

VIRGINIA BONOMO is an instructor in the Department of Early Childhood and Elementary Education at Blomsburg University of Pennsylvania.

ARTICLE 13

Classroom Assessment and Grading to Assure Mastery

Achieving learning standards is at the forefront of current educational philosophy, and is the goal of sound educational practice. That "all children can learn" and there will be "no child left behind" presume that teaching and assessment practices must benefit all children. Agreement in principle is nearly universal. Practical implementation, however, is another matter. One philosophy of learning and instruction that has a long history of targeting instruction and achievement for all students is mastery learning. This article examines (a) fundamental tenets that mastery learning is built upon, (b) the clear connection between learning standards and mastery learning, and (c) how mastery is often erroneously implemented. It then outlines the defining features of mastery and how to implement them. These defining features include developing clear objectives, setting a mastery standard, using criterion-referenced assessments, and grading incentives for students to learn beyond initial mastery.

JAMES P. LALLEY AND J. RONALD GENTILE

Who among us, when frustrated by the blank looks on our students' faces, has not uttered the phrase, "You've *had* this before!"? Of course, they had encountered it before, perhaps even passed a test on it, but they forgot it. The evidence has been clear (since Ebbinghaus, 1885/1964) that even when material is initially mastered to a high standard, much will be forgotten in a few hours or days. The good news is that relearning is faster—that is there is a savings of time in relearning over initial learning and that memory will continue to improve with additional practice beyond mastery—technically called *overlearning*. Under optimal conditions, such as practice to the point of automaticity (Schneider & Shiffrin, 1977) or sufficient distributed practice, organization, and use of material (Bahrick, 1984a, 1984b), knowledge and skills can achieve relative permanence.

This, of course, is the kind of memory developed by experts in a field, which allows them to more quickly access their memories to solve problems or acquire new information (Chi, Glaser, & Rees, 1982; deGroot, 1965; Halpern & Bower, 1982; Rumelhart & Norman, 1981). Learners who do not achieve mastery in the initial phase of learning show none of these benefits. Instead, they show considerable forgetting within hours or days, little (if any) savings in relearning, and no overlearning (by definition), because practice makes perfect only if the practice is essentially correct.

Figure 1 illustrates the ups and downs of learning/forgetting for initially successful and unsuccessful learners (masters and nonmasters, respectively). For a positive example (the learners portrayed in Figure 1A), consider your own experience as a teacher. The first time teaching a unit, there is quite a bit to learn, despite the courses you took at college. With each successive preparation for that unit, however, it is gratifying that relearning is not only quicker, but you are organizing the material better, as well as inventing new examples and exercises. By the tenth iteration of this unit, you experience virtual total recall, with a vast repertoire of examples on which to draw. The material is becoming so natural to you that you find yourself agreeing with other teachers that "the students seem less prepared every year." You are losing empathy with the beginning student, as relative experts often do. But this is the difference between an expert and a teacher: "An expert can do it; a teacher can do it but also remembers what it takes to progress from novice to expert" (Gentile & Lalley, 2003, p. 5).

For a negative example (Figure 1B), consider students who have been unsuccessful in their original learning of addition and subtraction of fractions. Their forgetting will likely be close to complete, because they learned so little in the first place. They are even likely to complain, when subsequently confronted with this material, that they "never had this before." This may not be just an excuse: They may really not remember it. Worse, their next attempt will probably also be unsuccessful because, after all, most teachers spend less time reviewing material than they spend teaching it originally. Thus, by the third or fourth encounter with fractions, these students will recall having had it before but they will also recall that they were not good at fractions. They are well on their way to learned helplessness, with the attendant cognitive, behavioral, and emotional baggage that is often called *math anxiety* (Gentile & Monaco, 1986; Peterson, Maier, & Seligman, 1993).

A. When Original Learning is Adequate (Mastery)

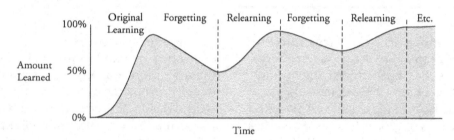

B. When Original Learning is Inadequate (Nonmastery)

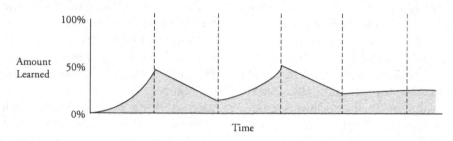

FIGURE 1   Hypothetical learning/forgetting curves, mastery versus nonmastery. Reprinted with permission of the publisher from Gentile, J. R. & Lalley, J. P. (2003). *Standards and Mastery Learning: Aligning Teaching and Assessment So All Children Can Learn.* Thousand Oaks, CA: Corwin Press, p. 6.

There is also a problem regarding prerequisite knowledge. When students have mastered prerequisites, they are ready for the current lesson, and thus can begin the upward acceleration toward mastery of the new material. If required prior knowledge is missing—or worse, incorrect—then students are not ready to learn to multiply or divide fractions, to continue the above example, and it takes a long time before they begin to show progress in learning the current lesson.

In general, from cognitive theory, and especially from the research on experts versus novices discussed below, each cognitive and perceptual act is an interpretation or construction of new information in terms of what is already known. Indeed, how could it be otherwise? Consider reading. Those who are better informed can understand what they read, learn to read better, and then are more prepared to learn from reading. Those who lack prerequisite knowledge and/or have difficulty reading will be unprepared to use reading to increase their knowledge. The rich get richer, the poor get poorer, and the learning/memory curves diverge further.

Mastery Learning and Assessment

The above discussion distinguishes between mastery and expertise, with the former being a necessary first step—but only a first step—toward what eventually might develop into the latter with concentrated, in-depth, and extended study and practice. In typical classrooms, one of the major goals is to introduce relative novices to ideas, skills, or strategies that are fundamental to a discipline and, therefore, prerequisites for more advanced courses and continued development in that discipline. Whatever else is taught in each course, we need to assure that each student masters those fundamentals as a criterion for a passing grade (Gentile, 2004).

Mastery learning requires that each student achieve a preestablished standard of performance on a specified set of instructional objectives in a criterion-referenced manner—that is, without regard to how well others are doing. well implemented programs:

1. identify significant mastery objectives in terms of their necessity as prerequisites for subsequent learning, requiring students to learn and relearn until they demonstrate their competence; and
2. provide enrichment objectives for students to go beyond initial mastery to expand, organize, apply, and teach their newly acquired knowledge and skills.

Of course, depending on curriculum and/or teachers' professional judgment, what is an enrichment objective for one course or grade level could be a mastery objective for another. As such, in the ideal educational world, instruction would be sequenced in a spiral curriculum (Bruner, 1960) and teachers would adapt instruction to the prior knowledge of each student. This would still not be easy, because each individual would remember different things from prior instruction, have somewhat different misconceptions to unlearn, and relearn at different rates.

As Black and Wiliam (1998) and Stiggins and Chappuis (2008) argued, we raise standards by focusing on formative assessment and providing timely feedback on students' progress in learning. Feedback, in this conception, is neither a grade nor a summative test score. Rather, it is specific information on what was correct, what was incorrect, and how to improve (Gentile, 1993; Hunter, 1982). This implies that an exercise, assignment, or test will be tried and tried again until it is adequate. Conceived of this way, there is no such thing as negative feedback; all feedback is positive in the sense that it points the way to improvements in knowledge, skill, and self-efficacy.

To provide formative assessment and timely feedback requires that assessment and grading be *criterion-referenced* (Glaser & Nitko, 1971; Popham, 1978), meaning that each student's performance is interpreted relative to established instructional goals and standards, independent of other students' performances. This is in contrast to more traditional *norm-referenced* assessment, in which a student's score or performance is compared with the norm or distribution of scores provided by other students. In Bloom's (1976) succinct analysis, norm-referenced assessment is useful for *selecting* talent, but criterion-referenced assessment has the goal of *developing* talent (see also Gentile, 2005). And developing talent is what teaching is all about.

Assessing and Grading to Ensure Mastery

When schools attempt to implement mastery learning—as in the recent movement toward achieving benchmarks—they usually make the following fatal errors: (a) demonstrating mastery is conceptualized as the endpoint rather than the initial phase of the learning/memory/application process, (b) mastery tests and activities are limited to the knowledge/comprehension end of the thinking continuum, (c) there is no requirement or grading incentive for going beyond initial mastery, and (d) assessment of student achievement remains embedded in a competitive or norm referenced grading system.

To avoid such implementation errors, we propose four ways to incorporate the defining features of a good mastery learning program (Block, Efthim, & Burns, 1989; Gentile & Lalley, 2003):

1. clearly stated and published objectives, sequenced to facilitate transfer of prior learning to current and future competencies;

2. a standard for passing mastery tests sufficiently high (e.g., 75% correct or better) to assure that initial learning, once forgotten (as is almost inevitable) can be relearned quickly;
3. multiple and parallel forms of criterion-referenced tests, with corrective exercises and retesting as needed to demonstrate initial mastery; and
4. grading incentives to encourage students to reach beyond initial mastery and strive for fluency in the material, to better organize, apply, and even teach it to others.

To facilitate the successful implementation of these ideas, we will elaborate these four defining features of a good mastery learning program.

Clearly Stated and Published Objectives

Every discipline has a set of objectives that are so basic that failure to master one or more of these fundamentals would elicit such comments as, "How can one of our graduates not understand that?" These fundamentals range from facts and principles to skills and research methods, from historical discoveries and personalities to current theories and controversies. Each course within a discipline is optimally designed to address a piece or stage of development on the journey toward such understanding. Either explicitly or implicitly, each course focuses on a portion of those essential objectives, in a context of assumed prior knowledge and promised future understandings and applications.

The purpose of this first defining feature of mastery learning is to be explicit about these fundamentals. We do this by identifying—and publishing for students, parents, and colleagues—those fundamental objectives and, moreover, by explicitly establishing mastery of those fundamentals as necessary for a passing grade in the course (e.g., *D* or *C*, or 60 or 70). If such fundamental objectives are not immediately obvious, two ways of establishing them are to identify competencies that (a) are considered prerequisites for the next unit or course in the discipline, or (b) have been common to standardized or instructor-made exams on this material in the recent past.

By definition, mastery of fundamentals is likely at lower levels of cognitive processing (e.g., Bloom's 1956 taxonomy), and every teacher strives for more than minimal competence. This is where all of the other course objectives—higher-order or analytical thinking, applications, inventions, etc.—enter into the course and grading scheme. For this to occur, teachers must analyze the curriculum to identify what content will be revisited, as well as why and how it will be revisited. This will assist them in identifying key fundamentals. For example, if students will be learning about the effects of pollution on the Great Lakes in the middle school grades, they will need to develop a solid understanding of pollution and fresh water during the primary grades. This will enable the middle school teacher to primarily focus on the complexities of pollution's impact (e.g., companies produce highly valued commodities while tainting fresh water supplies) and spend minimal time assisting students in relearning the basics of pollution and fresh water.

A Sufficiently High Standard for Demonstrating Mastery

As portrayed in Figure 1, initial learning must attain a relatively high standard or, after the nearly-inevitable forgetting that follows, there will be little or no residue in memory nor savings in relearning. How high is high enough for a standard is not easily empiri-

cally established, and may depend upon the discipline or level of the course. For example, 80% correct on times tables may be sufficient at first, but 90% correct within five seconds may be a reasonable requirement in a subsequent course.

For most fields, a minimum passing score of 75% or 80% correct on a multiple-choice test of knowledge or a commensurate high rating of initial competence in a skilled performance might be sufficient, but 60% or 65% is probably too low. A good model for this is the driving test on which, in most states, it is necessary to pass a written test at 80% correct on rules of the road and other essential facts, as well as to demonstrate competence in authentic skills of driving. The material to be tested and the passing standards for the driving test are published for all applicants, and passing both parts of the exam is necessary to receive a license to drive. Note also that a person who scores 80, one who scores 100, and one who needs three tries to attain at least an 80 are all treated the same: All are considered sufficiently competent to receive a license that allows them to begin their careers as drivers (with some restrictions in enlightened states).

Although the analogy to driving tests probably ends there, we teachers need to impress upon students as well as the general public that initial mastery is only that: the beginning. So we congratulate students by awarding them a pass in the course (a *D* or *C*, or 60 or 70) and encourage them as promising novices in the discipline to strive toward expert status. Therefore, even 100% correct on the initial mastery objective does not result in top level grades (an *A*). They can only be earned by completing additional assignments designed to reinforce the mastery objectives while expanding upon that learning. Conversely, if students are given top-level grades for high achievement of mastery objectives without revisiting those objectives, they are sure to forget a great deal of what was originally learned, and therefore short-circuit the cumulative effects of the learning process as we know it.

Multiple Forms of Criterion-Referenced Tests with Corrective Exercises and Retesting

Each mastery objective requires several test questions to be written and randomly assigned to several parallel forms of a test. For example, suppose you are teaching a beginning unit on division of fractions (for other illustrations in math, science, social studies, and language arts, see Gentile and Lalley, 2003). An initial mastery test might have the following objectives: that students (a) can correctly calculate such problems as 3/8 divided by 1/5 (the Knowledge level of Bloom's taxonomy); (b) can demonstrate why we have the rule "Invert, then multiply," showing all steps (the Comprehension level); and (c) can solve word problems in which they must decide whether division is the correct procedure, or invent word problems (Application level).

For each parallel form of the test, you will need, say, four items at each of those three levels of cognitive processing, which yields a 12-item mastery test. Because this is a beginning unit, a standard of 75% correct seems fair and would require that students solve 9 of the 12 items correctly to pass. Those who did not pass could now be diagnosed: Did they miss only the higher complexity items? Did they miss the computational items? Both?

Remedial exercises would now be necessary for those students, including reteaching, more examples, peer tutoring by those who did pass, for example. When they have shown sufficient progress in these exercises, they are then eligible to retake the second parallel form

of the test. Meanwhile, other students can work on enrichment objectives for this unit.

Writing of parallel forms of a test must be done before the course begins, because it is virtually impossible to create parallel test items—that is, questions that cover the same content at the same level of difficulty—after students did not pass the initial test. Another advantage of creating the tests before the course begins is that it helps define your fundamental objectives: If you cannot write good test questions for a concept, it is likely to be better assessed by a performance assessment such as a presentation, paper or project, rather than a mastery objective.

The goal of all of this, of course, is to facilitate teaching and learning. Good teachers continue to expand their repertoires of methods, which include finding alternate ways of helping each student succeed in the course. Parallel forms of the test remind us that not all students get it the first time and need additional attempts, and perhaps other methods or examples, before they try and try again. In addition, one of the parallel forms of the test can be used to review and test for prior knowledge from previous units or courses, instead of merely assuming it, so that new learning can truly build on those prerequisites. Parallel forms also enable periodic review, much as coaches require athletes to continue to review and automatize fundamental skills. Moreover, as Roediger and Karpicke (2006) concluded from their comprehensive review, testing is one of our most powerful tools for enhancing memory.

Grading Incentives to Encourage Reaching Beyond Initial Mastery

Passing a mastery test is often conceived as a benchmark or end point for learning, and earns a spuriously high grade for that unit.

Instead, initial mastery must be considered the beginning, and thus earn only the lowest passing grade for that unit. Higher grades are reserved for going beyond mastery to demonstrating fluency, ability to apply the material, analytical or creative skills, and the ability to teach the material to others.

Enter the enrichment objectives—those which are fundamental but not easily tested, or might be considered optional in that not all students need to know all of them, or that they require extended time frames to learn and be assessed. These should also be published as projects or exercises which, when judged OK, earn a higher grade or a specified number of points to add to the course grade (e.g., to move from a *D* to *C* with one satisfactory project, to *B* with two, etc.; or to add 10 points to the basic pass of 60 or 70 for this extended project, six points for a less difficult one, etc.). To earn an *OK* on the project may, of course, also require more than one attempt, with feedback and resubmissions, as necessary.

Enrichment projects include conducting an experiment, analyzing data, composing or creating a story or poem, doing critical reviews of literature, inventing problems or test items, and so forth. Such projects can be completed individually or, with appropriate procedures and supervision, as pairs or cooperative teams. And, in keeping with the emphasis on teaching to demonstrate learning, tutoring other students is an exemplary project: When the tutee passes the mastery test, the tutor earns an *OK* on an enrichment project.

The point of building enrichment exercises on top of mastered fundamentals is that we are encouraging students on the road toward expertise. Thus we must emphasize the cognitive growth that is accruing—fluency, application, creativity, memory, and coaching ability vis-àvis the material. That a higher grade follows is simply a well-deserved recognition of that additional competence.

Conclusion

One of the questions that always seems to arise during discussions of mastery learning is "What happens to the faster students while the slower ones are still trying to pass the mastery test?" The question is moot when the above principles of mastery learning are followed. The faster students are doing enrichment projects, including helping the slower ones, because they would never be permitted to settle for the lowest passing grade in the course. Along the way, they are doing more than they needed to do under competitive norm-referenced grading systems in which they only had to beat out their slower compatriots to get the highest grades in the course. Meanwhile, the slower students can also be doing enrichment exercises, earning *OKs* that will increase their grade when they finally pass the mastery test. In this criterion-referenced grading scheme, everyone has incentive: (a) to certify they are competent on the fundamentals (because it is the only way to pass the course), and (b) to go beyond initial mastery because it is the only way to get above the minimum passing grade.

That said, mastery learning might not affect the extant competitiveness among students, particularly if the rest of their schooling emphasizes class ranks. The fastest learners in a discipline are likely to get higher scores on the test, to master more quickly, to do more enrichment projects, and thus to earn higher grades. Nevertheless, their higher grades will have been earned by more advanced achievements, not by simply besting slower or less motivated learners. The slower learners can also be empowered because they, too, can succeed. Thus, even if our norm referenced and criterion-referenced measures of student achievement remain correlated, it is fundamentally different psychologically for both students and their teachers to conceive of passing a test as a certification of competence, rather than as a competition.

References

Bahrick, H. P. (1984a). Associations and organization in cognitive psychology: A reply to Neisser. *Journal of Experiment Psychology: General, 113,* 36–37.

Bahrick, H. P. (1984b). Semantic memory content in permastore: Fifty years of memory for Spanish learned in school. *Journal of Experiment Psychology: General, 113,* 1–29.

Black, P., & Wiliam, D. (1998). Inside the black box: Raising standards through classroom assessment. *Phi Delta Kappan, 80,* 139–148.

Block, J. H., Efthim, H. E., & Burns, R. B. (1989). *Building effective mastery learning schools.* New York: Longman.

Bloom, B. S. (Ed.). (1956). *Taxonomy of educational objectives: The classification of educational goals, handbook 1. Cognitive domain.* New York: McKay.

Bloom, B. S. (1976). *Human characteristics and school learning.* New York: McGraw-Hill.

Bruner, J. (1960). *The process of education.* New York: Vintage.

Chi, M. T. H., Glaser, R., & Rees, E. (1982). Expertise in problem solving. In R. J. Sternberg (Ed.), *Advances in the psychology of human intelligence, vol. 1.* (pp. 7–75). Hillside, NJ: Lawrence Erlbaum Associates.

deGroot, A. D. (1965). *Thought and choice in chess.* The Hague, The Netherlands: Mouton.

Ebbinghaus, H. (1964). *Memory: A contribution to experimental psychology* (H. A. Ruger & E. C. Bussenius, Trans.). New York: Dover. (Original work published 1885)

Gentile, J. R. (1993). *Instructional improvement: A summary and analysis of Madeline Hunter's essential elements of instruction and supervision* (2nd ed.). Oxford, OH: National Staff Development Council.

Gentile, J. R. (2004). Assessing fundamentals in every course through mastery learning. In M. V. Achacoso & M. D. Svinicki (Eds.), *Alternative strategies for evaluating student learning* (pp. 15–20). San Francisco: Jossey Bass.

Gentile, J. R. (2005). Improving college teaching productivity via mastery learning. In J. E. Groccia & J. E. Miller (Eds.), *On becoming a productive university* (pp. 291–301). Boston: Anker.

Gentile, J. R., & Lalley, J. P. (2003). *Standards and mastery learning: Aligning teaching and assessment so all children can learn.* Thousand Oaks, CA: Corwin Press.

Gentile, J. R., & Monaco, N. M. (1986). Learned helplessness in mathematics: What educators should know. *Journal of Mathematical Behavior, 5,* 159–178.

Glaser, R., & Nitko, A. J. (1971). Measurement in learning and instruction. In R. L. Thorndike (Ed.), *Educational measurement* (2nd ed., pp. 625–670). Washington, DC: American Council on Education.

Halpern, A. R., & Bower, G. H. (1982). Musical expertise and melodic structure in memory for musical notation. *American Journal of Psychology, 95,* 31–50.

Hunter, M. (1982). *Mastery teaching.* El Segundo, CA: TIP Publications.

Peterson, E., Maier, S. F., & Seligman, M. E. P. (1993). *Learned helplessness: A theory for the age of personal control.* New York: Oxford University Press.

Popham, W. J. (1978). *Criterion-referenced measurement.* Englewood Cliffs, NJ: Prentice-Hall.

Roediger, H. L., III, & Karpicke, J. D. (2006). The power of testing memory: Basic research and implications for educational practice. *Perspectives on Psychological Science, 1,* 181–210.

Rumelhart, D. E., & Norman, D.A. (1981).
Analogical processes in learning. In
J. R. Anderson (Ed.), *Cognitive skills and
their acquisition* (pp. 335–359). Hillsdale,
NJ: Lawrence Erlbaum Associates.

Schneider, W., & Shiffrin, R. M. (1977).
Controlled and automatic human
information processing: 1. Detection,
search, and attention. *Psychological
Review, 84,* 1–66.

Stiggins, R., & Chappuis, J. (2008). Enhancing
student learning. *District Administration,
44*(1), 42–44.

JAMES P. LALLEY is an associate professor of
education at D'Youville College in Buffalo, NY;
J. RONALD GENTILE is a SUNY Distinguished
Teaching Professor, Emeritus, at the University
at Buffalo.

Correspondence should be addressed to
James P. Lalley, Associate Professor of
Education, D'Youville College, 320 Porter
Avenue, Buffalo, NY 14201. E-mail:
lalleyj@dyc.edu

"To Find Yourself, Think for Yourself"

Using Socratic Discussions in Inclusive Classrooms

BARBARA FINK CHORZEMPA AND LAURIE LAPIDUS

Students in Ms. Lapidus's inclusion class have just finished reading Cinderella and are preparing for their first Socratic seminar. To do so, the students begin the process of questioning the components of the story, including the author's style and the literary elements, specifically the theme. Ms. Lapidus reminds the students to generate questions that should be supported with evidence from the text (i.e., inferential questions,) including those that can be open to interpretation. "For example," she says, "You can't ask any questions about the magic in the story because magic is an element of fairy tales. That is, we can't argue how the fairy godmother did the magic—just assume it's so." After all the students' questions have been recorded, the students collaboratively decide which 10 questions they would like to discuss during their seminar. Next, they independently search through the text to find support for their answer to each of the 10 questions, using sticky notes to mark the reference. The students are now ready for the Socratic seminar.

To facilitate a good discussion, the students move their desks to form a circle. As they do so, Ms. Lapidus reminds them of the rules for a Socratic discussion. Once the students are in place, she begins the discussion with one of the 10 inferential questions they identified (i.e., Was Cinderella able to find true happiness?). As the students are discussing this possibility, John, a student with a learning disability, responds with another question, "Why didn't the fairy god-mother just change Cinderella's life?" "Wow. That's a good question. Can you repeat that?" says Ms. Lapidus. After the question is repeated, Ms. Lapidus paraphrases the question and poses it to the students: "Why if the fairy godmother was capable of magic, did she not just change Cinderella's life? Who'd like to share their thoughts?" After reflecting, another student says, "Cinderella had to go to the ball to experience self-worth before she believed in herself." Knowing the students had reached one of the implied themes, Ms. Lapidus encourages them to wrap up their discussion and move into their writing assignment.

Aristotle said, "To find yourself, think for yourself" (Quotationspage.com). As schools and teachers strive to align instruction with state and national standards, teachers often struggle with developing students' abilities to think for themselves. As a result, students may find analyzing a piece of literature and writing proficiently about it to be a daunting task. Ms. Lapidus found in her classroom that although elementary students might be able to critically analyze a text reading through discussion, they often have difficulty doing so in their own writing. She related this challenge to her own training in education: Teacher preparation programs place a greater emphasis on teaching students to read than on teaching them how to write. For some students, particularly those with disabilities, writing is intimidating, challenging, and labor intensive (Fink-Chorzempa, Graham, & Harris, 2005; Graham, 2006). Thus teaching students how to write, especially when teachers have been taught only a few strategies themselves, can be a very difficult undertaking. These observations and beliefs are also documented in the research about writing instruction (cf., Graham & Perm, 2007; National Commission on Writing, 2006).

Realizing the challenges many of her students encountered, Ms. Lapidus was determined to improve their writing and thought that before she could do so, she needed to first teach students how to think using supporting details. She recalled professional development she received as a middle school teacher, learning how Socratic seminars can be used as a way to teach students to think critically, and she decided to explore how she could adapt that method to make it work in her elementary inclusive classroom.

What Are Socratic Seminars?

Socratic seminars, defined as "exploratory intellectual conversations centered on a text" (Lambright, 1995, p. 30), are a group-discussion model and are designed in such a way to resemble Socrates's instruction-through-questioning method (Chorzempa & Lapidus, 2006; Polite & Adams, 1997). They are held in a student-centered environment to foster authentic engagement and to prompt ideas to occur (Loan, 2003). Simply stated, this method involves students' reading a selection and then generating questions and exploring their ideas and questions in an open discussion (Queen, 2000). The open-discussion method not only allows students to support their own opinions with details but also strengthens their ability to exhibit a personal voice in their writing and improves the depth of their papers (Sorenson, 1993). Elder and Paul (1998) linked critical thinking, or establishing an "inner voice of rea-

son," and Socratic discussion as the public forum that cultivates it.

The procedures and justifications for the use of Socratic seminars as a means of developing critical thinking skills are well documented in middle and high school classrooms (cf., Loan, 2003; Mawhinney, 2000; Metzger, 1998; Polite & Adams, 1997; Queen, 2000; Strong, 1997; Tanner & Casados, 1998; Tredway, 1995). However, its use is rarely documented in elementary inclusive classrooms. Therefore, in light of the potential benefits of the Socratic seminar and using the experiences of Ms. Lapidus and her third- and fifth-grade students, this article provides a model and guidelines for using the Socratic method to develop students' critical thinking and writing skills within elementary inclusive classrooms.

The open-discussion method not only allows students to support their own opinions with details but also strengthens their ability to exhibit a personal voice in their writing

---

Establishing the Foundations

Prior to using the Socratic method, it is important to establish the foundations that help students engage in the Socratic method. Similar to other educators who use this approach, Ms. Lapidus realized the importance of developing in her classroom a sense of community that fosters mutual respect for one another. She encouraged her students to express their views and to disagree respectfully and appreciate the different perspectives held by their classmates while still holding on to their own perspectives without feeling insecure. She established this climate by employing trust-building activities in the beginning of the year, specifically during her morning meetings. Those meetings along with other group activities (e.g., academic games) always closed with students' reflection on the experience. That is, she asked students to consider such questions as what they did well and what they could do better. She also modeled how to provide constructive feedback to one another by giving specific praise to students for a response and offering a suggestion for next time.

Ms. Lapidus also ensured that all students had in-depth knowledge of the literary elements and devices (e.g., plot, setting, point of view, symbolism) before seminars were held, because these elements provide the basis for establishing literary connections among works and are needed to develop critical thinking skills, such as making inferences and identifying implicit themes. She frequently asked her students to engage in Reader's Theatre (see description under "Preparing for the Discussion") as a way to deepen their understanding of these elements.

Knowledge of the different types of questions that can be asked in response to a reading also needs to be established before students can engage in a Socratic seminar. Specifically, students need to know the difference between "in the book" and "in your head" questions, the two general types of questions used in the Question Answer Relationships (QAR) strategy (Raphael & Au, 2005). Ms. Lapidus referred to the literal questions as the "right there" questions to help her students understand that the answers to such questions can be found explicitly in the text. The "in your head" questions she explained as either inferential questions (i.e., those for which answers are obtained by reading between the lines or putting information together) or evaluative questions (i.e., those for which the answers are not in the text but rather come from within). To help her students learn how to distinguish and generate the different types of questions, Ms. Lapidus first modeled the use of them for her students. This familiarity is important not only because students

generate "in your head" questions when preparing for the Socratic seminars but also because 70% to 80% of the questions they face on high-stakes testing will be these types of questions (Raphael & Au, 2005).

Preparing for the Seminar

Before a Socratic seminar can be conducted, it is important for teachers to prepare for the seminar by selecting an appropriate story and becoming familiar with its elements. The selected text should be thought-provoking and at a level at which every reader in the class can successfully read. When selecting a piece of literature, Ms. Lapidus found the *Junior Great Books* (The Great Books Foundation, 2006) and *Touch-pepples* (Touchstones Discussion Project, 1993) to be excellent resources, as these texts contain readings with identifiable themes or issues that were familiar and relevant to her students and their lives.

Before introducing the story to students, teachers read through the text carefully and identify the main themes. Teachers then consider a final discussion topic, one that the students will be asked to reflect on in their writing at the conclusion of the seminar. The final discussion topic should be one that encourages students to analyze the text critically and requires them to provide support for their statements with details from the text. Although a final discussion topic is prepared in advance, teachers should be flexible and willing to revise their topic on the basis of student questions and interpretations during the seminar, thus making it more powerful and meaningful.

Conducting the Seminar

Once the planning has been carefully considered, teachers serve as facilitators of the process by first introducing the text to the students and then engaging them in their preparations for the Socratic seminar. During the seminar, both the students and teachers accomplish a variety of tasks, which are outlined in the following paragraphs.

The Students' Role

Preparing for the Discussion. Before the Socratic discussion is held, students should be exposed to the text at least three times. Teachers read through the text first, encouraging students to listen aesthetically, and then ask students what questions they have. All students' questions are accepted, as long as they are "in your head" questions, with each question written down on chart paper for later examination. For the second reading, students read the text independently to answer two to three guided questions, ones that begin to focus on the themes of the text. After they read the story the third time, teachers ask students to respond to the guided questions orally and then allow students to add any questions to their list. Often these questions are more insightful than the ones constructed after the first reading, and teachers should point out to students that each time a text is read, more details to reflect on often become apparent. For example, on the first reading of *Cinderella,* one student in Ms. Lapidus's class asked, "Why were the stepsisters so mean?" After the third reading of the text, Alice, a student with emotional disturbance and reading difficulties, asked the following question as students were discussing the story, "Why at midnight did everything change except for the glass slipper?"

Depending on the complexity of the text, students may use Reader's Theatre to present a scene or excerpt from the text. First, students work cooperatively in small groups to prepare what they consider an important scene from the text, one that focuses on a theme. Next, they perform the scene in front of the class,

thereby experiencing another way to interact with the text. Having students engage in this strategy allows them to assume the role of a character and view the story from the character's perspective, thus possibly broadening their view of the events in the text.

As the last step before the discussion is held, teachers and students analyze each question generated after the first and third readings. Students are reminded that although these may all be good questions, only questions that can be supported from the text should be used in the discussion. The list of questions is then narrowed to a reasonable number (i.e., 10 to 15) that can be answered in one Socratic discussion. Students are then given sticky notes to mark where the evidence in the text is found, reinforcing their ability to provide supporting statements.

Holding the Socratic Discussion. Once the students are ready to begin the Socratic discussion, teachers outline and discuss several rules and procedures for teachers and students to follow (see Figure 1), allowing for a successful discussion by the students. These differ slightly from procedures used in secondary classrooms, modified specifically for use in an elementary classroom. For example, in Ms. Lapidus's class she has students raise their hands and wait to be called on to speak, whereas a Socratic discussion usually involves free expression of ideas and thoughts by participants. She also explains to the class that this rule is necessary to reduce the chance that one or more students monopolize the discussion and to give all students opportunities to speak. She also tells her students that one of her goals for the end of the year is for them to engage in a literary dialogue without raising their hands.

Teachers open the discussion by asking students to discuss the 15 or so questions they generated, one at a time. Not all students

Procedures

1. Every time a discussion is held, teachers review the prodecures and rules with the students.
2. The students are to sit in a circle so that every student can see every other student as they speak.
3. Teachers sit in the circle as well but do not participate in the discussion except as the facilitators.
4. Teachers do not give an opinion until the reflection time and are the last to speak.
5. Preparing a final discussion topic before the seminar is held allows teachers to select particular students whose ideas allow the discussion to be guided toward the intended topic or theme.
6. Time must be left at the end of the discussion for reflection. This is the only time during the seminar that every student must contribute.

Rules for Students

1. Students must raise their hands during the discussion, waiting to be called on by a teacher before they share their ideas or thoughts.
2. Students are to listen attentively to one another, respecting the rule that one person speaks at a time.
3. Mutual respect for one another must be shown.

FIGURE 1 Rules and Procedures for the Socratic Discussion

are required to participate in the discussion; however, Ms. Lapidus has experienced that many of her students want to share their ideas with their peers or respond to comments made by others. She does, however, subtly encourage all students to participate through positive reinforcement. The only time every student is required to participate is at the end of the seminar when Ms. Lapidus asks them to reflect on the discussion by responding to two questions: What did you learn from this discussion? and What could be done differently next time to improve the discussion?

During the discussion, students are asked to look at their classmates, another goal set at the beginning of the year. Often when students are first engaged in the Socratic seminar, they will look to teachers for a reaction or confirmation when they make a point. As the year progresses, though, students naturally begin talking with one another, sensing they are in an environment of mutual respect. The teacher continues as facilitator of the discussion, but students begin to refer to one another's comments and build on one another's ideas. As one

fifth grade student with Asperger's syndrome articulated, "The Socratic discussion is like building a brick wall: Each idea is a brick, and when someone says something, another person builds on top of it. Because of that, it is never-ending."

Applying the Writing Component. After the seminar is completed, students are asked to respond to a written prompt. Students also are expected to write about points made in the discussion and to support their statements with examples from the text. As mentioned before, one of the purposes for holding the seminar is to help students identify their own thoughts on a topic and articulate their point of view in writing

The Teacher's Role

During the Seminar. The Socratic seminar requires teachers to assume a variety of roles as well. In the role of facilitator, teachers must refrain from sharing their thoughts throughout the discussion to allow the students to develop their own critical thinking skills.

Also, sometimes during the seminar, students stray from the original question and teachers must decide whether they should allow the discussion to continue or bring it back to the original question. Teachers should facilitate the discussion by capitalizing on the strengths of students. Knowing each student's particular strengths helps teachers guide the discussion in such a way that the students are able to reach an intended outcome without teachers' having to share their own views. For example, Ms. Lapidus realized that one of her students with impulsivity, Cindy, surpassed her peers in the ability to clearly articulate her thoughts. Therefore Ms. Lapidus facilitated participation during the discussion so that Cindy was often one of the last to contribute, allowing her the opportunity to connect many of the points made in response to a question.

Engaging students in literary dialogue encourages the complex thinking associated with the writing process

---

Teachers also may find it useful to paraphrase comments the students make. By doing so, teachers are able to highlight important points made, usually ones that focus on the themes or relate to the final discussion topic. Paraphrasing student comments also can help students with attention difficulties and second language learners pay attention to and understand the discussion. An example of how Ms. Lapidus used paraphrasing is provided in the opening vignette.

Addressing the Needs of All Learners. With a wide range of levels in her classroom, Ms. Lapidus has found several components of this method helpful for all levels of learners because although teachers serve as facilitators, the instruction is nonetheless structured with clear expectations.

Because most of the activities are done as a whole class and thoughts are articulated verbally, students are not asked to write their thoughts down. This approach allows students who have difficulty articulating themselves in writing to share their higher level thinking in an open-discussion format. Ms. Lapidus has observed that often these students become the leaders during the Socratic discussion and feel quite comfortable obtaining roles when engaged in the Reader's Theatre component of the seminar. Ms. Lapidus also uses the Socratic discussion to teach appropriate social and communication skills (e.g., making eye contact, waiting for your turn to speak, responding appropriately to another's comments.) that are included in her students' individualized education program.

Ms. Lapidus makes instructional accommodations to support the participation of her students with disabilities in the Socratic seminar; she has found these accommodations beneficial for all her students. When the text is beyond the independent reading level of one or more students, she works with them in a small group to read the text orally a second time, stopping during the reading to monitor each student's comprehension. She also has provided "miniworkshops" to students who need further instruction on necessary components. Mini-workshops also provide supplemental instruction on identifying the literary elements, as well as on generating in-your-head questions instead of right-there questions.

Ms. Lapidus also adapts the Socratic seminar's writing component to address her students' strengths and challenges. Although all students are encouraged to use the writing process, Ms. Lapidus holds conferences with the students who struggle with writing at all stages of the process. When necessary, she, a special education teacher, or a paraeduator serves as a scribe to assist students in noting their initial thoughts and then guides them as they use their prewriting to construct a draft.

Benefits and Outcomes
for Using Socratic Seminars

Just as Ms. Lapidus had envisioned when she began using Socratic seminars in her inclusive classrooms, engaging students in literary dialogue encourages the complex thinking associated with the writing process. In her inclusive classroom, students learned to analyze a text through questioning, find evidence in the text, explore the elements of the story through discussion, and finally prepare a written response reflecting the main themes of the story. She noted that these skills helped prepare students to respond to a document-based question, a task required on many state assessments.

Ms. Lapidus also observed that the seminars helped develop responsibility and independence in her students and promote a sense of community, which are important goals for inclusive classrooms (Salend, 2008). After using Socratic seminars, Ms. Lapidus noticed that her students felt more comfortable sharing their ideas, encouraging one another to "think out of the box." One of the most enjoyable moments of holding the seminars for Ms. Lapidus has been watching the students eagerly respond to one another in a positive way, allowing themselves to be open to others' viewpoints and not criticizing others for points that are not concurrent with their own point of view. They often then follow through with their own opinions, or personal voice, in their writing, but sometimes because of others' comments during the discussion, they reverse their initial feelings and their writing as a response to, or validation of, another's viewpoint. For example, during the discussion of *Cinderella,* Ms. Lapidus watched her students move from a literal interpretation of the text (i.e., the fairy tale as presented by Disney) to a deeper understanding about a journey of self-worth.

For her students with special needs, Mrs. Lapidus has found that the seminars have helped the students focus their thoughts, resulting in a more organized written product. One of her former students, Adam, a student with processing difficulties, was very creative in his writing; however, it lacked organization. He often included what Mrs. Lapidus referred to as "gems" in his writing, profound or insightful statements but that seemed out of place in the larger piece. The Socratic seminars provided him the opportunity to retrieve statements made during the discussions and make use of them to support his thoughts. One example that illustrates this development was following a discussion on "The Enchanted Sticks" (Meyers, 1979), a story in which the character used his mind to outwit others and in doing so, proved his strength through intellect. During the discussion of the text, Adam literally jumped out of his seat, screaming "I get it!" and became the leader of the Socratic discussion. This interaction between Adam and the text, which arose because of the discussion with his peers, led to a writing product that was not only insightful but well organized and full of supporting detail.

"True knowledge exists in knowing that you know nothing. And in knowing that you know nothing, that makes you the smartest of all. To find yourself, think for yourself" (Aristotle, Quotationspage.com). The third- and fifth-grade students in Ms. Lapidus's classes have shown in their discussions during the Socratic seminars and in their writing after the seminar that they think about the text not as how they think their teacher wants them to, but rather as what they perceive the story to be about. In Ms. Lapidus's class, the students often generate 70 or more questions after they listen to the story and read it themselves. They make Ms. Lapidus proud by truly thinking for themselves; she thinks Socrates and Aristotle would be proud, too.

References

Aristotle. Retrieved March 19, 2007, from http://www.quotationspage.com/quote/3079.html

Chorzempa, B. F., & Lapidus, L. (2006, November). *Using Socratic seminars with third graders to promote critical thinking.* Presentation at annual Council for Learning Disabilities (CLD) conference, November.

Elder, L., & Paul, R. (1998). The role of Socratic questioning in thinking, teaching, and learning. *Clearing House, 71,* 297–301.

Fink-Chorzempa, B., Graham, S., & Harris, K. R. (2005). What can I do to help young children who struggle with writing? *TEACHING Exceptional Children, 37*(5), 64–66.

Graham, S. (2006). Writing. In P. Alexander & P. Winne (Eds.), *Handbook of educational psychology* (2nd ed., pp. 457–478). Mahwah, NJ: Lawrence Erbaum.

Graham, S., & Perin, D. (2007). A meta analysis of writing instruction for adolescent students. *Journal of Educational Psychology, 99,* 445–476.

The Great Books Foundation. (2006). *Junior great books.* Chicago. Author.

Lambright, L. L. (1995). Creating a dialogue: Socratic seminars and educational reform. *Community College Journal, 65*(4), 30–34.

Loan, B. (2003). A strong case for more talk in a Montessori classroom. *Montessori Life, 15*(3), 40–42.

Mawhinney, T. S. (2000). Finding the answer. *Principal Leadership, 4*(1), 44, 46–48.

Metzger, M. (1998). Teaching reading. *Phi Delta Kappan, 80,* 240–247.

Myers, S. J. (1979). *The enchanted sticks.* New York. Penguin Group (USA).

National Commission on Writing. (2006, May). *Writing and school reform.* Retrieved January 12, 2008, from http://www.writingcommission.org/

Polite, V. C., & Adams, A. H. (1997). Critical thinking and values clarification through Socratic seminars. *Urban Education, 32,* 256–278.

Queen, J. A. (2000). Block scheduling revisited. *Phi Delta Kappan, 82,* 214–222.

Raphael, T. E., & Au, K. E. (2005). QAR: Enhancing comprehension and test taking across grades and content areas. *The Reading Teacher, 59,* 206–221.

Salend, S. (2008). *Creating inclusive classrooms: Effective and reflective practices* (6th ed.). Upper Saddle River, NJ: Pearson Education.

Sorenson, M. (1993). Teach each other: Connecting talking and writing. *English Journal, 82,* 42–47.

Strong, M. (1997). *The habit of thought: From Socratic seminars to Socratic practice.* Chapel Hill, NC: New View.

Tanner, M. L., & Casados, L. (1998). Promoting and studying discussions in math classes. *Journal of Adolescent and Adult Literacy, 41,* 342–350.

Tredway, L. (1995). Socratic seminars: Engaging students in intellectual discourse. *Educational Leadership, 53*(1), 26–20.

Touchstones Discussion Project. (1993). *Touchpepples.* Annapolis, MD. Author.

BARBARA FINK CHORZEMPA (CEC NY Federation), Assistant Professor, Department of Elementary Education, SUNY New Paltz, New York; and LAURIE LAPIDUS, Classroom Teacher, Monroe Woodbury Central School District, Monroe, New York.

Address correspondence to Barbara Fink Chorzempa, Department. of Elementary Education, SUNY New Paltz, 1 Hawk Drive, New Paltz, NY 12561 (e-mail: chorzemb@newpaltz.edu).

ARTICLE 15

What Is Technology Education?
A Review of the "Official Curriculum"

Abstract: Technology education, not to be confused with educational technology, has an "official curriculum." This article explores this "official curriculum" and answers the following questions; what are the goals of technology education, what should technology education look like in classrooms, and why technology education is important. This article provides a primer on technology education that would be helpful to educational professionals interested in helping students become more technologically literate.

Keywords: technology education, curriculum, standards, high school

RYAN A. BROWN AND JOSHUA W. BROWN

"What is technology education?" Technology educators have been asked this question for many years. The field of technology education is a distinct area with a particular value for middle schools, high schools, and postsecondary institutions. Inspired by *The Clearing House*'s recent special issue on technology in education (Vol. 82, no. 2) we developed an article to answer the question of "what is technology education?" This question is entirely different than, but equally as important, as the question, "what is educational technology?" The two concepts are often confused. Discussion about public misconceptions regarding terms such as *technology education*, *educational technology*, and *computer literacy* can be found in the technology education literature (Dugger and Naik 2001; McCade 2001; Weber 2005). Through an analysis of the "official curriculum," this article provides education professionals in middle schools, high schools, and postsecondary settings with a brief description of the technology education curriculum by describing its educational aims, classroom elements, and context.

Official Curriculum

Over the past several decades, the technology education field has attempted to solidify the content that is taught in technology education classrooms. This new vision of technology education is presented here as an "official curriculum." The official curriculum, which Eisner labeled as the *intended curriculum*, was identified as the "formal and public course of study for which students, teachers, and schools, in one way or another, are held accountable" (1990, 63). The technology education official curriculum in this article has been determined based on the analysis of several documents that include standards and technological literacy documents (International Technology Education Association (ITEA) 2000; ITEA 2003; Indiana Department of Education 2007; National Academy of Engineering and National Research Council 2006; National Academy of Engineering and National Research Council 2002), state course guides, textbooks, monographs (Maley 1995), and numerous journal articles. The documents were analyzed and organized by modifying a framework suggested by Madaus and Kellaghan (1992). The resulting categories include the curriculum's context, broad educational aims and outcomes, and classroom elements. The findings are presented here as three basic questions: (1) What are the goals of technology education? (broad educational aims and outcomes); (2) What should technology education look like in the classroom? (classroom elements); and (3) Why is technology education important? (context).

What Are the Goals of Technology Education?

The stated goal of technology education is to "produce students with a more conceptual understanding of technology and its place in society, who can thus grasp and evaluate new bits of technology that they might never have seen before" (ITEA 2000, 4). This understanding is called *technological literacy* and is seen as both an aim and a potential outcome of technology education. It is clear in the literature that technological literacy, divided into five distinct categories by the *Standards for Technological Literacy*, is at the heart of the purpose and goals of technology education and is essentially what should be taught in technology education classrooms (ITEA 2000).

Technological Literacy

The International Technology Education Association (ITEA) states that "technological literacy is what every person needs in order to be an informed and contributing citizen for the world of today and tomorrow" (2003, 10). Gagel, in an effort to better define technological literacy, conducted a study aimed at bringing "the profession closer to a shared and deeper understanding of technological literacy" (1997, 6). He studied over two hundred frequently cited works by authors and institu-

tions from a number of disciplines including anthropology, education, history, industry, technology, and theology to establish a clear meaning of technological literacy and found that there was little agreement on the meaning of the terms *technology* or *literacy*. Gagel's work did not develop a concrete definition of *technological literacy*, but it did determine the nature of such a notion. He concluded that technological literacy was a fluid idea, and that its utility would be judged on its ability to change or mirror evolving cultural traditions. Gagel likened technological literacy to Hirsch's concept of cultural literacy because it is difficult to list all the essential elements of both, yet both are proposed for all citizens. In the absence of a definition, Gagel concluded that if an "identity kit" were created to detect technological literacy, it would include "both technological and praxiological knowledge, a holistic understanding of technology's ambience, and a technical adaptability engendered by inventive and resourceful thinking" (25).

The National Academy of Engineering (NAE) and the National Research Council (NRC) have also attempted to define technological literacy, which they state is "more of a capacity to understand the broader technical world rather than the ability to work with specific pieces of it" (National Academy of Engineering and National Research Council 2002, 22). These organizations have identified knowledge, critical thinking and decision making, and capabilities as the three dimensions of technological literacy. The knowledge dimension includes the basic nature and fundamental concepts of technology. The understanding of technological benefits, risks, and trade-offs, and participation in discussions and debates constitute the critical thinking and decision-making dimension. The capabilities dimension consists of being able to use the design process, troubleshoot a mechanical or technological problem, and effectively use technology (National Academy of Engineering and National Research Council 2002; National Academy of Engineering and National Research Council 2006). Lastly, ITEA defines technological literacy as the ability to use, manage, evaluate, and understand technology (ITEA 2006).

When technological literacy was initially introduced as a goal of technology education, the creation of a deeper and more meaningful definition of technological literacy was seen as "an unexpectedly complex and difficult task" (Gagel 1997, 6). Schultz claimed that developing technological literacy in students is a "noble, but darn-near-impossible-to-achieve goal" (1999, 83). The outcome of technological literacy is, in reality, very difficult to assess. The National Academy of Engineering and the National Research Council state that the "assessment of technological literacy in the United States is in its infancy" (National Academy of Engineering and National Research Council 2006, 7).

Technology Education Standards

A more tangible and visible outcome of technology education resides in the content identified in the Standards for Technological Literacy ITEA 2000). The official curricula of the technology education field are outlined largely in standards that, in essence, identify the knowledge that is needed for students to achieve the educational aims of the official curriculum. The Standards for Technological Literacy promote what students should know and be able to do to gain technological literacy and, in the process, they attempt to clear up confusion about the aims of technology education. The standards are organized into five major categories: nature of technology, technology and society, design, abilities for a technological world, and the designed world.

Each category includes three to seven content standards, with a total of twenty standards for technological literacy overall. The standards are then broken down into a number of benchmarks for students in grades K–2, 3–5, 6–8, and 9–12.

The *nature of technology category* encompasses the understanding that technology extends potential human knowledge and includes knowledge, process, and artifacts. This category has similarities to the work of Carl Mitcham, a philosopher of technology, which stated that technology can be conceptualized using four main approaches: objects, knowledge, actions, and volition (de Vries 2005). This category also defines the main concepts of technology as systems, resources, requirements, optimization, processes, controls, and trade-offs. The linkage between technology and other subject areas, such as science, mathematics, and social studies, is also addressed by a standard in the nature of technology category (ITEA 2000).

The standards in the second category, *technology and society*, focus on the influence, role, and effects of technology. This category addresses the desirable and undesirable cultural, social, economic, and political effects of technology. Students also learn about the effects of technology on the environment and the values and beliefs that the use and development of technology reflect. Last, students are introduced to the history of the development of technology (ITEA 2000).

The third category relates to *design*. This group of standards focuses on the attributes of design, the engineering design process, and methods of problem solving. Design attributes include criteria, constraints, optimization, creativity, and the creation of possible solutions. Engineering design is presented as a process in which a designer identifies a problem, generates ideas, creates and tests prototypes, and then builds a final solution. In this category, students learn that problem solving involves processes such as research and development, invention and innovation, and experimentation (ITEA 2000). Design is an area that has been debated throughout the history of the field and is seen as "arguably the single most important content category set forth in the standards" (Lewis and Zuga 2005, 52).

The *abilities for a technical world* category continues the theme of design and includes other abilities that students should develop in technology education curricula. The first standard is the ability to apply the design process and solve technical problems. Skills in this standard include measuring, sketching, drawing, and computer skills. The second ability is to use and maintain technological products and systems, and it consists of using tools and processes to troubleshoot, test, diagnose, and use technological artifacts. The final ability required is the development of the capacity to assess the impact of products and systems. Forecasting, analyzing trends, and determining benefits and risks are all skills that are grouped under the ability to assess technology (ITEA 2000).

The *designed world* is the final and largest category of the Standards for Technological Literacy. The seven standards of this category each focus on one of the following areas: medicine, agriculture, energy and power, information and communication, transportation, manufacturing, and construction. Students that attain the benchmarks in this category will be able to select, use, and understand technologies from one of these seven areas. For example, regarding the transportation standard, students should understand transportation and vehicular systems, have experience designing and using transportation systems, and be able to discuss the positive and negative impacts of transportation technology (ITEA 2000). The areas represent the ways in which humankind uses technology and are sometimes referred to as the *contexts of technology*.

What Should Technology Education Look Like?

The official curriculum, as the question implies, includes the actions that take place inside the classroom, where teaching and learning occur. It comprises Madaus and Kellaghan's (1992) *objectives of specific curricula*, *curricular materials*, and *transactions and processes* categories, as well as assessment. This article presents a discussion of instructional methods and strategies, and assessment techniques.

Instructional Methods and Strategies

The technology education literature includes a number of suggestions regarding what technology education should "look like" and how students should learn about technology. Many of the references to teaching technology education revolve around the idea of student engagement. The descriptors "hands-on, minds-on education" and "action-based" are often used to describe technology education courses. Students should be engaged in cognitive and psychomotor activities that foster critical thinking, decision making, and problem solving (ITEA 2003). Activity-based learning is the main approach of technology education.

Design and problem-solving activities are strongly encouraged in the technology education literature. Students should be given opportunities to solve practical, "real-world" problems, and they should be engaged in the design process. Students in technology education courses should also be given the opportunity to use and maintain technological products (ITEA 2005a). *Realizing Excellence* (ITEA 2005b) calls for students to examine ideas from several perspectives, and several of the standards include affective elements, but, as a whole, methods to teach those aspects are not easily found in the technology education curriculum. The importance of affective learning is aptly described by de Vries, who labels technology education as a "poor situation if a technology is taught without any kind of reflection, just as a collection of bits and pieces of knowledge and skill" (2005, 8).

Assessment

Student assessment is fairly well described in *Advancing Excellence in Technological Literacy* (ITEA 2003), in which it is divided into five assessment standards. The document states that both formative and summative assessment should be used in program enhancement and to gauge student learning and inform teachers of the effectiveness of instruction. Although the official curriculum lacks instructional methods for the affective domain, all three domains are covered in the assessment category.

According to the official curriculum, student assessment should be consistent with the Standards for Technological Literacy and should "include cognitive learning elements for solving technological problems . . . [and] psychomotor learning elements for applying technology . . . and [they should] guide student abilities to operate within the affective domain" (ITEA 2003, 21). Cognitive assessment is designed to allow students to describe and apply their knowledge. Assessment of psychomotor learning should be performance-based and should allow the students to use and apply their tactile knowledge and skills. Affective domain assessment should require students to demonstrate their knowledge of impacts and consequences of technology, as well as their understanding of critical perspectives (ITEA 2003).

The Standards for Technological Literacy (ITEA 2000) also lists potential assessment tools such as daily records of student work, quizzes, tests, portfolios, and standardized tests. Demonstrations, design briefs, prototyping, multiple-choice and true-false tests, proj-

ects, and self and peer assessments are also identified as possible assessment tools in technology education courses (ITEA 2004). The assessment tools should aid technology teachers in checking student understanding and ensuring that students are reaching the desired outcomes.

Why Is Technology Education Important?

The focus on technological literacy and the creation of the Standards for Technological Literacy comes at a time in history when technology and technological advancements have taken center stage in our society. Bybee, however, suggests that "in contrast to the dominant role of technology in society[,] one finds a citizenry with little knowledge and understanding of technology" (2003, 26). ITEA (2006) warns of a widening gap between people who use technology, the average citizen, and the inventors and designers that create technology. As technology continues to become more advanced, "society has become more specialized. As a result, all of us know more about fewer things" (National Academy of Engineering and National Research Council 2002, 49).

This lack of understanding of and connection with technology is evident in two Gallup polls conducted to determine the public's view of technology and technological literacy (Rose and Dugger 2002; Rose et al. 2004). The studies found that 98 percent of all Americans polled believed that it was either *somewhat* or *very important* to understand and use technology. Eighty eight percent recognized the importance of knowing how various technologies work, and approximately 90 percent believed it is important to know whether it is better to repair or throw away products and to be able to develop solutions to practical technological problems (Rose et al. 2004).

These findings imply that society is interested in being able to understand and use technology. The respondents, however, generally felt uninformed and believed they had little influence in technological decisions. Nearly half of those surveyed believed they were either *not very* or *not at all* informed about various technologies, and over 60 percent of respondents stated that they have little or no influence in regards to technological issues such as automobile efficiency, road construction in the community, and genetically modified foods. Finally, when asked specifically about technology education, respondents were nearly unanimous in stating that technology education, as defined by the ITEA, should be included in the school curriculum, and almost two-thirds believed that it should be required for high school graduation (Rose et al. 2004).

If this poll is representative of society as a whole, then it would be fair to say that there is general agreement that technology and technology education are important to society. That being the case, Zilbert and Mercer (1992) still found that technology has no well-defined place in the curriculum taught to most students. Understanding technology and becoming technologically literate are believed to help students achieve a better understanding of the technological society in which they live, not through vocational or specific job training, but by developing a holistic understanding of technology (Seemann 2003).

Gagel (1997) suggests that a technologically literate person is someone who can stay abreast of new technology, solve technical problems, use technology effectively, and assess its impacts. Being technologically literate and understanding technology is also believed to benefit students personally, socially, and academically. The personal values found in the literature include exploring interests, achieving a feeling of success, developing both problem-solving and interpersonal skills, and developing "a broad sense of career

awareness" (Maley 1995, 7). In regard to personal development, ITEA states that "people benefit both at work and at home by being able to choose the best products for their purposes, to operate the products properly, and to troubleshoot them when something goes wrong" (2000, 2).

The societal values attributed to technology education are "those contributions that enhance and strengthen the individual's capabilities of functioning effectively as a citizen in a democratic, technological society" (Maley 1995, 3). These values include learning the skills required for proper selection and assessment of technology, developing informed citizens, heightening awareness of the social and environmental impacts of technology, and questioning the use, value, and abuse of technology. In support of the value of questioning technology, Gilberti says:

In a democracy, citizens and consumers are continually being asked to make evaluations of the applications and limitations of technology to human wants, desires, and problems. By providing students with the skills to evaluate the appropriateness of various technological devices and fixes, the curriculum area of technology education helps to promote a more just and sustainable future. (quoted in Maley 1995, 16)

The final area of values that can be attributed to technology education's official curriculum is academic values. These values "provide enrichment of the academic experience as well as its relevance—personal and social" (Maley 1995, 3). These values include the relevant integration of other subjects, the development of technological skills and understanding, the connection between theoretical and practical knowledge, the understanding of history and evolution of technology, and the development of inquiry, research, and problem-solving skills.

Conclusions

The personal, social, and academic values that have been attributed to technology, like technological literacy, are both very ambitious and difficult to quantify. They are, however, present in the "official curriculum," as are the answers to the questions posed throughout this article: what are our goals, how should we teach technology education, and why is it important. Teachers, administrators, and those interested in the difference between technology education and educational technology need only review the curricular documents to discover that there is an "official curriculum" of technology education. In doing so, they will find that the broad educational aims and outcomes of technology education focus on the goal of attaining technological literacy within the areas of the Standards for Technological Literacy. Instructional methods of the official curriculum focus mainly on student engagement with the subject of technology in activities, design problems, and problem-solving opportunities, while other methods discussed include presentations, debates, journals, and discussions. Teachers will also discover that student assessment should be designed to correspond with the aims of technology education and should measure students' understanding and abilities in the cognitive, psychomotor, and affective domains. Finally, it is clear that technology education can contribute to a range of personal, social, and academic values.

References

Bybee, R. 2003. Fulfilling a promise. *The Technology Teacher* 62(6): 23–26.

de Vries, M. J. 2005. *Teaching about technology*. Dordrecht, The Netherlands: Springer.

Dugger, W., and N. Naik. 2001. Clarifying misconceptions between technology education and educational technology. *The Technology Teacher* 61(1): 31–35.

Eisner, E. 1990. Creative curriculum development and practice. *Journal of Curriculum and Supervision* 6(1): 62–73.

Gagel, C. W. 1997. Literacy and technology: Reflections and insights for technological literacy. *Journal of Industrial Teacher Education* 34(3): 6–34.

Hirsch, Jr., E. D. 1998. *Cultural literacy: What every American needs to know*. New York: Vintage Books.

Indiana Department of Education. 2007. *Technology education content standards*. Indiana Department of Education 2004. http://www.doe.state.in.us/standards/docs-Technology/2006-08- 15-TechEd-Stds .pdf (accessed March 13, 2007).

International Technology Education Association (ITEA). 2000. *Standards for technological literacy: Content for the study of technology*. Reston, VA: ITEA.

——. 2003. *Advancing excellence in technological literacy: Student assessment, professional development, and program standards*. Reston, VA: ITEA.

——. 2004. *Measuring progress: Assessing students for technological literacy*. Reston, VA: ITEA.

——. 2005a. *Planning learning: Developing technology curricula*. Reston, VA: ITEA.

——. 2005b. *Realizing excellence: Structuring technology programs*. Reston, VA: ITEA.

——. 2006. *Technological literacy for all: A rationale and structure for the study of technology*. Reston, VA: ITEA.

Lewis, T., and K. Zuga. 2005. A conceptual framework of ideas and issues in technology education: National Science Foundation. http://teched.vt.edu/ctte/ImagesPDFs/ConceptualFramework2005 . pdf (accessed December 28, 2009).

Madaus, G., and T. Kellaghan. 1992.
Curriculum evaluation and assessment. In
Handbook of research on curriculum,
ed P. Jackson, 119–154. New York:
Macmillan.

Maley, D., ed. 1995. *Quotations in support
of technology education: A compendium
of positive outcome that may be
attributed to an effective program in the
area of technology education*. Reston, VA:
Council on Technology Teacher
Education.

McCade, J. 2001. Technology education and
computer literacy. *The Technology Teacher*
61(2): 9–13.

———. 2002. *Technically speaking: Why all
Americans need to know more about
technology*. Washington, DC: National
Academy Press.

National Academy of Engineering and
National Research Council. 2006. *Tech tally:
Approaches to assessing technological
literacy*. Washington, DC: National Academy
Press.

Rose, L., and W. Dugger. 2002. ITEA/
Gallup poll reveals what Americans think
about technology. *The Technology Teacher*
61(6): 1–8.

Rose, L., A. Gallup, W. Dugger, and
K. Starkweather. 2004. The second
installment of the ITEA/Gallup poll and
what it reveals as to how Americans think
about technology. *The Technology Teacher*
61(8): 1–8.

Schultz, A. E. 1999. What we teach and why
we teach it. *Journal of Industrial Teacher
Education* (1), http://scholar.lib.vt.edu/
ejournals/JITE/v37n1/schultz.html
(accessed March 14, 2008).

Seemann, K. 2003. Basic principles in holistic
technology education. *Journal of
Technology Education* 14(2): 28–39.

Weber, K. 2005. A proactive approach to
technological literacy. *The Technology
Teacher* 64(7): 28–30.

Zilbert, E., and J. Mercer. 1992. *Technology
competence: Learner goals for all
Minnesotans*. St. Paul, MN: Minnesota State
Council on Vocational Technical Education.

RYAN A. BROWN is an assistant professor in the
Department of Curriculum and Instruction,
Illinois State University, Normal, IL.

JOSHUA W. BROWN is an assistant professor in the
Department of Technology, Illinois State
University, Normal, IL.

ARTICLE 16

The Perils and Promises of Praise

The wrong kind of praise creates self-defeating behavior.
The right kind motivates students to learn.

CAROL S. DWECK

We often hear these days that we've produced a generation of young people who can't get through the day without an award. They expect success because they're special, not because they've worked hard.

Is this true? Have we inadvertently done something to hold back our students?

I think educators commonly hold two beliefs that do just that. Many believe that (1) praising students' intelligence builds their confidence and motivation to learn, and (2) students' inherent intelligence is the major cause of their achievement in school. Our research has shown that the first belief is false and that the second can be harmful—even for the most competent students.

As a psychologist, I have studied student motivation for more than 35 years. My graduate students and I have looked at thousands of children, asking why some enjoy learning, even when it's hard, and why they are resilient in the face of obstacles. We have learned a great deal. Research shows us how to praise students in ways that yield motivation and resilience. In addition, specific interventions can reverse a student's slide into failure during the vulnerable period of adolescence.

Fixed or Malleable?

Praise is intricately connected to how students view their intelligence. Some students believe that their intellectual ability is a fixed trait. They have a certain amount of intelligence, and that's that. Students with this fixed mind-set become excessively concerned with how smart they are, seeking tasks that will prove their intelligence and avoiding ones that might not (Dweck, 1999, 2006). The desire to learn takes a backseat.

Other students believe that their intellectual ability is something they can develop through effort and education. They don't necessarily believe that anyone can become an Einstein or a Mozart, but they do understand that even Einstein and Mozart had to put in years of effort to become who they were. When students believe that they can develop their intelligence, they focus on doing just that. Not worrying about how smart they will appear, they take on challenges and stick to them (Dweck, 1999, 2006).

More and more research in psychology and neuroscience supports the growth mind-set. We are discovering that the brain has more plasticity over time than we ever imagined (Doidge, 2007); that fundamental aspects of intelligence can be enhanced through learning (Sternberg, 2005); and that dedication and persistence in the face of obstacles are key ingredients in outstanding achievement (Ericsson, Charness, Feltovich, & Hoffman, 2006).

Alfred Binet (1909/1973), the inventor of the IQ test, had a strong growth mind-set. He believed that education could transform the basic capacity to learn. Far from intending to measure fixed intelligence, he meant his test to be a tool for identifying students who were not profiting from the public school curriculum so that other courses of study could be devised to foster their intellectual growth.

The Two Faces of Effort

The fixed and growth mind-sets create two different psychological worlds. In the fixed mind-set, students care first and foremost about how they'll be judged: smart or not smart. Repeatedly, students with this mind-set reject opportunities to learn if they might make mistakes (Hong, Chiu, Dweck, Lin, & Wan, 1999; Mueller & Dweck, 1998). When they do make mistakes or reveal deficiencies, rather than correct them, they try to hide them (Nussbaum & Dweck, 2007).

They are also afraid of effort because effort makes them feel dumb. They believe that if you have the ability, you shouldn't need effort (Blackwell, Trzesniewski, & Dweck, 2007), that ability should bring success all by itself. This is one of the worst beliefs that students can hold. It can cause many bright students to stop working in school when the curriculum becomes challenging.

Finally, students in the fixed mind-set don't recover well from setbacks. When they hit a setback in school, they *decrease* their efforts and consider cheating (Blackwell et al., 2007). The idea of fixed intelligence does not offer them viable ways to improve.

Let's get inside the head of a student with a fixed mind-set as he sits in his classroom, confronted with algebra for the first time. Up until then, he has breezed through math. Even when he barely paid attention in class and skimped on his homework, he always got As. But this is different. It's hard. The student feels anxious and thinks, "What if I'm not as good at math as I thought? What if other kids understand it and I don't?" At some level, he realizes that he has two choices: try hard, or turn off. His interest in math begins to wane, and his attention wanders. He tells himself, "Who cares about this stuff? It's for nerds. I could do it if I wanted to, but it's so boring. You don't see CEOs and sports stars solving for x and y."

By contrast, in the growth mind-set, students care about learning. When they make a mistake or exhibit a deficiency, they correct it (Blackwell et al., 2007; Nussbaum & Dweck, 2007). For them, effort is a *positive* thing: It ignites their intelligence and causes it to grow. In the face of failure, these students escalate their efforts and look for new learning strategies.

Let's look at another student—one who has a growth mind-set—having her first encounter with algebra. She finds it new, hard, and confusing, unlike anything else she has ever learned. But she's determined to understand it. She listens to everything the teacher says, asks the teacher questions after class, and takes her textbook home and reads the chapter over twice. As she begins to get it, she feels exhilarated. A new world of math opens up for her.

It is not surprising, then, that when we have followed students over challenging school transitions or courses, we find that those with growth mind-sets outperform their classmates with fixed mind-sets—even when they entered with equal skills and knowledge. A growth mind-set fosters the growth of ability over time (Blackwell et al., 2007; Mangels, Butterfield, Lamb, Good, & Dweck, 2006; see also Grant & Dweck, 2003).

The Effects of Praise

Many educators have hoped to maximize students' confidence in their abilities, their enjoyment of learning, and their ability to thrive in school by praising their intelligence. We've studied the effects of this kind of praise in children as young as 4 years old and as old as adolescence, in students in inner-city and rural settings, and in students of different ethnicities—and we've consistently found the same thing (Cimpian, Arce, Markman, & Dweck, 2007; Kamins & Dweck, 1999; Mueller & Dweck, 1998): Praising students' intelligence gives them a short burst of pride, followed by a long string of negative consequences.

In many of our studies (see Mueller & Dweck, 1998), 5th grade students worked on a task, and after the first set of problems, the teacher praised some of them for their intelligence ("You must be smart at these problems") and others for their effort ("You must have worked hard at these problems"). We then assessed the students' mind-sets. In one study, we asked students to agree or disagree with mind-set statements, such as, "Your intelligence is something basic about you that you can't really change." Students praised for intelligence agreed with statements like these more than students praised for effort did. In another study, we asked students to define intelligence. Students praised for intelligence made significantly more references to innate, fixed capacity, whereas the students praised for effort made more references to skills, knowledge, and areas they could change through effort and learning. Thus, we found that praise for intelligence tended to put students in a fixed mind-set (intelligence is fixed, and you have it), whereas praise for effort tended to put them in a growth mind-set (you're developing these skills because you're working hard).

We then offered students a chance to work on either a challenging task that they could learn from or an easy one that ensured error-free performance. Most of those praised for intelligence wanted the easy task, whereas most of those praised for effort wanted the challenging task and the opportunity to learn.

Next, the students worked on some challenging problems. As a group, students who had been praised for their intelligence *lost* their confidence in their ability and their enjoyment of the task as soon as they began to struggle with the problem. If success meant they were smart, then struggling meant they were not. The whole point of intelligence praise is to boost confidence and motivation, but both were gone in a flash. Only the effort-praised kids remained, on the whole, confident and eager.

When the problems were made somewhat easier again, students praised for intelligence did poorly, having lost their confidence and motivation. As a group, they did worse than they had done initially on these same types of problems. The students praised for effort showed excellent performance and continued to improve.

Finally, when asked to report their scores (anonymously), almost 40 percent of the intelligence-praised students lied. Apparently, their egos were so wrapped up in their performance that they couldn't admit mistakes. Only about 10 percent of the effort-praised students saw fit to falsify their results.

Praising students for their intelligence, then, hands them not motivation and resilience but a fixed mind-set with all its vulnerability. In contrast, effort or "process" praise (praise for engagement, perseverance, strategies, improvement, and the like) fosters hardy motivation. It tells students what they've done to be successful and what they need to do to be successful again in the future. Process praise sounds like this:

- You really studied for your English test, and your improvement shows it. You read the material over several times, outlined it, and tested yourself on it. That really worked!
- I like the way you tried all kinds of strategies on that math problem until you finally got it.

- It was a long, hard assignment, but you stuck to it and got it done. You stayed at your desk, kept up your concentration, and kept working. That's great!
- I like that you took on that challenging project for your science class. It will take a lot of work—doing the research, designing the machine, buying the parts, and building it. You're going to learn a lot of great things.

What about a student who gets an *A* without trying? I would say, "All right, that was too easy for you. Let's do something more challenging that you can learn from." We don't want to make something done quickly and easily the basis for our admiration.

What about a student who works hard and *doesn't* do well? I would say, "I liked the effort you put in. Let's work together some more and figure out what you don't understand." Process praise keeps students focused, not on something called ability that they may or may not have and that magically creates success or failure, but on processes they can all engage in to learn.

Motivated to Learn

Finding that a growth mind-set creates motivation and resilience—and leads to higher achievement—we sought to develop an intervention that would teach this mind-set to students. We decided to aim our intervention at students who were making the transition to 7th grade because this is a time of great vulnerability. School often gets more difficult in 7th grade, grading becomes more stringent, and the environment becomes more impersonal. Many students take stock of themselves and their intellectual abilities at this time and decide whether they want to be involved with school. Not surprisingly, it is often a time of disengagement and plunging achievement.

We performed our intervention in a New York City junior high school in which many students were struggling with the transition and were showing plummeting grades. If students learned a growth mind-set, we reasoned, they might be able to meet this challenge with increased, rather than decreased, effort. We therefore developed an eight-session workshop in which both the control group and the growth-mind-set group learned study skills, time management techniques, and memory strategies (Blackwell et al., 2007). However, in the growth-mind-set intervention, students also learned about their brains and what they could do to make their intelligence grow.

They learned that the brain is like a muscle—the more they exercise it, the stronger it becomes. They learned that every time they try hard and learn something new, their brain forms new connections that, over time, make them smarter. They learned that intellectual development is not the natural unfolding of intelligence, but rather the formation of new connections brought about through effort and learning.

Students were riveted by this information. The idea that their intellectual growth was largely in their hands fascinated them. In fact, even the most disruptive students suddenly sat still and took notice, with the most unruly boy of the lot looking up at us and saying, "You mean I don't have to be dumb?"

Indeed, the growth-mind-set message appeared to unleash students' motivation. Although both groups had experienced a steep decline in their math grades during their first months of junior high, those receiving the growth-mind-set intervention showed a significant rebound. Their math grades improved. Those in the control group, despite their excellent study skills intervention, continued their decline.

What's more, the teachers—who were unaware that the intervention workshops

110

differed—singled out three times as many students in the growth-mindset intervention as showing marked changes in motivation. These students had a heightened desire to work hard and learn. One striking example was the boy who thought he was dumb. Before this experience, he had never put in any extra effort and often didn't turn his homework in on time. As a result of the training, he worked for hours one evening to finish an assignment early so that his teacher could review it and give him a chance to revise it. He earned a *B+* on the assignment (he had been getting *C*s and lower previously).

Other researchers have obtained similar findings with a growth-mind-set intervention. Working with junior high school students, Good, Aronson, and Inzlicht (2003) found an increase in math and English achievement test scores; working with college students, Aronson, Fried, and Good (2002) found an increase in students' valuing of academics, their enjoyment of schoolwork, and their grade point averages.

To facilitate delivery of the growth-mind-set workshop to students, we developed an interactive computer-based version of the intervention called *Brainology*. Students work through six modules, learning about the brain, visiting virtual brain labs, doing virtual brain experiments, seeing how the brain changes with learning, and learning how they can make their brains work better and grow smarter.

We tested our initial version in 20 New York City schools, with encouraging results. Almost all students (anonymously polled) reported changes in their study habits and motivation to learn resulting directly from their learning of the growth mind-set. One student noted that as a result of the animation she had seen about the brain, she could actually "picture the neurons growing bigger as they make more connections." One student

referred to the value of effort: "If you do not give up and you keep studying, you can find your way through."

Adolescents often see school as a place where they perform for teachers who then judge them. The growth mind-set changes that perspective and makes school a place where students vigorously engage in learning for their own benefit.

Going Forward

Our research shows that educators cannot hand students confidence on a silver platter by praising their intelligence. Instead, we can help them gain the tools they need to maintain their confidence in learning by keeping them focused on the *process* of achievement.

Maybe we have produced a generation of students who are more dependent, fragile, and entitled than previous generations. If so, it's time for us to adopt a growth mind-set and learn from our mistakes. It's time to deliver interventions that will truly boost students' motivation, resilience, and learning.

References

Aronson, J., Fried, C., & Good, C. (2002). Reducing the effects of stereotype threat on African American college students by shaping theories of intelligence. *Journal of Experimental Social Psychology, 38*, 113–125.

Binet, A. (1909/1973). *Les idées modernes sur les enfants* [Modern ideas on children]. Paris: Flamarion. (Original work published 1909)

Blackwell, L., Trzesniewski, K., & Dweck, C. S. (2007). Implicit theories of intelligence predict achievement across an adolescent transition: A longitudinal study and an intervention. *Child Development, 78*, 246–263.

Cimpian, A., Arce, H., Markman, E. M., & Dweck, C. S. (2007). Subtle linguistic cues impact children's motivation. *Psychological Science, 18*, 314–316.

Doidge, N. (2007). *The brain that changes itself: Stories of personal triumph from the frontiers of brain science.* New York: Viking.

Dweck, C. S. (1999). *Self-theories: Their role in motivation, personality and development.* Philadelphia: Taylor and Francis/Psychology Press.

Dweck, C. S. (2006). *Mindset: The new psychology of success.* New York: Random House.

Ericsson, K. A., Charness, N., Feltovich, P. J., & Hoffman, R. R. (Eds.). (2006). *The Cambridge handbook of expertise and expert performance.* New York: Cambridge University Press.

Good, C., Aronson, J., & Inzlicht, M. (2003). Improving adolescents' standardized test performance: An intervention to reduce the effects of stereotype threat. *Journal of Applied Developmental Psychology, 24*, 645–662.

Grant, H., & Dweck, C. S. (2003). Clarifying achievement goals and their impact. *Journal of Personality and Social Psychology, 85*, 541–553.

Hong, Y. Y., Chiu, C., Dweck, C. S., Lin, D., & Wan, W. (1999). Implicit theories, attributions, and coping: A meaning system approach. *Journal of Personality and Social Psychology, 77*, 588–599.

Kamins, M., & Dweck, C. S. (1999). Person vs. process praise and criticism: Implications for contingent self-worth and coping. *Developmental Psychology, 35*, 835–847.

Mangels, J. A., Butterfield, B., Lamb, J., Good, C. D., & Dweck, C. S. (2006). Why do beliefs about intelligence influence learning success? A social-cognitive-neuroscience model. *Social, Cognitive, and Affective Neuroscience, 1*, 75–86.

Mueller, C. M., & Dweck, C. S. (1998). Intelligence praise can undermine motivation and performance. *Journal of Personality and Social Psychology, 75*, 33–52.

Nussbaum, A. D., & Dweck, C. S. (2007). Defensiveness vs. remediation: Self-theories and modes of self-esteem maintenance. *Personality and Social Psychology Bulletin*.

Sternberg, R. (2005). Intelligence, competence, and expertise. In A. Elliot & C. S. Dweck (Eds.), *The handbook of competence and motivation* (pp. 15–30). New York: Guilford Press.

CAROL S. DWECK is the Lewis and Virginia Eaton Professor of Psychology at Stanford University and the author of *Mindset: The New Psychology of Success* (Random House, 2006).

ARTICLE 17

Should Learning Be Its Own Reward?

How does the mind work—and especially how does it learn? Teachers' instructional decisions
are based on a mix of theories learned in teacher education, trial and error, craft knowledge,
and gut instinct. Such gut knowledge often serves us well, but is there anything sturdier to rely on?

Cognitive science is an interdisciplinary field of researchers from psychology,
neuroscience, linguistics, philosophy, computer science, and anthropology who seek to
understand the mind. In this regular American Educator column, we consider findings
from this field that are strong and clear enough to merit classroom application.

Daniel T. Willingham

Question: In recent months, there's been a big uproar about students being paid to take standardized tests—and being paid even more if they do well. Can cognitive science shed any light on this debate? Is it harmful to students to reward them like this? What about more typical rewards like a piece of candy or five extra minutes of recess?

There has been much debate recently about boosting standardized test scores by paying students. Here are a few examples that I read about in the news. In Coshocton, Ohio, third- and sixth-graders are being paid up to $20 for earning high scores on standardized tests. In New York City, fourth-grade students will receive $5 for each standardized test they take throughout the year, and up to $25 for each perfect score. Seventh-graders will get twice those amounts. In Tucson, Ariz., high school juniors selected from low-income areas will be paid up to $25 each week for attendance. These and similar programs affect just a tiny fraction of students nationwide. But rewarding students with things like small gifts, extra recess time, stickers, certificates, class parties and the like is actually pretty common. Most teachers have the option of distributing rewards in the classroom, and many do. For example, in a recent survey of young adults, 70 percent said that their elementary school teachers had used candy as a reward (Davis, Winsler, and Middleton, 2006).

So whether or not your district offers cash rewards for standardized test scores or attendance, you've probably wondered if rewarding your students for their classwork is a good idea. Some authors promise doom if a teacher rewards students, with the predicted negative effects ranging from unmotivated pupils to a teacher's moral bankruptcy (e.g., Kohn, 1993). Others counter that rewards are harmless or even helpful (e.g., Cameron, Banko, and Pierce, 2001; Chance, 1993). Where does the truth lie? In the middle. There is some merit to the arguments on both sides. Concrete rewards can motivate students to attend class, to behave well, or to produce better work. But if you are not careful in choosing what you reward, they can prompt students to produce shoddy work—and worse, they can cause students to actually like school subjects less. The important guidelines are these: Don't use rewards unless you have to, use rewards for a specific reason, and use them for a limited time. Let's take a look at the research behind these guidelines.

Concrete rewards can motivate students to attend class, to behave well, or to produce better work. But if you are not careful in choosing what you reward, they can prompt students to produce shoddy work— and worse, they can cause students to actually like school subjects less.

Do Rewards Work?

Rewarding students is, from one perspective, an obvious idea. People do things because they find them rewarding, the reasoning goes, so if students don't find school naturally rewarding (that is, interesting and fun), make it rewarding by offering them something they do like, be it cash or candy.

In this simple sense, rewards usually work. If you offer students an appealing reward, the targeted behavior will generally increase (for reviews, see O'Leary and Drabman, 1971; Deci, Koestner, and Ryan, 1999). Teachers typically use rewards like candy, stickers, small prizes, or extra recess time. They use them to encourage student behaviors such as completing assignments, producing good work, and so on. In one example (Hendy, Williams, and Camise, 2005) first-, second-, and fourth-graders were observed in the school cafeteria to see how often they ate fruits and vegetables. Once this baseline measure was taken, they were rewarded for eating one or the other. Students received a token for each day that they ate the assigned food, and tokens could be redeemed for small prizes at the end of the week. Not surprisingly, students ate more of what they were rewarded for eating.

But things don't always go so smoothly. If you mistakenly offer a reward that students don't care for, you'll see little result. Or, if you reward the wrong behavior, you'll see a result you don't care for. When I was in fourth grade, my class was offered a small prize for each

book we read. Many of us quickly developed a love for short books with large print, certainly not the teacher's intent. In the same way, if you reward people to come up with ideas, but don't stipulate that they must be good ideas, people will generate lots of ideas in order to gain lots of rewards, but the ideas may not be especially good (Ward, Kogan, and Pankove, 1972). It's often possible to correct mistakes such as these. Unappealing rewards can be replaced by valued rewards. The target behavior can be changed. My fourth-grade teacher stipulated that books had to be grade-appropriate and of some minimum length.

Because rewards are generally effective, people's objection to them in the classroom is seldom that they won't work. The op-ed newspaper articles I have seen about the student payment plans described above don't claim that you can't get students to go to school by paying them (e.g., Carlton, 2007; Schwartz, 2007). They raise other objections.

The common arguments against rewards fall into three categories. Let me state each one in rather extreme terms to give you the idea, and then I'll consider the merits of each in more detail. The first objection is that using rewards is immoral. You might toss your dog a treat when he shakes hands, but that is no way to treat children. Classrooms should be a caring community in which students help one another, not a circus in which the teacher serves as ringmaster. The second objection is that offering rewards is unrealistic. Rewards can't last forever, so what happens when they stop? Those who make this argument think it's better to help students appreciate the subtle, but real rewards that the world offers for things like hard work and politeness. After all, adults don't expect that someone will toss them a candy bar every time they listen politely, push their chair under a table, or complete a report on time. The third objection is that offering rewards can actually decrease motivation. Cognitive science has found that this is true, but only under certain conditions. For example, if you initially enjoy reading and I reward you for each book you finish, the rewards will make you like reading less. Below, I'll explain how and why that happens. Let's consider each of these arguments in turn.

Are Rewards Immoral?

Don't rewards control students? Aren't rewards dehumanizing? Wouldn't it be better to create a classroom atmosphere in which students wanted to learn, rather than one in which they reluctantly slogged through assignments, doing the minimal work they thought would still earn the promised reward? Cognitive science cannot answer moral questions. They are outside its purview. But cognitive science can provide some factual background that may help teachers as they consider these questions.

It is absolutely the case that trying to control students is destructive to their motivation and their performance. People like autonomy, and using rewards to control people definitely reduces motivation. Even if the task is one students generally like, if they sense that you're trying to coerce them, they will be less likely to do it (e.g., Ryan, Mims, and Koestner, 1983). It is worth pointing out, however, that rewards themselves are not inherently controlling. If students are truly offered a choice—do this and get a reward, don't do it and get no reward—then the student maintains control. Within behavioral science, it is accepted that rewards themselves are coercive if they are excessive (e.g., National Commission for the Protection of Human Subjects of Biomedical and Behavioral Research, 1978). In other words, if I offer you $200 to take a brief survey, it's hard to know that you're freely choosing to take the survey.

Rewards in classrooms are typically not excessive, and so are not, themselves, controlling. Rather, rewards might be an occasion for control if the teacher makes it quite clear that the student is expected to do the required work and collect his or her reward. That is, the teacher uses social coercion. So too, we've all known people we would call "manipulative," and those people seldom manipulate us via rewards. They use social means. In sum, the caution against controlling students is well-founded, but rewards are not inherently controlling.

Are rewards dehumanizing? Again, it seems to me that the answer depends on how the student construes the reward. If a teacher dangles stickers before students like fish before a seal, most observers will likely wince. But if a teacher emphasizes that rewards are a gesture of appreciation for a job well done, that probably would not appear dehumanizing to most observers.[1] Even so, rather than offer rewards, shouldn't teachers create classrooms in which students love learning? It is difficult not to respond to this objection by saying "Well, duh." I can't imagine there are many teachers who would rather give out candy than have a classroom full of students who are naturally interested and eager to learn. The question to ask is not "Why would you use rewards instead of making the material interesting?" Rather, it is "After you've wracked your brain for a way to make the material interesting for students and you still can't do it, then what?" Sanctimonious advice on the evils of rewards won't get chronically failing students to have one more go at learning to read. I think it unwise to discourage teachers from using any techniques in the absolute; rather, teachers need to know what research says about the benefits and drawbacks of the techniques, so that they can draw their own conclusions about whether and when to use them. Considering the merits of the two other objections will get us further into that research.

> Sanctimonious advice on the evils
> of rewards won't get chronically failing
> students to have one more go at learning
> to read. I think it unwise to discourage
> teachers from using any techniques in the
> absolute; rather, teachers need to know
> what research says about the benefits
> and drawbacks of the techniques.

What Happens When Rewards Stop?

This objection is easy to appreciate. If I'm working math problems because you're paying me, what's going to happen once you stop paying me? Your intuition probably tells you that I will stop doing problems, and you're right. In the fruits and vegetables study described earlier, students stopped eating fruits and vegetables soon after the reward program stopped.

Although it might seem obvious that this would happen, psychologists initially thought that there was a way around this problem. Many studies were conducted during the 1960s using token economies. A token economy is a system by which rewards are administered in an effort to change behavior. There are many variants but the basic idea is that every time the student exhibits a targeted behavior (e.g., gets ready to work quickly in the morning), he or she gets a token (e.g., a plastic chip). Students accumulate tokens and later trade them for rewards (e.g., small prizes). Token economies have some positive effects, and have been used not only in classrooms, but in clinical settings (e.g., Dickerson, Tenhula, and Green-Paden, 2005).

When the idea of a token economy was developed, the plan was that the rewards would be phased out. Once the desired behavior was occurring frequently, you would not give the reward every time, but give it ran-

domly, averaging 75 percent of the time, then 50 percent of the time, and so on. Thus, the student would slowly learn to do the behavior without the external reward. That works with animals, but normally not with humans. Once the rewards stop, people go back to behaving as they did before (Kazdin, 1982; O'Leary and Drabman, 1971).[2]

Well, one might counter, it may be true that students won't spontaneously work math problems once we stop rewarding them, but at least they will have worked more than they otherwise would have! Unfortunately, there is another, more insidious consequence of rewards that we need to consider: Under certain circumstances, they can actually decrease motivation.

How Can Rewards Decrease Motivation?

The previous section made it sound like rewards boost desired behavior so long as they are present, and when they are removed behavior falls back to where it started. That's true sometimes, but not always. If the task is one that students like, rewards will, as usual, make it more likely they'll do the task. But after the rewards stop, students will actually perform the previously likable task *less* than they did when rewards were first offered.

A classic study on this phenomenon (Lepper, Greene, and Nisbett, 1973) provides a good illustration. Children (aged 3 to 5 years old) were surreptitiously observed in a classroom with lots of different activities available. The experimenters noted how much time each child spent drawing with markers. The markers were then unavailable to students for two weeks. At the end of the two weeks, students were broken into three groups. Each student in the first group was taken to a separate room and was told that he or she could win an attractive "Good Player" certificate by drawing a picture with the markers. Each was eager to get the certificate and drew a picture. One-by-one, students in a second group were also brought to a separate room, encouraged to draw, and then given a certificate, but the certificate came as a surprise; when they started drawing, they didn't know that they would get the certificate. A third group of students served as a control group. They had been observed in the first session, but didn't draw or get a certificate in this second session. After another delay of about two weeks, the markers again appeared in the classroom, and experimenters observed how much children used them. The students in the first group—those who were promised the certificate for drawing—used the markers about half as much as students in the other two groups. Promising and then giving a reward made children like the markers less. But giving the reward as a surprise (as with the second group of students) had no effect.

This has been replicated scores of times with students of different ages, using different types of rewards, and in realistic classroom situations (see Deci et al., 1999 for a review). What is going on? How can getting a reward reduce your motivation to do something? The answer lies in the students' interpretation of why they chose to use the markers. For students who either didn't get a reward or who didn't expect a reward, it's obvious that they weren't drawing for the sake of the reward; they drew pictures because they liked drawing. But for the children who were promised a reward, the reason is less clear. A student might not remember that he drew because he wanted to draw, but rather he remembered really wanting the certificate. So when the markers were available again but no certificate was promised, the student may well have thought "I drew because I wanted that certificate; why should I draw now for nothing?"

The analogy to the classroom is clear. Teachers seek to create lifelong learners. We don't just want children to read, we want children to learn to love reading. So if, in an effort to get children to read more, we promise to reward them for doing so, we might actually make them like reading less! They will read more in order to get the pizza party or the stickers, but once the teacher is no longer there to give out the rewards, the student will say "Why should I read? I'm not getting anything for it."

The key factor to keep in mind is that rewards only decrease motivation for tasks that students initially like. If the task is dull, motivation might drop back down to its original level once the rewards stop, but it will not drop below its original level. Why does the appeal of the task make a difference? As I mentioned, rewards hurt motivation because of the way students construe the situation: "I drew with markers in order to get a certificate," instead of "I drew with markers because I like to draw with markers." But if the task is dull, students won't make that mistaken interpretation. They never liked the task in the first place. That hypothesis has been confirmed in a number of studies showing that once the reward is no longer being offered, having received a reward in the past harms the motivation for an interesting task, but not for a dull task (e.g., Daniel and Esser, 1980; Loveland and Olley, 1979; Newman and Layton, 1984).

The key factor to keep in mind is that rewards only decrease motivation for tasks that students initially like. If the task is dull, motivation might drop back down to its original level once the rewards stop, but it will not drop below its original level.

This finding might make one wonder whether rewards, in the form of grades, are behind students' lack of interest in schoolwork; by issuing grades, we're making students like school less (Kohn, 1993). It is true that students like school less and less as they get older. But it is wise to remember that motivation is a product of many factors. Researchers often distinguish between extrinsic motivators (e.g., concrete rewards or grades that are external to you) and intrinsic motivators (things that are internal to you such as your interest in a task). The effect described above can be succinctly summarized: Extrinsic rewards can decrease intrinsic motivation. We would thus expect that intrinsic and extrinsic motivation would be negatively correlated. That is, if you work mostly for the sake of getting good grades and other rewards, then you aren't very intrinsically motivated, and if you are highly intrinsically motivated, that must mean you don't care much about rewards. That's true to some extent, but the relationship is far from perfect. College students whose intrinsic and extrinsic motivation have been measured usually show a modest negative correlation, around $-.25$[3] (Lepper, Corpus, and Iyengar, 2005). This seems reasonable since motivation is actually pretty complex—we rarely do things for just one reason.

What Makes Rewards More or Less Effective?

If you decide to use rewards in the classroom, how can you maximize the chances that they will work? Three principles are especially important. Rewards should be desirable, certain, and prompt.

The importance of desirability is obvious. People will work for rewards that appeal to them, and will work less hard or not at all for rewards that are not appealing.[4] That is self-evident, and teachers likely know which rewards would appeal to their students and which would mean little to them.

> If you decide to use rewards in the classroom, how can you maximize the chances that they will work? Three principles are especially important. Rewards should be desirable, certain, and prompt.

Less obvious is the importance of the certainty of a reward, by which I mean the probability that a student will get a reward if he or she attempts to do the target behavior. What if you've set a target that seems too difficult to the student, and he won't even try? Or what if the target seems achievable to the student, he makes an attempt and does his best, but still fails? Either reduces the likelihood that the student will try again. Both problems can be avoided if the reward is contingent on the student trying his best, and not on what he achieves. But that has its drawbacks, as well. It means that you must make a judgment call as to whether he tried his best. (And you must make that judgment separately for each student.) It is all too likely that some students will have an inflated view of their efforts, and your differing assessment will lead to mistrust. Ideally, the teacher will select specific behaviors for each student as targets, with the target titrated to each student's current level of ability.

A corollary of rewards being desirable is that they be prompt. A reward that is delayed has less appeal than the same reward delivered immediately. For example, suppose I gave you this choice: "You can have $10 tomorrow, or $10 a week from tomorrow." You'd take the $10 tomorrow, right? Rewards have more "oomph"—that is, more power to motivate—when you are going to get them soon. That's why, when my wife calls me from the grocery store, it's easy for me to say "Don't buy ice cream. I'm trying to lose weight." But when I'm at home it's difficult for me to resist ice cream that's in the freezer. In the first situation, I'm denying myself ice cream sometime in the distant future, but in the second I would be denying myself ice cream right at that moment. The promise of ice cream two minutes from now has higher value for me than the promise of ice cream hours from now.

It is possible to measure how much more desirable a reward is when given sooner rather than later. In one type of experiment, subjects participate in an auction and offer sealed bids for money that will be delivered to them later. Thus, each subject might be asked "What is the maximum you would pay right now for a reward of $10, to be delivered

tomorrow?"[5] Subjects are asked to make bids for a variety of rewards to be delivered at delays varying from one to 30 days. Then, researchers use subjects' bids to derive a relationship between the amount of time that the reward is delayed and how much people value the delayed reward. Subjects typically show a steep drop off in how much they value the reward—with a one-day delay, $20 is worth about $18 to most subjects, and with a one-week delay, the value is more like $15 (e.g., Kirby, 1997). In other words, there is a significant cost to the reward value for even a

---

What Is the Difference between Rewards and Praise?

You may have noticed that I have limited my discussion to the effects of concrete rewards—candy, cash, and so on. Isn't praise a reward as well? It can be, but praise as it's usually administered has some important differences. The most important is that praise is usually given unpredictably. The student doesn't think to himself, "If I get 90 percent or better on this spelling test, the teacher will say 'Good job, Dan!'" Rewards are different. There is usually an explicit bargain in the classroom, with the understanding that a particular behavior (e.g., 90 percent or better on a spelling test) merits a reward. As described in the main article, the decrease in motivation for a task only occurs if the reward was expected (and if the students enjoy the task). Since praise is not expected, it does not lead to an immediate decrement to motivation.

Another important difference between praise and concrete rewards is that the former is often taken as a more personal comment on one's abilities. Rewards typically don't impart information to the student. But praise can carry quite a bit of meaning. For starters, it tells the student that she did something noteworthy enough to merit praise. Then too, the student learns what the teacher considers important by listening to what she praises. A student may be told that she's smart, or that she tried hard, or that she's improving. In the short run, sincere praise will provide a boost to motivation (Deci et al., 1999), but in the long run, the content of praise can have quite different effects on the students' self-concept and on future efforts (e.g., Henderlong and Lepper, 2002;

Mueller and Dweck, 1998). The key is in what type of praise is given. When faced with a difficult task, a child who has been praised in the past for her *effort* is likely to believe that intelligence increases as knowledge increases and, therefore, will work harder and seek more experiences from which she can learn. In contrast, a student who has been praised for her *ability* will likely believe that intelligence is fixed (e.g., is genetically determined) and will seek to maintain the "intelligent" label by trying to look good, even if that means sticking to easy tasks rather than more challenging tasks from which more can be learned.

A final difference between praise and rewards lies in students' expectations of encountering either in school. At least in the U.S., praise is part of everyday social interaction. If someone displays unusual skill or determination or kindness, or any other attribute that we esteem, it is not unusual to offer praise. In fact, a teacher who never praised her students might strike them as cold, or uncaring. No such expectation exists for rewards, however. It is hard to imagine teaching students without ever praising them. It is easy to imagine teaching students without ever offering them a concrete reward.

For more on praise and its effects, see "Ask the Cognitive Scientist," *American Educator,* Winter 2005–2006, available at www.aft.org/pubs-reports/american_educator/issues/winter05–06/cogsci.htm.

—D.W.

brief delay. Other studies show that the cost is greater for elementary school students than college students (e.g., Green, Fry and Myerson, 1994). That finding probably matches your intuition: As we get older, we get better at delaying gratification. Distant rewards become more similar to immediate rewards.

In this section I've summarized data showing that rewards should be desirable, certain, and prompt if they are to be effective. These three factors provide some insight into the extrinsic (but non-tangible) rewards that almost all schools offer: grades and graduation. Grades are not as rewarding as we might guess because they are seldom administered right after the required behavior (studying), and the reward of a diploma is, of course, even more distant. Then too, low-achieving students likely perceive these rewards as highly uncertain. That is, hard work does not guarantee that they will receive the reward.

Putting It All Together: Are Rewards Worth It?

When all is said and done, are rewards worth it? I liken using rewards to taking out a loan. You get an immediate benefit, but you know that you will eventually have to pay up, with interest. As with loans, I suggest three guidelines to the use of rewards: 1) try to find an alternative; 2) use them for a specific reason, not as a general strategy; and 3) plan for the ending.

Try to Find an Alternative

It is very difficult to implement rewards without incurring some cost. If the reward system is the same for all class members, it won't work as well as an individualized approach and you will likely reward some students for tasks they already like. If you tailor the rewards to individual students, you vastly increase your workload, and you

increase the risk of students perceiving the program as unfair.

The size of the costs to motivation, although real, should not be overstated. As mentioned earlier, there are many contributors to motivation, and putting a smiley sticker on a spelling test will probably not rank high among them. Still, why incur the cost at all, if an alternative is available? The obvious alternative is to make the material intrinsically interesting. Indeed, if you follow that precept, you will never offer an extrinsic reward for an intrinsically interesting task, which is when the trouble with motivation really starts.

It is also worth considering whether student motivation is the real reason you use rewards. Do you put stickers on test papers in the hopes that students will work harder to earn them, or just for a bit of fun, a colorful diversion? Do you throw a class pizza party to motivate students, or to increase the class's sense of community? You might still distribute stickers and throw the party, but not make them explicitly contingent on performance beforehand. Announce to the class that they have done such a good job on the most recent unit that a party seems in order. Thus, the party is still an acknowledgement of good work and still might contribute to a positive class atmosphere, but it is not offered as a reward contingent on performance.

Use Rewards for a Specific Reason

A wise investor understands that taking out a loan, although it incurs a cost, might be strategic in the long run. So too, although a rewards program may incur some cost to motivation, there are times when the cost might be worth it. One example is when students must learn or practice a task that is rather dull, but that, once mastered, leads to opportunities for greater interest and motivation. For example, learning the times tables might be dull, but if students can get over that hump of boredom, they are ready to take on more interesting work. Rewards might also be useful when a student has lost confidence in himself to the point that he is no longer willing to try. If he'll attempt academic work to gain a desirable extrinsic reward and succeeds, his perception of himself and his abilities may change from self-doubt to recognition that he is capable of academic work (Greene and Lepper, 1974). Thereafter, the student may be motivated by his sense of accomplishment and his expectation that he will continue to do well.

Although a rewards program may incur some cost to motivation, there are times that the cost might be worth it. For example, learning the times tables might be dull, but if students can get over that hump of boredom, they are ready to take on more interesting work.

Use Rewards for a Limited Time

No one wants to live with chronic debt, and no one should make rewards a long-term habit. Although the cost of using rewards may not be large, that cost likely increases as rewards are used for a longer time. In addition, there would seem to be an advantage to the program having a natural ending point. For example, students are rewarded for learning their times tables, and once they are learned, the rewards end. The advantage is that any decrease in motivation might stick to the task. In other words, students will think "times tables are boring, and we need to be rewarded to learn them" rather than "math is boring, and we need to be rewarded to learn it." In addition, if students are told at the start of the program when it will end, there may be fewer complaints when the goodies are no longer available.

Notes

1. Such positive framing of rewards does not reverse the negative impact of rewards on motivation, but telling students that rewards signal acknowledgement of good work, rather than the closing of a bargain, seems more in keeping with the spirit of education.

2. Readers who are familiar with interventions to reduce students' aggressive or antisocial behavior may be surprised at this finding. Such interventions do often use rewards and then phase them out. But keep in mind that the rewards are just one part of a complex intervention and that in order to be effective, such interventions must be implemented in full. To learn more about the use of rewards in such an intervention, see "Heading Off Disruption: How Early Intervention Can Reduce Defiant Behavior—and Win Back Teaching Time," *American Educator*, Winter 2003–2004, available at www.aft.org/pubs-reports/american_educator/winter03-04/index.html.

3. A correlation of zero would indicate that they were unrelated, and a correlation of −1.0 would indicate that they were perfectly related.

4. There are exceptions to this generalization, notably in the social realm. People will work hard without reward as part of a social transaction. In such situations a small reward will actually make people less likely to work (e.g., Heyman and Ariely, 2004). For example, if an acquaintance asks you to help her move a sofa, you would assume that she's asking a favor as a friend, and you might well help. But if she offers you $5 to move the sofa you think of the request as a business transaction, and $5 may not seem like enough money. These social

concerns could apply to the classroom; some students might work to please the teacher. But such social transactions rest on reciprocity. If your friend with the poorly placed sofa never helps you out, you will get tired of her requests. It would be difficult to set up a classroom relationship that used social reciprocity between teachers and students.

5. The procedure is actually what researchers call a second-bid auction; the highest bidder wins the auction, but pays the price of the second highest bid. This procedure is meant to ensure that people bid exactly what the item is worth to them. The workings of the auction are explained in detail to subjects.

References

Cameron, J., Banko, K.M., and Pierce, D. (2001). Pervasive negative effects of rewards on intrinsic motivation: The myth continues. *The Behavior Analyst*, 24, p. 1–44.

Carlton, S. (May 30, 2007). Paying kids to pass tests gets an *F. St. Petersburg Times*, p. 1B.

Chance, P. (1993). Sticking up for rewards. *Phi Delta Kappan*, 74, p. 787–790.

Daniel, T.L. and Esser, J.K. (1980). Intrinsic motivation as influenced by rewards, task interest, and task structure. *Journal of Applied Psychology*, 65, p. 566–573.

Davis, K.D., Winsler, A., and Middleton, M. (2006). Students' perceptions of rewards for academic performance by parents and teachers: Relations with achievement and motivation in college. *Journal of Genetic Psychology*, 167, p. 211–220.

Deci, E.L., Koestner, R., and Ryan, R.M. (1999). A meta-analytic review of experiments examining the effects of extrinsic rewards on intrinsic motivation. *Psychological Bulletin*, 125, p. 627–668.

Dickerson, F. B., Tenhula, W.N., and Green-Paden, L.D. (2005). The token economy for schizophrenia: Review of the literature and recommendations for future research. *Schizophrenia Research*, 75, p. 405–416.

Green, L., Fry, A. F., and Myerson, J. (1994). Discounting of delayed rewards: A life-span comparison. *Psychological Science*, 5, p. 33–36.

Greene, D. and Lepper, M.R. (1974). Intrinsic motivation: How to turn play into work. *Psychology Today*, 8, p. 49–54.

Henderlong, J. and Lepper, M.R. (2002). The effects of praise on children's intrinsic motivation: A review and synthesis. *Psychological Bulletin*, 128, p. 774–795.

Hendy, H.M., Williams, K. E., and Camise, T. S. (2005). "Kids Choice" school lunch program increases children's fruit and vegetable acceptance. *Appetite*, 45, p. 250–263.

Heyman, J. and Ariely, D. (2004). Effort for payment: A tale of two markets. *Psychological Science*, 15, p. 787–793.

Kazdin, A.E. (1982). The token economy: A decade later. *Journal of Applied Behavior Analysis*, 15, p. 431–445.

Kirby, K.N. (1997). Bidding on the future: Evidence against normative discounting of delayed rewards. *Journal of Experimental Psychology: General*, 126, p. 54–70.

Kohn, A. (1993). *Punished by Rewards*. Boston: Houghton Mifflin.

Lepper, M.R., Corpus, J.H., and Iyengar, S.S. (2005). Intrinsic and extrinsic motivational orientations in the classroom: Age differences and academic correlates. *Journal of Educational Psychology*, 97, p. 184-196.

Lepper, M.R., Greene, D., and Nisbett, R.E. (1973). Undermining children's intrinsic interest with extrinsic reward: A test of the "overjustification" hypothesis. *Journal of Personality and Social Psychology*, 28, p. 129-137.

Loveland, K.K. and Olley, J.G. (1979). The effect of external reward on interest and quality of task performance in children of high and low intrinsic motivation. *Child Development*, 50, p. 1207-1210.

Mueller, C.M. and Dweck, C.S. (1998). Praise for intelligence can undermine children's motivation and performance. *Journal of Personality and Social Psychology*, 75, p. 33-52.

Newman, J. and Layton, B.D. (1984). Overjustification: A self-perception perspective. *Personality and Social Psychology Bulletin*, 10, p. 419-425.

National Commission for the Protection of Human Subjects of Biomedical and Behavioral Research (1978). *Ethical Principles and Guidelines for the Protection of Human Subjects of Research*. Available at www.hhs.gov/ohrp/humansubjects/guidance/belmont.htm, retrieved 10-1-07.

O'Leary, K.D. and Drabman, R. (1971). Token reinforcement programs in the classroom: A review. *Psychological Bulletin*, 75, p. 379-398.

Ryan, R. M., Mims, V., and Koestner, R. (1983). Relation of reward contingency and interpersonal context to intrinsic motivation: A review and test using cognitive evaluation theory. *Journal of Personality and Social Psychology*, 45, p. 736-750.

Schwartz, B. (July 2, 2007). Money for nothing. *New York Times*, p. A19.

Ward, W.C., Kogan, N., and Pankove, E. (1972). Incentive effects in children's creativity. *Child Development*, 43, p. 669-676.

DANIEL T. WILLINGHAM is professor of cognitive psychology at the University of Virginia and author of *Cognition: The Thinking Animal*. His research focuses on the role of consciousness in learning. Readers can pose specific questions to "Ask the Cognitive Scientist," American Educator, 555 New Jersey Ave. N.W., Washington, DC 20001, or to amered@aft.org. Future columns will try to address readers' questions.

Beyond Content: How Teachers Manage Classrooms to Facilitate Intellectual Engagement for Disengaged Students

This article explores how teachers manage classrooms to facilitate the intellectual engagement of disengaged students. The author proposes that teachers create an environment conducive to intellectual engagement when students perceive: (a) that there are opportunities for them to succeed, (b) that flexible avenues exist through which learning can occur, and (c) that they are respected as learners because teachers convey the belief that students are capable of learning. When teachers purposefully manage classrooms so that these elements intersect optimally, students perceive that they are known and valued. Furthermore, opportunities for success, flexibility, and respect generally are present when teachers challenge their students at appropriate levels, provide academic support, use instructional techniques that convey excitement for the content, and make learning relevant. To illuminate how teachers succeed in managing classrooms for intellectual engagement, the author provides numerous quotes from students attending an alternative high school designed for disengaged students who possess academic potential.

DEBORAH L. SCHUSSLER

[Here] I'm more, I guess, a free thinker or something. . . . [The teachers] don't rush us, they don't force us. But they don't make it easy and they don't give us forever. . . . At my other school I just kind of felt like they're giving all this stuff to me because I had to do it, and they didn't care. . . . Here it's just different. I care about what I'm doing. (Peter,[1] 10th grade)

Peter was once at risk of dropping out of school. Despite attending a middle-class, suburban, comprehensive high school where the average SAT score was 1126 and the percent of students on free or reduced lunch was 8%, Peter almost decided to quit. Although most of his grades were passing, Peter had disengaged from school on all levels—behavioral, emotional, and cognitive (Fredricks, Blumenfeld, & Paris, 2004). Osterman (1998) summarized Peter's situation quite well: "Even for those students who succeed in school on standard achievement criteria, lack of engagement with learning is a serious problem" (p. 41). Fortunately, Peter had the option to attend a small, alternative school that followed the Middle College concept. Middle Colleges are public high schools collaborating with local colleges. They seek to prevent capable students from dropping out of school by creating academically enriched environments that also support students' social and personal development.[2] For Peter, who is not unlike many high school students, the issue was not whether he was capable of challenging intellectual work; he was capable. The issue involved whether Peter was in an environment conducive to his engagement in learning.

What was it about the alternative school that kept Peter, and others like him, from dropping out? Even more importantly, what was it that captured his interest and helped him care about what he was doing academically? The brief quote from Peter provides powerful clues into ways teachers can engage disengaged students in intellectual work. Contrary to the beliefs of legislators myopically focused on accountability, it has little to do with helping students meet proficiency requirements on standardized tests, though accountability and proficiency are important. Contrary to the beliefs of those preoccupied with particular instructional strategies, it extends beyond the actual content of what teachers teach (Ritchhart, 2002) and the mere elimination of student misbehavior (McCaslin & Good, 1992). Teachers can create an environment conducive to intellectual engagement when students perceive three pervasive elements are a part of all classroom discourse:

1. There are opportunities for students to succeed.
2. Flexible avenues exist through which learning can occur.
3. Students are respected as learners because teachers convey the belief that students are capable of achieving academic success.

It seems so basic. Yet disengaged students perceive opportunities for success, flexibility, and respect as pervasively lacking in schools (Altenbaugh, 1998; Liaupsin, Umbreit, Ferro, Urso, & Upreti, 2006; Pressley, Gaskins, Solic, & Collins, 2006). In this article, I explain how teachers can manage classrooms to facilitate these three pervasive elements that are cru-

cial to engaging students intellectually. To augment the explanations, I provide quotes from students—primarily Peter's classmates at a Middle College in a suburban district in the southeastern United States. I use these students' voices for two reasons. First, students are frequently ignored in conversations of educational policy and practice (Cook-Sather, 2002; Yazzie-Mintz, 2006), yet students decide their engagement or disengagement in school. Second, Middle College students provide a unique glimpse into aspects of engagement. These 126 students possessed academic potential, but for any number of reasons—from academic to social—disengaged from their previous schools only to re-engage at Middle College. Their insights suggest that effective classroom management and pedagogy that supports intellectual engagement are inextricably linked, as they involve knowing the students well and finding where opportunities for success, flexibility, and respect intersect optimally.

Before proceeding, I should explain what I mean by intellectual *engagement*. Although some define engagement in learning as the tangible behaviors that students exhibit in the classroom (Greenwood, Horton, & Utley, 2002) or outside the classroom related to homework and study habits (Yazzie-Mintz, 2006), I take a more comprehensive view. Engagement in learning involves formulating a deeper connection between the student and the material whereby a student develops an interest in the topic or retains the learning beyond the short term. There are no precise formulas for managing a classroom for intellectual engagement. However, opportunities for success, flexibility, and respect generally are present when teachers challenge their students at appropriate levels, provide academic support, use instructional techniques that convey excitement for the content, and make learning relevant. I describe these in greater detail in the next sections.

Academic Challenge

They'll make you seep in as much as you can right up to the point that you'd turn it off . . . and then it's pulled back a little bit. (James, 11th grade)

Lack of academic challenge has often been attributed to the "bargains" (Sedlak, Wheeler, Pullin, & Cusick, 1986) or "compromises" (Sizer, 1984) teachers establish with students, whereby students tacitly agree to maintain order and teachers tacitly agree to hold expectations to a minimum. However, substantial evidence exists that students across school contexts want teachers to challenge them academically (Sizer & Sizer, 1999; Yazzie-Mintz, 2006). The desire for a challenge is especially true when classroom discourse mirrors authentic conversations, as opposed to typical classroom talk, and includes issues students perceive are relevant (Alpert, 1991; Sizer & Sizer, 1999). Furthermore, it is imperative that teachers couple academic challenge with academic support.

It becomes more obvious why academic challenge must operate in tandem with academic support when one considers how the three pervasive elements intersect to portray a *sweet spot* for achieving engagement. Students feel appropriately challenged when teachers combine flexibility with opportunities to succeed, which results in the students feeling respected as students and having a positive attitude toward their academics (Turner & Meyer, 2004). When students perceive academic work as too difficult or too easy, which usually means there is either no flexibility or too much flexibility in how students achieve academic success, they feel a lack of respect. Lack of respect generally manifests in a negative attitude toward their academics. Compare James's words to those of a student in Pittsburgh who eventually decided to drop out of school, a decision he attributed

to his reaction toward the "cynical and calloused teachers" who did little more than pass students along: " 'they sort of had an 'I don't care' attitude. Get you in and get you out. Just so long as you get that D' " (Altenbaugh, 1998, p. 60). This student perceived a lack of respect because teachers did not care enough to challenge him. In contrast, James described the sweet spot of where the optimal academic challenge exists. Students have to feel pushed. When they do not feel pushed, students disengage. When they are asked to "seep in" more than they can handle, students disengage.

The challenge for teachers, then, is to determine how much to push students. Where is the sweet spot? As the Pittsburgh student's quote indicates, it stems from teachers' attitudes. A combination of care and high expectations is essential for students to reach their highest capacity as evidenced in academic achievement and motivation (Gay, 2000; Turner & Meyer, 2004; Wentzel, 1997), positive social outcomes (Wentzel, 1997), and increased ownership (Stefanou, Perencevich, DiCintio, & Turner, 2004). This is true for students across school contexts. Teachers create a synergy of care and high expectations when they provide opportunities for students to succeed, both for the present-oriented purpose of achieving good grades and for the future-oriented purpose of living a good life. Kathleen, a 10th grader, highlighted how care and high expectations operated synergistically for present and future purposes when she said, "They care about your grades and they want you to succeed and it just made me feel like there's somebody that wants me to graduate; there's somebody that wants me to do something with my life."

Teachers foster opportunities to succeed and provide flexibility through a curriculum that is student-driven, rather than curriculum-driven. Curricular flexibility means demonstrating both acute awareness of ways students understand the material and responsiveness to student needs. The idea of responsiveness is prevalent in research on at-risk students (Catterall, 1998), culturally relevant pedagogy (Gay, 2000), and special education (Fuchs, Mock, Morgan, & Young, 2003). Across these bodies of literature, the most compelling commonality that applies to all teachers, regardless of context, is the importance of knowing and responding to students' needs, as individuals. This means meeting students where they are, which seems obvious, but for a variety of reasons often does not occur in high schools. When describing her teachers at Middle College, Stephanie, an 11th grader, said, "They'll actually help you with what you don't know . . . When I came here I didn't have like really any study skills . . . because I had been moving around so much . . . In Geometry she's taught different ways that you can study for tests and how to prepare for certain things." When James says teachers "make you seep in as much as you can right up to the point that you'd turn it off," this implies that teachers know how much each student can seep in and also know the point where each student would turn it off. In other words, for each individual student, teachers provide just the right amount of challenge, along with just the right amount of support.

Academic Support

Teachers should teach so everybody can understand, not just so a few elite kids can know what's going on. (Peter, 10th grade)

Students who disengage academically from school often feel as though success is meant only for certain elite students, or those who have experienced success in the past, or those who are just lucky (Altenbaugh, 1998). To complicate matters, intellectual disengagement frequently occurs as a result of students'

emotional and behavioral disengagement (Fredricks et al., 2004). In other words, students who do not feel that they belong on the football field or in the student council also feel that they do not belong in the classroom. To engage students, teachers must make them feel like they not only belong in the classroom, but also that they are capable of doing challenging intellectual work. This means not just pushing them to achieve, but also providing the support through which achievement is possible.

Academic support is possible when teachers convey an attitude that students can succeed. This attitude should mirror those of high-reliability organizations, such as air traffic control towers; those working in such organizations view success as the expectation, not a chance occurrence, and they do everything possible to create conditions that facilitate success (Irmsher, 1997). At her alternative school, Leah describes her teachers as having exactly this attitude toward student success: "They'll do anything they can because they know we can do it. . . . They all know us, and they're going to keep pushing us to do it." Leah's perception that her teachers possessed a steadfast belief in her ability to achieve led her to adopt this same belief.

As Leah also indicates, teachers must know students individually in order to translate their beliefs into actions. Because each student varies in terms of learning style, interests, background knowledge, culture, and cognitive scaffolding, teachers must make efforts to know students within these various dimensions and to respond accordingly. Only through such knowing can teachers provide the appropriate type and amount of academic support.

My teacher actually sat there and watched me do some math problems. I didn't know she was watching me and she was like, "You're a very verbal learner." . . . I'd never thought about it. . . . She had observed how I learned and she had noticed that when I was doing really well on a problem, I was talking my way through it. (James, 11th grade)

Not only did his teacher become aware of James's learning style, the teacher also helped James become aware of his own learning style. This was accomplished through a very simple technique: observation. James's teacher simply observed him as he engaged in the learning process. Obviously, this takes time. However, when the goal is curriculum coverage, a likely end result is teachers covering more and students engaging less (Ritchhart, 2002).

The three pervasive elements—opportunities to succeed, flexibility, and respect—are readily apparent in the specific ways teachers provide academic support to facilitate students' engagement. These include conducting diagnostic assessments as a way of knowing students' strengths and needs. These assessments may include formal instruments, like a learning styles inventory, but most are the result of simply observing students. The informal assessment James's teacher conducted provided valuable information to both James and the teacher about how he worked through math problems. To help James engage, and therefore succeed, the teacher can be flexible in allowing James to talk his way through his work. James will feel respected because not only will he know a strategy he needs to function successfully in math class, but he will also be encouraged to use it.

Formative assessment and differentiated instruction are other specific ways teachers provide academic support to facilitate students' engagement. Bob, an 11th grader in a challenging math class, highlighted the importance of formative assessment when he noted, "She makes sure that we know how to do it before we take a test, before we leave that

classroom." When teachers frequently check on students' understanding, through low-risk assessments, students know that teachers want them to succeed academically. When teachers use differentiated instruction, modifying the content, process, or products of learning, students know there is flexibility in how they can develop and demonstrate their understanding (King-Shaver & Hunter, 2003). A classroom that accommodates this level of academic support must be very organized. Teachers must be purposeful about determining students' strengths and needs and about ensuring the availability of appropriate resources, described next.

Instruction

High school isn't all about necessarily learning facts. . . . [Teachers] are so concerned with "Am I going to meet my deadline? Are my standardized tests going to be up to par?" that they don't have time to stop and think about it. (James, 11th grade)

When monotony and task completion characterize a majority of classroom instruction, students are less likely to engage intellectually. In contrast, when students perceive they have opportunities to succeed on authentic tasks through the flexible instruction of their teachers, they are more likely to engage. Teachers manage classrooms to facilitate student engagement when they demonstrate enthusiasm for authentic content and purposefully use instructional strategies to capture students' interest.

As James and Peter noted, students equate learning disparate facts from the book with rigidity and lack of instructional creativity on the part of the teacher. In the mind of the students, when a teacher teaches straight from the book, it is the teacher being lazy; students then have little motivation to complete academic work, much less become excited about it. They may demonstrate overt misbehavior or quietly subversive resistance through non-participation in classroom discourse (Alpert, 1991). In contrast, a number of students at Middle College mentioned the infectious enthusiasm of the ecology teacher who had worked in the private sector before teaching at the college level then teaching at Middle College. Caesar, a 12th grader, said, "The teachers here cover more, like the ecology teacher. She gets really into it because she's a big environmentalist. . . . She just talks from personal experience and incorporates things. She's a very good teacher." Caesar wanted to engage in the content because the teacher combined knowledge with a desire to share her passions with her students.

No single instructional technique operates as a panacea for increasing student interest in course content. In fact, when Bryk, Lee, and Holland (1993) investigated the educational processes of Catholic high schools, they were surprised to find "students' positive reactions to rather ordinary teaching" (p. 99). Despite ubiquitously traditional pedagogy, the researchers observed "high levels of engagement with classroom activities" (p. 99). They found that the "quality of human relations" (p. 99) was more important than specific instructional techniques. My own work exploring care in educational contexts supports the conclusion that how students perceive teachers' attitudes is one of the most important factors in determining the extent of their intellectual engagement (Schussler, 2006). When teachers structure instruction in ways that demonstrate their desire to interest students in the content, students notice. It is not that the instructional techniques are unimportant; rather, it is that the attitude with which the teacher employs the techniques is more important. Knowing how to structure instruction entails knowing the students,

specifically, knowing how to challenge and support students, as well as how to tap into their interests and demonstrate the relevance of the content.

Relevance

I can tell that I'm learning in his class because outside of his class I'll be flipping through the channels and something on history will come on and I'll be like, "Let's watch this." It's an interest. (Trixie, 11th grade)

In a study of over 80,000 students at 110 high schools, researchers found that when asked why they were bored in class, 75% of students said because the material was not interesting and 39% said the material was not relevant to them (Yazzie-Mintz, 2006). Teachers help increase students' interest in academic content, and their engagement, by giving students authentic tasks. Authentic tasks include opportunities to problem solve situations that mirror the kind of ambiguity students face in real life (Alpert, 1991; Ritchhart, 2002). In describing how to help students put intelligence into action, Ritchhart advocated "conditional instruction" (p. 140). In conditional instruction, teachers present facts open-endedly. For example, students are told, "This may be the cause of the evolution of city neighborhoods," instead of "The cause of [the] evolution of city neighborhoods is . . ." (p. 140). Studies on conditional instruction found that students in both conditions retained the information equally well, but students who received the information via conditional language demonstrated more creativity and flexibility in being able to solve problems. They also shifted from being passive to being more active learners, developing "a sense of their own agency," (p. 141) as they attempted to make sense of ambiguous situations.

Thinking about the curriculum outside of traditional, academic content is also crucial to helping students see the relevance in what they are learning. Noddings (2006) emphasized the importance of being purposeful about teaching personal and social skills that students will use throughout their lives. "Possibly no goal of education is more important—or more neglected—than self-understanding" (p. 10). These goals should not exist as separate from, but rather as integrated with, the academic curriculum. Notice that David, a 12th grader, does not view the academic and personal curricula as mutually exclusive, but rather as infinitely relevant: "I'm learning about me and who I want to be. . . . Basically with what I'm concentrating on—writing or trying to figure out some economic equation—I'm trying to figure out what I want to do, where I want to be five, ten years down the road." Similarly, Kathleen, a 10th grader, notes how the social skills were important for her life-long learning: "I'm not only learning the actual curriculum stuff, but here you're also learning . . . adult skills. . . . You learn how to communicate with people. . . . They're preparing you for life here."

Clearly, academic content is not unimportant. However, it becomes more relevant when it is purposefully integrated with the development of social and personal skills. As adults, we do not choose to engage in tasks in which we see no relevance. We should not expect students to be any different.

Concluding Comments

Middle College does not represent the traditional high school, yet all schools can learn something about classroom management and intellectual engagement from a school that succeeds in engaging previously disengaged students. Opportunities to succeed, flexibility,

and respect undergird students' experiences at Middle College. More specifically, teachers purposefully balance offering an academic challenge with support, use instructional techniques that convey excitement for the content, and make learning relevant. Managing a classroom within these pedagogical parameters means moving beyond thinking primarily about content and into thinking about knowing students as individuals. Certainly, many teachers pursue this goal. Small alternative schools do not hold sole proprietorship on holding the students central. It may be that alternative schools are more purposeful about creating an environment that enables teachers to know students well. Maybe this is where future reform efforts should focus.

Notes

1. All proper names have been changed.
2. For more information about the Middle College concept, see Weschler (2001).
3. All students are from Middle College unless otherwise noted.

References

Alpert, B. (1991). Students' resistance in the classroom. *Anthropology and Education Quarterly, 22*(4), 350–366.

Altenbaugh, R. J. (1998). "Some teachers are ignorant": Teachers and teaching through urban school leavers' eyes. In B. M. Franklin (Ed.), *When children don't learn: Student failure and the culture of teaching* (pp. 52–71). New York: Teachers College Press.

Bryk, A. S., Lee, V. E., & Holland, P. B. (1993). *Catholic schools and the common good.* Cambridge, MA: Harvard University Press.

Catterall, J. S. (1998). Risk and resilience in student transitions to high school. *American Journal of Education, 106*(2), 302–333.

Cook-Sather, A. (2002). Authorizing students' perspectives: Toward trust, dialogue, and change in education. *Educational Researcher, 31*(4), 3–14.

Fredricks, J. A., Blumenfeld, P. C., & Paris, A. H. (2004). School engagement: Potential of the concept, state of the evidence. *Review of Educational Research, 74*(1), 59–109.

Fuchs, D., Mock, D., Morgan, P. L., & Young, C. L. (2003). Responsiveness-to-intervention: Definitions, evidence, and implications for the learning disabilities construct. *Learning Disabilities Research & Practice, 18*(3), 157–171.

Gay, G. (2000). *Culturally responsive teaching: Theory, research, and practice.* New York: Teachers College Press.

Greenwood, C. R., Horton, B. T., & Utley, C. A. (2002). Academic engagement: Current perspectives on research and practice. *School Psychology Review, 31*(3), 328–349.

Irmsher, K. (1997). *Education reform and students at risk: ERIC Digest, Number 112* (No. ERIC Document Reproduction Service ED 405 642). Eugene, OR: ERIC Clearinghouse on Educational Management.

King-Shaver, B., & Hunter, A. (2003). *Differentiated instruction in the English classroom.* Portsmouth, NH: Heinemann.

Liaupsin, C. J., Umbreit, J., Ferro, J. B., Urso, A., & Upreti, G. (2006). Improving academic engagement through systematic, function-based intervention. *Education and Treatment of Children, 29*(4), 572–589.

McCaslin, M., & Good, T. L. (1992). Compliant cognition: The misalliance of management and instructional goals in current school reform. *Educational Researcher, 21*(3), 4–17.

Noddings, N. (2006). *Critical lessons: What our schools should teach.* Cambridge, MA: Cambridge University Press.

Osterman, K. F. (1998, April). *Student community within the school context: A research synthesis.* Paper presented at the Annual Meeting of the American Educational Research Association.

Pressley, M., Gaskins, I. W., Solic, K., & Collins, S. (2006). A portrait of Benchmark School: How a school produces high achievement in students who previously failed. *Journal of Educational Psychology, 98*(2), 282–306.

Ritchhart, R. (2002). *Intellectual character: What it is, why it matters, and how to get it.* San Francisco: Jossey-Bass.

Schussler, D. L. (2006). An empirical exploration of the who? what? and how? of school care. *Teachers College Record, 108*(7), 1460–1495.

Sedlak, M., Wheeler, C. W., Pullin, D. C., & Cusick, P. A. (1986). *Selling students short: Classroom bargains and academic reform in the American high school.* New York: Teachers College Press.

Sizer, T. R. (1984). *Horace's compromise: The dilemma of the American high school.* Boston: Houghton Mifflin Company.

Sizer, T. R., & Sizer, N. F. (1999). *The students are watching: Schools and the moral contract.* Boston: Beacon Press.

Stefanou, C. R., Perencevich, K. C., DiCintio, M., & Turner, J. C. (2004). Supporting autonomy in the classroom: Ways teachers encourage student decision making and ownership. *Educational Psychologist, 39*(2), 97–110.

Turner, J. C., & Meyer, D. K. (2004). A classroom perspective on the principle of moderate challenge in mathematics. *Journal of Educational Research, 97*(6), 311–318.

Wechsler, H. S. (2001). *Access to success in the urban high school: The Middle College movement.* New York: Teachers College Press.

Wentzel, K. R. (1997). Student motivation in middle school: The role of perceived pedagogical caring. *Journal of Educational Psychology, 89*(3), 411–419.

Yazzie-Mintz, E. (2006). *Voices of students on engagement: A report on the 2006 high school survey of student engagement.* Bloomington, IN: Center for Evaluation and Education Policy.

DEBORAH L. SCHUSSLER is an associate professor of education and human services at Villanova University.

Correspondence should be addressed to: Deborah L. Schussler, Department of Education and Human Services, Villanova University, 800 Lancaster Ave., Villanova, PA 19085. E-mail: deborah.schussler@villanova.edu

ARTICLE 19

Classroom Management Strategies for Difficult Students: Promoting Change through Relationships

MARY ELLEN BEATY-O'FERRALL, ALAN GREEN, AND FRED HANNA

Teachers in middle level schools face overwhelming demands and challenges in their classrooms. They are expected to know content and pedagogy, develop engaging lessons that meet the needs of diverse learners, and use a variety of instructional strategies that will boost student achievement while they simultaneously develop positive relationships with, on average, 125 students each day who are experiencing the personal, social, and cognitive challenges and opportunities of early adolescence (Carnegie Council on Adolescent Development, 1995; Schmakel, 2008).

Teaching is complex and cannot be reduced to discrete tasks that can be mastered one at a time. Teachers must "win their students' hearts while getting inside their students' heads" (Wolk, 2003, p. 14). As Haberman (1995) suggested, this winning of the hearts occurs through very personal interactions, one student at a time. This perspective is supported by research suggesting that teachers who develop such relationships experience fewer classroom behavior problems and better academic performance (Decker, Dona, & Christenson, 2007; Marzano, Marzano, & Pickering, 2003).

How can teachers engage students through enhanced personal interactions while simultaneously managing classroom climate and instruction? The purpose of this article is to suggest specific strategies that integrate knowledge and skills from education, counseling, and psychotherapy to help teachers develop a strong management system based on the development of personal relationships with students. These techniques are specifically adapted for use by teachers and more clearly delineate the nature of developing relationships and deepening them for the purpose of making education more effective.

Classroom Management and Relationship Building

Research indicates that teachers' actions in their classrooms have twice as much impact on student achievement as assessment policies, community involvement, or staff collegiality; and a large part of teachers' actions involves the management of the classroom (Marzano, 2003; Marzano & Marzano, 2003). Classroom management is critically important in the middle grades years when students are more likely to experience declines in academic motivation and self-esteem (Anderman, Maehr, & Midgley, 1999). Research indicates that these declines can be linked to the classroom, and particularly to teacher-student relationships (Furrer & Skinner, 2003). When surveyed about their goals, adolescents have claimed that academics and the completion of their education are important to them. However, repeated studies of sixth through ninth graders have shown interest in academics, motivation for academics, and academic achievement levels decline dramatically during early adolescence, and especially during seventh grade (Carnegie Council on Adolescent Development, 1995).

One of the keys to effective classroom management is the development of a quality relationship between the teacher and the students in the classroom. Marzano, Marzano, and Pickering (2003), in a meta-analysis of more than 100 studies, reported that teachers who had high-quality relationships with students had 31% fewer discipline problems, rule violations, and other related problems over a year's time than did teachers who did not. This significant statistic justifies further investigation into developing relationships.

A critical component of developing relationships is knowing and understanding the learner. Teachers must take steps to learn and understand the unique qualities of middle grades students, who are at a crucial time in their development. Although they are good at disguising their feelings, they have been described as actually craving positive social interaction with peers and adults; limits on behavior and attitudes; meaningful participation in families, school, and community; and opportunities for self-definition (Wormeli, 2003). Teaching middle grades students is unique in its demand for unconventional thinking; therefore, middle grades teachers must be willing to break the rules and transcend convention. The strategies that will be described for dealing with the most difficult of students are in many ways just that—unconventional.

Teachers who adopt a relationship-building approach to classroom management by focusing on developing the whole person are more likely to help students develop positive, socially-appropriate behaviors. The characteristics of effective teacher-student relationships are not related to the teacher's personality or whether the teacher is well liked by the students. Instead, the relationships are characterized by specific behaviors, strategies, and fundamental attitudes demonstrated by the teacher (Bender, 2003) This approach involves taking personal interest in students; establishing clear learning goals; and modeling assertive, equitable, and positive behaviors (Hall & Hall, 2003; Rogers & Renard, 1999).

Research indicates that the most effective classroom managers do not treat all students the same. Effective managers employed different strategies with different types of students (Brophy, 1996; Brophy & McCaslin, 1992). Teachers with effective classroom management skills are aware of high needs students and have a repertoire of specific techniques for meeting some of their needs (Marzano & Marzano, 2003).

Adelman and Taylor (2002) reported that 12% to 22% of all students in schools suffer from mental, emotional, and behavioral disorders, and relatively few receive mental health services. The Association of School Counselors noted that close to one in five students has special needs and requires extraordinary interventions and treatments beyond the typical resources available to classroom teachers (Dunn & Baker, 2002). It is often these very students who create the most daunting challenges for teachers.

Strategies for Building Relationships

According to Wolk (2003), "Teacher-student relationships permeate the classroom, with relationships both helping and hindering learning and affecting everything from curriculum to choice of teaching methods." Wolk asserted that for most teachers, "their relationships are their teaching" (p. 14). Current literature on building relationships as a means to manage classrooms includes recommendations such as using gentle interventions, finding time for bonding, avoiding punishments, and building activities that ensure success for all students (Hall & Hall, 2003).

These strategies, though helpful, may still leave teachers struggling with the most difficult students. Ideas from the fields of counseling and psychotherapy can be applied to these classroom struggles. Rogers and Renard (1999) asserted that we need to understand the needs and beliefs of our students as they are—not as we think they ought to be" (p. 34). What follows are specific strategies from the fields of counseling and psychology that teachers can apply in classroom settings when dealing with difficult students. The strategies of empathy, admiring negative attitudes, leaving the ego at the door, and multicultural connections will be explored.

Building Empathy

Probably the most important aspect of a positive helping relationship is empathy on the part of the helper (Garfield, 1994; Goldfried, Greenberg, & Marmar, 1990; Luborsky, Crits-Christoph, Mintz, & Auerbach, 1988; Orlinsky, Grawe, & Parks, 1994; Sexton & Whiston, 1994). In actual practice, empathy on the part of the teacher results in the student feeling understood. Empathetic relationships are especially important for difficult adolescents (Bernstein, 1996; Mordock, 1991). Unfortunately in education, empathy is a concept largely misunderstood and even trivialized as a form of affection or caring. To the contrary, caring and empathy are not at all the same. Adler (1956) defined empathy as "seeing with the eyes of another, hearing with the ears of another, and feeling with heart of another" (p. 135). The end result of having been shown empathy is that the person "feels understood." This is crucial to reaching and relating to young adolescents (Hanna, Hanna, & Keys, 1999).

Many teachers simply assume they understand the student's problems and dilemmas, and mistakenly try to communicate their understanding in ways that only distance the student. For example, a female middle grades student once told a disappointed teacher that things were really hard at home and studying was difficult. The teacher responded by saying, "Well, you have to get past it and study anyway. I have been teaching for a long time, and there isn't any excuse I haven't heard." The student, of course, had no indication that the teacher understood at all and was actually discouraged by the teacher's unempathetic response. If this teacher had taken the time to show that she understood the student's dilemma, she would have learned that the parents of the student were verbally fighting with each other every day, threatening each other with divorce, and arguing over custody of the children. They also fought about the father's drinking.

The teacher could have easily encouraged the student with an empathetic response such as, "It must be really difficult trying to study while listening to your parents fighting and wondering what is going to happen with your family." Such a response would have communicated understanding to the student that she would have found valuable and that would have enhanced the level of respect she had for the teacher. Such a response also would have encouraged the student to communicate with the teacher so that the teacher and student could brainstorm ways to keep the student on task with her various assignments.

Admiring Negative Attitudes and Behaviors

At first glance, this approach would seem to violate all that we know about behavior modification, but it is based on a well established area of research called "positive psychology"

(Seligman, 1999). This approach looks upon negative student behavior as a skill he or she has been practicing and refining for many years. Most of these skills have their beginning in the student's family life. In the case of a manipulative female teen, for example, being manipulative might have been the only or best way of getting her needs met in her family. It is to be entirely expected that she would bring these same skills to school in an effort to meet her needs there as well.

Rather than engage in a power struggle with such a student, a teacher should acknowledge the skill that the student has worked so hard to develop—and then redirect it. Give her credit for all of the years she has practiced the skill. This will also lead to an increase in the student's perceived empathy from the teacher. After acknowledging the skill, reframe the skill and then redirect it. It is important that this skill be applied with sincerity. Any hint of sarcasm could lead to further alienation between the student and the teacher.

Let us extend the example of a manipulative, young adolescent girl. She is engaged in a behavior that, in all likelihood, annoys both adults and her peers. However, there is a skill that may be present in the girl that can be reframed as the "ability to influence people." Rather than address the girl's manipulations as such, mention to her, "I have noticed that you have the ability to influence people, is that true?" She will probably reply with something like, "What do you mean?" The teacher can respond by saying, "Well, I have noticed that you can get people to do what you want them to do. Am I wrong?" It would help if the teacher used specific examples. At this point, the student will likely look at the teacher somewhat suspiciously and smile, saying, "Well that's true sometimes, I guess." The teacher can then respond, saying, "You have a valuable skill there. If you used it in other

ways, you may find more successful ways of getting your needs met. This skill could be valuable in certain careers, such as corporate management, sales, or even counseling." The young adolescent is usually quite surprised to hear something that she has previously been criticized for now being admired and looked upon as something potentially valuable.

Another example of the application of this approach would be the case of a young adolescent who consistently displays the infamous "bad attitude." Quite at variance with the usual characterization of the bad attitude, we look at it as a skill that is often practiced and has a particular goal. The goal is to display and announce defiance and, to a certain degree, independence. Instead of fighting the attitude, punishing it, or even ridiculing it, try admiring it, putting aside any disgust or exasperation. "Wow," the teacher might say, "You sure do have an impressive attitude. It is very well constructed, and I can tell you have been working on it for years." One's first thought on reading this might be to conclude that such an approach is simply crazy. However, a large percentage of young adolescents respond to this tactic with a smile and a greater willingness to continue the discussion. Admiration is extremely rare in the lives of young adolescents, and we dare say, much rarer than love. To receive it from an adult is precious indeed, and it often inspires immediate loyalty and respect toward a teacher. When communicated genuinely and honestly, it also increases the level of perceived empathy from an adult.

Disruptive behaviors, when displayed by a student who takes charge in his or her own way, can sometimes be reframed as great leadership skills. The teacher can ask the student to use those abilities to help lead the class. In the case of the disruptive class clown, the reframe would be along the lines of admiring the student, then reframing the clown act as natural comedic skill. A possible redirect could consist of a challenge to the student to use that skill in a creative way and in an appropriate setting that can be set up by the teacher according to the personality of the student.

Disruptive behaviors, when displayed by a student who takes charge in his or her own way, can sometimes be reframed as great leadership skills.

Leaving the Ego at the Door

It is readily apparent that to follow this relationship approach, a teacher or school administrator must have the capacity to suspend the flaring up of his or her own impulses, issues, and negative reactions. Young adolescents are highly skilled at reading teachers and identifying the things that make them impatient, rigid, angry, and upset. Young adolescents often share insights with each other about what annoys teachers and school administrators. The ability to manage one's own issues as they arise is one of the counselor's most demanding skills. It also marks the difference between the effective and the ineffective counselor (Van Wagoner, Gelso, Hayes, & Diemer, 1991). It is also an assessment of truly effective relationship-based teaching. Once a professional gives in to emotions such as anger, exasperation, or displeasure, his or her ability to function becomes impaired to a degree. It seems no one knows this better than some young adolescents, who may be quite aware of the effects they have on adults.

When a teacher takes the comments and manipulations of students personally, interpersonal chaos is likely to follow. Thus, it is a good idea for a teacher to learn to suspend his or her own issues as they arise—to "place them on the shelf," so to speak, to be addressed later. One of the hidden advantages of working with young adolescents is that they have much to teach us about our own reactions and habitual ways of interacting. All too often, the student becomes the teacher of lessons that may not be learned in any other context (Hanna, 2002). Suspending one's own reactions is a skill, to be sure, and it is a skill that can be improved with practice.

Leaving the ego at the door of the classroom is perhaps the most valuable suggestion we have to offer, along with showing empathy. Without this, however, empathy may never get a chance to emerge. Young adolescents closely watch the reactions of adults to see if they practice what they preach. For example, if Tom, a seventh grade student, erupts in class one day because he is being teased for being a "suck-up," a very typical teacher response is, "Just try to ignore what the other kids are saying." However, if a teacher or counselor tells a student to "ignore" the taunts or insults of another and then reacts angrily to being disrespected, the student, like most of us, will have little respect for what amounts to hypocrisy. Demanding respect is not as effective as earning it, and how the teacher comports himself or herself has much to do with how he or she is viewed and respected by students. To successfully build relationships and apply the skills mentioned in this article, leaving the ego at the door can be viewed as a prerequisite. At various times, leaving the ego at the door can be connected to issues of culture as well.

When a disruptive young adolescent routinely pushes a teacher's buttons, that teacher has an ideal opportunity to apply the practice of leaving the ego at the door. It is human nature for teachers, or anyone for that matter, to get upset when an adolescent pokes fun at a personally sensitive topic or issue. This is especially true when it comes to the topic of authority. Many teachers believe that they must have absolute authority in the classroom. They also believe that this authority comes automatically with their status as the teacher and does not necessarily have to be earned. When students question this authority by being non-compliant or engaging in disruptive behaviors, they may easily trigger an emotional reaction from the teacher. For example, Sammy, an eighth grade student, might say, "Why should I listen to you? You're just a middle school teacher. Why don't you have a good job?" The unexamined response that a teacher might give is this: "You have no right speaking to me like this. I know a lot more than you do, and I know you have detention today. See me after school." Because teachers do have authority and certain privileges afforded to them by their position, anger and frustration often lead to the abuse of power in punitive ways. This usually happens when the adult does not take the opportunity to examine his or her own vulnerabilities on a regular basis. When the disruptive adolescent repeatedly insults or disobeys the teacher, the teacher's ego takes over, demanding respect.

If the teacher had taken the time to examine his or her own vulnerabilities, he or she might have said, "You sound like my mother. She didn't think I should become a teacher either. She wanted me to wear a starched shirt and tie every day and work in a big law firm. But I tell her I get to be a part of the lives of more than 120 seventh graders—including yours, Sammy. What more power do I need?" Then the teacher can turn the topic around to question the student by saying, "What does your family say to you about what you hope to do someday?"

When a teacher is self-aware of vulnerabilities, such as the need for power, he or she is more likely to respond strategically rather than emotionally. For example, a teacher who knows he is sensitive to students questioning his authority can anticipate that middle grades students will, in fact, question his authority. Such awareness can lead to the use of empathy or the admiration of negative behaviors, as previously discussed. In essence, the key to leaving one's ego at the door is awareness.

Multicultural Connections

Developing relationships with students who come from culturally different backgrounds can be challenging and requires specific skills from new and experienced teachers alike (Nieto, 1999a, 1999b, 2008). The recommendations for forming relationships made earlier in this article are essential when cultural differences are present. That is, having empathy, admiring negative behaviors, and leaving one's ego at the door can go a long way toward bridging the gap between culturally or linguistically different (CLD) learners and the teacher.

The challenges within the cross-cultural encounter lie in overcoming the additional barriers that prevent teachers from letting down their guard to empathize and develop stronger relationships with students. These barriers exist due to a fear of the culturally different, a lack of knowledge about the differences and similarities between cultures, persistent negative stereotyping, and general intolerance. To overcome these barriers and develop multicultural competence, a teacher must overcome his or her fears and unresolved issues regarding cultural difference. This can be achieved by gaining deeper knowledge about himself or herself and the culturally different student. (Bradfield-Kreider, 2001).

Practices from the field of counseling have great promise for enhancing relationships in the culturally diverse classroom. In counseling, multicultural competence consists of being acutely aware of cultural attitudes, beliefs, knowledge, and skills of both the counselor and the client (Arredondo, 2003). Training new counselors involves an examination of how the new counselors feel about themselves and culturally different clients. Such competencies can easily be used as a guide for classroom teachers who want to enhance their relationships with CLD students.

It is important to help teachers become aware of how their racial and cultural heritages may impact their classroom climates. This awareness helps prepare teachers to identify and work through any existing intolerance they may have for students who come from different ethnic, racial, class, or religious backgrounds. It is equally important for teachers to be aware of their negative and positive emotional reactions to CLD students. For example, if the disruptive adolescent described in the previous scenario happens to come from a racial or ethnic background that is different from that of the teacher, checking one's ego becomes more complicated. It is, therefore, vital for the teacher to be aware of his or her cultural and personal biases and the connections between the two. Then, when challenges to authority occur, the teacher who is aware of his or her "stuff" is better equipped to respond in more strategic ways. Such self-examination helps teachers leave their egos at the door and ultimately develop empathy for those they teach.

For teachers to engage in successful intercultural interactions, they must maintain an astute approach to learning relationships and be aware of the ways schooling helps to reinforce social class differences (Hipolito-Delgado & Lee, 2007). Marginalization refers to the historic and systemic ways in which people are adversely affected by racism, poverty, and other forms of oppression (Green, Conley, & Barnett, 2005). Teachers who are vested in educating students who come from such backgrounds should develop relationships by making meaning of the curriculum as it relates to their lived experiences outside the school. Taking this approach allows teachers to share their own personal experiences about hardship, triumph, and failure, regardless of the similarities or differences with the student's life.

Programs such as *Facing History and Ourselves* (www.facinghistory.org) and *Rethinking Schools* (www.rethinkingschools.com) provide curricular materials that are designed to provide these kinds of shared self-examination experiences in the classroom. *Facing History and Ourselves* engages students from diverse backgrounds in an examination of racism and prejudice to promote a more informed and tolerant citizenship. Through study and discussions of current and past historical events, students are encouraged to analyze their own thinking, see the world from more than one perspective, and place themselves in someone else's shoes as they examine events from history around the world. Together, students and teachers struggle to form judgments about human behaviors. Curricular materials expose students to such topics as violence in Northern Ireland, genocide in Cambodia, AIDS victims in Africa, anti-Semitism in London, or Mexican immigration struggles in California. Even though many of these events may occur miles away in different states and different countries, many of the core issues are still the same. When teachers use curriculum and content that hold personal meaning to them and their students, barriers are more likely to break down for everyone, and relationship building has a better chance.

One strategy from *Facing History and Ourselves* is called the Life Road Map (www.facinghistory.org), which allows teachers and students to develop a map of their lives by creating sequences of events, including important decisions and inspirations. This strategy would be useful to a teacher with students who have recently immigrated to the United States. It would promote an appreciation for one's own culture and for the cultures of others that are represented in the classroom. It also would provide a forum for sharing difficulties that teachers and students have faced, some of which will be a result of culture and race.

A similar strategy, developed by *Rethinking Schools,* provides a template for teachers and students to write a poem called "Where I'm From" that reveals information about their lives outside school (Christensen, 2002). Students are encouraged to include information in the poem by studying items found in their homes, in their yards, and in their neighborhoods and the names of relatives, foods, and places they keep in their childhood memories. For a teacher with students from a variety of cultures in one classroom, these poems could be read aloud and posted to provide a powerful way of building relationships and community in the classroom. For both of these strategies, it is critical that the teacher participate by completing the assignments and sharing them as well.

When teachers use curriculum and content that hold personal meaning to them and their students, barriers are more likely to break down for everyone, and relationship building has a better chance.

Conclusion

Efforts to improve education must focus on the single most important component: the classroom teacher (Ingwalson & Thompson, 2007). Teachers in middle level schools must be well prepared to face the challenges of working with young adolescents; and critical components of teacher preparation are the knowledge and skills from education and related fields that will enable them to develop effective, and often unconventional, management systems in their classrooms. This effort must begin with a new paradigm in which teachers view classroom management as an ongoing exercise in building relationships.

For dealing with the most challenging of students, teachers can learn and apply strategies used in the field of counseling and psychotherapy, such as building empathy, admiring negative attitudes and behaviors, and leaving one's ego at the door. It seems particularly important to provide specific strategies for dealing with what can often be the problems that prevent us from persevering in the important work of helping students learn. In the area of classroom management, it is critical that teachers find ways of building relationships with *all* students, from the most motivated to the most difficult. To borrow the words of Rogers and Renard (1999), when we enter into understanding human needs and relationship-driven teaching, "amazing things can happen" (p. 34).

Extensions

Identify three obstacles that interfere with your ability to make meaningful connections with your students.

Think of an educator from your past with whom you did not connect. What would you say to that educator about building relationships with students?

References

Adelman, H. S., & Taylor, L. (2002). School counselors and school reform: New directions. *Professional School Counseling, 5,* 235–248.

Adler, A. (1956). *The individual psychology of Alfred Adler: A systematic presentation in selections from his writings.* New York: Harper & Row.

Anderman, E. M., Maehr, M., & Midgley, C. (1999). Declining motivation after the transition to middle school: Schools can make a difference. *Journal of Research and Development in Education, 32*(3), 131–147.

Arredondo, P. (2003). *Applying multicultural competencies in white institutions of higher education.* In G. Roysircar, D. S. Sandhu, & V. B. Bibbins (Eds.), *A guidebook: Practices of multicultural competencies* (pp. 229–242). Alexandria, VA: ACA Press.

Bender, W. L. (2003). *Relational discipline: Strategies for in-your-face students.* Boston: Pearson.

Bernstein, N. (1996). *Treating the unmanageable adolescent: A guide to oppositional defiant and conduct disorders.* Northvale, NJ: Jason Aronson.

Bradfield-Kreider, P. (2001). Personal transformations from the inside out: Nurturing monoculture teachers' growth toward multicultural competence. *Multicultural Education, 8*(4), 31–34.

Brophy, J. E. (1996). *Teaching problem students.* New York: Guilford.

Brophy, J. E., & McCaslin, N. (1992). Teachers' reports of how they perceive and cope with problem students. *Elementary School Journal, 93*(1), 63–68.

Carnegie Council on Adolescent Development. (1995). *Great transitions: Preparing adolescents for a new century.* Waldorf, MD: Carnegie Corporation of New York.

Christensen, L. (2002). Where I'm from: Inviting student lives into the classroom. In B. Bigelow (Ed.), *Rethinking our classrooms volume 2: Teaching for equity and justice,* (p. 6). Milwaukee, WI: Rethinking Schools.

Decker, D. M., Dona, D. P., & Christenson, S. L. (2007). Behaviorally at-risk African-American students: The importance of student-teacher relationships for student outcomes. *Journal of School Psychology, 45*(1), 83–109.

Dunn, N. A., & Baker, S. B. (2002). Readiness to serve students with disabilities: A survey of elementary school counselors. *Professional School Counseling, 5,* 277–284.

Furrer, C., & Skinner, E. (2003). Sense of relatedness as a factor in children's academic engagement and performance. *Journal of Educational Psychology, 95,* 148–162.

Garfield, S. L. (1994). Research on client variables in psychotherapy. In A. E. Bergin & S. L. Garfield (Eds.), *Handbook of psychotherapy and behavior change* (4th ed.) (pp. 190–228). New York: John Wiley.

Goldfried, M. R., Greenberg, L. S., & Marmar, C. (1990). Individual psychotherapy: Process and outcome. *Annual Review of Psychology, 41,* 659–688.

Green, A., Conley, J. A., & Barnett, K. (2005). Urban school counseling: Implications for practice and training. *Professional School Counseling, 8,* 189–195.

Haberman, M. (1995). *STAR teachers of poverty.* Bloomington, IN: Kappa Delta Pi.

Hall, P. S., & Hall, N. D. (2003). Building relationships with challenging children. *Educational Leadership, 61*(1), 60–63.

Hanna, F. J. (2002). *Therapy with difficult clients: Using the precursors model to awaken change.* Washington, DC: American Psychological Association.

Hanna, F. J., Hanna, C. A., & Keys, S. G. (1999). Fifty strategies for counseling defiant and aggressive adolescents: Reaching, accepting, and relating. *Journal of Counseling and Development, 77,* 395–404.

Hipolito-Delgado, C. P., & Lee, C. C. (2007). Empowerment theory for the professional school counselor: A manifesto for what really matters. *Professional School Counseling, 10,* 327–332.

Ingwalson, G., & Thompson, J., Jr. (2007). A tale of two first-year teachers: One likely to continue, one likely to drop out. *Middle School Journal, 39*(2), 43–49.

Luborsky, L., Crits-Christoph, P., Mintz, J., & Auerbach, A. (1988). *Who will benefit from psychotherapy: Predicting therapeutic outcomes.* New York: Basic Books.

Marzano, R. J. (2003). *What works in schools.* Alexandria, VA: Association for Supervision and Curriculum Development.

Marzano, R. J., & Marzano, J. S. (2003). The key to classroom management. *Educational Leadership, 61*(1), 6–13.

Marzano, R. J., Marzano, J. S., & Pickering, D. J. (2003). *Classroom management that works.* Alexandria, VA: Association for Supervision and Curriculum Development.

Mordock, J. B. (1991). *Counseling the defiant child.* New York: Crossroad Publishing.

Nieto, S. (1999a). *Affirming diversity: The sociopolitical context of multicultural education.* Boston: Pearson/Allyn & Bacon.

Nieto, S. (1999b). *The light in their eyes: Creating a multicultural learning community.* New York: Teachers College Press.

Nieto, S. (2008). *Affirming diversity: The sociopolitical context of multicultural education* (5th ed.). New York: Allyn & Bacon.

Orlinsky, D. E., Grawe, K., & Parks, B. K. (1994). Process and outcome in psychotherapy. In A. E. Bergin & S. L. Garfield (Eds.), *Handbook of psychotherapy and behavior change* (4th ed.) (pp. 270–376). New York: Wiley.

Rogers, S., & Renard, L. (1999). Relationship-driven teaching. *Educational Leadership, 57*(1), 34–37.

Schmakel, P. O. (2008). Early adolescents' perspectives on motivation and achievement. *Urban Education, 43,* 723–749.

Seligman, M. E. (1999). The president's address. *American Psychologist, 54,* 599–567.

Sexton, T. L., & Whiston, S. C. (1994). The status of the counseling relationship: An empirical review, theoretical implications, and research directions. *The Counseling Psychologist, 22*(1), 6–78.

Van Wagoner, S. L., Gelso, C. J., Hayes, J. A., & Diemer, R. A. (1991). Countertransference and the reputedly excellent therapist. *Psychotherapy, 28,* 411–421.

Wang, M. C., Haertel, G. D., & Walberg, H. J. (1993). Toward a knowledge base for school learning. *Review of Educational Research, 63*(3), 249–294.

Wolk, S. (2003). Hearts and minds. *Educational Leadership, 61*(1), 14–18.

Wormeli, R. (2003). *Day one and beyond: Practical matters for middle-level teachers.* Portland, ME: Stenhouse.

MARY ELLEN BEATY-O'FERRALL is associate professor of education at the Johns Hopkins University School of Education in Baltimore, MD. E-mail: mebo@jhu.edu.

ALAN GREEN is an associate professor of clinical education and school counseling program lead at the Rossier School of Education, University of Southern California, Los Angeles, CA. E-mail: alangree@usc.edu.

FRED HANNA is professor and director of the School of Applied Psychology and Counselor Education at the University of Northern Colorado, Greeley. E-mail: fred.hanna@unco.edu.

ARTICLE 20

Using Self-Assessment to Chart Students' Paths

Margaret Heritage

Emergent economies of the last several decades have created a global market in which international competition is a reality. At the same time, knowledge and information are growing exponentially, and it is almost certain that the skills of today will not be the skills of tomorrow. Learning how to learn (LtL) is, thus, a critical life and career skill that students must develop long before they exit the formal education system.

New developments in the science of learning emphasize the importance of learners taking control of their own learning. These metacognitive approaches to learning increase the degree to which students transfer learning to new settings and include sense-making, self-assessment, and reflection on learning strategies—in other words, learning how to learn (Bransford, Brown, & Cocking, 2000).

While schools have traditionally concerned themselves with what students are to learn, less attention has been paid to these metacognitive dimensions of learning. This is, perhaps, especially evident in the field of assessment. Large-scale assessments, such as annual state tests, evaluate how well students meet state standards. Interim or quarterly assessments determine whether students are on the way to meeting state standards, and classroom assessments are typically used to decide whether students have learned what they are supposed to learn for a given period of instruction. What is missing in contemporary assessment practices is any involvement of students in evaluating their own learning and making decisions about how they can improve. However, U.S. educators are increasingly recognizing the need to alter the balance away from assessment in which students are passive recipients toward assessment that involves them as active participants. This student-involved approach to assessment is not intended to replace accountability measures. After all, for a total outlay of approximately $500 billion for public education in fiscal year 2005 (National Center for Education Statistics, 2008), schools should be accountable for the effectiveness of this expenditure. Rather, involving students in assessment is an educational approach in its own right: it is a means of helping them develop the skills of learning how to learn.

Ripe for Learning How to Learn

Middle school students are beginning the developmental transition from childhood dependency to adult independence and, ultimately, to the world of work. As they develop independence, they are still reliant on guidance and help from adults. They are becoming increasingly self-aware, more able to reflect on themselves, and conscious of their strengths and weaknesses. Consequently, this period of schooling is a time when students are ripe for developing an increased awareness of themselves as learners. Developmentally, middle school students have the capacity to become effective in monitoring and evaluating their own learning, and to build a repertoire of learning strategies they can employ strategically during the course of learning. Schools must take advantage of this developmental capacity and ensure that learning how to learn is an integral part of middle school education. Indeed, if middle school students are not on track with LtL skills by this stage of their education, they could well find the train leaving the station in high school. Worse, by the time they reach higher education and the workplace, the train definitely will have left with many students remaining on the platform. Fortunately, teachers can adopt assessment practices that will foster students' abilities to learn how to learn through student self-assessment.

Formative Assessment

Due, in part, to literature suggesting that formative assessment can have a powerful effect on student learning (e.g., Black & Wiliam, 1998; Black, Harrison, Lee, Marshall, & Wiliam, 2003; Brookhart, 2007), it has attracted the attention of educators across the U.S. in recent years. Formative assessment is assessment that is carried out during instruction for the purpose of improving teaching or learning (Shepard, et al., 2005). It is important to recognize that, according to these and other scholars, the purpose of formative assessment is not just to improve teaching but also to improve *learning*. Improving learning must involve students, because, in the end, no one else can learn for them.

Formative assessment requires teachers to gather evidence of how student learning is progressing toward desired goals during instruction and partner with students in a process of reciprocal feedback to improve learning: teacher feedback resulting from interpretation of evidence gathered and student feedback as a result of self-assessment. In their landmark review of formative assessment research, Black and Wiliam (1998) concluded that student self-assessment is an essential part of formative assessment, noting that when people are trying to learn, they need information about the goal, evidence about where they are in relation to the goal, and an understanding of what they must do to close the gap between the two. Self-assessment, as a means to improve learning, includes two components: monitoring learning and managing learning. When students are involved in self-assessment, they monitor how well their learning is developing toward specific goals, and in self-management, they select from a repertoire of learning strategies to make adjustments to how they are learning to keep their learning on course. The students' actions in formative assessment very much mirror the teachers'; teachers monitor the effectiveness of their teaching in moving students toward the learning goal and select from a repertoire of pedagogical strategies when they want to make adjustments to teaching.

The Educational Environment

Self-assessment requires an educational environment in which students are able to take responsibility for their own learning. To take responsibility, students must be clear about learning goals—what it is they are going to learn and why. They must have the opportunity to develop and exercise the skills of monitoring their learning toward the goal and be able to use internal feedback to make adjustments to their learning when they are not moving successfully toward the goal. However, this is far from the school experience of many middle school students. Their experience is still very much as Mary Alice White observed in 1971 when she likened students at school to being on a ship sailing across an unknown sea to an unknown destination. The students know they are going to the school, but the compass and chart are neither available nor intelligible to the students. Instead of the voyage and its destination being all-important, the daily life aboard ship, the chores, the demands, and the inspections are all that count (White, 1971). What can be done to change students' experience of school, to involve them in learning, and enable them to become self-directed and responsible for their own learning?

Teaching and Learning as a Partnership

Watkins (2003) argued that learning is constituted of three elements: being taught, individual sense making, and building knowledge as part of interactions with others. The dominant conception of learning in the U.S. has focused almost exclusively on the first of these: that learning is being taught. To be taught, students are provided with activities, often without a real grasp or understanding of their purpose, leading to the common response of "the teacher told me to" when asked what they are doing and why they are doing it—hardly a response from students who are taking responsibility for learning and learning how to learn!

If we are serious about middle school students learning how to learn, we must address the other constituents of learning: individual sense making and building knowledge by doing things with others. Individual sense making requires students to be reflective about what they are learning and to have the strategies to take action if things are not making sense. For example, students who are reflecting on their learning in science or math might choose from a range of learning strategies such as reorganizing the information, doing a drawing, making a table, or finding more information that will fill gaps in knowledge. Doing things with others means working with and learning from peers, but it also means partnering with teachers. A partner relationship with teachers capitalizes on the developmental characteristics of middle school students; they are seeking independence from adults, yet still need adult support and guidance.

Imagine a classroom in which students are clear about learning goals and the criteria for success in meeting those learning goals. Through exemplars and discussions with the teacher, the students have a conception of what success means in the context of their own work. The students know what they are learning and why, and they have been taught the skills of self assessment and reflection. They have also developed a repertoire of strategies to adjust their learning when their self-assessment against the success criteria indicates to them that they are not moving forward. They use this internal feedback, together with the external feedback provided by their teachers, to discuss how their learning is progressing and what needs to be done to move forward. Teachers make adjustments to teaching and students to learning. In this scenario, teachers and students are partners who share responsibility for learning. And most important, the students are developing the lifelong skills of learning how to learn.

Teacher Practices

Making student self-assessment a widespread reality in middle school classrooms will necessitate some changes in teacher knowledge, skills, attitudes, and practices. For many teachers and students, this may involve a fundamental shift in the ecology of classroom environments that is both new and motivating. Teachers must first understand how to use formative assessment and have the skills to implement formative assessment in their classrooms. They must understand what student self-assessment entails and be able to teach students the skills of self-monitoring and self-management. They can begin by asking the students to reflect on their performance on the assessment relative to the criteria for success using questions like "Do you think that your response demonstrated understanding of . . . ? If yes, why do you think this? If not, why do you think you did not demonstrate understanding?" From this basis, students can learn to be more independent and recognize when they do not understand and when they need to do something about it.

By giving students feedback about strategies that they can use to improve learning, rather than telling them what the solutions are, teachers can help students develop awareness of how to make adaptations to learning. Consider this example. In a science class, the students were focusing on designing a fair test. The criteria for success were that the students would be specific about what they wanted to measure, identify the key variable and which factors remain constant, and

then show a plan to conduct the test. One student wrote in his design that he was going to measure the time it takes a parachute to fall to the ground. He noted that he would change the size of the parachute, but keep the weight and shape of the parachute the same and the length and thickness of the parachute strings the same.

The feedback the teacher gave to this student was,

> Your design shows that you are clear about what you want to measure and that you have listed four factors that should remain constant in your test and one that will change. For your test to be fair, there is one other factor that must remain constant. You are planning to measure the time parachutes of different sizes take fall to the ground. With this in mind, can you review your plan and think about what else needs to be constant? I will be back in a few moments to see what you have come up with.

The student reviewed his plan and realized that the height from which the parachute is dropped needs to be constant. The next round of feedback for this student from the teacher was,

> You have planned your fair test in general terms. Now think about how you would conduct your test in a systematic way so that you can draw conclusions from your test. Go back to some of the examples of fair tests we looked at from last year's students and consider how you will conduct your measurements and record your data in systematic ways so that you can compare your results.

Through the use of strategic feedback, the teacher successfully assisted the student in moving forward and understanding how to conduct a fair test.

Teachers must also have the skills to create a classroom culture that is conducive to self-assessment. Middle school students are very self-conscious and sensitive to the opinions of their peers. For self-assessment, they need a classroom culture in which they feel it is acceptable to admit they do not understand something or are having difficulties and need to work on solutions. It is essential that the classroom culture is characterized by respect, trust, and individual self-worth so that students can be reflective about learning without any threats to their self-esteem.

Finally, teachers must have the attitude that self assessment is beneficial and will make a difference in students' abilities to learn in the near- and long-term. They must also see the value of partnering with students and be willing, in many cases, to change the classroom contract from one in which learning is a product of teaching, to one in which learning is a shared responsibility between teachers and students.

Charting the Course

Rather than experiencing school as a journey on a unknown sea to an unknown destination, it is possible for students to use formative self-assessment as a navigational chart and compass—to know where they are going, how they are going to get there, and whether they need to make learning adjustments along the way. In short, to chart the course of their learning. At a time when lifelong learning is an expectation for personal and societal success, it is incumbent upon middle school educators to take advantage of their students' stage of development and make self-assessment, as a means of learning how to learn, an essential part of teaching and assessment practices. Without it, we risk limiting the potential and prospects of our students, which is something we must not do.

References

Black, P., Harrison, C., Lee, C., Marshall, B., & Wiliam, D. (2003). *Assessment for learning: Putting it into practice.* Berkshire, England: Open University Press.

Black, P., & Wiliam, D. (1998). Assessment and classroom learning. *Assessment in Education: Principles, Policy and Practice, 5*(1), 7–73.

Bransford, J. D., Brown, A. L., & Cocking, R. R. (Eds.). (2000). *How people learn: Brain, mind, experience, and school.* (Committee on Developments in the Science and Learning, Commission on Behavioral and Social Sciences and Education, National Research Council). Washington, DC: National Academy Press.

Brookhart, S. M. (2007). Expanding views about formative classroom assessment: A review of the literature. In J. H. McMillan (Ed.), *Formative classroom assessment: Research, theory and practice* (pp. 43-62). New York: Teachers College Press.

National Center for Education Stastictics. (2008). *Digest of Education Statistics, 2007* (NCES 2008-022). Washington, DC: U.S. Department of Education.

Shepard, L. A., Hammerness, K., Darling-Hammond, L., Rust, F., Snowden, J. B., Gordon, E., et al. (2005). Assessment. In L. Darling-Hammond & J. Bransford (Eds.), *Preparing teachers for a changing world: What teachers should learn and be able to do* (pp. 275-236). San Francisco: Jossey-Bass.

Watkins, C. (2003). *Learning: a sense-maker's guide.* London: Association of Teachers and Lecturers.

White, M.A. (1971). The view from the pupil's desk. In M. Silberman (Ed.), *The experience of schooling* (pp. 337-345). New York: Rinehart and Winston.

MARGARET HERITAGE is assistant director for professional development at the National Center for Research on Evaluation, Standards, and Student Testing and an expert on formative assessment at the University of California at Los Angeles. E-mail: mheritage@ucla.edu.

ARTICLE 21

Students' Reactions to a "No Failure" Grading System and How They Informed Teacher Practice

This article briefly describes the central tenets of a program several low-income middle schools implemented to remove failure as a choice students could make in completing their assignments. Instead of doling out Fs for poor and nonexistent work, teachers devised a variety of options students had to follow to demonstrate eventual mastery of critical skills and knowledge. This article draws on nearly five years of interviews the authors did in the buildings with both educators and students and found that in sharing their reactions to the initiative, young people spoke not with a voice but with voices. Teachers learned that the program's effectiveness improved as they paid attention to, and gave credibility to, the students' varied reactions. The article concludes with an oft-repeated but not yet widely adhered to call to allow students to actually participate in reform efforts rather than just be the beneficiaries of them.

DICK CORBETT AND BRUCE WILSON

Students are clear about what they want to see in their teachers. They want teachers who are willing to help—whenever and however help is needed, who explain material and assignments clearly and repeat those explanations as often as requested, who can control their classes, who make sure all students do their work, who vary their activities from time to time, and who establish relationships with their students (Wilson & Corbett, 2001). And students have a single word under which they bundle these six qualities of a good teacher: caring. For students, caring is all about teachers not giving up on them, as these urban middle school youth explain:

S: A good teacher is someone who stays on top of you and gives you homework. Someone who prepares you for the next grade. A good teacher cares about you.

I: What do you mean by cares?

S: If you don't do it, she doesn't just say "it's on you" to get the work in.

S: I like the ones that don't allow excuses. It's my turn to get an education. I need to have someone to tell me when I'm tired and don't feel like doing the work that I should do it anyway.

Caring, then, is often hard-nosed, in students' opinion, as one marveled about her teacher: "My teacher is mean, out of the kindness of her heart."

We have visited nearly 500 low achieving schools, K–12, around the country over the last 30 years. They all have some teachers who behave in the student-preferred ways, but it is rare to find an entire faculty that adopts, with a single mind, the perspective that it is solely their responsibility to insure students' success (Corbett, Wilson, & Williams, 2005). Thus, most students tend to get a *luck-based* education. That is, they have to be fortunate enough to be placed in classrooms where their teachers refuse to let them fail. The unlucky ones are left to endure the "I already told you that," "I'm not going to keep repeating myself," and "You'll have to catch yourself up" statements that signal to students that their teachers are not very concerned whether they learn. Indeed, an all-too-prevalent pattern in schools is for teachers to settle for using good instructional practices and leaving it up to students to decide if they want to do their part. Tragically, in urban schools especially, many students—when given the choice to fail—do.

Imagine, however, a school environment where every teacher insists that every student must complete every assignment well—in other words, a school where teachers simply do not let students shrug off their work. We have come across a handful of such schools. These buildings took part in the Academy for Educational Development's Middle Start program (http://www. middlestart.org/) and adopted a specific strand of the overall initiative known as Achievement by Continual Improvement (ABCI; http://www.middlestart .org/what/abci.cfm). As independent, third-party evaluators of the program since 1999, we conducted yearly in-depth interviews with educators and students to document their perceptions of and reactions to ABCI. The educators said that they were less concerned with heightening student motivation and increasing parental involvement than with altering their own beliefs and actions. Put simply, they decided that they had to assume responsibility for student success and not worry with success factors out of their control. Otherwise, they argued, learning would be left to the vagaries of youthful whim and to the taxed energy of multitasking adults. To that end, the schools adopted ABCI, the core principle of which, according to participants, was failure is not an option.

This article briefly describes the central tenets of the program and then details students' reactions to it. It draws on the 5 years of interviews with nearly every teacher and more than 50 students across all performance levels in several low-income, urban middle schools in Michigan. These schools were typical of many of the nation's urban schools, with high concentrations of students of color and achievement levels well below state averages. At first blush, one might predict that students would have enthusiastically welcomed seeing all of their teachers begin to act in ways that communicated to students that the adults cared about their learning. However, the students spoke not with a voice but with voices, and so the faculties discovered that ABCI's effectiveness improved as they paid attention to, and gave credibility to, young people's varied reactions. The article concludes with an oft repeated, but not yet widely adhered to call, to allow students to actually participate in reform efforts rather than just be the beneficiaries of them (Fullan & Steigelbauer, 1991).

The Program's Features

Educators participating in ABCI attempted to create four essential conditions in their buildings:

1. Educators assumed responsibility for student success.
2. Schools instituted a no-failure grading system.
3. Staff established numerous interventions.
4. Teachers reassessed the definition of assignments.

The first condition involves educators assuming responsibility for student success. Students, parents, and teachers are joined at the hip in the search for ways to enable all students to enjoy academic excellence and healthy development. Conventional wisdom says that none can succeed at this task without the full cooperation of the others. However, ABCI argued that the responsibility for producing desired outcomes resided with educators. Educators recognized that motivated students and actively engaged parents make life a lot easier, but understood that they only had control over what happened at school. Thus, "It's on us," they concluded, because once they relinquished the responsibility for success to students or parents, the game was lost. Many exasperated teachers have thrown up their hands and said, "I've done all I can do; you've had your opportunity to do this and so you'll get a zero." But the educators in these schools decided that they would never again say this.

The second condition involves the development of a no failure grading system. All the *D*s, *E*s, or *F*s were removed from the grade books. And the zeroes disappeared, too. Instead, teachers graded only work that had been done to an acceptable level of quality—an *A* or *B* or *C*. They used placeholders for work that had not yet met the desired standard—an *I* for incomplete, an *NY* for not yet quality, or an *NQ* for not quality. The philosophy underlying this idea is not new. After all, *mastery learning* has been around a long time (Bloom, 1971). The novel part was that an entire school's operation became organized around the principle that every student could and would do quality work. Some students might take longer than others, but no teacher would ever signal the end of an assignment with an *F* or zero. Furthermore, every student was expected to do every assignment. No grade was forthcoming until every piece of work was completed to an acceptable level of quality.

One of the complications with doing this was that there were always at least two possible reasons why someone did not do an assignment to the desired level of quality— either the student did not understand what

he or she was doing or the student just did not want to do it. The former obviously should set in motion some form of reteaching; the latter warranted further prodding. Teachers could not say "You've had enough time" or "You've passed up your last chance." Students could not settle for responding "So, just give me a zero" or "Whatever." Thus, the schools had to put in place *interventions* to help the students who needed more time and to motivate or, more accurately, annoy the students who were persistent procrastinators. These included Saturday School, before and after school tutoring, lunch time makeup sessions, various tangible incentives, reteaching and enrichment periods during the day, and, ultimately, summer school, as well as the teachers themselves doing professional development that would help them develop engaging, thought-provoking, and rigorous lessons.

Consequently, teachers began to reassess the quality and quantity of their graded assignments. They realized that if students were going to have to go to summer school to finish certain tasks, then the assignment had better be pretty worthwhile to begin with. In other words, having a bunch of kids completing word search puzzles in June was not an appealing image of an improved education. Teachers said that, as a result, they had numerous conversations among themselves about what a good assignment should look like and what criteria they should use for judging whether to include an assignment in their array of requirements. A parallel benefit was that teachers discovered having deeper and richer collegial discussions than they had ever had before.

Students' Reflections on the Program

Given students' near universal desire to see signs of caring from their teachers, one might have suspected a ready acceptance of putting the ideas discussed above into practice. And, in fact, many students did embrace the major changes they saw in their instructors, especially the unwavering insistence that all students must do all the assigned work. For instance: "The program is good because it makes us get our work done. We have to pay attention." Or "You learn more because you have to do all the work, not some of it."

Students especially seemed to like the idea of getting second chances. A common complaint among students was that they often did not understand a concept the first time or the first way a teacher explained it. The program acknowledged explicitly that students might need extra chances to get the work done to an acceptable level and students embraced that idea: "If we get lower than a C, we have to do the assignment over again. It's good because it gives us a chance to pass."

S: If I fall behind, I can make it up and I won't just flunk because I didn't get it the first time.

I: Are you a better student now?

S: Yes, now when I get an *NQ* it better prepares me to make up the work. I would rather do the work again than take a *D* or *F.* That way I will be better prepared for the next grade.

Students also pointed out the value of an increased sense of accountability brought on by the new practices. Instead of the old system where students accepted whatever grade they were issued, what students have previously referred to as "It is what it is," students were now always striving to do better, and there were important implications associated with the kind of progress they were making: "We didn't have this program last year and people didn't care about their grades. There were no real consequences. This year it affects everything."

I: Are you learning more here? [Compared to the student's other middle school]

S: Yes. Here they challenge you more.

I: What do you mean?

S: There is no way you can fail and get away with it.

Or, as a teacher phrased the same idea, "We've made the invisible students visible." In fact, the tone of the schools had changed enough that one eighth grade student was prompted to advise her younger sibling:

My sister is in sixth grade here. I tell her that she's not focused enough on her schoolwork. She's got to be more responsible for her assignments and for asking for help when she needs it. That's what the teachers here expect.

However, it seemed students liked for their teachers to push them and give chances to them, in particular, but were not so generous with their underperforming peers. Like many adults, some students clearly felt that it was the responsibility of students to do the work and if they chose not to do it, then the consequence would be straightforward and simple—lower grades, less comprehension, and a higher risk of failure. Accurately reflecting a concern of many teachers, a student pointed out that "I don't like that kids can wait all year to make up their work because they can just mess around until the end."

For some students, *D*s, *E*s, *F*s, and zeroes had been solutions, not problems. For example, a student explained that he would rather have the choice of getting an E because, (a) he knew what he would get if he did not do his work—"I know if I don't do my work, I'll get an *E*"—instead of facing a continuous barrage of reminders and work sessions to make it up and, (b) by actually receiving a grade, even if it were an *E*, the student could still average it in with better grades and pass the class: "This is my opinion. I'd rather get an *E*. If you do get an *E*, at least you get a grade. And if you pass, you pass with whatever you get." Complaints surfaced about being penalized for having just one missing assignment: "I like the chance to make up work, but I hate that with all *A*s and *B*s an *I* can still make you fail." To be accurate, the student would not fail with an *I*, but would have to keep the *I* until the assignment was completed, but students regarded summer school as having failed.

Students with generally good grades sometimes chafed at teachers' insistence on completing all of their assignments. For example, a couple of *A* middle schoolers did poorly on a specific assignment, well below a *C*. However, averaging the lower grade in with their other results would not have affected their overall *A*, so they did not want to retake the test until they got a *C*. The teacher explained:

> I had two very good students in my class. They got 60s on an assignment. Even with the 60s, they were still carrying an *A*. I returned the assignment to them and told them they still had to get at least 70. "We have an *A* and you're making us do it again?" I said that everything has to be quality.

The students' parents stepped in and argued that there was no reason for them to go back and restudy the now past material. The teacher did not give in, much to the students' and parents' dismay, and said that since the tested content was deemed necessary to learn, it had to be learned at an acceptable level—by everyone.

Teachers realized, then, that if they were going to be instructionally stubborn and enforce the completion of all assignments, they needed to take a very careful look at what they were asking students to do and make sure that the work was worth doing in the first place.

We try to keep assessments at the level of higher order thinking. We've actually raised the bar because every kid is accountable for the benchmarks. What is the purpose of an assignment after all? To show that they attained the benchmarks.

Students picked up on the consequences: "The program makes teachers give better assignments because they don't want to fight with us about stupid things."

But being able to make up the work was not without its challenges for struggling students. As one student observed, teachers did not just put new work completely on hold, unless the whole class was struggling. Instead, some students had to juggle making up work while also trying to keep up with new work: "They give us lots of chances to make up work, but teachers still give new assignments, which makes it hard to catch up."

However, the dissenters often ended up realizing that what they said actually made the case for the program. For instance, one student grimaced somewhat shyly after saying: "Ms. M—is so mean. She expects us to do all the assignments and then to do them over if they're not good enough!" Likewise, another student recognized the potential good embedded in his criticism: "I don't like it because I am not that good in school and if I don't do well, I get an *I*. I have to redo my work and pass. . . . I guess it gives me a chance to do my work better."

It was unclear, to the interviewer at least, whether the following student saw the irony of her comment: "It works for some students, but not me because I do my work. It may not always be *C* quality but I'm fine with that and sometimes I just want to move on."

Ultimately, for every "I hate it" there was an "It makes you buckle down and finish things." Sometimes students made the point-counterpoint in the same answer: "I used to be a *C* student but now I am *A* and *B*. It helped me a lot. I try harder now. I try not to get *I*'s cause it's annoying and it's just better to do it right the first time." Taken together, the positive and negative reactions of students still underscored the central premise of ABCI: If allowed to fail, some students would. And that was the condition that prompted the schools to be so keen on using work completion as the primary academic lever.

Educators' Responses to Students' Reactions

The principles behind this idea and the appealing simplicity of not permitting failure made the program particularly attractive to adults, at least on an intellectual level. But students' less than wholehearted acceptance and their specific reactions prompted educators to make a host of adjustments that they did not anticipate having to make ahead of time.

For example, legitimate absences and procrastination together conspired to generate a plethora of *I*s. Students worried that they would never catch up and teachers became overwhelmed with all the attendant record keeping. Moreover, students were apparently going to resist *busy work* no matter how hard their teachers urged them to do it. Teachers obviously had to get a handle on which assignments were worth being graded.

This topic became the subject of much faculty discussion. As part of Middle Start, teachers had worked hard to form effectively functioning grade-level teams. During their common planning times, they kept each other informed about the number of *I*s that students were accumulating and discussed which interventions might work best. Noting the statistics prompted them to consider the relationship between assigned tasks and the emergence of *I*s. They discovered that one problem was the quantity of graded assign-

ments, and that many of these mostly reinforced desired skills, instead of instigating new learning or demonstrating proficiency. Only the latter two tasks, they reasoned, really needed to be graded. Reinforcement was tantamount to practice and whether a student had engaged in enough practice would be patently clear by their efforts on culminating tasks. This caused them to reclassify homework and much of the students' daily work as non-graded activities. An easy out? Teachers worried about this but, as several maintained, the change also put the burden on teachers to come up with meaningful ways of making sure that students could actually demonstrate skill mastery. At the time this article was written, teachers acknowledged that they still had a lot of work to do in this respect, but they felt that their foray into considering the quality of assignments—precipitated by students' reactions to their initial efforts—had put them on the path to improving instruction in significant ways.

Teachers also realized that they needed to put two types of interventions into place: extra time and alternative tasks for students who were struggling with comprehension, and annoyances like lunch study for students who did not need extra time but chose to put off doing something they were perfectly capable of completing on time. Giving good students the freedom to procrastinate—and watching them take advantage of it—was probably the most surprising and frustrating development, according to teachers.

Educators had to work even harder than the kids just to get students to do their work. This caused them to constantly question whether the results were worth the effort. Five years into the ABCI reform, however, teachers continued to answer in the affirmative and stridently reaffirmed that going back to blaming students and parents for poor performance and to failing scores of students each year was not what they wanted to do.

Ultimately, the program was, at its core, a way of thinking about schooling more than it was a set of practices to put into place, and it was an arduous task to manifest those thoughts in daily school life. Teachers did not go into ABCI imagining that doing so would force them to match wits with students. But it did. In hindsight, the educators realized that the program might work best if all participants, younger and older, started out as mutual advocates for change, rather than potential adversaries.

The nuanced comments of students showed that doing something for them will not succeed without also inviting them to be partners alongside the reformers. For example, some students readily blamed peers for their failure and thought it fair that they did so, just as many adults would. The teachers had spent a long time examining this issue and determined that they were not willing to accept the status quo. Students might well have benefited from having opportunities to foreshadow what was to come and to reconcile their beliefs ahead of time with those the program espoused. Indeed, had they been involved in early reform conversations, they might also have begun to take some ownership for its implementation. And, instead of having a good number of them trying to *game the system,* students might have done their part to see that things worked more smoothly.

Therein lies the real value of learning about students' perspectives on schooling. Fullan and Steigelbauer (1991) offered the stark assessment that "Unless they [students] have some meaningful role in the enterprise, most educational change, indeed most education, will fail" (p. 170). In light of what we have learned from students' reactions to a reform based on principles they valued in the first place (i.e., teachers who did not give up on them), just having adults work harder at putting a program into place will not be sufficient. Students need to be participants and not just beneficiaries of the reform. A critical piece of that involves listening carefully to their opinions and inviting them to be part of the process of modifying the reform in ways that take their perspectives seriously.

References

Bloom, B. S. (1971). Mastery learning. In J. H. Block (Ed.), *Mastery learning: Theory and practice* (pp. 47-63). New York: Holt, Rinehart, & Winston.

Corbett, D., Wilson, B., & Williams, B. (2005). No choice but success. *Educational Leadership, 62*(6), 8-13.

Fullan, M., & Stiegelbauer, S. (1991). *The new meaning of educational change* (2nd ed.). New York: Teachers College Press.

Wilson, B. L., & Corbett, H. D. (2001). *Listening to urban kids: School reform and the teachers they want.* Albany, NY: SUNY Press.

DICK CORBETT and BRUCE WILSON are independent educational researchers. Correspondence should be addressed to Bruce Wilson, 11 Linden Avenue, Merchantville, NJ 08109. E-mail: bruce.wilson8@verizon.net

ARTICLE 22

Taking Play Seriously

ROBIN MARANTZ HENIG

On a drizzly Tuesday night in late January, 200 people came out to hear a psychiatrist talk rhapsodically about play—not just the intense, joyous play of children, but play for all people, at all ages, at all times. (All species too; the lecture featured touching photos of a polar bear and a husky engaging playfully at a snowy outpost in northern Canada.) Stuart Brown, president of the National Institute for Play, was speaking at the New York Public Library's main branch on 42nd Street. He created the institute in 1996, after more than 20 years of psychiatric practice and research persuaded him of the dangerous long-term consequences of play deprivation. In a sold-out talk at the library, he and Krista Tippett, host of the public-radio program "Speaking of Faith," discussed the biological and spiritual underpinnings of play. Brown called play part of the "developmental sequencing of becoming a human primate. If you look at what produces learning and memory and well-being, play is as fundamental as any other aspect of life, including sleep and dreams."

The message seemed to resonate with audience members, who asked anxious questions about what seemed to be the loss of play in their children's lives. Their concern came, no doubt, from the recent deluge of eulogies to play. Educators fret that school officials are hacking away at recess to make room for an increasingly crammed curriculum. Psychologists complain that overscheduled kids have no time left for the real business of childhood: idle, creative, unstructured free play. Public health officials link insufficient playtime to a rise in childhood obesity. Parents bemoan the fact that kids don't play the way they themselves did—or think they did. And everyone seems to worry that without the chance to play stickball or hopscotch out on the street, to play with dolls on the kitchen floor or climb trees in the woods, today's children are missing out on something essential.

The success of "The Dangerous Book for Boys"—which has been on the best-seller list for the last nine months—and its step-by-step instructions for activities like folding paper airplanes is testament to the generalized longing for play's good old days. So were the questions after Stuart Brown's library talk; one woman asked how her children will learn trust, empathy and social skills when their most frequent playing is done online. Brown told her that while video games do have some play value, a true sense of "interpersonal nuance" can be achieved only by a child who is engaging all five senses by playing in the three-dimensional world.

This is part of a larger conversation Americans are having about play. Parents bobble between a nostalgia-infused yearning for their children to play and fear that time spent playing is time lost to more practical pursuits. Alarming headlines about U.S. students falling behind other countries in science and math, combined with the ever-more-intense competition to get kids into college, make parents rush to sign up their children for piano lessons and test-prep courses instead of just leaving them to improvise on their own; playtime versus résumé building.

Discussions about play force us to reckon with our underlying ideas about childhood, sex differences, creativity and success. Do boys play differently than girls? Are children being damaged by staring at computer screens and video games? Are they missing something when fantasy play is populated with characters from Hollywood's imagination and not their own? Most of these issues are too vast to be addressed by a single field of study (let alone a magazine article). But the growing science of play does have much to add to the conversation. Armed with research grounded in evolutionary biology and experimental neuroscience, some scientists have shown themselves eager—at times perhaps a little too eager—to promote a scientific argument for play. They have spent the past few decades learning how and why play evolved in animals, generating insights that can inform our understanding of its evolution in humans too. They are studying, from an evolutionary perspective, to what extent play is a luxury that can be dispensed with when there are too many other competing claims on the growing brain, and to what extent it is central to how that brain grows in the first place.

Scientists who study play, in animals and humans alike, are developing a consensus view that play is something more than a way for restless kids to work off steam; more than a way for chubby kids to burn off calories; more than a frivolous luxury. Play, in their view, is a central part of neurological growth and development—one important way that children build complex, skilled, responsive, socially adept and cognitively flexible brains.

Their work still leaves some questions unanswered, including questions about play's darker, more ambiguous side: is there really an evolutionary or developmental need for dangerous games, say, or for the meanness and hurt feelings that seem to attend so much child's play? Answering these and other ques-

tions could help us understand what might be lost if children play less.

"See how that little boy reaches for a pail?" Stuart Brown asked one morning last fall, standing with me on the fringes of a small playground just north of the Central Park Zoo. "See how he curves his whole body around it?" Brown had flown to New York from his home in California to pitch a book about play to publishers. (He sold the idea to an editor at Penguin.) He agreed to meet me at the zoo while he was in town, to help me observe playfulness in the young members of many animal species, including our own.

Social play has its own vocabulary. Dogs have a particular body posture called the "play bow"—forelegs extended, rump in the air—that they use as both invitation and punctuation. A dog will perform a play bow at the beginning of a bout, and he will crouch back into it if he accidentally nips too hard and wants to assure the other dog: "Don't worry! Still playing!"

Other species have play signals, too. Chimps put on a "play face," an open-mouthed expression that is almost like a face of aggression except that the muscles are relaxed into something like a smile. Baboons bend over and peer between their legs as an invitation to play, beavers roll around, goats gambol in a characteristic "play gait." In fact, most species have from 10 to 100 distinct play signals that they use to solicit play or to reassure one another during play-fighting that it's still all just in fun. In humans, the analogue to the chimp's play face is a child's smile, an open expression that indicates there is no real anger involved even in gestures that can look like a fight.

The day Brown met me in the park was a cold one, and the kids were bundled up like Michelin Men, adding more than the usual heft and waddle to their frolicking. Even beneath the padding, though, Brown could detect some typical gestures that these 2- and 3-year-olds were using instinctively to let one another know they were playing. "Play movement is curvilinear," he said. "If that boy was reaching for something in a nonplay situation, his body would be all straight lines. But using the body language of play, he curves and embraces."

In their play—climbing up a slide, running around, passing buckets back and forth—the kids we watched were engaging in a pattern of behavior that many scientists believe is hard-wired. Their mothers and nannies were watching, too, no doubt having dragged the kids out of comfortable Upper East Side apartments because they thought daily play was important somehow, perhaps the first step in the long march toward Yale. To me all that little-kid motion looked just a bit silly— because play is, in many ways, a silly thing. Indeed, an essential component of play is its frivolity; biologists generally use phrases like "apparently purposeless activity" in their definitions of play. The definition proposed by Gordon Burghardt, an evolutionary psychologist at the University of Tennessee, refines that phrase a little. In his 2005 book, "The Genesis of Animal Play," he wrote that play is an activity of "limited immediate function."

Burghardt included several other factors in his definition too. Play is an activity that is different from the nonplay version of that activity (in terms of form, sequence or the stage of life in which it occurs), is something the animal engages in voluntarily and repeatedly and occurs in a setting in which the animal is "adequately fed, healthy and free from stress." That last part of the definition—that play requires that an animal be stress-free and secure— suggests that play is the biological equivalent of a luxury item, the first thing to go when an animal or child is hungry or sick.

This makes evolutionary scientists prick up their ears. How can a behavior be crucial and expendable at the same time? And play is

indeed expendable. Studies of vervet monkeys found that playtime decreased to almost zero during periods of drought in East Africa. Squirrel monkeys won't play when their favorite food sources are unavailable. In humans under stress, what happens with play is more complicated. Even under devastating circumstances, the drive to play is unquenchable. As George Eisen wrote in "Children and Play in the Holocaust": "Children's yearning for play naturally burst forth even amidst the horror. . . . An instinctual, an almost atavistic impulse embedded in the human consciousness."

Yet play does diminish when children suffer long-term, chronic deprivation, either one at a time in abusive or neglectful homes, or on a massive scale in times of famine, war or forced relocation. And children can still survive, albeit imperfectly, without it.

For humans and animals alike, truly vigorous, wholehearted, spontaneous play is something of a biological frill. This suggests one possible evolutionary function: that in its playfulness, an animal displays its own abundant health and suitability for breeding. But a skeptic might see it differently: if a behavior is this easy to dispense with when times are hard, it might suggest that the behavior is less essential than some advocates claim.

If play is an extravagance, why has it persisted? It must have some adaptive function, or at least a benefit that outweighs its cost, or it would have been winnowed out by the forces of natural selection. One answer can be found through ethology, the study of animal behavior, which takes as one of its goals the explication of how and why a behavior evolved. Nonhuman animals can be more easily studied than humans can: the conditions under which they are raised can be manipulated, their brains altered and probed. And if there is an evolutionary explanation for a human behavior, it could reveal itself in the study of the analogous behavior in animals. Because of nature's basic parsimony, many aspects of the brain and behavior have been conserved through evolution, meaning that many of the observations that ethologists make in rats, mice and monkeys could apply to humans too.

When it comes to animal play, scientists basically agree that it's mostly mammals that do it, and they basically agree that it's a mystery why they do it, since there are so many good reasons not to. It all seems incredibly wasteful, and nature does not usually tolerate waste.

Play can be costly in terms of energy expenditure. Juveniles spend an estimated 2 to 15 percent of their daily calorie budget on play, using up calories the young animal could more profitably use for growing. Frisky playing can also be dangerous, making animals conspicuous and inattentive, more vulnerable to predators and more likely to hurt themselves as they romp and cavort. Biologists have observed many play-related calamities, like bighorn lambs being injured on cactus plants as they frolicked. One of the starkest measures of the risk of play was made by Robert Harcourt, a zoologist now at Macquarie University in Sydney, Australia, who spent nine months in 1988 observing seal pups off the coast of Peru. Harcourt witnessed 102 seal pups attacked by southern sea lions; 26 of them were killed. "Of these observed kills," Harcourt reported in the British journal *Animal Behaviour,* "22 of the pups were playing in the shallow tidal pools immediately before the attack and appeared to be oblivious to the other animals fleeing nearby." In other words, nearly 85 percent of the pups that were killed had been playing.

So play can be risky. And, under stress, it tends to disappear. What then would justify, in evolutionary terms, the prevalence of play?

One popular view is the play-as-preparation hypothesis. In this perspective, play evolved because it is good preparation for adulthood. It is a chance for young animals to learn and rehearse the skills they will need for the rest of their lives, and to do so in a secure environment, where mistakes will have few consequences. Proponents of this hypothesis say play is a way—and, not incidentally, a pleasurable way—of getting into muscle memory the generalized movements of survival: chasing, running, probing, tussling. Through play, these movements can be learned when the stakes are low and then retrieved in adulthood, when the setting is less safe and the need more urgent.

The play-as-preparation hypothesis seems logical, and each new observation seems to confirm it. Watch wolf pups at play, and it is easy to see how the biting and wrangling could be baby versions of the actions the pups will need later to assert their dominance or to help the pack kill its prey. Watch 2-year-olds playing at a toy workbench with little wooden mallets and blocks, and you can picture them as adults employing those same muscles to wield a full-size hammer.

But one trouble with the hypothesis is that the gestures of play, while similar, are not literally the same as the gestures of real life. In fact, the way an animal plays is often the exact opposite of the way it lives. In play-fighting, if one player starts to edge toward victory, he will suddenly reverse roles and move from the dominant to the submissive posture. Or he will stop fighting as hard, something the ethologists call self-handicapping. This is rarely done in real fighting, when the whole point is winning. The targets of play are different, too. In rats, real fighters try to bite one another on the back and the lower flanks; in play fights, they go for the nape of the neck. The gestures players use to nuzzle the neck are not the same ones they need to rehearse if they are to win a serious fight.

Nor is there much experimental evidence to support a connection between youthful playing and adult expertise. One Scottish study of kittens, for instance, tested the hypothesis that ample object play early in life would lead to better hunting later on. The investigator, a psychologist named T. M. Caro then at the University of St. Andrews, found no difference in hunting skills between one group of 11 cats that had been exposed to toys in their youth and a control group of 8 cats that had not.

Now an alternative view is taking hold, based on a belief that there must be something else going on—play not as a literal rehearsal, but as something less direct and ultimately more important. It focuses on the way that play might contribute to the growth and development of the brain.

John Byers started thinking about the brain and play almost by accident. A zoologist at the University of Idaho, Byers had spent years studying the playful antics of deer, pronghorn antelopes and the wild mountain goats called ibex. He knew that play was risky—he had observed ibex kids falling off steep cliffs as they romped—and at first he thought maybe the animals were taking such risks because the motor training helped them get in physical shape for adulthood. But something about this idea troubled him. Play can be exercise, he reasoned, but it was of too short duration to lead to long-term fitness or build muscle tone.

Byers preferred an alternate theory. In almost every species studied, a graph of playfulness looked like an inverted U, increasing during the juvenile period and then falling off around puberty, after which time most animals don't play much anymore. One winter afternoon in 1993, Byers was roaming the stacks at the University of Idaho library, flipping through books the way you do when you're not quite sure what you're looking for. One book contained a graph of the growth curve of one important region of the brain, the cerebellum, over the juvenile period in the mouse. The growth curve of the mouse

cerebellum was nearly identical to the curve of mouse playfulness.

"It was like a light went on in my head," Byers told me from Washington, D.C., where he is temporarily working at the National Science Foundation. "I wasn't thinking specifically about play, but I sort of had a long-term interest in behavioral development." And there it was: a chart that made it look as if rates of play in mice synchronized almost perfectly with growth rates in one critical region of the brain, the area that coordinates movements originating in other parts of the brain.

Intrigued, Byers enlisted the help of a graduate student, Curt Walker, who looked through the scientific literature on cerebellum development in rats and cats. "Then we compared those rates to what was known about the rates of play in those species," Byers said. "And rats and cats showed the same relationship as mice: a match between when they were playing and when the cerebellum was growing."

The synchrony suggested a few things to Byers: that play might be related to growth of the cerebellum, since they both peak at about the same time; that there is a sensitive period in brain growth, during which time it's important for an animal to get the brain-growth stimulation of play; and that the cerebellum needs the whole-body movements of play to achieve its ultimate configuration.

This opened up new lines of research, as neuroscientists tried to pinpoint just where in the brain play had its most prominent effects—which gets to the heart of the question of what might be lost when children do not get enough play. Most of this work has been done in rats. Sergio Pellis, a neuroscientist at the University of Lethbridge in Alberta, Canada, is one of these investigators. He studies how brain damage in rats affects play behavior, and whether the relationship works in reverse: that is, not only whether brain-damaged rats play abnormally but also whether play-deprived rats develop abnormalities in their brains. Pellis's research indicates that the relationship might indeed work in both directions.

In a set of experiments conducted last year, Pellis and his colleagues raised 12 female rats from the time they were weaned until puberty under one of two conditions. In the control group, each rat was caged with three other female juveniles. In the experimental group, each rat was caged with three female adults. Pellis knew from previous studies that the rats caged with adults would not play, since adult rats rarely play with juveniles, even their own offspring. They would get all the other normal social experiences the control rats had—grooming, nuzzling, touching, sniffing—but they would not get play. His hypothesis was that the brains in the experimental rats would reflect their play-deprived youth, especially in the region known as the prefrontal cortex.

At puberty the rats were euthanized so the scientists could look at their brains. What Pellis and his collaborators found was the first direct evidence of a neurological effect of play deprivation. In the experimental group—the rats raised in a play-deprived environment—they found a more immature pattern of neuronal connections in the medial prefrontal cortex. (This is distant from the cerebellum; it is part of the cerebrum, which constitutes the bulk of the mammalian brain.) Rats, like other mammals, are born with an overabundance of cortical brain cells; as the animal matures, feedback from the environment leads to the pruning and selective elimination of these excess cells, branchings and connections. Play is thought to be one of the environmental influences that help in the pruning—and, this research showed, play deprivation interferes with it.

Figuring out what these findings mean in terms of function involves a certain amount of conjecture. Pellis interprets his observation of a more tangled, immature medial prefrontal cortex in play-deprived rats to mean that the rat will be less able to make subtle adjustments to the social world. But maybe the necessary pruning can happen later in life, through other feedback mechanisms having little to do with play. Maybe there were already compensatory changes happening elsewhere in the brains of these young rats where no one had thought to look. Current research in Pellis's lab, in which the brain is damaged first and the rat's playing ability is measured afterward, seems to confirm that the medial prefrontal cortex has an important role in play. But the exact nature of its action is still not clear.

Many of the other important studies on play and the brain have come from the lab of Jaak Panksepp, a behavioral neuroscientist who trained most of the neurological investigators in the field during the three decades he was at Bowling Green State University in Ohio (though Pellis, who studied at Australia's Monash University, was not among them). In the 1980s, Panksepp and a graduate student, Stephen Siviy, located the play drive in the thalamus, a primitive region of the brain that receives sensory information and relays it to the cortex. More recently, Panksepp has been exploring the connections among the play drive and certain human conditions, in particular attention deficit hyperactivity disorder (A.D.H.D.).

Panksepp has been studying A.D.H.D. in rats since the 1990s. In one experiment, to create a rat model of A.D.H.D., he and his colleagues took 32 newborn rats and destroyed in each the right frontal cortex, the region of the brain responsible for paying attention, planning ahead and being sensitive to social cues. (Human studies have shown that in children with A.D.H.D., frontal-lobe development is often delayed.) As a control, they performed sham surgery on 32 other rats, making the incisions but leaving the brain intact to be sure that any observed change would be due to the cortical destruction rather than the surgery itself. When the scientists compared the play behavior of the two groups, they found that the rats with the damaged right frontal cortex had higher levels of overall activity, as well as increased rates of rough-and-tumble play, as compared with the controls. The rats with damaged frontal cortices behaved much like children described as hyperactive.

Panksepp and his colleagues then exposed these superplayers to extra opportunities for play. One extra hour a day of play, which generally took the form of play-fighting during a critical early stage, sufficed to reduce hyperactivity. The scientists thought similar play therapy might work for children with A.D.H.D., particularly if it was undertaken in early childhood—between ages 3 and 7—when the urges are "especially insistent."

Panksepp's current view of human A.D.H.D., he told me from his office at Washington State University, where he moved two years ago, is that it is in part "overactivity of play urges in the nervous system." His ideas have made some impression on the human A.D.H.D. community, but not much. Benedetto Vitiello, the head of child and adolescent treatment and research at the National Institute of Mental Health, remembers hearing Panksepp give a talk at the institute around the time his article appeared in 2003. But he said he has not heard of any clinical studies since then that investigate whether extra play in early childhood helps ease the symptoms of A.D.H.D. Besides, Vitiello adds, there are many differences between a rat with a brain injury and a child with an intact but slowly developing brain. So even though he considers Panksepp's research "interesting," he says that it has not quite led to a complete animal model of A.D.H.D.

Animal-play experiments have focused largely on the most vivid form of play—social play, in particular the kind of social play known as play-fighting. But it's clear to anyone who thinks about it that play-fighting is a very narrow definition of play. Wrestling is not the same as chasing. For that matter, playing tag is not the same as playing dress up; playing in a soccer league is not the same as shooting hoops in a neighborhood park; and none of these are the same as playing Scrabble or Uno or video games. For all its variety, however, there is something common to play in all its protean forms: variety itself. The essence of play is that the sequence of actions is fluid and scattered. In the words of Marc Bekoff, an evolutionary biologist at the University of Colorado, play is at its core "a behavioral kaleidoscope."

In fact, it's this kaleidoscopic quality that led Bekoff and others to think of play as the best way for a young animal to gain a more diverse and responsive behavioral repertory. Thus, the currently fashionable flexibility hypothesis, a revival of an idea Bekoff first proposed in the 1970s. If a single function can be ascribed to every form of play, in every playful species, according to this way of thinking, it is that play contributes to the growth of more supple, more flexible brains.

"I think of play as training for the unexpected," Bekoff says. "Behavioral flexibility and variability is adaptive; in animals it's really important to be able to change your behavior in a changing environment." Play, he says, leads to mental suppleness and a broader behavioral vocabulary, which in turn helps the animal achieve success in the ways that matter: group dominance, mate selection, avoiding capture and finding food.

The flexibility hypothesis is something of a bridge between the play-as-preparation hypothesis and more recent findings about play and neurological growth. It works best when explaining play-fighting. With its variable tempo, self-handicapping and role reversals, play-fighting is like the improvisation of a jazz quartet, forcing an animal to respond rapidly to change.

Players riff off one another. One thrusts, the other parries; suddenly the one that was on top is pinned on the bottom and then just as suddenly is on top again. As in jazz, the smoothness of the improvisation matters as much as the gestures themselves. "Ability to use and switch among alternative sequences," Maxeen Biben, an ethologist formerly at the National Institutes of Health, wrote in an essay in "Animal Play," "may be as valuable as getting a lot of practice at the most effective sequences."

The physical movements of playfighting provide the environmental input needed to prune the developing cortex, as Sergio Pellis's research suggested. This pruning is one way an animal achieves the ability to predict and respond to another animal's shifting movements. Some play scholars say that such skills will come in handy in adulthood, not only in fighting but in other real-life situations as well, like evading capture and finding food. A more skeptical view would be that play-fighting might not really teach much at all about an animal's subsequent skills—there was that Scottish study about object play in kittens, remember, that showed no connection to hunting ability in adulthood—but it does one thing for sure: it makes the animal that play-fights a better play-fighter. And there might be something to be said for that. The more a young animal plays, the richer the animal's life, the more fun, the more stimulated, the more social. There might possibly be an immediate benefit just from that simple fact.

Which reveals an important rift in the study of the purpose of play: a debate among play scholars about how to tell the story of play's possible short-term and long-term bene-

fits. The flexibility hypothesis imposes one such story, but it might not be the best story. Just because it's possible to see how playing might contribute to a suppler brain and a more varied behavioral repertoire, it does not follow that playing is the only way to achieve such flexibility. This relates to the concept of equifinality, an idea from systems theory that says there are usually more ways than one to arrive at a particular end. The fact that play offers one way of getting to an end need not mean it is the only way—nor need it mean that getting to that end is the ultimate purpose of play.

The problem of equifinality troubled Anthony Pellegrini, a psychologist at the University of Minnesota, when he tried to interpret his findings about rough-and-tumble play in fifth-grade boys. He and his colleagues studied the recess behavior of 37 boys and scored a play episode as rough-and-tumble when a boy engaged in one from a list of behaviors—"tease, hit and kick at, chase, poke, pounce, sneak up, carry child, pile on, play-fight, hold and push"—while displaying a wide smile or "play face." Knowing that earlier studies found a connection between rough-and-tumble play and a child's peer affiliation and social problem-solving flexibility, the scientists hypothesized that the most vigorous players would also be the most socially competent. But Pellegrini found no clear benefits in the boys who played the most. Maybe, he wrote in an essay about this research in "The Future of Play Theory," it's because other things that happen at recess—"cooperative social games, comfort contact and conversation"—might be just as good as pouncing or chasing at achieving a sense of connection.

"Developmental systems tend to be highly redundant," wrote Patrick Bateson, a noted biologist at Cambridge University, in a book of essays called "The Nature of Play." This means, Bateson wrote, "that if an endpoint is not achieved by one route, it is achieved by another. Playing when young is not the only way to acquire knowledge and skills; the animal can delay acquisition until it is an adult."

Nonetheless, even Bateson, a prominent play scholar who recognizes the quandary posed by equifinality, suggested that play is the best way to reach certain goals. Through play, an individual avoids what he called the lure of "false endpoints," a problem-solving style more typical of harried adults than of playful youngsters. False endpoints are avoided through play, Bateson wrote, because players are having so much fun that they keep noodling away at a problem and might well arrive at something better than the first, good-enough solution.

But maybe the flexibility hypothesis is itself a false endpoint. Maybe the idea that play is the best route to a whole host of good results—creativity, social agility, overall mental suppleness—is just the first idea scientists landed on, and they were inclined to accept it because it fit so well with their innate ideas about the nature of childhood. This is the view of a small group of play scholars we'll call the play skeptics. What worries the play skeptics is that most people in the industrialized West—scientists in the field, play advocates and all the rest of us, parents, teachers, doctors, scholars, all the children and all the aging children—have been ensnared by what skeptics call the "play ethos." By this they mean the reflexive, unexamined belief that play is an unmitigated good with a crucial, though vaguely defined, evolutionary function.

"Play ethos" comes from Peter Smith, a psychology professor at the University of London and a leading authority on play's effect on children's emotional development. He uses it as a cautionary term, a reminder that most conclusions about play's adaptive function have so far been based not on scientific evidence but on wishful thinking.

For Smith to suggest that scientists have fallen under the spell of the play ethos is a kind of apostasy, because some of the earliest bits of evidence used to establish the play ethos in the first place came out of Smith's own laboratory at the University of London in the late 1970s. But it was in the execution of those experiments, and the follow-up studies that revealed their fatal flaw, that Smith came to understand, more than most, the importance of caution.

In one of his early experiments, Smith and his colleagues put 3- and 4-year-olds in two different play settings. In one group the children were allowed to play, in whatever way they felt like, with several wooden sticks. In the other group they were shown by an adult "play tutor" how to fit two sticks together to make a longer one. Then the children were given two tasks. First they had to retrieve a marble by connecting two sticks. Both groups performed this task, which Smith called "direct" problem solving, about equally well. Then they had to retrieve a marble that had been pushed farther away, so they could reach it only by connecting three sticks, not just two—what Smith called "innovative" problem solving. The children who had played with the sticks performed this task significantly better than the ones who had been shown how to join together only two sticks.

"At this point I was happy," Smith recalled years later, writing in "The Future of Play Theory." His findings were taken as evidence that spontaneous free play led to more creative thinking. But then he started to wonder whether he himself had fallen victim to the play ethos.

A single investigator had conducted the entire experiment, serving as both play tutor and evaluator on the problem-solving task. Might the experimenter subconsciously have favored the free-play children, Smith asked himself, maybe by giving subtle nonverbal cues or scoring more leniently? He ran the experiment again, bringing in a second investigator who could test the children without knowing whether they were in the free-play or the tutored group.

This time Smith found no difference in innovative problem solving between the two groups. At first he didn't believe his new results, thinking that maybe the sample size was too small or that the groups were somehow poorly matched. But further studies bore out this nonfinding, and Smith realized, on reflection, that he and his colleagues had probably been giving inadvertent hints to the free-play group the first time around. He ascribed it to his own subconscious idealization of play.

Idealization is a trap. And it seems most seductive when it comes to play, especially one particular kind: pretend play. This is the kind ethologists tend to ignore, since it is difficult to argue—though a few scientists have tried—that animals are capable of pretending. Yet for humans, pretend play is one of the most crucial forms of play, occupying at its peak at about age 4 some 20 percent of a child's day. It includes some of the most wondrous moments of childhood: dramatic play, wordplay, ritual play, symbolic play, games, jokes and imaginary friends. And it is the kind of play that positively screams out for hyperbole when outsiders try to describe it. This is where even coolheaded scientists get florid in their prose—and where play advocates like Stuart Brown and play skeptics like Peter Smith engage in their most vivid disagreements about the ultimate purpose of play.

Brown talked about pretend play at the New York Public Library last month, saying that a playful imagination "can infuse the moment with a sense of magic." But skeptics find such comments annoying. "Despite the heartwarming rhetoric we dish out in our teacher-training classes, children do *not* have unlimited imagination," wrote David Lancy, an anthropologist at Utah State University. "Their make-believe and, by extension, other play forms, is constrained by the roles, scripts and props of the culture they live in." Lancy pointed to field studies of a Mayan community in which children teach their younger siblings how to pretend in the most pedestrian of ways, "focusing their attention on washing, caring for babies and cooking"—no magic there.

The skeptical Smith does see some value to fantasy play: when children dress up, make and use props and devise story lines to playact, he says, they learn to use sophisticated language, negotiate roles and exchange information. But he adds that many of these benefits could be gained just as well through other forms of play, work activities and plain old-fashioned instruction. Smith does not deny that playing is great fun—his own children were playing noisily in the background when I phoned him at his home in London, and he never once asked them to hush—but he wants everyone to keep it all in perspective.

Keeping play in perspective means looking at it not just clearly but fully. Not everything about childhood play is sweetness and light, no matter how much we romanticize it. Play can be dangerous or scary. It can be disturbing, destabilizing, aggressive. It can lead to misunderstandings and hurt feelings, leaving children out of the charmed circle of the schoolyard. The other side of playing is teasing, bullying, scapegoating, excluding, hurting.

I well remember this darker side of play from my own girlhood. Like many other klutzy kids, I hated recess, since it stripped me of the classroom competence that was such good cover for my shyness. Out in the schoolyard, there was no raising your hand with the right answer. I had to wait to be asked to play jumprope and had to face embarrassment if I missed a skip or—worse, much worse—if nobody ended up asking me. Even pretend play could take an ugly turn if my playmates made their dolls say nasty things.

Recognizing play's dark side is not difficult, if we are really willing to search our memories. To play scholars, thinking about play's negatives can be clarifying and might even generate new ideas, not only about play but also about the double-edged nature of pleasure itself. Why is it that something so joyous, something children yearn for so forcefully, can be so troubling too? If you're accustomed to looking for evolutionary explanations for perplexing behavior, here is something meaty to chew on: what could be the adaptive advantage of using play to wrestle your demons?

Demons do indeed emerge at playtime, in part because children carve out play spaces that have no room for the civilizing influence of adults. This is what happened in the recess "fort culture" that arose spontaneously in 1990 at the Lexington Montessori School in Massachusetts, when the elementary-age children shunned the organized play their teachers had arranged and instead started building forts on their own in the surrounding woods. An intricate and rule-bound subculture developed, one that is still going on.

Mark Powell, then a graduate student at Lesley University in Cambridge nearby, observed the recess fort culture for several years in the 1990s and described it in 2007 in the journal Children, Youth and Environments. For the first few years, he wrote, petty conflicts, stick stealing and ejections for minor infractions were a constant background hum in a play culture that was otherwise high-spirited and fun. But it finally erupted into a miniwar one autumn, sparked by the hostile actions of a fort of 6-year-olds headed by a tyrannical little boy who called himself the General. Within a month of the General's appearance, Powell wrote, the fantasy war play "had become a reality with daily raids and counterattacks, yelling, the occasional physical scrape and lots of hurt feelings." It took the intervention of some other children, teachers and the General's parents finally to persuade the child to call a truce.

Brian Sutton-Smith, one of the nation's most eminent play scholars, has seen eruptions like the General's many times before, but they don't worry him. In fact, he embraces them. In such an elaborate play culture, he wrote, where so many harsh human truths come to the fore, "children learn all those necessary arts of trickery, deception, harassment, divination and foul play that their teachers won't teach them but are most important in successful human relationships in marriage, business and war."

Sutton-Smith's 1997 classic, "The Ambiguity of Play," reflects in its title his belief that play's ultimate purpose can be found in its paradoxes. During his years at Columbia's Teachers College and the University of Pennsylvania, Sutton-Smith, a psychologist and folklorist, took careful note of how play could be destabilizing, destructive or disturbing. He collected renditions of the stories children told in their imaginative or dramatic play, stories of "being lost, being stolen, being bitten, dying, being stepped on, being angry, calling the police, running away or falling down." Are these really the thoughts percolating inside our children? And is expressing these thoughts through play somehow good for them? Sutton-Smith called this underbelly of imaginative play part of the "phantasmagoria," where children's thoughts run wild and all the chaotic bits of the real world get tumbled together and pulled haphazardly apart in new, sometimes even scarier confabulations.

Why would such an enriching activity as play also be a source of so much anarchy and fear? Sutton-Smith found one possible answer by reading Stephen Jay Gould, the author and evolutionary biologist. The most highly adaptive organisms, Gould wrote, are those that embody both the positive and the negative, organisms that "possess an opposite set of attributes usually devalued in our culture: sloppiness, broad potential, quirkiness, unpredictability and, above all, massive redundancy."

Finely tuned specific adaptations can lead to blind alleys and extinction, he wrote; "the key is flexibility."

What Gould called quirkiness, Sutton-Smith called play. "Animal play has been described by many investigators as fragmentary, disorderly, unpredictable and exaggerated," Sutton-Smith wrote, and "child play has been said to be improvised, vertiginous and nonsensical." The adaptive advantage to a behavior that is multifaceted, then, is that pursuing it, enjoying it, needing it to get through the day, allows for a wider range in a play-loving person's behavioral repertoire, which is always handy, just in case.

Playing might serve a different evolutionary function too, he suggests: it helps us face our existential dread. The individual most likely to prevail is the one who believes in possibilities—an optimist, a creative thinker, a person who has a sense of power and control. Imaginative play, even when it involves mucking around in the phantasmagoria, creates such a person. "The adaptive advantage has often gone to those who ventured upon their possibility with cries of exultant commitment," Sutton-Smith wrote. "What is adaptive about play, therefore, may be not only the skills that are a part of it but also the willful belief in acting out one's own capacity for the future."

It's a pretty idea, the notion that play gives you hope for a better tomorrow, but science demands something a little less squishy. Science demands that if there are important long-term benefits to play, they must be demonstrated. That is why studies of play-deprived rats are so fascinating; they offer objective evidence that in at least some animals, insufficient play can have serious consequences.

Even when science suggests certain answers, however, it cannot easily make the leap from young rats to young humans, nor tell us much of anything about how those young children should behave. What if all the things we hope children derive from free play—cognitive flexibility, social competence, creative problem-solving, mastery of their own bodies and their own environments—can be learned just as well by teaching these skills directly? What if the only clear advantage to the vanishing 20-minute recess is that it makes kids less restless in class, something that can be just as easily accomplished by a jog around the all-purpose room?

Which brings us back to wondering what would be lost if the Cassandras are right, whether children would suffer if free play really does turn out to be a thing of the past. It seems almost ludicrous to ask such a question. Of course play is good for something; it is the essence of good. Watch children at play, and the benefits are so obvious: just look at those ecstatic faces, just listen to those joyful squeals. Stuart Brown alluded to it in his library talk last month. "Look at life without play, and it's not much of a life," he told the audience. "If you think of all the things we do that are playrelated and erase those, it's pretty hard to keep going." Without play, he said, "there's a sense of dullness, lassitude and pessimism, which doesn't work well in the world we live in."

In the end, it comes down to a matter of trade-offs. There are only six hours in a school day, only another six or so till bedtime, and adults are forever trying to cram those hours with activities that are productive, educational and (almost as an afterthought) fun. Animal findings about how play influences brain growth suggest that playing, though it might look silly and purposeless, warrants a place in every child's day. Not too overblown a place, not too sanctimonious a place, but a place that embraces all styles of play and that recognizes play as every bit as essential to healthful neurological development as test-taking drills, Spanish lessons or Suzuki violin.

ARTICLE 23

The Moral Instinct

STEVEN PINKER

Which of the following people would you say is the most admirable: Mother Teresa, Bill Gates or Norman Borlaug? And which do you think is the least admirable? For most people, it's an easy question. Mother Teresa, famous for ministering to the poor in Calcutta, has been beatified by the Vatican, awarded the Nobel Peace Prize and ranked in an American poll as the most admired person of the 20th century. Bill Gates, infamous for giving us the Microsoft dancing paper clip and the blue screen of death, has been decapitated in effigy in "I Hate Gates" Web sites and hit with a pie in the face. As for Norman Borlaug . . . who the heck is Norman Borlaug?

Yet a deeper look might lead you to rethink your answers. Borlaug, father of the "Green Revolution" that used agricultural science to reduce world hunger, has been credited with saving a billion lives, more than anyone else in history. Gates, in deciding what to do with his fortune, crunched the numbers and determined that he could alleviate the most misery by fighting everyday scourges in the developing world like malaria, diarrhea and parasites. Mother Teresa, for her part, extolled the virtue of suffering and ran her well-financed missions accordingly: their sick patrons were offered plenty of prayer but harsh conditions, few analgesics and dangerously primitive medical care.

It's not hard to see why the moral reputations of this trio should be so out of line with the good they have done. Mother Teresa was the very embodiment of saintliness: white-clad, sad-eyed, ascetic and often photographed with the wretched of the earth. Gates is a nerd's nerd and the world's richest man, as likely to enter heaven as the proverbial camel squeezing through the needle's eye. And Borlaug, now 93, is an agronomist who has spent his life in labs and nonprofits, seldom walking onto the media stage, and hence into our consciousness, at all.

I doubt these examples will persuade anyone to favor Bill Gates over Mother Teresa for sainthood. But they show that our heads can be turned by an aura of sanctity, distracting us from a more objective reckoning of the actions that make people suffer or flourish. It seems we may all be vulnerable to moral illusions the ethical equivalent of the bending lines that trick the eye on cereal boxes and in psychology textbooks. Illusions are a favorite tool of perception scientists for exposing the workings of the five senses, and of philosophers for shaking people out of the naïve belief that our minds give us a transparent window onto the world (since if our eyes can be fooled by an illusion, why should we trust them at other times?). Today, a new field is using illusions to unmask a sixth sense, the moral sense. Moral intuitions are being drawn out of people in the lab, on Web sites and in brain scanners, and are being explained with tools from game theory, neuroscience and evolutionary biology.

"Two things fill the mind with ever new and increasing admiration and awe, the oftener and more steadily we reflect on them," wrote Immanuel Kant, "the starry heavens above and the moral law within." These days, the moral law within is being viewed with increasing awe, if not always admiration. The human moral sense turns out to be an organ of considerable complexity, with quirks that reflect its evolutionary history and its neuro-biological foundations.

These quirks are bound to have implications for the human predicament. Morality is not just any old topic in psychology but close to our conception of the meaning of life. Moral goodness is what gives each of us the sense that we are worthy human beings. We seek it in our friends and mates, nurture it in our children, advance it in our politics and justify it with our religions. A disrespect for morality is blamed for everyday sins and history's worst atrocities. To carry this weight, the concept of morality would have to be bigger than any of us and outside all of us.

So dissecting moral intuitions is no small matter. If morality is a mere trick of the brain, some may fear, our very grounds for being moral could be eroded. Yet as we shall see, the science of the moral sense can instead be seen as a way to strengthen those grounds, by clarifying what morality is and how it should steer our actions.

The Moralization Switch

The starting point for appreciating that there *is* a distinctive part of our psychology for morality is seeing how moral judgments differ from other kinds of opinions we have on how people ought to behave. Moralization is a psychological state that can be turned on and off like a switch, and when it is on, a distinctive mind-set commandeers our thinking. This is the mind-set that makes us deem actions immoral ("killing is wrong"), rather than merely disagreeable ("I hate brussels sprouts"), unfashionable ("bell-bottoms are out") or imprudent ("don't scratch mosquito bites").

The first hallmark of moralization is that the rules it invokes are felt to be universal. Prohibitions of rape and murder, for example, are felt not to be matters of local custom but to be universally and objectively warranted. One can easily say, "I don't like brussels sprouts, but I don't care if you eat them," but no one would say, "I don't like killing, but I don't care if you murder someone."

The other hallmark is that people feel that those who commit immoral acts deserve to be punished. Not only is it allowable to inflict pain on a person who has broken a moral rule; it is wrong *not* to, to "let them get away with it." People are thus untroubled in inviting divine retribution or the power of the state to harm other people they deem immoral. Bertrand Russell wrote, "The infliction of cruelty with a good conscience is a delight to moralists—that is why they invented hell."

We all know what it feels like when the moralization switch flips inside us—the righteous glow, the burning dudgeon, the drive to recruit others to the cause. The psychologist Paul Rozin has studied the toggle switch by comparing two kinds of people who engage in the same behavior but with different switch settings. Health vegetarians avoid meat for practical reasons, like lowering cholesterol and avoiding toxins. Moral vegetarians avoid meat for ethical reasons: to avoid complicity in the suffering of animals. By investigating their feelings about meat-eating, Rozin showed that the moral motive sets off a cascade of opinions. Moral vegetarians are more likely to treat meat as a contaminant—they refuse, for example, to eat a bowl of soup into which a drop of beef broth has fallen. They are more likely to think that other people ought to be vegetarians, and are more likely to imbue their dietary habits with other virtues, like believing that meat avoidance makes people less aggressive and bestial.

Much of our recent social history, including the culture wars between liberals and conservatives, consists of the moralization or amoralization of particular kinds of behavior. Even when people agree that an outcome is desirable, they may disagree on whether it should be treated as a matter of preference and prudence or as a matter of sin and virtue. Rozin notes, for example, that smoking has lately been moralized. Until recently, it was understood that some people didn't enjoy smoking or avoided it because it was hazardous to their health. But with the discovery of the harmful effects of secondhand smoke, smoking is now treated as immoral. Smokers are ostracized; images of people smoking are censored; and entities touched by smoke are felt to be contaminated (so hotels have not only nonsmoking rooms but nonsmoking *floors*). The desire for retribution has been visited on tobacco companies, who have been slapped with staggering "punitive damages."

At the same time, many behaviors have been amoralized, switched from moral failings to lifestyle choices. They include divorce, illegitimacy, being a working mother, marijuana use and homosexuality. Many afflictions have been reassigned from payback for bad choices to unlucky misfortunes. There used to be people called "bums" and "tramps"; today they are "homeless." Drug addiction is a "disease"; syphilis was rebranded from the price of wanton behavior to a "sexually transmitted disease" and more recently a "sexually transmitted infection."

This wave of amoralization has led the cultural right to lament that morality itself is under assault, as we see in the group that anointed itself the Moral Majority. In fact there seems to be a Law of Conservation of Moralization, so that as old behaviors are taken out of the moralized column, new ones are added to it. Dozens of things that past generations treated as practical matters are now ethical battlegrounds, including disposable diapers, I.Q. tests, poultry farms, Barbie dolls and research on breast cancer. Food alone has become a minefield, with critics sermonizing about the size of sodas, the chemistry of fat, the freedom of chickens, the price of coffee beans, the species of fish and now the distance the food has traveled from farm to plate.

Many of these moralizations, like the assault on smoking, may be understood as practical tactics to reduce some recently identified harm. But whether an activity flips our mental switches to the "moral" setting isn't just a matter of how much harm it does. We don't show contempt to the man who fails to change the batteries in his smoke alarms or takes his family on a driving vacation, both of which multiply the risk they will die in an accident. Driving a gas-guzzling Hummer is reprehensible, but driving a gas-guzzling old Volvo is not; eating a Big Mac is unconscionable, but not imported cheese or crème brûlée. The reason for these double standards is obvious: people tend to align their moralization with their own lifestyles.

Reasoning and Rationalizing

It's not just the content of our moral judgments that is often questionable, but the way we arrive at them. We like to think that when we have a conviction, there are good reasons that drove us to adopt it. That is why an older approach to moral psychology, led by Jean Piaget and Lawrence Kohlberg, tried to document the lines of reasoning that guided people to moral conclusions. But consider these situations, originally devised by the psychologist Jonathan Haidt:

> Julie is traveling in France on summer vacation from college with her brother Mark. One night they decide that it would be interesting and fun if they tried making love. Julie was already taking

birth-control pills, but Mark uses a condom, too, just to be safe. They both enjoy the sex but decide not to do it again. They keep the night as a special secret, which makes them feel closer to each other. What do you think about that—was it O.K. for them to make love?

A woman is cleaning out her closet and she finds her old American flag. She doesn't want the flag anymore, so she cuts it up into pieces and uses the rags to clean her bathroom.

A family's dog is killed by a car in front of their house. They heard that dog meat was delicious, so they cut up the dog's body and cook it and eat it for dinner.

Most people immediately declare that these acts are wrong and then grope to justify *why* they are wrong. It's not so easy. In the case of Julie and Mark, people raise the possibility of children with birth defects, but they are reminded that the couple were diligent about contraception. They suggest that the siblings will be emotionally hurt, but the story makes it clear that they weren't. They submit that the act would offend the community, but then recall that it was kept a secret. Eventually many people admit, "I don't know, I can't explain it, I just know it's wrong." People don't generally engage in moral reasoning, Haidt argues, but moral *rationalization*: they begin with the conclusion, coughed up by an unconscious emotion, and then work backward to a plausible justification.

The gap between people's convictions and their justifications is also on display in the favorite new sandbox for moral psychologists, a thought experiment devised by the philosophers Philippa Foot and Judith Jarvis Thomson called the Trolley Problem. On your morning walk, you see a trolley car hurtling down the track, the conductor slumped over the controls. In the path of the trolley are five

men working on the track, oblivious to the danger. You are standing at a fork in the track and can pull a lever that will divert the trolley onto a spur, saving the five men. Unfortunately, the trolley would then run over a single worker who is laboring on the spur. Is it permissible to throw the switch, killing one man to save five? Almost everyone says "yes."

Consider now a different scene. You are on a bridge overlooking the tracks and have spotted the runaway trolley bearing down on the five workers. Now the only way to stop the trolley is to throw a heavy object in its path. And the only heavy object within reach is a fat man standing next to you. Should you throw the man off the bridge? Both dilemmas present you with the option of sacrificing one life to save five, and so, by the utilitarian standard of what would result in the greatest good for the greatest number, the two dilemmas are morally equivalent. But most people don't see it that way: though they would pull the switch in the first dilemma, they would not heave the fat man in the second. When pressed for a reason, they can't come up with anything coherent, though moral philosophers haven't had an easy time coming up with a relevant difference, either.

When psychologists say "most people" they usually mean "most of the two dozen sophomores who filled out a questionnaire for beer money." But in this case it means most of the 200,000 people from a hundred countries who shared their intuitions on a Web-based experiment conducted by the psychologists Fiery Cushman and Liane Young and the biologist Marc Hauser. A difference between the acceptability of switch-pulling and man-heaving, and an inability to justify the choice, was found in respondents from Europe, Asia and North and South America; among men and women, blacks and whites, teenagers and octogenarians, Hindus, Muslims, Buddhists, Christians, Jews and atheists; people with elementary-school educations and people with Ph.D.'s.

176

Joshua Greene, a philosopher and cognitive neuroscientist, suggests that evolution equipped people with a revulsion to manhandling an innocent person. This instinct, he suggests, tends to overwhelm any utilitarian calculus that would tot up the lives saved and lost. The impulse against roughing up a fellow human would explain other examples in which people abjure killing one to save many, like euthanizing a hospital patient to harvest his organs and save five dying patients in need of transplants, or throwing someone out of a crowded lifeboat to keep it afloat.

By itself this would be no more than a plausible story, but Greene teamed up with the cognitive neuroscientist Jonathan Cohen and several Princeton colleagues to peer into people's brains using functional M.R.I. They sought to find signs of a conflict between brain areas associated with emotion (the ones that recoil from harming someone) and areas dedicated to rational analysis (the ones that calculate lives lost and saved).

When people pondered the dilemmas that required killing someone with their bare hands, several networks in their brains lighted up. One, which included the medial (inward-facing) parts of the frontal lobes, has been implicated in emotions about other people. A second, the dorsolateral (upper and outer-facing) surface of the frontal lobes, has been implicated in ongoing mental computation (including nonmoral reasoning, like deciding whether to get somewhere by plane or train). And a third region, the anterior cingulate cortex (an evolutionarily ancient strip lying at the base of the inner surface of each cerebral hemisphere), registers a conflict between an urge coming from one part of the brain and an advisory coming from another.

But when the people were pondering a hands-off dilemma, like switching the trolley onto the spur with the single worker, the brain reacted differently: only the area involved in rational calculation stood out. Other studies have shown that neurological patients who have blunted emotions because of damage to the frontal lobes become utilitarians: they think it makes perfect sense to throw the fat man off the bridge. Together, the findings corroborate Greene's theory that our nonutilitarian intuitions come from the victory of an emotional impulse over a cost-benefit analysis.

A Universal Morality?

The findings of trolleyology—complex, instinctive and worldwide moral intuitions—led Hauser and John Mikhail (a legal scholar) to revive an analogy from the philosopher John Rawls between the moral sense and language. According to Noam Chomsky, we are born with a "universal grammar" that forces us to analyze speech in terms of its grammatical structure, with no conscious awareness of the rules in play. By analogy, we are born with a universal moral grammar that forces us to analyze human action in terms of its moral structure, with just as little awareness.

The idea that the moral sense is an innate part of human nature is not far-fetched. A list of human universals collected by the anthropologist Donald E. Brown includes many moral concepts and emotions, including a distinction between right and wrong; empathy; fairness; admiration of generosity; rights and obligations; proscription of murder, rape and other forms of violence; redress of wrongs; sanctions for wrongs against the community; shame; and taboos.

The stirrings of morality emerge early in childhood. Toddlers spontaneously offer toys and help to others and try to comfort people they see in distress. And according to the psychologists Elliot Turiel and Judith Smetana, preschoolers have an inkling of the difference between societal conventions and moral principles. Four-year-olds say that it is not O.K. to wear pajamas to school (a convention) and also not O.K. to hit a little girl for no reason (a moral principle). But when asked whether these actions would be O.K. if the teacher allowed them, most of the children said that wearing pajamas would now be fine but that hitting a little girl would still not be.

Though no one has identified genes for morality, there is circumstantial evidence they exist. The character traits called "conscientiousness" and "agreeableness" are far more correlated in identical twins separated at birth (who share their genes but not their environment) than in adoptive siblings raised together (who share their environment but not their genes). People given diagnoses of "antisocial personality disorder" or "psychopathy" show signs of morality blindness from the time they are children. They bully younger children, torture animals, habitually lie and seem incapable of empathy or remorse, often despite normal family backgrounds. Some of these children grow up into the monsters who bilk elderly people out of their savings, rape a succession of women or shoot convenience-store clerks lying on the floor during a robbery.

Though psychopathy probably comes from a genetic predisposition, a milder version can be caused by damage to frontal regions of the brain (including the areas that inhibit intact people from throwing the hypothetical fat man off the bridge). The neuroscientists Hanna and Antonio Damasio and their colleagues found that some children who sustain severe injuries to their frontal lobes can grow up into callous and irresponsible adults, despite normal intelligence. They lie, steal, ignore punishment, endanger their own children and can't think through even the simplest moral dilemmas, like what two people should do if they disagreed on which TV channel to watch or whether a man ought to steal a drug to save his dying wife.

The moral sense, then, may be rooted in the design of the normal human brain. Yet for all the awe that may fill our minds when we reflect on an innate moral law within, the idea is at best incomplete. Consider this moral dilemma: A runaway trolley is about to kill a schoolteacher. You can divert the trolley onto a sidetrack, but the trolley would trip a switch sending a signal to a class of 6-year-olds, giving them permission to name a teddy bear Muhammad. Is it permissible to pull the lever?

This is no joke. Last month a British woman teaching in a private school in Sudan allowed her class to name a teddy bear after the most popular boy in the class, who bore the name of the founder of Islam. She was jailed for blasphemy and threatened with a public flogging, while a mob outside the prison demanded her death. To the protesters, the woman's life clearly had less value than maximizing the dignity of their religion, and their judgment on whether it is right to divert the hypothetical trolley would have differed from ours. Whatever grammar guides people's moral judgments can't be all *that* universal. Anyone who stayed awake through Anthropology 101 can offer many other examples.

Of course, languages vary, too. In Chomsky's theory, languages conform to an abstract blueprint, like having phrases built out of verbs and objects, while the details vary, like whether the verb or the object comes first. Could we be wired with an abstract spec sheet that embraces all the strange ideas that people in different cultures moralize?

The Varieties of Moral Experience

When anthropologists like Richard Shweder and Alan Fiske survey moral concerns across the globe, they find that a few themes keep popping up from amid the diversity. People everywhere, at least in some circumstances and with certain other folks in mind, think it's bad to harm others and good to help them. They have a sense of fairness: that one should reciprocate favors, reward benefactors and punish cheaters. They value loyalty to a group, sharing and solidarity among its members and conformity to its norms. They believe that it is right to defer to legitimate authorities and to respect people with high status. And they exalt purity, cleanliness and sanctity while loathing defilement, contamination and carnality.

The exact number of themes depends on whether you're a lumper or a splitter, but Haidt counts five—harm, fairness, community (or group loyalty), authority and purity—and suggests that they are the primary colors of our moral sense. Not only do they keep reappearing in cross-cultural surveys, but each one tugs on the moral intuitions of people in our own culture. Haidt asks us to consider how much money someone would have to pay us to do hypothetical acts like the following:

Stick a pin into your palm.

Stick a pin into the palm of a child you don't know. (Harm.)

Accept a wide-screen TV from a friend who received it at no charge because of a computer error.

Accept a wide-screen TV from a friend who received it from a thief who had stolen it from a wealthy family. (Fairness.)

Say something bad about your nation (which you don't believe) on a talk-radio show in your nation.

Say something bad about your nation (which you don't believe) on a talk-radio show in a foreign nation. (Community.)

Slap a friend in the face, with his permission, as part of a comedy skit.

Slap your minister in the face, with his permission, as part of a comedy skit. (Authority.)

Attend a performance-art piece in which the actors act like idiots for 30 minutes, including flubbing simple problems and falling down on stage.

Attend a performance-art piece in which the actors act like animals for 30 minutes, including crawling around naked and urinating on stage. (Purity.)

In each pair, the second action feels far more repugnant. Most of the moral illusions we have visited come from an unwarranted intrusion of one of the moral spheres into our judgments. A violation of community led people to frown on using an old flag to clean a bathroom. Violations of purity repelled the people who judged the morality of consensual incest and prevented the moral vegetarians and nonsmokers from tolerating the slightest trace of a vile contaminant. At the other end of the scale, displays of extreme purity lead people to venerate religious leaders who dress in white and affect an aura of chastity and asceticism.

The Genealogy of Morals

The five spheres are good candidates for a periodic table of the moral sense not only because they are ubiquitous but also because they appear to have deep evolutionary roots. The impulse to avoid harm, which gives trolley ponderers the willies when they consider throwing a man off a bridge, can also be found in rhesus monkeys, who go hungry rather than pull a chain that delivers food to them and a shock to another monkey. Respect for authority is clearly related to the pecking orders of dominance and appeasement that are widespread in the animal kingdom. The purity-defilement contrast taps the emotion of disgust that is triggered by potential disease vectors like bodily effluvia, decaying flesh and unconventional forms of meat, and by risky sexual practices like incest.

The other two moralized spheres match up with the classic examples of how altruism can evolve that were worked out by sociobiologists in the 1960s and 1970s and made famous by Richard Dawkins in his book "The Selfish Gene." Fairness is very close to what scientists call reciprocal altruism, where a willingness to be nice to others can evolve as long as the favor helps the recipient more than it costs the giver and the recipient returns the favor when fortunes reverse. The analysis makes it sound as if reciprocal altruism comes out of a robotlike calculation, but in fact Robert Trivers, the biologist who devised the theory, argued that it is implemented in the brain as a suite of moral emotions. Sympathy prompts a person to offer the first favor, particularly to someone in need for whom it would go the furthest. Anger protects a person against cheaters who accept a favor without reciprocating, by impelling him to punish the ingrate or sever the relationship. Gratitude impels a beneficiary to reward those who helped him in the past. Guilt prompts a cheater in danger of being found out to repair the relationship by redressing the misdeed and advertising that he will behave better in the future (consistent with Mencken's definition of *conscience* as "the inner voice which warns us that someone might be looking"). Many experiments on who helps whom, who likes whom, who punishes whom and who feels guilty about what have confirmed these predictions.

Community, the very different emotion that prompts people to share and sacrifice without an expectation of payback, may be rooted in nepotistic altruism, the empathy and solidarity we feel toward our relatives (and which evolved because any gene that pushed an organism to aid a relative would have helped copies of itself sitting inside that relative). In humans, of course, communal feelings can be lavished on nonrelatives as well. Sometimes it pays people (in an evolutionary sense) to love their companions because their interests are yoked, like spouses with common children, in-laws with common relatives, friends with common tastes or allies with common enemies. And sometimes it doesn't pay them at all, but their kinship-detectors have been tricked into treating their groupmates as if they were relatives by tactics like kinship metaphors (*blood brothers*, *fraternities*, *the fatherland*), origin myths, communal meals and other bonding rituals.

Juggling the Spheres

All this brings us to a theory of how the moral sense can be universal and variable at the same time. The five moral spheres are universal, a legacy of evolution. But how they are ranked in importance, and which is brought in to moralize which area of social life—sex, government, commerce, religion, diet and so on—depends on the culture. Many of the flabbergasting practices in faraway places become more intelligible when you recognize that the same moralizing impulse that Western elites channel toward violations of harm and fairness (our moral obsessions) is channeled elsewhere to violations in the other spheres. Think of the Japanese fear of nonconformity (community), the holy ablutions and dietary restrictions of Hindus and Orthodox Jews (purity), the outrage at insulting the Prophet among Muslims (authority). In the West, we believe that in business and government, fairness should trump community and try to root out nepotism and cronyism. In other parts of the world this is incomprehensible—what heartless creep would favor a perfect stranger over his own brother?

The ranking and placement of moral spheres also divides the cultures of liberals and conservatives in the United States. Many bones of contention, like homosexuality, atheism and one-parent families from the right, or racial imbalances, sweatshops and executive pay from the left, reflect different weightings of the spheres. In a large Web survey, Haidt found that liberals put a lopsided moral weight on harm and fairness while playing down group loyalty, authority and purity. Conservatives instead place a moderately high weight on all five. It's not surprising that each side thinks it is driven by lofty ethical values and that the other side is base and unprincipled.

Reassigning an activity to a different sphere, or taking it out of the moral spheres altogether, isn't easy. People think that a behavior belongs in its sphere as a matter of sacred necessity and that the very act of questioning an assignment is a moral outrage. The psychologist Philip Tetlock has shown that the mentality of taboo—a conviction that some thoughts are sinful to think—is not just a superstition of Polynesians but a mind-set that can easily be triggered in college-educated Americans. Just ask them to think about applying the sphere of reciprocity to relationships customarily governed by community or authority. When Tetlock asked subjects for their opinions on whether adoption agencies should place children with the couples willing to pay the most, whether people should have the right to sell their organs and whether they should be able to buy their way out of jury duty, the subjects not only disagreed but felt personally insulted and were outraged that anyone would raise the question.

The institutions of modernity often question and experiment with the way activities are assigned to moral spheres. Market economies tend to put everything up for sale. Science amoralizes the world by seeking to understand phenomena rather than pass judgment on them. Secular philosophy is in the business of scrutinizing all beliefs, including those entrenched by authority and tradition. It's not surprising that these institutions are often seen to be morally corrosive.

Is Nothing Sacred?

And "morally corrosive" is exactly the term that some critics would apply to the new science of the moral sense. The attempt to dissect our moral intuitions can look like an attempt to debunk them. Evolutionary psychologists seem to want to unmask our noblest motives as ultimately self-interested—to show that our love for children, compassion for the unfortunate and sense of justice are just tactics in a Darwinian struggle to perpetuate our genes. The explanation of how different cultures appeal to different spheres could lead to a spineless relativism, in which we would never have grounds to criticize the practice of another culture, no matter how barbaric, because "we have our kind of morality and they have theirs." And the whole enterprise seems to be dragging us to an amoral nihilism, in which morality itself would be demoted from a transcendent principle to a figment of our neural circuitry.

In reality, none of these fears are warranted, and it's important to see why not. The first misunderstanding involves the logic of evolutionary explanations. Evolutionary biologists sometimes anthropomorphize DNA for the same reason that science teachers find it useful to have their students imagine the world from the viewpoint of a molecule or a beam of light. One shortcut to understanding the theory of selection without working through the math is to imagine that the genes are little agents that try to make copies of themselves.

Unfortunately, the meme of the selfish gene escaped from popular biology books and mutated into the idea that organisms (including people) are ruthlessly self-serving. And this doesn't follow. Genes are not a reservoir of our dark unconscious wishes. "Selfish" genes are perfectly compatible with selfless organisms, because a gene's metaphorical goal of selfishly replicating itself can be implemented by wiring up the brain of the organism to do unselfish things, like being nice to relatives or doing good deeds for needy strangers. When a mother stays up all night comforting a sick child, the genes that endowed her with that tenderness were "selfish" in a metaphorical sense, but by no stretch of the imagination is *she* being selfish.

Nor does reciprocal altruism—the evolutionary rationale behind fairness—imply that people do good deeds in the cynical expectation of repayment down the line. We all know of unrequited good deeds, like tipping a waitress in a city you will never visit again and falling on a grenade to save platoonmates. These bursts of goodness are not as anomalous to a biologist as they might appear.

In his classic 1971 article, Trivers, the biologist, showed how natural selection could push in the direction of true selflessness. The emergence of tit-for-tat reciprocity, which lets organisms trade favors without being cheated, is just a first step. A favor-giver not only has to avoid blatant cheaters (those who would accept a favor but not return it) but also prefer generous reciprocators (those who return the biggest favor they can afford) over stingy ones (those who return the smallest favor they can get away with). Since it's good to be chosen as a recipient of favors, a competition arises to be the most generous partner around. More accurately, a competition arises to *appear* to be the most generous partner around, since the favor-giver can't literally read minds or see into the future. A reputation for fairness and generosity becomes an asset.

Now this just sets up a competition for potential beneficiaries to inflate their reputations without making the sacrifices to back them up. But it also pressures the favor-giver to develop ever-more-sensitive radar to distinguish the genuinely generous partners from the hypocrites. This arms race will eventually reach a logical conclusion. The most effective way to *seem* generous and fair, under harsh scrutiny, is to be generous and fair. In the long run, then, reputation can be secured only by commitment. At least some agents evolve to be genuinely high-minded and self-sacrificing— they are moral not because of what it brings them but because that's the kind of people they are.

Of course, a theory that predicted that everyone always sacrificed themselves for another's good would be as preposterous as a theory that predicted that no one ever did. Alongside the niches for saints there are niches for more grudging reciprocators, who attract fewer and poorer partners but don't make the sacrifices necessary for a sterling reputation. And both may coexist with outright cheaters, who exploit the unwary in one-shot encounters. An ecosystem of niches, each with a distinct strategy, can evolve when the payoff of each strategy depends on how many players are playing the other strategies. The human social environment does have its share of generous, grudging and crooked characters, and the genetic variation in personality seems to bear the fingerprints of this evolutionary process.

Is Morality a Figment?

So a biological understanding of the moral sense does not entail that people are calculating maximizers of their genes or self-interest. But where does it leave the concept of morality itself?

Here is the worry. The scientific outlook has taught us that some parts of our subjective experience are products of our biological makeup and have no objective counterpart in the world. The qualitative difference between red and green, the tastiness of fruit and foulness of carrion, the scariness of heights and prettiness of flowers are design features of our common nervous system, and if our species had evolved in a different ecosystem or if we were missing a few genes, our reactions could go the other way. Now, if the distinction between right and wrong is also a product of brain wiring, why should we believe it is any more real than the distinction between red and green? And if it is just a collective hallucination, how could we argue that evils like genocide and slavery are wrong for everyone, rather than just distasteful to us?

Putting God in charge of morality is one way to solve the problem, of course, but Plato made short work of it 2,400 years ago. Does God have a good reason for designating certain acts as moral and others as immoral? If not—if his dictates are divine whims—why should we take them seriously? Suppose that God commanded us to torture a child. Would that make it all right, or would some other standard give us reasons to resist? And if, on the other hand, God was forced by moral reasons to issue some dictates and not others—if a command to torture a child was never an option—then why not appeal to those reasons directly?

This throws us back to wondering where those reasons could come from, if they are more than just figments of our brains. They certainly aren't in the physical world like wavelength or mass. The only other option is that moral truths exist in some abstract Platonic realm, there for us to discover, perhaps in the same way that mathematical truths (according to most mathematicians) are there for us to discover. On this analogy, we are born with a rudimentary concept of number, but as soon as we build on it with formal mathematical reasoning, the nature of mathematical reality forces us to discover some truths and not others. (No one who understands the concept of two, the concept of four and the concept of addition can come to any conclusion but that 2 + 2 = 4.) Perhaps we are born with a rudimentary moral sense, and as soon as we build on it with moral reasoning, the nature of moral reality forces us to some conclusions but not others.

Moral realism, as this idea is called, is too rich for many philosophers' blood. Yet a diluted version of the idea—if not a list of cosmically inscribed Thou-Shalts, then at least a few If-Thens—is not crazy. Two features of reality point any rational, self-preserving social agent in a moral direction. And they could provide a benchmark for determining when the judgments of our moral sense are aligned with morality itself.

One is the prevalence of nonzero-sum games. In many arenas of life, two parties are objectively better off if they both act in a non-selfish way than if each of them acts selfishly. You and I are both better off if we share our surpluses, rescue each other's children in danger and refrain from shooting at each other, compared with hoarding our surpluses while they rot, letting the other's child drown while we file our nails or feuding like the Hatfields and McCoys. Granted, I might be a bit better off if I acted selfishly at your expense and you played the sucker, but the same is true for you with me, so if each of us tried for these advantages, we'd both end up worse off. Any neutral observer, and you and I if we could talk it over rationally, would have to conclude that the state we should aim for is the one in which we both are unselfish. These spreadsheet projections are not quirks of brain wiring, nor are they dictated by a supernatural power; they are in the nature of things.

The other external support for morality is a feature of rationality itself: that it cannot depend on the egocentric vantage point of the reasoner. If I appeal to you to do anything that affects me—to get off my foot, or tell me the time or not run me over with your car—then I can't do it in a way that privileges my interests over yours (say, retaining my right to run you over with my car) if I want you to take me seriously. Unless I am Galactic Overlord, I have to state my case in a way that would force me to treat you in kind. I can't act as if my interests are special just because

I'm me and you're not, any more than I can persuade you that the spot I am standing on is a special place in the universe just because I happen to be standing on it.

Not coincidentally, the core of this idea—the interchangeability of perspectives—keeps reappearing in history's best-thought-through moral philosophies, including the Golden Rule (itself discovered many times); Spinoza's Viewpoint of Eternity; the Social Contract of Hobbes, Rousseau and Locke; Kant's Categorical Imperative; and Rawls's Veil of Ignorance. It also underlies Peter Singer's theory of the Expanding Circle—the optimistic proposal that our moral sense, though shaped by evolution to overvalue self, kin and clan, can propel us on a path of moral progress, as our reasoning forces us to generalize it to larger and larger circles of sentient beings.

Doing Better by Knowing Ourselves

Morality, then, is still something larger than our inherited moral sense, and the new science of the moral sense does not make moral reasoning and conviction obsolete. At the same time, its implications for our moral universe are profound.

At the very least, the science tells us that even when our adversaries' agenda is most baffling, they may not be amoral psychopaths but in the throes of a moral mind-set that appears to them to be every bit as mandatory and universal as ours does to us. Of course, some adversaries really are psychopaths, and others are so poisoned by a punitive moralization that they are beyond the pale of reason. (The actor Will Smith had many historians on his side when he recently speculated to the press that Hitler thought he was acting morally.) But in any conflict in which a meeting of the minds is not completely hopeless, a recognition that the other guy is acting from

moral rather than venal reasons can be a first patch of common ground. One side can acknowledge the other's concern for community or stability or fairness or dignity, even while arguing that some other value should trump it in that instance. With affirmative action, for example, the opponents can be seen as arguing from a sense of fairness, not racism, and the defenders can be seen as acting from a concern with community, not bureaucratic power. Liberals can ratify conservatives' concern with families while noting that gay marriage is perfectly consistent with that concern.

The science of the moral sense also alerts us to ways in which our psychological makeup can get in the way of our arriving at the most defensible moral conclusions. The moral sense, we are learning, is as vulnerable to illusions as the other senses. It is apt to confuse morality per se with purity, status and conformity. It tends to reframe practical problems as moral crusades and thus see their solution in punitive aggression. It imposes taboos that make certain ideas indiscussible. And it has the nasty habit of always putting the self on the side of the angels.

Though wise people have long reflected on how we can be blinded by our own sanctimony, our public discourse still fails to discount it appropriately. In the worst cases, the thoughtlessness of our brute intuitions can be celebrated as a virtue. In his influential essay "The Wisdom of Repugnance," Leon Kass, former chair of the President's Council on Bioethics, argued that we should disregard reason when it comes to cloning and other biomedical technologies and go with our gut: "We are repelled by the prospect of cloning human beings . . . because we intuit and feel, immediately and without argument, the violation of things that we rightfully hold dear. . . . In this age in which everything is held to be permissible so long as it is freely done . . .

repugnance may be the only voice left that speaks up to defend the central core of our humanity. Shallow are the souls that have forgotten how to shudder."

There are, of course, good reasons to regulate human cloning, but the shudder test is not one of them. People have shuddered at all kinds of morally irrelevant violations of purity in their culture: touching an untouchable, drinking from the same water fountain as a Negro, allowing Jewish blood to mix with Aryan blood, tolerating sodomy between consenting men. And if our ancestors' repugnance had carried the day, we never would have had autopsies, vaccinations, blood transfusions, artificial insemination, organ transplants and in vitro fertilization, all of which were denounced as immoral when they were new.

There are many other issues for which we are too quick to hit the moralization button and look for villains rather than bug fixes. What should we do when a hospital patient is killed by a nurse who administers the wrong drug in a patient's intravenous line? Should we make it easier to sue the hospital for damages? Or should we redesign the IV fittings so that it's physically impossible to connect the wrong bottle to the line?

And nowhere is moralization more of a hazard than in our greatest global challenge. The threat of human-induced climate change has become the occasion for a moralistic revival meeting. In many discussions, the cause of climate change is overindulgence (too many S.U.V.'s) and defilement (sullying the atmosphere), and the solution is temperance (conservation) and expiation (buying carbon offset coupons). Yet the experts agree that these numbers don't add up: even if every last American became conscientious about his or her carbon emissions, the effects on climate change would be trifling, if for no other reason than that two billion Indians and Chinese are unlikely to copy our born-again abstemiousness. Though voluntary conservation may be one wedge in an effective carbon-reduction pie, the other wedges will have to be morally boring, like a carbon tax and new energy technologies, or even taboo, like nuclear power and deliberate manipulation of the ocean and atmosphere. Our habit of moralizing problems, merging them with intuitions of purity and contamination, and resting content when we feel the right feelings, can get in the way of doing the right thing.

Far from debunking morality, then, the science of the moral sense can advance it, by allowing us to see through the illusions that evolution and culture have saddled us with and to focus on goals we can share and defend. As Anton Chekhov wrote, "Man will become better when you show him what he is like."

STEVEN PINKER is the Johnstone Family Professor of Psychology at Harvard University and the author of "The Language Instinct" and "The Stuff of Thought: Language as a Window Into Human Nature."

ARTICLE 24

What If the Secret to Success Is Failure?

PAUL TOUGH

Dominic Randolph can seem a little out of place at Riverdale Country School—which is odd, because he's the headmaster. Riverdale is one of New York City's most prestigious private schools, with a 104-year-old campus that looks down grandly on Van Cortlandt Park from the top of a steep hill in the richest part of the Bronx. On the discussion boards of UrbanBaby.com, worked-up moms from the Upper East Side argue over whether Riverdale sends enough seniors to Harvard, Yale and Princeton to be considered truly "TT" (top-tier, in UrbanBabyese), or whether it is more accurately labeled "2T" (second-tier), but it is, certainly, part of the city's private-school elite, a place members of the establishment send their kids to learn to be members of the establishment. Tuition starts at $38,500 a year, and that's for prekindergarten.

Randolph, by contrast, comes across as an iconoclast, a disrupter, even a bit of an eccentric. He dresses for work every day in a black suit with a narrow tie, and the outfit, plus his cool demeanor and sweep of graying hair, makes you wonder, when you first meet him, if he might have played sax in a ska band in the '80s. (The English accent helps.) He is a big thinker, always chasing new ideas, and a conversation with him can feel like a one-man TED conference, dotted with references to the latest work by behavioral psychologists and management gurus and design theorists. When he became headmaster in 2007, he swapped offices with his secretary, giving her the reclusive inner sanctum where previous headmasters sat and remodeling the small outer recep-

tion area into his own open-concept work space, its walls covered with whiteboard paint on which he sketches ideas and slogans. One day when I visited, one wall was bare except for a white sheet of paper. On it was printed a single black question mark.

For the headmaster of an intensely competitive school, Randolph, who is 49, is surprisingly skeptical about many of the basic elements of a contemporary high-stakes American education. He did away with Advanced Placement classes in the high school soon after he arrived at Riverdale; he encourages his teachers to limit the homework they assign; and he says that the standardized tests that Riverdale and other private schools require for admission to kindergarten and to middle school are "a patently unfair system" because they evaluate students almost entirely by I.Q. "This push on tests," he told me, "is missing out on some serious parts of what it means to be a successful human."

The most critical missing piece, Randolph explained as we sat in his office last fall, is *character*—those essential traits of mind and habit that were drilled into him at boarding school in England and that also have deep roots in American history. "Whether it's the pioneer in the Conestoga wagon or someone coming here in the 1920s from southern Italy, there was this idea in America that if you worked hard and you showed real grit, that you could be successful," he said. "Strangely, we've now forgotten that. People who have an easy time of things, who get 800s on their SAT's, I worry that those people get feedback that everything they're doing is great. And I think as a result, we are actually setting them up for long-term failure. When that person suddenly has to face up to a difficult moment, then I think they're screwed, to be honest. I don't think they've grown the capacities to be able to handle that."

Randolph has been pondering throughout his 23-year career as an educator the question of whether and how schools should impart good character. It has often felt like a lonely quest, but it has led him in some interesting directions. In the winter of 2005, Randolph read "Learned Optimism," a book by Martin Seligman, a psychology professor at the University of Pennsylvania who helped establish the Positive Psychology movement. Randolph found the book intriguing, and he arranged a meeting with the author. As it happened, on the morning that Randolph made the trip to Philadelphia, Seligman had scheduled a separate meeting with David Levin, the co-founder of the KIPP network of charter schools and the superintendent of the KIPP schools in New York City. Seligman decided he might as well combine the two meetings, and he invited Christopher Peterson, a psychology professor at the University of Michigan, who was also visiting Penn that day, to join him and Randolph and Levin in his office for a freewheeling discussion of psychology and schooling.

Levin had also spent many years trying to figure out how to provide lessons in character to his students, who were almost all black or Latino and from low-income families. At the first KIPP school, in Houston, he and his co-founder, Michael Feinberg, filled the walls with slogans like "Work Hard" and "Be Nice" and "There Are No Shortcuts," and they developed a system of rewards and demerits designed to train their students not only in fractions and algebra but also in perseverance and empathy. Like Randolph, Levin went to Seligman's office expecting to talk about opti-

mism. But Seligman surprised them both by pulling out a new and very different book, which he and Peterson had just finished: "Character Strengths and Virtues: A Handbook and Classification," a scholarly, 800-page tome that weighed in at three and a half pounds. It was intended, according to the authors, as a "manual of the sanities," an attempt to inaugurate what they described as a "science of good character."

It was, in other words, exactly what Randolph and Levin had been looking for, separately, even if neither of them had quite known it. Seligman and Peterson consulted works from Aristotle to Confucius, from the Upanishads to the Torah, from the Boy Scout Handbook to profiles of Pokémon characters, and they settled on 24 character strengths common to all cultures and eras. The list included some we think of as traditional noble traits, like bravery, citizenship, fairness, wisdom and integrity; others that veer into the emotional realm, like love, humor, zest and appreciation of beauty; and still others that are more concerned with day-to-day human interactions: social intelligence (the ability to recognize interpersonal dynamics and adapt quickly to different social situations), kindness, self-regulation, gratitude.

In most societies, Seligman and Peterson wrote, these strengths were considered to have a moral valence, and in many cases they overlapped with religious laws and strictures. But their true importance did not come from their relationship to any system of ethics or moral laws but from their practical benefit: cultivating these strengths represented a reliable path to "the good life," a life that was not just happy but also meaningful and fulfilling.

Six years after that first meeting, Levin and Randolph are trying to put this conception of character into action in their schools. In the process, they have found themselves wrestling with questions that have long confounded not just educators but anyone trying to nurture a thriving child or simply live a good life. What is good character? Is it really something that can be taught in a formal way, in the classroom, or is it the responsibility of the family, something that is inculcated gradually over years of experience? Which qualities matter most for a child trying to negotiate his way to a successful and autonomous adulthood? And are the answers to those questions the same in Harlem and in Riverdale?

Levin had believed in the importance of character since KIPP's inception. But on the day of his trip to see Seligman, he was feeling a new urgency about the subject. Six years earlier, in 1999, the first group of students to enter KIPP Academy middle school, which Levin founded and ran in the South Bronx, triumphed on the eighth-grade citywide achievement test, graduating with the highest scores in the Bronx and the fifth-highest in all of New York City. Every morning of middle school they passed a giant sign in the stairwell reminding them of their mission: "Climb the Mountain to College." And as they left KIPP for high school, they seemed poised to do just that: not only did they have outstanding academic results, but most of them also won admission to highly selective private and Catholic schools, often with full scholarships.

But as Levin told me when we spoke last fall, for many students in that first cohort, things didn't go as planned. "We thought, O.K., our first class was the fifth-highest-performing class in all of New York City," Levin said. "We got 90 percent into private and parochial schools. It's all going to be solved. But it wasn't." Almost every member of the cohort did make it through high school, and more than 80 percent of them enrolled in college. But then the mountain grew steeper, and every few weeks, it seemed, Levin got word of another student who decided to drop out. According to a report that KIPP issued last spring, only 33 percent of students who grad-

uated from a KIPP middle school 10 or more years ago have graduated from a four-year college. That rate is considerably better than the 8 percent of children from low-income families who currently complete college nationwide, and it even beats the average national rate of college completion for all income groups, which is 31 percent. But it still falls well short of KIPP's stated goal: that 75 percent of KIPP alumni will graduate from a four-year college, and 100 percent will be prepared for a stable career.

As Levin watched the progress of those KIPP alumni, he noticed something curious: the students who persisted in college were not necessarily the ones who had excelled academically at KIPP; they were the ones with exceptional character strengths, like optimism and persistence and social intelligence. They were the ones who were able to recover from a bad grade and resolve to do better next time; to bounce back from a fight with their parents; to resist the urge to go out to the movies and stay home and study instead; to persuade professors to give them extra help after class. Those skills weren't enough on their own to earn students a B.A., Levin knew. But for young people without the benefit of a lot of family resources, without the kind of safety net that their wealthier peers enjoyed, they seemed an indispensable part of making it to graduation day.

What appealed to Levin about the list of character strengths that Seligman and Peterson compiled was that it was presented not as a finger-wagging guilt trip about good values and appropriate behavior but as a recipe for a successful and happy life. He was wary of the idea that KIPP's aim was to instill in its students "middle-class values," as though well-off kids had some depth of character that low-income students lacked. "The thing that I think is great about the character-strength approach," he told me, "is it is fundamentally devoid of value judgment."

Still, neither Levin nor Dominic Randolph had a clear vision of how to turn an 800-page psychology text into a practical program. After that first meeting in Seligman's office, Levin and Randolph kept in touch, calling and e-mailing, swapping articles and Web links, and they soon discovered that they shared a lot of ideas and interests, despite the very different school environments in which they worked. They decided to join forces, to try to tackle the mysteries of character together, and they turned for help to Angela Duckworth, who at the time was a graduate student in Seligman's department (she is now an assistant professor). Duckworth came to Penn in 2002 at the age of 32, after working for a decade as a teacher and a charter-school consultant. When she applied to the Ph.D. program at Penn, she wrote in her application essay that her experiences in schools had given her "a distinctly different view of school reform" than the one she started out with in her 20s. "The problem, I think, is not only the schools but also the students themselves," she wrote. "Here's why: learning is hard. True, learning is fun, exhilarating and gratifying—but it is also often daunting, exhausting and sometimes discouraging. . . . To help chronically low-performing but intelligent students, educators and parents must first recognize that character is at least as important as intellect."

Duckworth's early research showed that measures of self-control can be a more reliable predictor of students' grade-point averages than their I.Q.'s. But while self-control seemed to be a critical ingredient in attaining basic success, Duckworth came to feel it wasn't as relevant when it came to outstanding achievement. People who accomplished great things, she noticed, often combined a passion for a single mission with an unswerving dedication to achieve that mission, whatever the obstacles and however long it might take. She decided she needed to name this quality, and she chose the word "grit."

She developed a test to measure grit, which she called the Grit Scale. It is a deceptively simple test, in that it requires you to rate yourself on just 12 questions, from "I finish whatever I begin" to "I often set a goal but later choose to pursue a different one." It takes about three minutes to complete, and it relies entirely on self-report—and yet when Duckworth took it out into the field, she found it was remarkably predictive of success. At Penn, high grit ratings allowed students with relatively low college-board scores to nonetheless achieve high G.P.A.'s. Duckworth and her collaborators gave their grit test to more than 1,200 freshman cadets as they entered West Point and embarked on the grueling summer training course known as Beast Barracks. The military has developed its own complex evaluation, called the Whole Candidate Score, to judge incoming cadets and predict which of them will survive the demands of West Point; it includes academic grades, a gauge of physical fitness and a Leadership Potential Score. But at the end of Beast Barracks, the more accurate predictor of which cadets persisted and which ones dropped out turned out to be Duckworth's 12-item grit questionnaire.

Levin and Randolph asked Duckworth to use the new methods and tools she was developing to help them investigate the question of character at KIPP and Riverdale, and she and a handful of Penn graduate students began making regular treks from Philadelphia to New York. The first question Duckworth addressed, again, was the relative importance of I.Q. and self-control. She and her team of researchers gave middle-school students at Riverdale and KIPP a variety of psychological and I.Q. tests. They found that at both schools, I.Q. was the better predictor of scores on statewide achievement tests, but measures of self-control were more reliable indicators of report-card grades.

Duckworth's research convinced Levin and Randolph that they should try to foster self-control and grit in their students. Yet those didn't seem like the only character strengths that mattered. The full list of 24, on the other hand, felt too unwieldy. So they asked Peterson if he could narrow the list down to a more manageable handful, and he identified a set of strengths that were, according to his research, especially likely to predict life satisfaction and high achievement. After a few small adjustments (Levin and Randolph opted to drop love in favor of curiosity), they settled on a final list: zest, grit, self-control, social intelligence, gratitude, optimism and curiosity.

Over the course of the next year and a half, Duckworth worked with Levin and Randolph to turn the list of seven strengths into a two-page evaluation, a questionnaire that could be completed by teachers or parents, or by students themselves. For each strength, teachers suggested a variety of "indicators," much like the questions Duckworth asked people to respond to on her grit questionnaire, and she road-tested several dozen of them at Riverdale and KIPP. She eventually settled on the 24 most statistically reliable ones, from "This student is eager to explore new things" (an indicator of curiosity) to "This student believes that effort will improve his or her future" (optimism).

For Levin, the next step was clear. Wouldn't it be cool, he mused, if each student graduated from school with not only a G.P.A. but also a C.P.A., for character-point average? If you were a college-admissions director or a corporate human-resources manager selecting entry-level employees, wouldn't you like to know which ones scored highest in grit or optimism or zest? And if you were a parent of a KIPP student, wouldn't you want to know how your son or daughter stacked up next to the rest of the class in character as well as in

reading ability? As soon as he got the final list of indicators from Duckworth and Peterson, Levin started working to turn it into a specific, concise assessment that he could hand out to students and parents at KIPP's New York City schools twice a year: the first-ever character report card.

Back at Riverdale, though, the idea of a character report card made Randolph nervous. "I have a philosophical issue with quantifying character," he explained to me one afternoon. "With my school's specific population, at least, as soon as you set up something like a report card, you're going to have a bunch of people doing test prep for it. I don't want to come up with a metric around character that could then be gamed. I would hate it if that's where we ended up."

Still, he did think that the inventory Duckworth and Peterson developed could be a useful tool in communicating with students about character. And so he has been taking what one Riverdale teacher described as a "viral approach" to spreading the idea of this new method of assessing character throughout the Riverdale community. He talks about character at parent nights, asks pointed questions in staff meetings, connects like-minded members of his faculty and instructs them to come up with new programs. Last winter, Riverdale students in the fifth and sixth grades took the 24-indicator survey, and their teachers rated them as well. The results were discussed by teachers and administrators, but they weren't shared with students or parents, and they certainly weren't labeled a "report card."

As I spent time at Riverdale last year, it became apparent to me that the debate over character at the school wasn't just about how best to evaluate and improve students' character. It went deeper, to the question of what "character" really meant. When Randolph arrived at Riverdale, the school already had in place a character-education program, of a sort. Called CARE, for Children Aware of Riverdale Ethics, the program was adopted in 1989 in the lower school, which at Riverdale means prekindergarten through fifth grade. It is a blueprint for niceness, mandating that students "Treat everyone with respect" and "Be aware of other people's feelings and find ways to help those whose feelings have been hurt." Posters in the hallway remind students of the virtues related to CARE ("Practice Good Manners . . . Avoid Gossiping . . . Help Others"). In the lower school, many teachers describe it as a proud and essential part of what makes Riverdale the school that it is.

When I asked Randolph last winter about CARE, he was diplomatic. "I see the character strengths as CARE 2.0," he explained. "I'd basically like to take all of this new character language and say that we're in the next generation of CARE."

In fact, though, the character-strength approach of Seligman and Peterson isn't an expansion of programs like CARE; if anything, it is a repudiation of them. In 2008, a national organization called the Character Education Partnership published a paper that divided character education into two categories: programs that develop "moral character," which embodies ethical values like fairness, generosity and integrity; and those that address "performance character," which includes values like effort, diligence and perseverance. The CARE program falls firmly on the "moral character" side of the divide, while the seven strengths that Randolph and Levin have chosen for their schools lean much more heavily toward performance character: while they do have a moral component, strengths like zest, optimism, social intelligence and curiosity aren't particularly heroic; they make you think of Steve Jobs or Bill Clinton more than the Rev. Martin Luther King Jr. or Gandhi.

The two teachers Randolph has chosen to oversee the school's character initiative are K.C. Cohen, the guidance counselor for the middle and upper schools, and Karen Fierst, a learning specialist in the lower school. Cohen is friendly and thoughtful, in her mid-30s, a graduate of Fieldston, the private school just down the road from Riverdale. She is intensely interested in character development, and like Randolph, she is worried about the character of Riverdale students. But she is not yet entirely convinced by the seven character strengths that Riverdale has ostensibly chosen. "When I think of good character, I think: Are you fair? Are you honest in dealings with other people? Are you a cheater?" she told me. "I don't think so much about: Are you tenacious? Are you a hard worker? I think, Are you a good person?"

Cohen's vision of character is much closer to "moral character" than "performance character," and so far, that vision remains the dominant one at Riverdale. When I spent a day at the school in March, sitting in on a variety of classes and meetings, messages about behavior and values permeated the day, but those messages stayed almost entirely in the moral dimension. It was a hectic day at the middle school—it was pajama day, plus there was a morning assembly, and then on top of that, the kids in French class who were going on the two-week trip to Bordeaux for spring break had to leave early in order to make their overnight flight to Paris. The topic for the assembly was heroes, and a half-dozen students stood up in front of their classmates— about 350 kids, in all—and each made a brief presentation about a particular hero he or she had chosen: Ruby Nell Bridges, the African-American girl who was part of the first group to integrate the schools in New Orleans in 1960; Mohamed Bouazizi, the Tunisian fruit vendor whose self-immolation helped spark the recent revolt in that country; the actor and activist Paul Robeson.

In the assembly, in classes and in conversations with different students, I heard a lot of talk about values and ethics, and the values that were emphasized tended to be social values: inclusion, tolerance, diversity. (I heard a lot more about black history at Riverdale than I did at the KIPP schools I visited.) One eighth-grade girl I asked about character said that for her and her friends, the biggest issue was inclusion—who was invited to whose bat mitzvah; who was being shunned on Facebook. Character, as far as I could tell, was being defined at Riverdale mostly in terms of helping other people—or at least not hurting their feelings.

Randolph told me that he had concerns about a character program that comprised only those kind of nice-guy values. "The danger with character is if you just revert to these general terms—respect, honesty, tolerance—it seems really vague," he said. "If I stand in front of the kids and just say, 'It's really important for you to respect each other,' I think they glaze over. But if you say, 'Well, actually you need to exhibit self-control,' or you explain the value of social intelligence—this will help you collaborate more effectively—then it seems a bit more tangible."

When I spoke to Karen Fierst, the teacher who was overseeing the character project for the Riverdale lower school, she said she was worried that it would be a challenge to convince the students and their parents that there was anything in the 24 character strengths that might actually benefit them. For KIPP kids, she said, the notion that character could help them get through college was a powerful lure, one that would motivate them to take the strengths seriously. For kids at Riverdale, though, there was little doubt that they would graduate from college. "It will just happen," Fierst explained. "It happened to every generation in their family before them. And so it's harder to get them to invest in this

idea. For KIPP students, learning these strengths is partly about trying to demystify what makes other people successful—kind of like, 'We're letting you in on the secret of what successful people are like.' But kids here already live in a successful community. They're not depending on their teachers to give them the information on how to be successful."

At KIPP Infinity middle school, which occupies one floor of a school on West 133rd Street, across from the M.T.A.'s giant Manhattanville bus depot, report-card night last winter fell on a cold Thursday at the beginning of February. Report-card night is always a big deal at KIPP schools—parents are strongly urged to attend, and at Infinity, almost all of them do—but this particular evening carried an extra level of anxiety for both the administrators and the parents, because students were receiving their very first character report cards, and no one knew quite what to expect.

Logistically, the character report card had been a challenge to pull off. Teachers at all four KIPP middle schools in New York City had to grade every one of their students, on a scale of 1 to 5, on every one of the 24 character indicators, and more than a few of them found the process a little daunting. And now that report-card night had arrived, they had an even bigger challenge: explaining to parents just how those precise figures, rounded to the second decimal place, summed up their children's character. I sat for a while with Mike Witter, a 31-year-old eighth-grade English teacher, as he talked through the character report card with Faith Flemister and her son Juaquin Bennett, a tall, hefty eighth grader in a gray hooded sweatshirt.

"For the past few years we've been working on a project to create a clearer picture for parents about the character of your child," Witter explained to Flemister. "The categories that we ended up putting together represent qualities that have been studied and determined to be indicators of success. They mean you're more likely to go to college. More likely to find a good job. Even surprising things, like they mean you're more likely to get married, or more likely to have a family. So we think these are really important."

Flemister nodded, and Witter began to work his way down the scores on Juaquin's character report card, starting with the good news: every teacher had scored him as a perfect 5 on "Is polite to adults and peers," and he did almost as well on "Keeps temper in check." They were both indicators for interpersonal self-control.

"I can tell this is a real strength for you," Witter said, turning to Juaquin. "This kind of self-control is something you've developed incredibly well. So that makes me think we need to start looking at: What's something we can target? And the first thing that jumps out at me is this." Witter pulled out a green felt-tip marker and circled one indicator on Juaquin's report card. " 'Pays attention and resists distraction,' " Witter read aloud, an indicator for academic self-control. "That's a little lower than some of the other numbers. Why do you think that is?"

"I talk too much in class," Juaquin said, a little sheepishly, looking down at his black sneakers. "I sometimes stare off into space and don't pay attention."

The three of them talked over a few strategies to help Juaquin focus more in class, and by the end of the 15-minute conversation, Flemister seemed convinced by the new approach. "The strong points are not a surprise," she said to Witter as he got up to talk to another family. "That's just the type of person Juaquin is. But it's good how you pinpoint what he can do to make things easier on himself. Then maybe his grades will pick up."

A month later, I returned to KIPP to visit Witter's classroom. By that point in the school year, character language had permeated Infinity. Kids wore T-shirts with the slogan "Infinite Character" and Seligman's 24 character strengths listed on the back. The walls were covered with signs that read "Got self-control?" and "I actively participate!" (one indicator for zest). There was a bulletin board in the hallway topped with the words "Character Counts," where students filled out and posted "Spotted!" cards when they saw a fellow student performing actions that demonstrate character. (Jasmine R. cited William N. for zest: "William was in math class and he raised his hand for every problem.")

I came to Witter's class to observe something that Levin was calling "dual-purpose instruction," the practice of deliberately working explicit talk about character strengths into every lesson. Levin wanted math teachers to use the strengths in word problems; he explained that history teachers could use them to orient a class discussion about Harriet Tubman and the Underground Railroad. And when I arrived in Witter's class at 7:45 on a Thursday morning in March, he was leading a discussion about Chinua Achebe's novel "Things Fall Apart." Above Witter's head, at the front of the class, the seven character strengths were stenciled in four-inch-high letters, white on blue, from optimism to social intelligence. He asked his students to rank Okonkwo, the protagonist, on his various character strengths. There was a lot of back and forth, but in the end, most students agreed that Okonkwo rated highest on grit and lowest on self-control. Then a student named Yantzee raised his hand. "Can't a trait backfire at you?" he asked.

"Sure, a trait can backfire," Witter said. "Too much grit, like Okonkwo, you start to lose your ability to have empathy for other people. If you're so gritty that you don't understand why everyone's complaining about how hard things are, because nothing's hard for you, because you're Mr. Grit, then you're going to have a hard time being kind. Even love—being too loving might make you the kind of person who can get played." There was a ripple of knowing laughter from the students. "So, yes, character is something you have to be careful about. Character strengths can become character weaknesses."

Though the seven character strengths aren't included in every lesson at KIPP, they do make it into most conversations about discipline. One day last winter, I was speaking with Sayuri Stabrowski, a 30-year-old seventh-and-eighth-grade reading teacher at KIPP Infinity, and she mentioned that she caught a girl chewing gum in her class earlier that day. "She denied it," Stabrowski told me. "She said, 'No, I'm not, I'm chewing my tongue.' " Stabrowski rolled her eyes as she told me the story. "I said, 'O.K. fine.' Then later in the class, I saw her chewing again, and I said: 'You're chewing gum! I see you.' She said, 'No, I'm not, see?' and she moved the gum over in her mouth in this really obvious way, and we all saw what she was doing. Now, a couple of years ago, I probably would have blown my top and screamed. But this time, I was able to say: 'Gosh, not only were you chewing gum, which is kind of minor, but you lied to me twice. That's a real disappointment. What does that say about your character?' And she was just devastated."

Stabrowski was worried that the girl, who often struggled with her behavior, might have a mini-meltdown—a "baby attack," in KIPP jargon—in the middle of the class, but in fact, the girl spit out her gum and sat through the rest of the class and then afterward came up to her teacher with tears in her eyes. "We had a long conversation," Stabrowski told me. "She said: 'I'm trying so hard to just grow up. But nothing ever changes!' And I said: 'Do you know what does change? You didn't have a baby attack in front of the other kids, and two weeks ago, you would have.' "

To Tom Brunzell, who as the dean of students at KIPP Infinity oversaw the implementation of the character report card, what is going on in character conversations like that one isn't academic instruction at all, or even discipline; it's therapy. Specifically, it's a kind of cognitive behavioral therapy, the very practical, nuts-and-bolts psychological technique that provides the theoretical underpinning for the whole positive psychology field. Cognitive behavioral therapy, or C.B.T., involves using the conscious mind to understand and overcome unconscious fears and self-destructive habits, using techniques like "self-talk"—putting an immediate crisis in perspective by reminding yourself of the larger context. "The kids who succeed at KIPP are the ones who can C.B.T. themselves in the moment," Brunzell told me. Part of the point of the character initiative, as he saw it, was to give their students the tools to do that. "All kids this age are having mini-implosions every day," he said. "I mean, it's middle school, the worst years of their lives. But the kids who make it are the ones who can tell themselves: 'I can rise above this little situation. I'm O.K. Tomorrow is a new day.' "

For Randolph, the experience that Brunzell was describing—the struggle to pull yourself through a crisis, to come to terms on a deep level with your own shortcomings and to labor to overcome them—is exactly what is missing for so many students at academically excellent schools like Riverdale. And perhaps surprisingly, it may turn out to be an area where the students at KIPP have a real advantage over Riverdale kids. On the professional development day in February when I visited Riverdale, Randolph had arranged a screening for his entire faculty of "Race to Nowhere," a movie about the stresses facing mostly privileged American high-school students that has become an underground hit in many wealthy suburbs, where one-time showings at schools, churches and community centers bring out hundreds of concerned parents. The movie paints a grim portrait of contemporary adolescence, rising in an emotional crescendo to the story of an overachieving teenage girl who committed suicide, apparently because of the ever-increasing pressure to succeed that she felt both at school and at home. At Riverdale, the film seemed to have a powerful effect on many of the staff; one teacher who came up to Randolph afterward had tears in her eyes.

"Race to Nowhere" has helped to coalesce a growing movement of psychologists and educators who argue that the systems and methods now in place to raise and educate well-off kids in the United States are in fact devastating them. One central figure in the movie is Madeline Levine, a psychologist in Marin County who is the author of a best-selling book, "The Price of Privilege: How Parental Pressure and Material Advantage Are Creating a Generation of Disconnected and Unhappy Kids." In her book, Levine cites studies and surveys to back up her contention that children of affluent parents now exhibit "unexpectedly high rates of emotional problems beginning in junior high school." This is no accident of demographics, Levine says, but instead is a direct result of the child-raising practices that prevail in well-off American homes; wealthy parents today, she argues, are more likely to be emotionally distant from their children, and at the same time to insist on high levels of achievement, a potentially toxic blend of influences that can create "intense feelings of shame and hopelessness" in affluent children.

Cohen and Fierst told me that they also see many Riverdale parents who, while pushing their children to excel, also inadvertently shield them from exactly the kind of experience that can lead to character growth. As Fierst put it: "Our kids don't put up with a lot

of suffering. They don't have a threshold for it. They're protected against it quite a bit. And when they do get uncomfortable, we hear from their parents. We try to talk to parents about having to sort of make it O.K. for there to be challenge, because that's where learning happens."

Cohen said that in the middle school, "if a kid is a C student, and their parents think that they're all-A's, we do get a lot of pushback: 'What are you talking about? This is a great paper!' We have parents calling in and saying, for their kids, 'Can't you just give them two more days on this paper?' Overindulging kids, with the intention of giving them everything and being loving, but at the expense of their character—that's huge in our population. I think that's one of the biggest problems we have at Riverdale."

This is a problem, of course, for all parents, not just affluent ones. It is a central paradox of contemporary parenting, in fact: we have an acute, almost biological impulse to provide for our children, to give them everything they want and need, to protect them from dangers and discomforts both large and small. And yet we all know—on some level, at least—that what kids need more than anything is a little hardship: some challenge, some deprivation that they can overcome, even if just to prove to themselves that they can. As a parent, you struggle with these thorny questions every day, and if you make the right call even half the time, you're lucky. But it's one thing to acknowledge this dilemma in the privacy of your own home; it's quite another to have it addressed in public, at a school where you send your kids at great expense.

And it's that problem that Randolph is up against as he tries to push forward this new kind of conversation about character at Riverdale. When you work at a public school, whether it's a charter or a traditional public school, you're paid by the state, responsible, on some level, to your fellow citizens for the job you do preparing your students to join the adult world. When you work at a private school like Riverdale, though, even one with a long waiting list, you are always conscious that you're working for the parents who pay the tuition fees. Which makes a campaign like the one that Randolph is trying to embark on all the more complicated. If your premise is that your students are lacking in deep traits like grit and gratitude and self-control, you're implicitly criticizing the parenting they've received—which means you're implicitly criticizing your employers.

When I asked Randolph to explain just what he thought Riverdale students were missing out on, he told me the story of his own scholastic career. He did well in boarding school and was admitted to Harvard, but when he got to college, he felt lost, out of step with the power-tie careerism of the Reagan '80s. After two years at Harvard, Randolph left for a year to work in a low-paying manual job, as a carpenter's helper, trying to find himself. After college, he moved for a couple of years to Italy, where he worked odd jobs and studied opera. It was an uncertain and unsettled time in his life, filled with plenty of failed experiments and setbacks and struggles. Looking back on his life, though, Randolph says that the character strengths that enabled him to achieve the success that he has were not built in his years at Harvard or at the boarding schools he attended; they came out of those

years of trial and error, of taking chances and living without a safety net. And it is precisely those kinds of experiences that he worries that his students aren't having.

"The idea of building grit and building self-control is that you get that through failure," Randolph explained. "And in most highly academic environments in the United States, no one fails anything."

Most Riverdale students can see before them a clear path to a certain type of success. They'll go to college, they'll graduate, they'll get well-paying jobs—and if they fall along the way, their families will almost certainly catch them, often well into their 20s or even 30s, if necessary. But despite their many advantages, Randolph isn't yet convinced that the education they currently receive at Riverdale, or the support they receive at home, will provide them with the skills to negotiate the path toward the deeper success that Seligman and Peterson hold up as the ultimate product of good character: a happy, meaningful, productive life. Randolph wants his students to succeed, of course—it's just that he believes that in order to do so, they first need to learn how to fail.

PAUL TOUGH (inquiries@paultough.com), a contributing writer, is the author of "Whatever It Takes: Geoffrey Canada's Quest to Change Harlem and America." His book "The Success Equation" will be published next year.

ARTICLE 25

Teenage Brains

Beautiful Brains

Moody. Impulsive. Maddening. Why do teenagers act the way they do? Viewed through the eyes of evolution, their most exasperating traits may be the key to success as adults.

DAVID DOBBS

Although you know your teenager takes some chances, it can be a shock to hear about them.

One fine May morning not long ago my oldest son, 17 at the time, phoned to tell me that he had just spent a couple hours at the state police barracks. Apparently he had been driving "a little fast." What, I asked, was "a little fast"? Turns out this product of my genes and loving care, the boy-man I had swaddled, coddled, cooed at, and then pushed and pulled to the brink of manhood, had been flying down the highway at 113 miles an hour.

"That's more than a little fast," I said.

He agreed. In fact, he sounded somber and contrite. He did not object when I told him he'd have to pay the fines and probably for a lawyer. He did not argue when I pointed out that if anything happens at that speed—a dog in the road, a blown tire, a sneeze—he dies. He was in fact almost irritatingly reasonable. He even proffered that the cop did the right thing in stopping him, for, as he put it, "We can't all go around doing 113."

He did, however, object to one thing. He didn't like it that one of the several citations he received was for reckless driving.

"Well," I huffed, sensing an opportunity to finally yell at him, "what would you call it?"

"It's just not accurate," he said calmly. 'Reckless' sounds like you're not paying attention. But I was. I made a deliberate point of doing this on an empty stretch of dry interstate, in broad daylight, with good sight lines and no traffic. I mean, I wasn't just gunning the thing. I was driving.

"I guess that's what I want you to know. If it makes you feel any better, I was really focused."

Actually, it did make me feel better. That bothered me, for I didn't understand why. Now I do.

My son's high-speed adventure raised the question long asked by people who have pondered the class of humans we call teenagers: What on Earth was he doing? Parents often phrase this question more colorfully. Scientists put it more coolly. They ask, What can explain this behavior? But even that is just another way of wondering, What is wrong with these kids? Why do they act this way? The question passes judgment even as it inquires.

Through the ages, most answers have cited dark forces that uniquely affect the teen. Aristotle concluded more than 2,300 years ago that "the young are heated by Nature as drunken men by wine." A shepherd in William Shakespeare's *The Winter's Tale* wishes "there were no age between ten and three-and-twenty, or that youth would sleep out the rest; for there is nothing in the between but getting wenches with child, wronging the ancientry, stealing, fighting." His lament colors most modern scientific inquiries as well. G. Stanley Hall, who formalized adolescent studies with his 1904 *Adolescence: Its Psychology and Its Relations to Physiology, Anthropology, Sociology, Sex, Crime, Religion and Education,* believed this period of "storm and stress" replicated earlier, less civilized stages of human development. Freud saw adolescence as an expression of torturous psychosexual conflict; Erik Erikson, as the most tumultuous of life's several identity crises. Adolescence: always a problem.

Such thinking carried into the late 20th century, when researchers developed brain-imaging technology that enabled them to see the teen brain in enough detail to track both its physical development and its patterns of activity. These imaging tools offered a new way to ask the same question—What's wrong with these kids?—and revealed an answer that surprised almost everyone. Our brains, it turned out, take much longer to develop than we had thought. This revelation suggested both a simplistic, unflattering explanation for teens' maddening behavior—and a more complex, affirmative explanation as well.

The first full series of scans of the developing adolescent brain—a National Institutes of Health (NIH) project that studied over a hundred young people as they grew up during the 1990s—showed that our brains undergo a massive reorganization between our 12th and 25th years. The brain doesn't actually grow very much during this period. It has already reached 90 percent of its full size by the time a person is six, and a thickening skull accounts for most head growth afterward. But as we move through adolescence, the brain undergoes extensive remodeling, resembling a network and wiring upgrade.

For starters, the brain's axons—the long nerve fibers that neurons use to send signals to other neurons—become gradually more insulated with a fatty substance called myelin (the brain's white matter), eventually boosting the axons' transmission speed up to a hundred times. Meanwhile, dendrites, the branch-like extensions that neurons use to receive signals from nearby axons, grow twiggier, and the most heavily used synapses—the little chemical junctures across which axons and dendrites pass notes—grow richer and stronger. At the same time, synapses that see little use begin to wither. This synaptic pruning, as it is called, causes the brain's cortex—the outer layer of gray matter where we do much of our conscious and complicated thinking—to become thinner but more efficient. Taken together, these changes make the entire brain a much faster and more sophisticated organ.

This process of maturation, once thought to be largely finished by elementary school, continues throughout adolescence. Imaging work done since the 1990s shows that these physical changes move in a slow wave from the brain's rear to its front, from areas close to the brain stem that look after older and more behaviorally basic functions, such as vision, movement, and fundamental processing, to the evolutionarily newer and more complicated thinking areas up front. The corpus callosum, which connects the brain's left and right hemispheres and carries traffic essential to many advanced brain functions, steadily thickens. Stronger links also develop between the hippocampus, a sort of memory directory, and frontal areas that set goals and weigh different agendas; as a result, we get better at integrating memory and experience into our decisions. At the same time, the frontal areas develop greater speed and richer connections, allowing us to generate and weigh far more variables and agendas than before.

When this development proceeds normally, we get better at balancing impulse, desire, goals, self-interest, rules, ethics, and even altruism, generating behavior that is more complex and, sometimes at least, more sensible. But at times, and especially at first, the brain does this work clumsily. It's hard to get all those new cogs to mesh.

Beatriz Luna, a University of Pittsburgh professor of psychiatry who uses neuroimaging to study the teen brain, used a simple test that illustrates this learning curve. Luna scanned the brains of children, teens, and twentysomethings while they performed an antisaccade task, a sort of eyes-only video game where you have to stop yourself from looking at a suddenly appearing light. You view a screen on which the red crosshairs at the center occasionally disappear just as a light flickers elsewhere on the screen. Your instructions are to not look at the light and instead to look in the opposite direction. A sensor detects any eye movement. It's a tough assignment, since flickering lights naturally draw our attention. To succeed, you must override both a normal impulse to attend to new information and curiosity about something forbidden. Brain geeks call this response inhibition.

Ten-year-olds stink at it, failing about 45 percent of the time. Teens do much better. In fact, by age 15 they can score as well as adults if they're motivated, resisting temptation about 70 to 80 percent of the time. What Luna found most interesting, however, was not those scores. It was the brain scans she took while people took the test. Compared with adults, teens tended to make less use of brain regions that monitor performance, spot errors, plan, and stay focused—areas the adults seemed to bring online automatically. This let the adults use a variety of brain resources and better resist temptation, while the teens used those areas less often and more readily gave in to the impulse to look at the flickering light—just as they're more likely to look away from the road to read a text message.

If offered an extra reward, however, teens showed they could push those executive regions to work harder, improving their scores. And by age 20, their brains respond to this task much as the adults' do. Luna suspects the improvement comes as richer networks and faster connections make the executive region more effective.

These studies help explain why teens behave with such vexing inconsistency: beguiling at breakfast, disgusting at dinner; masterful on Monday, sleepwalking on Saturday. Along with lacking experience generally, they're still learning to use their brains' new networks. Stress, fatigue, or challenges can cause a misfire. Abigail Baird, a Vassar psychologist who studies teens, calls this neural gawkiness—an equivalent to the physical awkwardness teens sometimes display while mastering their growing bodies.

The slow and uneven developmental arc revealed by these imaging studies offers an alluringly pithy explanation for why teens may do stupid things like drive at 113 miles an hour, aggrieve their ancientry, and get people (or get gotten) with child: They act that way because their brains aren't done! You can see it right there in the scans!

This view, as titles from the explosion of scientific papers and popular articles about the "teen brain" put it, presents adolescents as "works in progress" whose "immature brains" lead some to question whether they are in a state "akin to mental retardation."

The story you're reading right now, however, tells a different scientific tale about the teen brain. Over the past five years or so, even as the work-in-progress story spread into our culture, the discipline of adolescent brain studies learned to do some more-complex thinking of its own. A few researchers began to view recent brain and genetic findings in a brighter, more flattering light, one distinctly colored by evolutionary theory. The resulting account of the adolescent brain—call it the adaptive-adolescent story—casts the teen less as a rough draft than as an exquisitely sensitive, highly adaptable creature wired almost perfectly for the job of moving from the safety of home into the complicated world outside.

This view will likely sit better with teens. More important, it sits better with biology's most fundamental principle, that of natural selection. Selection is hell on dysfunctional traits. If adolescence is essentially a collection of them—angst, idiocy, and haste; impulsiveness, selfishness, and reckless bumbling—then how did those traits survive selection? They couldn't—not if they were the period's most fundamental or consequential features.

The answer is that those troublesome traits don't really characterize adolescence; they're just what we notice most because they annoy us or put our children in danger. As B. J. Casey, a neuroscientist at Weill Cornell Medical College who has spent nearly a decade applying brain and genetic studies to our understanding of adolescence, puts it, "We're so used to seeing adolescence as a problem. But the more we learn about what really makes this period unique, the more adolescence starts to seem like a highly functional, even adaptive period. It's exactly what you'd need to do the things you have to do then."

To see past the distracting, dopey teenager and glimpse the adaptive adolescent within, we should look not at specific, sometimes startling, behaviors, such as skateboarding down stairways or dating fast company, but at the broader traits that underlie those acts.

Let's start with the teen's love of the thrill. We all like new and exciting things, but we never value them more highly than we do during adolescence. Here we hit a high in what behavioral scientists call sensation seek-

ing: the hunt for the neural buzz, the jolt of the unusual or unexpected.

Seeking sensation isn't necessarily impulsive. You might plan a sensation-seeking experience—a skydive or a fast drive—quite deliberately, as my son did. Impulsivity generally drops throughout life, starting at about age 10, but this love of the thrill peaks at around age 15. And although sensation seeking can lead to dangerous behaviors, it can also generate positive ones: The urge to meet more people, for instance, can create a wider circle of friends, which generally makes us healthier, happier, safer, and more successful.

This upside probably explains why an openness to the new, though it can sometimes kill the cat, remains a highlight of adolescent development. A love of novelty leads directly to useful experience. More broadly, the hunt for sensation provides the inspiration needed to "get you out of the house" and into new terrain, as Jay Giedd, a pioneering researcher in teen brain development at NIH, puts it.

Also peaking during adolescence (and perhaps aggrieving the ancientry the most) is risk-taking. We court risk more avidly as teens than at any other time. This shows reliably in the lab, where teens take more chances in controlled experiments involving everything from card games to simulated driving. And it shows in real life, where the period from roughly 15 to 25 brings peaks in all sorts of risky ventures and ugly outcomes. This age group dies of accidents of almost every sort (other than work accidents) at high rates. Most long-term drug or alcohol abuse starts during adolescence, and even people who later drink responsibly often drink too much as teens. Especially in cultures where teenage driving is common, this takes a gory toll: In the U.S., one in three teen deaths is from car crashes, many involving alcohol.

Are these kids just being stupid? That's the conventional explanation: They're not thinking, or by the work-in-progress model, their puny developing brains fail them.

Yet these explanations don't hold up. As Laurence Steinberg, a developmental psychologist specializing in adolescence at Temple University, points out, even 14- to 17-year-olds—the biggest risk takers—use the same basic cognitive strategies that adults do, and they usually reason their way through problems just as well as adults. Contrary to popular belief, they also fully recognize they're mortal. And, like adults, says Steinberg, "teens actually overestimate risk."

So if teens think as well as adults do and recognize risk just as well, why do they take more chances? Here, as elsewhere, the problem lies less in what teens lack compared with adults than in what they have more of. Teens take more risks not because they don't understand the dangers but because they weigh risk versus reward differently: In situations where risk can get them something they want, they value the reward more heavily than adults do.

A video game Steinberg uses draws this out nicely. In the game, you try to drive across town in as little time as possible. Along the way you encounter several traffic lights. As in real life, the traffic lights sometimes turn from green to yellow as you approach them, forcing a quick go-or-stop decision. You save time—and score more points—if you drive through before the light turns red. But if you try to drive through the red and don't beat it, you lose even more time than you would have if you had stopped for it. Thus the game rewards you for taking a certain amount of risk but punishes you for taking too much.

When teens drive the course alone, in what Steinberg calls the emotionally "cool" situation of an empty room, they take risks at about the same rates that adults do. Add stakes that the teen cares about, however, and the situation changes. In this case Steinberg

added friends: When he brought a teen's friends into the room to watch, the teen would take twice as many risks, trying to gun it through lights he'd stopped for before. The adults, meanwhile, drove no differently with a friend watching.

To Steinberg, this shows clearly that risk-taking rises not from puny thinking but from a higher regard for reward.

"They didn't take more chances because they suddenly downgraded the risk," says Steinberg. "They did so because they gave more weight to the payoff."

Researchers such as Steinberg and Casey believe this risk-friendly weighing of cost versus reward has been selected for because, over the course of human evolution, the willingness to take risks during this period of life has granted an adaptive edge. Succeeding often requires moving out of the home and into less secure situations. "The more you seek novelty and take risks," says Baird, "the better you do." This responsiveness to reward thus works like the desire for new sensation: It gets you out of the house and into new turf.

As Steinberg's driving game suggests, teens respond strongly to social rewards. Physiology and evolutionary theory alike offer explanations for this tendency. Physiologically, adolescence brings a peak in the brain's sensitivity to dopamine, a neurotransmitter that appears to prime and fire reward circuits and aids in learning patterns and making decisions. This helps explain the teen's quickness of learning and extraordinary receptivity to reward—and his keen, sometimes melodramatic reaction to success as well as defeat.

The teen brain is similarly attuned to oxytocin, another neural hormone, which (among other things) makes social connections in particular more rewarding. The neural networks and dynamics associated with general reward and social interactions overlap heavily. Engage one, and you often engage the other. Engage them during adolescence, and you light a fire.

This helps explain another trait that marks adolescence: Teens prefer the company of those their own age more than ever before or after. At one level, this passion for same-age peers merely expresses in the social realm the teen's general attraction to novelty: Teens offer teens far more novelty than familiar old family does.

Yet teens gravitate toward peers for another, more powerful reason: to invest in the future rather than the past. We enter a world made by our parents. But we will live most of our lives, and prosper (or not) in a world run and remade by our peers. Knowing, understanding, and building relationships with them bears critically on success. Socially savvy rats or monkeys, for instance, generally get the best nesting areas or territories, the most food and water, more allies, and more sex with better and fitter mates. And no species is more intricately and deeply social than humans are.

This supremely human characteristic makes peer relations not a sideshow but the main show. Some brain-scan studies, in fact, suggest that our brains react to peer exclusion much as they respond to threats to physical health or food supply. At a neural level, in other words, we perceive social rejection as a threat to existence. Knowing this might make it easier to abide the hysteria of a 13-year-old deceived by a friend or the gloom of a 15-year-old not invited to a party. These people! we lament. They react to social ups and downs as if their fates depended upon them! They're right. They do.

Excitement, novelty, risk, the company of peers. These traits may seem to add up to nothing more than doing foolish new stuff with friends. Look deeper, however, and you see that these traits that define adolescence make us more adaptive, both as individuals

and as a species. That's doubtless why these traits, broadly defined, seem to show themselves in virtually all human cultures, modern or tribal. They may concentrate and express themselves more starkly in modern Western cultures, in which teens spend so much time with each other. But anthropologists have found that virtually all the world's cultures recognize adolescence as a distinct period in which adolescents prefer novelty, excitement, and peers. This near-universal recognition sinks the notion that it's a cultural construct.

Culture clearly shapes adolescence. It influences its expression and possibly its length. It can magnify its manifestations. Yet culture does not create adolescence. The period's uniqueness rises from genes and developmental processes that have been selected for over thousands of generations because they play an amplified role during this key transitional period: producing a creature optimally primed to leave a safe home and move into unfamiliar territory.

The move outward from home is the most difficult thing that humans do, as well as the most critical—not just for individuals but for a species that has shown an unmatched ability to master challenging new environments. In scientific terms, teenagers can be a pain in the ass. But they are quite possibly the most fully, crucially adaptive human beings around. Without them, humanity might not have so readily spread across the globe.

This adaptive-adolescence view, however accurate, can be tricky to come to terms with—the more so for parents dealing with teens in their most trying, contrary, or flat-out scary moments. It's reassuring to recast worrisome aspects as signs of an organism learning how to negotiate its surroundings. But natural selection swings a sharp edge, and the teen's sloppier moments can bring unbearable consequences. We may not run the risk of being killed in ritualistic battles or being eaten by leopards, but drugs, drinking, driving, and crime take a mighty toll. My son lives, and thrives, sans car, at college. Some of his high school friends, however, died during their driving experiments. Our children wield their adaptive plasticity amid small but horrific risks.

We parents, of course, often stumble too, as we try to walk the blurry line between helping and hindering our kids as they adapt to adulthood. The United States spends about a billion dollars a year on programs to counsel adolescents on violence, gangs, suicide, sex, substance abuse, and other potential pitfalls. Few of them work.

Yet we can and do help. We can ward off some of the world's worst hazards and nudge adolescents toward appropriate responses to the rest. Studies show that when parents engage and guide their teens with a light but steady hand, staying connected but allowing independence, their kids generally do much better in life. Adolescents want to learn primarily, but not entirely, from their friends. At some level and at some times (and it's the parent's job to spot when), the teen recognizes that the parent can offer certain kernels of wisdom—knowledge valued not because it comes from parental authority but because it comes from the parent's own struggles to learn how the world turns. The teen rightly perceives that she must understand not just her parents' world but also the one she is entering. Yet if allowed to, she can appreciate that her parents once faced the same problems and may remember a few things worth knowing.

Meanwhile, in times of doubt, take inspiration in one last distinction of the teen brain— a final key to both its clumsiness and its remarkable adaptability. This is the prolonged plasticity of those late-developing frontal areas as they slowly mature. As noted earlier,

these areas are the last to lay down the fatty myelin insulation—the brain's white matter— that speeds transmission. And at first glance this seems like bad news: If we need these areas for the complex task of entering the world, why aren't they running at full speed when the challenges are most daunting?

The answer is that speed comes at the price of flexibility. While a myelin coating greatly accelerates an axon's bandwidth, it also inhibits the growth of new branches from the axon. According to Douglas Fields, an NIH neuroscientist who has spent years studying myelin, "This makes the period when a brain area lays down myelin a sort of crucial period of learning—the wiring is getting upgraded, but once that's done, it's harder to change."

The window in which experience can best rewire those connections is highly specific to each brain area. Thus the brain's language centers acquire their insulation most heavily in the first 13 years, when a child is learning language. The completed insulation consolidates those gains—but makes further gains, such as second languages, far harder to come by.

So it is with the forebrain's myelination during the late teens and early 20s. This delayed completion—a withholding of readiness— heightens flexibility just as we confront and enter the world that we will face as adults.

This long, slow, back-to-front developmental wave, completed only in the mid-20s, appears to be a uniquely human adaptation. It may be one of our most consequential. It can seem a bit crazy that we humans don't wise up a bit earlier in life. But if we smartened up sooner, we'd end up dumber.

DAVID DOBBS is the author of *Reef Madness*, on Darwin's controversial theory of coral reef origins.

ARTICLE 26

Students with Intellectual Disabilities Going to College? *Absolutely!*

In a pilot project in Kentucky, called SHEP, young people with intellectual disabilities are pursuing career goals and learning important life skills. They participate in college courses, work with mentors and coaches, and experience supported employment opportunities—all through partnerships among school systems, institutions of higher learning, and community agencies. For example, one student pursuing a career in graphic design works at a screen printing business while simultaneously taking college courses to pursue his career goal. This article describes the rationale for such programs, the scope of the programs, and benefits to students and the community.

HAROLD L. KLEINERT, MELISSA M. JONES, KATHLEEN SHEPPARD-JONES, BEVERLY HARP, AND ELIZABETH M. HARRISON

Postsecondary education and students with intellectual disabilities have not historically been viewed as compatible. In fact, it was only with the 1977 implementation of the Education for All Handicapped Children Act (Public Law 94-142) that students with the most significant disabilities were guaranteed a public education at all, much less the opportunity to attend postsecondary programs. Yet with subsequent reauthorizations of IDEA, including the Individuals With Disabilities Education Act (IDEA) of 2004 (Public Law 108-446), we have come to realize that all students should have the opportunity to learn age-appropriate academic content and engage in activities alongside their peers without disabilities. In this article, we propose a model of postsecondary education for students with intellectual disabilities (ID); this model extends the notion of inclusive education to the next level—going to college.

Though tremendous overall gains have occurred in the past 15 years in the percentage of students with disabilities who have attended some form of postsecondary education (Newman, Wagner, Cameto, Knokey, & Shaver, 2010), the lowest percentage of students from *any* disability category attending postsecondary education has been that of students with ID (Wagner, Newman, Cameto, Garza, & Levine, 2005). Until recently, few educators or community members held expectations that students with ID would continue their education after high school. Indeed, the historical exclusion of students with ID from postsecondary experiences has played a significant role in the perpetuation of a cycle of low expectations and poor adult outcomes overall (Grigal, Hart, & Paiewonsky, 2010).

In recent years, a growing number of colleges have offered opportunities for students with intellectual disabilities (Think

College, 2011a). Students taking part in some of these programs are often dually enrolled by finishing their final years of high school in a college setting with the additional support required in the postsecondary environment provided by public school special education staff, as a part of these students' transition services (Hall, Kleinert, & Kearns, 2000). Some students, however, participate in programs designed for high school graduates, entering college through non-degreeseeking options or open enrollment programs. Not surprisingly, the students served in these programs indicate goals similar to those of their peers—to get a job, to be independent, to have friendships with peers, and to go to class and social events (Moon, Grigal, & Neubert, 2001). A college or university campus is an ideal venue for gaining the skills needed to achieve these goals.

Along with the students' own goals for postsecondary education, family expectations have also evolved, as families of students who have succeeded in inclusive general education classes with individualized supports now envision age-appropriate options for their students as they graduate (Think College, 2011b). Legislative impetus is occurring, as well, with the Higher Education Opportunities Act of 2008 (HEOA), which supports the transition of students with ID into higher education. The HEOA provides not only new avenues for accessing postsecondary education, but also federal and financial support not formerly available to students with ID. In the wake of these changes, it is imperative for teachers and individualized education program (IEP) team members to (a) recognize the benefits of postsecondary education for students with ID, (b) become familiar with the various avenues that exist to accessing postsecondary education, and (c) identify the skills needed to support students with ID to transition into a postsecondary setting.

A Rationale for Postsecondary Education for Students with Intellectual Disabilities

So what is the value of postsecondary education for students with intellectual disabilities? In pilot studies, higher education opportunities for students with ID have been shown to correlate with improved employment outcomes and increased participation in communities. For example, Migliore, Butterworth, and Hart (2009) noted a correlation between participation in *both* postsecondary education *and* vocational rehabilitation and positive employment outcomes. Young adults with ID who took advantage of both were 26% more likely to exit with paid jobs than those who used only vocational rehabilitation services as their postsecondary experience, with an average 73% higher income than those who only received vocational rehabilitation services.

Moreover, students with ID who participated in inclusive postsecondary education also reported increased satisfaction across several life domains, including emotional well-being, interpersonal relationships, personal development, self-determination, and social inclusion (Hughson, Moodie, & Uditsky, 2006). For campus communities, the presence of students with ID offers invaluable opportunities for students to engage in learning alongside peers with different educational experiences and learning styles. For universities and colleges seeking to broaden the diversity of their student populations, the presence of students with ID adds to the campus and academic life for all students, incorporating opportunities for mentoring and friendships.

The Higher Education Opportunities Act of 2008 (HEOA)

The HEOA provides opportunities for students with ID who are enrolled in a Comprehensive Transition and Postsecondary Program (CTP) approved by the U.S. Department of Education, including eligibility for Pell Grants and Federal Work Study Programs. Whereas colleges and universities must first apply to offer a CTP, what is new to these programs is that students with ID may access such federal support (e.g., Pell Grants, Work-Study) if they are working toward an educational credential (not necessarily a degree), as specifically defined by the institution in its CTP application. This credential, which can reflect personalized student goals designed to address employment, independent living, and educational outcomes, can include audited courses (as well as for-credit courses), job internships, and other on-campus activities designed to lead to enhanced independence and employment. Most important, students with ID may qualify to participate in a CTP even if they do *not* have a standard high school diploma, or if they do not meet the requirements to enroll in a regular degree program at the institution. Figure 1 illustrates how the supports now available to students with ID under CTPs build on, and yet are distinct from, the services and accommodations that an institution of higher education (IHE) must offer, under the requirements of Section 504 of the Rehabilitation Act of 1973, to all students with documented disabilities who enroll at that institution. (See Gil (2007) for a full explanation of the allowable supports under Section 504 for students with disabilities.)

A National Network of Postsecondary Programs

To further enable young adults with intellectual disabilities to gain access to, and complete postsecondary education, the HEOA authorized the funding of postsecondary Transition Programs for Students With Intellectual Disabilities (TPSID). Twenty-seven TPSID grants were awarded in the fall of 2010 to colleges and universities, or IHEs, around the United States. According to the U.S. Department of Education (2010), TPSIDs are funded to serve students with intellectual disabilities by providing individualized supports and services with respect to academic, social, and vocational goals.

A National Resource: Think College

In addition to providing competitive funding for the 27 different model programs, the TPSID initiative also authorized the Institute for Community Inclusion at the University of Massachusetts, Boston (www.thinkcollege.net) for colleges and universities that operates as a national clearinghouse for educators, students, and families regarding postsecondary education programs for students with ID.

Types of Postsecondary Education Programs: What Do They Look Like?

Though postsecondary programs for students with ID can be shaped quite differently, they are often classified in terms of being stand-alone (separate), mixed, or integrated (Hart, Grigal, Sax, Martinez, & Will, 2006). A *stand-alone* program, although located on a 2- or 4-year college campus, might offer specific classes aimed solely at students with ID. Such a program may also include a residential component for students to live away from home in dorms or apartments with other students. An *integrated* program uses existing coursework at the college or university so students with and without disabilities take classes together. The residential component would also be integrated with students without disabilities. A *mixed* program draws on aspects from both the stand-alone and integrated program types (e.g., separate coursework for students with intellectual disabilities but inclusion in residential life and extracurricular activities).

Student Provision	Participation, Supports, and Services in Postsecondary Education Programs for Students with Disabilities Under Section 504	CTP Provisions for Eligibility and Participation for Students with Intellectual Disabilities
Completion of regular high school diploma	Required for college entrance.	Students with ID may enroll in a CTP without a regular high school diploma.
College entrance or placement exams	Students must pass entrance or college placement tests to enroll in program and/or specific coursework.	Students with ID may enroll in a CTP without passing entrance, placement, or other "ability to benefit" tests.
Pell Grants and Federal Work-Study	Students are eligible if they meet financial means test and they maintain satisfactory academic progress, as defined by the university or college, for all students.	Students with ID are eligible if they meet financial means test and they maintain satisfactory academic progress, as defined by the CTP within that college or university.
Academic coursework and degree	Courses are taken for academic credit and typically lead to a degree.	Courses are taken either for credit or as audit, and they lead towards a certificate or meaningful credential, which can be individualized to meet the needs of the student.
Reasonable accommodations	Students with documented disabilities have the right to reasonable accommodations to ensure academic access, but such accommodations *cannot* alter the course content or objectives.	Students with ID also have the right to reasonable accommodations to ensure academic access, including courses not taken for credit.
Course modifications	Students are not eligible for course modifications.	If taking courses for audit, and with permission of the instructor, students with ID may have course modifications that *do* alter the course content to meet their individualized learning objectives. Audited courses can count towards the CTP certificate.
Advising	Students participate in advising in the same fashion as all other students on campus.	CTP must include an advising and curriculum structure for enrolled students that is a part of the campus advising structure for all students.

FIGURE 1   Comparison of Student Provisions in Comprehensive Transition and Postsecondary Programs (CTPs) for Students with Intellectual Disabilities (ID) with Allowable Accommodations and Services for all Students with Disabilities Under Section 504

> **Interagency partnerships and the use of shared funding streams enable students with ID to attend college and choose careers, rather than only attending day programs or sheltered workshops.**

An example of an integrated approach, being applied from a statewide perspective, is the Supported Higher Education Project (SHEP) of Kentucky. The goal of SHEP, funded through a 5-year grant from the U.S. Office on Postsecondary Education as one of the TPSIDs, is to build capacity across colleges and universities in the state, so that students with ID have a choice of college programs. This project developed partnerships with key state agencies including the Kentucky Department of Education (KDE), the Kentucky Office of Vocational Rehabilitation (OVR), the Kentucky Division of Developmental and Intellectual Disabilities (DIDD), and the Commonwealth Council on Developmental Disabilities (CCDD). Interagency partnerships and the use of shared funding streams enable students with ID to attend college and choose careers, rather than only attending day programs or sheltered workshops.

The partnership with the state vocational rehabilitation agency led to a pilot project for several of the SHEP students. The intent is for students to gain college experiences and exposure to life skills and knowledge through coursework paired with internships or work study opportunities. The expectation is for gainful employment in a field that is meaningful to the individual. The pilot project is structured around (a) the development of a relevant course of study, (b) the use of academic/employment coaches to coordinate individualized supports, (c) the development of peer and natural supports, (d) an involvement in extracurricular and campus activities, and (e) access to financial supports. Currently, seven students are involved in the pilot program; five of the seven are taking postsecondary classes and working part-time. SHEP staff work with supported employment agencies to ensure that each student learns objectives related to his or her internship or work study, that progress is systematically documented, and any gaps in supports are identified. For example, one student pursuing a career in graphic design works at a screen printing business while simultaneously taking college courses to pursue his career goal.

In addition to the seven students participating in the SHEP supported employment pilot, SHEP is working with 30 additional students, who are enrolled in classes or preparing to enter college. Some of the courses students have taken (either for credit or on audit basis) include Introduction to Information Systems, Introductory Art, Beginning Web Design, Foundations of College Writing, Introduction to Computers, Experiential Education, Introduction to Graphic Design, Pre-Algebra, and Basic Algebra With Measurement.

Keys to Success

One of the greatest barriers to creating inclusive campus communities are the attitudes and preconceived notions about the limited ability of students with ID to meaningfully contribute to the collegiate environment. Through SHEP we strive to create an environment where other members of the university community recognize students with ID as members of the community who can actively contribute and participate. Signs of meaningful involvement in campus life include helping out with a collegiate sports team, participating in intramurals, engaging in campus events, attending campus theater productions, volunteering, joining clubs, and simply eating lunch with peers at the usual campus hangouts. By setting the stage through a coordinated set of

> Signs of meaningful involvement in campus life include helping out with a collegiate sports team, participating in intramurals, engaging in campus events, attending campus theater productions, volunteering, joining clubs, and simply eating lunch with peers.

practices geared toward communication and collaboration, the barriers created by historical biases and misinformation can be effectively dismantled.

An Individualized Support Model

Maintaining a focus on an "inclusive individual support model" (Hart et al., 2006, p. 1), planning should be student centered and individualized, based on the talents, strengths, and interests of each student with ID. Using a person centered planning approach (O'Brien & O'Brien, 2002) for each SHEP student, small teams who have a stake in the inclusive outcomes work together to identify the student's dreams, future goals, skills upon which to build, possible supports, and action steps with agreed upon timelines. In most cases, the teams consist of the student, her or his parent(s), the coordinator of the inclusive initiative, and whenever possible, past and present peer supports. Invitations can also be extended to staff members in formalized support roles such as vocational rehabilitation counselors, professors, and disability service personnel, as warranted.

A variety of processes can be used to facilitate this collaborative effort of customizable supports including Planning Alternative Tomorrows With Hope (PATH; Pierpoint, O'Brien, & Forest, 2011), the McGill Action Planning System (MAPS; Kellems & Morningstar, 2010), or Supporting Social Roles (SSR) scales (O'Brien, 2010). The end result should be a clearly articulated picture of the

goals for participation in college, as well as action steps for achieving those goals including academic, career, and social activities. (See Figure 2 for an example of a PATH for one of the students in the SHEP program.) Person-centered planning for postsecondary education can (and should) start while students are in high school. Whereas Figure 2 illustrates a PATH for a student enrolled in college, this process is equally valid for IEP transition teams in high school to ensure that a student has all of the necessary supports in place *before* he enrolls in college.

Peer Mentors

Peer mentors can play a vital role in supporting students with ID on campus. A peer mentor is another college student who agrees to support the student with ID to successfully navigate the campus culture such as supporting a student to actively engage in a class, tutoring, academic coaching outside of class, and socializing either on or off campus (Jones, Weir, & Hart, 2011). When developing peer mentoring programs, remember that "mentors are not born but developed" (Ramani, Gruppen, & Kachur, 2006, p. 404), and peer mentor development is an evolving process. Therefore, providing the necessary mentor training is imperative to assure the mentors understand what is expected of them from the start. Each mentor will gain skills in collaboration and accommodation along the way, but starting with some level of confidence enhances the mentoring relationship. Most important, the foundation of an effective mentoring partnership is equality between the mentor and mentee, with each learning and gaining skills as a result of interacting with the other (Stoddard, 2003; Zachary, 2005). To maintain parity in the relationship, mentoring partners should prioritize socializing and fun as much as they do academics, with fun being the equalizer in the partnership.

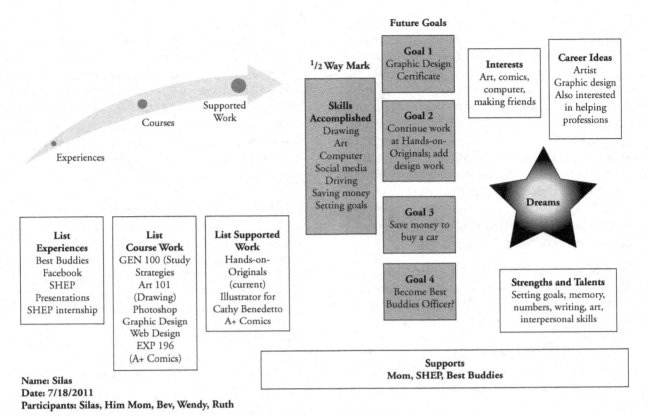

Future Goals

¹/₂ **Way Mark**

Goal 1
Graphic Design
Certificate

Interests
Art, comics,
computer,
making friends

Career Ideas
Artist
Graphic design
Also interested
in helping
professions

Skills Accomplished
Drawing
Art
Computer
Social media
Driving
Saving money
Setting goals

Goal 2
Continue work
at Hands-on-
Originals; add
design work

Dreams

Goal 3
Save money to
buy a car

List Experiences
Best Buddies
Facebook
SHEP
Presentations
SHEP internship

List Course Work
GEN 100 (Study
Strategies
Art 101
(Drawing)
Photoshop
Graphic Design
Web Design
EXP 196
(A+ Comics)

List Supported Work
Hands-on-
Originals
(current)
Illustrator for
Cathy Benedetto
A+ Comics

Goal 4
Become Best
Buddies Officer?

Strengths and Talents
Setting goals, memory,
numbers, writing, art,
interpersonal skills

Supports
Mom, SHEP, Best Buddies

Name: Silas
Date: 7/18/2011
Participants: Silas, Him Mom, Bev, Wendy, Ruth

Note. PATH = Planning Alternative Tomorrows With Hope; SHEP = Supported Higher Education Project

FIGURE 2   Sample PATH for Student

Through SHEP, we found it helpful to provide course or project credit for mentoring to increase accountability and consistency on the mentor. Formal peer mentors, however, are not the only option when creating a supportive environment. The occurrence of natural supports, students in the same class simply stepping up and offering or agreeing to provide assistance when needed, is a growing trend in many college classes. When this occurs, the dream of an inclusive culture is realized. These natural supports can be cultivated in the high school setting as peers who plan on attending the same college or university as the student with ID are identified, and connections are nurtured while the students are still in high school.

Mentoring partnerships between mentors and mentees need to be supportive relationships, in which both parties understand the boundaries of a friendship. It is the expectation that mentoring partners, whether in high school or college, honor one another and treat each other with the utmost respect. Maintaining trust is crucial in every relationship and the mentors must learn the importance of confidentiality and also understand that what the mentoring partner tells them should be treated as confidential unless there is a clear responsibility for sharing that information. Mentors are expected to (a) commit to a mentoring schedule; (b) introduce themselves to the course instructors ahead of time; (c) provide support in the classroom in the least intrusive manner possible; and (d) look for opportunities to build upon their mentee's strengths and interests through extracurricular activities, campus events, and organizations (for more information on mentor responsibilities see www.shep.org). These strategies are very similar to peer-support strategies (Carter, Cushing, & Kennedy, 2009) that are effective in supporting high school students with significant disabilities in general education classes and other school activities.

Working with Local Colleges to Develop New Programs

As educators of students with intellectual disabilities approach colleges and other postsecondary programs about the possibility of students with ID attending, there are a few questions we have found that college administrators nearly always ask. Here are some of the most frequently asked questions (FAQs), as well as responses we found effective.

FAQs

- *What is the benefit for students with ID to attend college?* Although we have tried to answer this question throughout this paper (e.g., enhanced employability in chosen career or opportunities for developing increased social and life skills), we have found it helpful to also emphasize that the presence on campus of individuals with ID can be a key element in embracing diversity. Disability is a natural part of the human experience, and the presence of individuals who have different gifts and challenges enriches the campus environment.
- *Won't a CTP program create inordinate work for our faculty, who are already overburdened by numerous demands in their work?* Answers we have given to this question include (a) having students

initially enroll in courses in which the instructor *explicitly* consents to participate in the CTP, (b) offering both training and ongoing support to participating faculty, and (c) working with college students who wish to mentor students with ID in courses and other campus activities. We discussed with both administrators and faculty that mentorship can be a valuable service learning or field experience for students from a variety of disciplines.

- *Is it fair to provide course modifications (i.e., modifications in course content) to students with ID when other students have to master all of the content?* If students with ID are *auditing* a class as part of their CTP credential, then they are not receiving official university credit, and it is reasonable to modify course content, in collaboration with the course instructor. However, if a student with ID is taking the course *for credit*, then that student must attempt to master all of the material which other students are expected to learn, receiving reasonable accommodations to do so. In this instance, course content would not be altered.

Two Student Examples

Jillian. Jillian is a 21-year-old college student attending classes part time. She enjoys staying active and would love to teach young children. She started on this career path through her paid summer job at a local preschool and volunteer work in the Early Childhood Center of the university she attends. She studies hard and is a diligent student, with professors exclaiming they wish all their students were as committed to learning as Jillian.

Jillian works with peer mentoring partners who support her inclusion in both the campus culture and the community. She receives assistance with note-taking, determining key points from lectures and texts, and studying, but otherwise is a very self-sufficient and independent young woman. Although Jillian is enrolled in college as a non-degree-seeking student and audits her classes, she consistently strives to do her best to gain knowledge and skills from each of her courses. Each semester, her mother, past and present mentoring partners, the program coordinator, and Jillian meet to discuss Jillian's progress toward her goals, review her semester schedule, and determine what types of supports they believe she will need to fully benefit from her college classes and experiences. Timelines are reviewed and mentoring plans are revised accordingly.

As many college students do, Jillian balances her academic coursework with the demands of a part-time job. As an assistant manager for the men's collegiate basketball team, Jillian is required to attend all practices and home games during the season. Her responsibilities include running the warm-up sessions for players and managing the equipment during games and practices. As one member of the team explained, "She knows how to find the good in everything. I probably play the least of anyone on the team, but she still manages to make me feel like the star player. I love her for that." (Donaldson, 2011, p. 23). Through this experience, Jillian has multiple opportunities to meet new people, engage socially with other college students, and be a valued and contributing member of a group on campus.

When Jillian was in elementary and high school, her parents made sure she was always included in the general education environment, even though she received special education services. As an individual with Down syndrome and ID, Jillian inadvertently challenged notions of inability through her determination, the same determination demonstrated on the university campus. As Jillian stated, "Don't give me the answers, just read the questions. I can answer them myself." Her success is not measured by a passing test grade, but rather by her independence, persistence, self-advocacy, and belonging as related to her personal goals for attending college.

Silas. From a young age, Silas had known he wanted to attend college. Because he had received special education services and had been diagnosed with ID, few people believed that he would attain this goal. His mother struggled with teachers who did not understand how to accommodate his learning styles and with a vocational counselor who proclaimed that Silas would not be able to work. Silas never gave up on himself or his quest to be "the ultimate artist." After high school, he continued to volunteer at his former school's office. There he learned of a new pilot project that might help him find his place in higher education.

With art as his leading interest, Silas enrolled in a Photoshop course at a community college. He earned an "A" in the course and subsequently took classes in graphic design, drawing, and an academic skills program. He gained general business skills through an experiential education course and he earned credit by working in a local comic book store. In his third semester, Silas was recruited to illustrate a science fiction book by a local author. Now a participant in the SHEP program, Silas is employed at a screen print business where he assists with the production of t-shirts 3 days a week. His employers are impressed by his dependability and work ethic and have offered him the opportunity to work with one of their graphic designers for an hour each day before beginning his regular duties.

SHEP staff members meet regularly with Silas to discuss plans for the future, provide tutoring, and encourage his ever-growing independence. Since beginning his journey to college, Silas became a member of the workforce, maintained a 3.5 grade point average, earned his driver's license, developed many friendships, and became a great advocate for other students with disabilities. He participates in the campus Best Buddies Program, in which students with ID are matched with other students on campus, and he is considering becoming an officer in that program. He believes that "people with disabilities will always succeed with the patience and help of friends, [supportive staff], and family." See Figure 2 for Silas's PATH, indicating his goals and his plans for achieving them.

Implications for Teachers

New postsecondary education opportunities for students with ID have tremendous implications for goal setting and transition planning that IEP teams should prioritize with students. Along with the specific IDEA transition requirements for students to learn about and explore postsecondary opportunities, the reality that students with ID are actually attending colleges and universities should compel IEP teams to prepare students for such experiences. As noted earlier, teachers can institute such person-centered planning processes as PATH (see Figure 2), to help students prepare for the transition to postsecondary education.

Moving beyond exploration to a focus on problem solving and increased independence has become a necessity as possibilities open for students with ID. Students with ID are not limited to traditional structured employment and leisure activities; it is critical that teachers start early in teaching self-advocacy skills to students with ID (J. Kleinert, Harrison, Fisher, & H. Kleinert, 2010). In preparation for postsecondary education in which students must direct their own learning, students need to be empowered as self-advocates, gain a better understanding of their abilities, and take a greater ownership of their own IEP meetings (Jones, 2006; Test et al., 2004). These skills should be taught and nurtured early in a student's school career, embedding skill develop-

> **Moving beyond exploration to a focus on problem solving and increased independence has become a necessity as possibilities open for students with ID.**

ment for fostering self-determination in elementary school, leading toward meaningful engagement of students in their IEPs at least by the time the students enter high school.

Aside from a focus on self-determination and self-advocacy, elementary and secondary teachers, from preschool to 12th grade, also need to ensure that students have the necessary supports for involvement in preferred extracurricular activities (H. Kleinert, Miracle, & Sheppard-Jones, 2007) including opportunities for community and service learning, academic clubs (e.g., Foreign Language, Yearbook, or Future Farmers of America), and special interest clubs (e.g., Photography and Computer), to develop the confidence and skills to continue these activities in college or other postsecondary settings. Through meaningful involvement in these activities, students with ID develop socialization and problem-solving skills necessary for inclusive experiences on a college or university campus. In many instances, we have found the social aspect of college to be even more important for promoting student growth and independence than the academics.

Teachers also need to ensure that students with ID have access to the grade-level general curriculum. Strategies to enable students to understand more complex academic content and build valued social relationships, including peer-support strategies (Carter et al., 2009) are important, so that when learning new things together they can provide both academic and social supports to their peers with significant disabilities. Many of the college students who volunteer to mentor a peer with a disability describe having a similar mentoring experience while still in high school. Fostering relationships such as these early on helps students recognize the benefits of interacting with others of varying ability and paves the way for the development of natural supports on a college campus.

Access remains a daunting barrier to many students with ID who wish to continue their formal learning beyond high school. Institutions of higher education are becoming increasingly technologically savvy, requiring students to enter college with more than basic skills in accessing and using technology. Beyond the required technology, however, is also the need for high school students with ID to have access to and experience with the assistive technology necessary for academic success in college, such as the use of iPAD applications that combine the power of augmentative communication systems with word-processing capabilities for college assignments.

Finally, like all high school students who are planning their futures, students with ID need the opportunity to receive assistance from school guidance counselors, specifically trained in helping students to identify sources of financial aid and college opportunities to address their career goals. Awareness of the resources students need to independently negotiate college expectations is paramount for contemporary IEP transition teams. Otherwise, valuable learning opportunities are lost, stunting the potential growth of young adults with ID.

Final Thoughts

Times are changing, as evidenced through the myriad of opportunities that now exist nationwide for students with disabilities, particularly students with ID. Thirty-five years ago, advocates fought for students with disabilities to have a right to a P–12 education; now we are talking about students with ID meaningfully participating in institutions of higher education. In recognition of these changes, intervention specialists can now begin assisting IEP teams in imagining what a postsecondary experience might look like for a student, and start the planning process, working toward this possibility.

In this article we have described the new opportunities for postsecondary education available to students with ID through the Higher Education Opportunities Act of 2008. We have also attempted to describe why these opportunities are important to students with ID, and key strategies for ensuring that their college experience is an important next step to a valued career, new friendships and interests, and ultimately, a fulfilling life. Indeed, these are the things we want for all students!

References

Carter, E., Cushing, L., & Kennedy, C. (2009). *Peer support strategies for improving all students' social lives and learning.* Baltimore, MD: Brookes.

Donaldson, B. (2011). Jillian the magnificent: Meet NKU's guardian angel maker. *Northern Magazine, 9*(2), 20-23.

Gil, L. (2007). Bridging the transition gap from high school to college. *TEACHING Exceptional Children, 40*(2), 12-16.

Grigal, M., Hart, D., & Paiewonsky, M. (2010). Postsecondary education: The next frontier for individuals with intellectual disabilities. In M. Grigal & D. Hart (Eds.), *Think college: Postsecondary education options for students with intellectual disabilities* (pp. 1–28). Baltimore, MD: Brookes.

Hall, M., Kleinert, H., & Kearns, J. (2000). College connection: New directions in post-secondary programs for students with moderate and severe disabilities. *TEACHING Exceptional Children, 32*(3), 58-65.

Hart, D., Grigal, M., Sax, C., Martinez, D., & Will, M. (2006). Postsecondary education options for students with intellectual disabilities, *Research to Practice*, *45*, 1–4. Retrieved from http://www.thinkcollege.net/for-professionals/pathways-to-postsecondary-education

Higher Education Opportunities Act of 2008, Public Law 110-315, 20 U.S.C. §§ 1001 *et seq.*

Hughson, E.A., Moodie, S., & Uditsky, B. (2006). *The story of inclusive post secondary education in Alberta: Final research report 2004–2005.* Retrieved from http://www.steps-forward.org/The_Story_of_Inclusive_Post_Secondary_Education_in_Alberta.pdf

Individuals With Disabilities Education Act (IDEA) of 2004, Public Law 108-446, 20 U.S.C. §§ 1400 *et seq.*

Jones, M. (2006). Teaching self-determination: Empowered teachers, empowered Students. *TEACHING Exceptional Children*, *39*(1), 12–17.

Jones, M., Weir, C., & Hart, D. (2011). Impact on teacher education programs of students with intellectual disabilities attending college, *Insight: A Think College Brief on Policy, Research, & Practice*, *6*. Retrieved from http://www.thinkcollege.net

Kellems, R., & Morningstar, M. (2010). Tips for transition. *TEACHING Exceptional Children*, *43*(2), 60–68.

Kleinert, H., Miracle, S., & Sheppard-Jones, K. (2007). Including students with moderate and severe disabilities in extracurricular and community recreation activities: Steps to success! *TEACHING Exceptional Children*, *39*(6), 33–38.

Kleinert, J., Harrison, B., Fisher, T., & Kleinert, H. (2010). "I can and I did"— Self-advocacy for young students with developmental disabilities. *TEACHING Exceptional Children*, *43*(2), 16–26.

Migliore, A., Butterworth, J., & Hart, D. (2009). Postsecondary education and employment outcomes for youth with intellectual disabilities. *Think College Fast Facts, 1.* Retrieved from http://www.thinkcollege.net

Moon, M. S., Grigal, M., & Neubert, D. (2001). High school and beyond: Students with significant disabilities complete high school through alternative programs in post-secondary settings. *Exceptional Parent, 31*(7), 52–57.

Newman, L., Wagner, M., Cameto, R., Knokey, A., & Shaver, D. (2010). *Comparisons across time of the outcomes of youth with disabilities up to 4 years after high school. A report of findings from the National Longitudinal Transition Study (NLTS) and the National Longitudinal Transition Study-2 (NLTS2)* (NCSER 2010-3008). Menlo Park, CA: SRI International.

O'Brien, J. (2010). *Supporting social roles: A second bottom line for services to people with developmental disabilities.* San Francisco, CA: Creative Commons. Retrieved from http://www.inclusion.com

O'Brien, J., & O'Brien, C. L. (Ed.). (2002). *Implementing person-centered planning: Voices of experience. Volume II.* Toronto, ON: Inclusion Press.

Pierpoint, J., O'Brien, J., & Forest, M. (2011). *Path: Planning possible positive futures: Planning alternative tomorrows with hope* (2nd ed.). Toronto, ON: Inclusion Press.

Ramani, S., Gruppen, L., & Kachur, E. K. (2006). Twelve tips for developing effective mentors. *Medical Teacher, 28,* 404–408. doi:10.1080/01421590600825326

Stoddard, D. A. (2003). *The heart of mentoring Ten proven principles for developing people to their fullest potential.* Colorado Springs, CO: NavPress.

Test, D., Mason, C., Hughes, C., Konrad, M., Neal, M., & Wood, W. (2004). Student involvement in individualized education program meetings. *Exceptional Children, 70,* 391–412.

Think College. (2011a). *Postsecondary education initiatives for students with intellectual disabilities.* Retrieved from http://www.thinkcollege.net/databases/programs-database? view=programsdatabase

Think College. (2011b). *Should I even think about college for my son or daughter?* Retrieved from http://www.thinkcollege.net/for-families

U.S. Department of Education. (2010). *Transition and postsecondary programs for students with intellectual disabilities.* Retrieved from http://www2.ed.gov/programs/tpsid/index.html

Wagner, M., Newman, L., Cameto, R., Garza, N., & Levine, P. (2005). *After high school: A first look at the postschool experiences of youth with disabilities. A report from the National Longitudinal Transition Study-2 (NLTS2).* Menlo Park, CA: SRI International. Retrieved from www.nlts2.org/reports/2005_04/nlts2_report_2005_04_complete.pdf.

Zachary, L. J. (2005). *Creating a mentoring culture: The organization's guide.* San Francisco, CA: Jossey-Bass.

HAROLD L. KLEINERT (Kentucky CEC), Executive Director, Human Development Institute, University of Kentucky, Lexington.

MELISSA M. JONES (Kentucky CEC), Associate Professor of Special Education, Department of Teacher Education, Northern Kentucky University, Highland Heights.

KATHLEEN SHEPPARD-JONES, Training Director, Human Development Institute.

BEVERLY HARP, Postsecondary Program Specialist, Supported Higher Education Project, Human Development Institute.

ELIZABETH M. HARRISON, Principal Investigator, Supported Higher Education Project, Human Development Institute, University of Kentucky, Lexington.

Address correspondence concerning this article to Harold L. Kleinert, Human Development Institute, University of Kentucky, 126 Mineral Industries Building, Lexington, KY 40506-0051 (e-mail: hklein@uky.edu). This article was supported in part by a grant from the U.S. Department of Education Office of Postsecondary Education Programs (Grant P407A100005). However, the opinions expressed do not necessarily reflect the position or policy of the Office of Postsecondary Education Programs, and no official endorsement should be inferred.

ARTICLE 27

Anatomy of a Scare

Newsweek, March 2, 2009

When one study linked childhood vaccines to autism, it set off a panic.
The research didn't hold up, but some wounded families can't move on.

SHARON BEGLEY, WITH JENEEN INTERLANDI

Like many people in London on that bleak February day in 1998, biochemist Nicholas Chadwick was eager to hear what the scientists would say. The Royal Free Hospital, where he was a graduate student in the lab of gastroenterologist Andrew Wakefield, had called a press conference to unveil the results of a new study. With flashbulbs popping, Wakefield stepped up to the bank of microphones: he and his colleagues, he said, had discovered a new syndrome that they believed was triggered by the MMR (measles, mumps, rubella) vaccine. In eight of the 12 children in their study, being published that day in the respected journal *The Lancet,* they had found severe intestinal inflammation, with the symptoms striking six days, on average, after the children received the MMR.

But hospitals don't hold elaborate press conferences for studies of gut problems. The reason for all the hoopla was that nine of the children in the study also had autism, and the tragic disease had seized them between one and 14 days after their MMR jab. The vaccine, Wakefield suggested, had damaged the intestine—in particular, the measles part had caused serious inflammation—allowing harmful proteins to leak from the gut into the bloodstream and from there to the brain, where they damaged neurons in a way that triggered autism. Although in their paper the scientists noted that "we did not prove an association" between the MMR and autism, Wakefield was adamant. "It's a moral issue for me," he said, "and I can't support the continued use of [the MMR] until this issue has been resolved."

That's strange, thought Chadwick. For months he had been extracting genetic material from children's gut biopsies, looking for evidence of measles from the MMR. That was the crucial first link in the chain of argument connecting the MMR to autism: the measles virus infects the gut, causing inflammation and leakage, then gut leakage lets neurotoxic compounds into the blood and brain. Yet Chadwick kept coming up empty-handed. "There were a few cases of false positives, [but] essentially all the samples tested were negative," he later told a judicial hearing. When he explained the negative results, he told *Newsweek,* Wakefield "tended to shrug his shoulders. Even in lab meetings he would only talk about data that supported his hypothesis. Once he had his theory, he stuck to it no matter what." Chadwick was more disappointed than upset, figuring little would come from the *Lancet* study. "Not many people thought [Wakefield] would be taken that seriously," Chadwick recalls. "We thought most people would see the *Lancet* paper for what it was—a very preliminary collection of [only 12] case reports. How wrong we were."

The next day, headlines in the British press screamed, DOCTORS LINK AUTISM TO MMR VACCINE AND BAN THREE-IN-ONE JAB, URGE DOCTORS AFTER NEW FEARS. That was mild compared with what followed. Hysteria over childhood vaccinations built to such a crescendo that Wakefield's nuanced warning—that it was specifically the triple vaccine, not single-disease vaccines (even measles), that posed a threat—was drowned out. In 2001, Prime Minister Tony Blair and his wife, Cherie, refused to say whether their son, then 19 months old, had received the MMR; rumors swirled that they had gone to France so the child could receive the measles vaccine alone. In 2003, a docudrama about Wakefield ran on British TV, depicting him as having his files stolen and his phone tapped by evil pharmaceutical companies intent on protecting their vaccines. As one reviewer described the show: "The MMR vaccine is coming to get our kids."

The MMR vaccine is the same on both sides of the Atlantic, so fears of childhood vaccines (of which U.S. health officials recommend 35 by age 6) started a backlash in the United States, too, fueled in no small part by the fact that the incidence of autism was rising for reasons scientists could not fully explain. In California, for instance, the incidence of autism had risen from 6.2 per 10,000 births in 1990 to 42.5 in 2001. Groups of parents began refusing vaccines for their children. Within a few years of Wakefield's announcement, rates of MMR vaccinations in Britain fell from 92 percent to below 80 percent. Although there was no comparable nationwide decrease in the United States, pockets of resistance to vaccination appeared throughout the country, laying the groundwork for a sevenfold increase in measles outbreaks. Looking back from the perspective of 11 years, the panic seems both inevitable and inexplicable.

Inevitable, because legitimate scientists publishing in respected journals produced evidence of a link between vaccines and autism, and because the press as well as politicians and even public-health officials stoked the mounting hysteria. Inexplicable because, by the early 2000s, scientific support for that link had evaporated as completely as the red dot on a baby's vaccinated thigh.

Scientists and government officials who defended the safety of childhood vaccines were not shy about attributing the fears to the science illiteracy of the public and the fearmongering of the press. In truth, however, after Wakefield's announcement there was a steady drumbeat of studies—not from kooks in basement labs but from real scientists working at real institutions and publishing in real, peer-reviewed journals—that backed him up. In 2002, pathologist John O'Leary of Coombe Women's Hospital in Dublin reported that he had found RNA from the measles virus in 7 percent of normal children—but in 82 percent of those with autism, suggesting that some children are unable to clear the vaccinated virus from their systems, resulting in autism. That same year, a Utah State University biologist reported finding high levels of antibodies against the measles virus in the blood and spinal fluid of autistic children; the MMR, he postulated, had triggered a hyperimmune response that attacked the children's brains. In 2003, gastroenterologist Arthur Krigsman, then at New York University School of Medicine, reported finding what Wakefield had: that the guts of 40 autistic children were severely inflamed, lending support to the idea that leaks allowed pernicious compounds to make a beeline for the brain.

But these studies and others supporting the link between autism and the MMR were nothing compared with an extraordinary step that had been taken by the U.S. government and by one of the country's leading medical organizations. On July 7, 1999, the American

Academy of Pediatrics (AAP) and the U.S. Public Health Service issued a warning about the preservative in many vaccines. Called thimerosal, it contains 49.6 percent ethylmercury by weight and had been used in vaccines since the 1930s, including the diphtheria/tetanus/pertussis (DTP) and Haemophilus influenzae (Hib) vaccines (but not the MMR). The experts tried to be reassuring, saying in a statement there are "no data or evidence of any harm" from thimerosal. But, they continued, children's cumulative exposure to mercury from vaccines "exceeds one of the federal safety guidelines" for mercury. (By 2003, most childhood vaccines did not contain thimerosal, though flu vaccines still did.) The AAP statement did not mention autism.

But on April 6, 2000, Rep. Dan Burton did. Burton had previously distinguished himself by his support for laetrile, the quack cancer remedy. Now he was chairing a congressional hearing on the link between vaccines and autism. His own grandson, Burton told an overflow audience filled with antivaccine activists, was perfectly normal until he received "nine shots on one day," after which he "quit speaking, ran around banging his head against the wall, screaming and hollering and waving his hands." Witnesses testified about their own tragedies, such as a child's "journey into silence" soon after receiving the MMR vaccine. Wakefield, too, testified. Since his *Lancet* paper, he said, he had studied scores more children, identifying almost 150 in whom MMR had triggered autism. O'Leary, the Irish scientist who had confirmed Wakefield's finding of measles virus in the guts of children with autism, pronounced himself "here to say that Wakefield's hypothesis is correct." Now there were two explosive theories about the dangers of childhood vaccines: Wakefield's, that the MMR caused gut inflammation and the release of autism-causing proteins into the blood and brain, and the thimerosal theory, that the mercury in child-

hood vaccines damages the immune system and, possibly, the brain.

Burton's hearing was widely covered in the press, but the attention was nothing compared with the flood of stories that were about to be unleashed. That November "60 Minutes" aired a segment featuring children who "appeared normal" until getting the MMR. On Nov. 10, 2002, *The New York Times Magazine* ran an article on "The Not-So-Crackpot Autism Theory," about thimerosal. It included news of an August 2002 study by the father-and-son team Mark and David Geier, who combed a federal database of reported "adverse events" after vaccinations. They found "increases in the incidence of autism" after children got thimerosal-containing vaccines compared with thimerosal-free vaccines. The following spring, the Geiers published another study: the more mercury in their vaccines, the more likely children were to develop autism.

By this time, mistrust of the scientific establishment—and of anyone defending vaccines—had mushroomed into something decidedly uglier. When pediatrician Paul Offit, a vaccine expert at the Children's Hospital of Philadelphia, testified before Burton's panel, he said that he had had his own children vaccinated, and gave their names. At a break, a congressional staffer pulled him aside and said, "Never, never mention the names of your own children in front of a group like this." The following year he received an e-mail threatening to "hang you by your neck until you are dead." The FBI deemed it credible and assigned him an armed guard during vaccine meetings at the U.S. Centers for Disease Control and Prevention.

The first cracks in the vaccine theories of autism appeared in early 2004. An investigation by British journalist Brian Deer in *The Sunday Times of London* revealed that the children Wakefield described in the *Lancet* study had not simply arrived on the doorstep of the Royal Free. At least five were clients of an attorney who was working on a case against vaccine makers alleging that the MMR caused the children's autism. In addition, two years before the *Lancet* paper Wakefield had received £55,000 from Britain's Legal Aid Board, which supports research related to lawsuits. After meeting with Deer, *Lancet* editor Richard Horton told the British press, "If we knew then what we know now, we certainly would not have published the part of the paper that related to MMR . . . There were fatal conflicts of interest." On March 6, 10 of Wakefield's 12 coauthors formally retracted the paper's suggestion that the MMR and autism were linked.

Wakefield did not join them. Now executive director of a Texas nonprofit called Thoughtful House, which offers treatments for autism, he admits he was retained and paid by the lawyer for the parents of autistic children but denies that posed a conflict of interest. "At the time the children were referred to the Royal Free, none of the parents were involved in litigation, though some went on to do so," he says. The legal board's payment supported other vaccine-autism research he was conducting, Wakefield says, not that in the *Lancet* paper. "I will not be deterred from continuing to look after these children and research their problems," says Wakefield.

In 2005 Britain's General Medical Council, which licenses physicians, began a hearing in which Wakefield was charged with professional misconduct for, among other things, the alleged financial conflict of interest in the *Lancet* study. The investigation has since expanded, with new charges by journalist Deer that Wakefield or his coauthors misrepresented the children's medical records. In particular, Deer reported that the children's gut and autism symptoms appeared long before their MMR rather than, as the 1998

Lancet study reported, right after. Wakefield denies doing anything improper, saying he "merely entered the documented findings into the *Lancet* paper."

The charges against Wakefield were the least of what was undermining the vaccine theory of autism. What would eventually become an overwhelming body of evidence showing that childhood vaccines did not increase the risk of autism began to pile up. In 2002 scientists led by Brent Taylor of the Royal Free reported that their study of 473 children had found no difference in the rates of autism between those who had received the MMR and those who had not, providing "further evidence against involvement of MMR vaccine in the initiation of autism," they wrote. Scientists in Finland, studying 2 million children, reached the same conclusion in a 2000 paper. So did scientists at Boston University, studying the medical records of 3 million children, in 2001. In 2004 a study of the medical records of 14,000 children in Britain found that the more thimerosal the children had been exposed to through vaccines, the less likely they were to have neurological problems. Also that year, the Institute of Medicine (IOM) in the United States, having reviewed 200-plus studies, rejected the vaccine-autism hypothesis. Not only did it find no evidence of a link—and, indeed, evidence against the existence of a link—but it took aim at the original 1998 *Lancet* paper by Wakefield's group. Because autism symptoms typically appear at the same age that children get the MMR, the panel said, it was inevitable that some children would first show symptoms of autism soon after being vaccinated. Coincidence is not causality.

If the IOM panel thought that would be the end of it, they were naive. From the halls of Congress to the airwaves to the pages of leading newspapers, true believers went at the vaccine-autism link more passionately than ever. After the IOM released its report, Rep. Dave Weldon of Florida, a physician, took to the House floor to denounce the CDC for its vaccine-autism research. The agency, Weldon charged, was guilty of "selective use of the data to make the associations [between vaccines and autism] disappear" and had engaged in "a public-relations campaign [on behalf of vaccines] rather than sound science."

The following year, a story by environmental lawyer Robert F. Kennedy Jr. called "Deadly Immunity" made the case against thimerosal in *Rolling Stone*. Activists used large chunks of the money they were raising from terrified parents to spread their message. On June 8, a full-page ad for Generation Rescue, which had been founded the month before to push the thimerosal theory, ran in *The New York Times,* proclaiming, "Mercury Poisoning and Autism: It Isn't a Coincidence." It included quotes from several politicians, with Burton stressing research that "indicated a direct link between exposure to mercury and autism," and Sen. John Kerry saying "mercury has been linked to autism." Later that year, a book titled "Evidence of Harm: Mercury in Vaccines and the Autism Epidemic," by journalist David Kirby, got huge attention in the media. Kirby appeared on "Imus in the Morning" several times, as did politicians supporting his thesis. Sen. Joseph Lieberman, citing the growing incidence of autism coupled with the increase in the number of required vaccines, said, "Make sure your kids are getting vaccines without thimerosal."

Throughout this saga, the "vaccines cause autism" side could claim more powerful persuaders than the dry-as-dust scientific papers and even drier scientists trying to reassure parents. On Sept. 18, 2007, model and actress Jenny McCarthy appeared on "The Oprah Winfrey Show" to promote her new book, "Louder Than Words," in which she describes curing her son Evan's autism—which she blames on

the MMR—with diet and chelation, a process that chemically binds heavy compounds in the body so they can be excreted. Asked about the CDC statement that science does not link vaccines to autism, McCarthy said, "My science is Evan." Researchers were dumbfounded that so many parents rejected the conclusions of the CDC, the Institute of Medicine and the American Academy of Pediatrics (which after its thimerosal debacle had put itself foursquare behind childhood vaccines). "The issue for people like Jenny McCarthy isn't that doctors and scientists and public-health officials haven't listened to parents," writes Paul Offit in his 2008 book "Autism's False Prophets: Bad Science, Risky Medicine and the Search for a Cure." "It's that they've been unable to find any evidence to validate parents' concern."

The anti-vaccine campaign was having an effect. As parents postponed vaccinating their children, or refused vaccines entirely, children were suddenly catching preventable diseases, and some were dying. The number of measles cases in the United States reached 131 in 2008, the highest in decades. Last month five children in Minnesota became infected with Hib. Four developed serious complications; the fifth child died. Other parents, believing that yanking mercury out would cure a child's autism, opted for chelation. Unfortunately, it can pull out vital metals such as iron and calcium as well as toxic mercury and lead.

An overwhelming majority of vaccine and autism experts were convinced that parents were putting their children at real risk over a phantom fear. But perhaps no one understood that the MMR theory, in particular, was a house of cards better than molecular biologist Stephen Bustin of the University of London. In 2004 the U.K. High Court asked him to inspect the Dublin lab that had reported measles genes in the guts of autistic children right after they received the MMR, an important confirmation of Wakefield's theory. It was an uncomfortable situation, Bustin recalls, playing cop at another scientist's lab. But he discovered a number of problems. The genetic material the lab had found was DNA, but measles genes are made of RNA. The equipment was so poorly calibrated that its results depended on where in the machine the sample was placed. Wakefield defends his collaborator, saying that a later test confirmed "the fidelity and high quality of [the Dublin lab's] methods . . . The original results that found measles virus genetic material in intestinal biopsies in 75 percent of the autistic children compared with 6 percent of the nonautistic controls still stand."

Under U.S. law, families who believe their child has been injured by a vaccine have their claims heard by a special "vaccine court." Since 1999 some 5,000 families had filed claims asserting that vaccines caused their child's autism. That is too many to try individually, so in 2004 they were combined into three test cases. One would represent the claim that MMR caused the children's autism, one that thimerosal in vaccines other than MMR did and one that the combination did. The last theory was tested with the case of Michelle Cedillo, a 12-year-old with severe autism; hearings began on June 11, 2007. Before it was over, the evidence would include 939 papers from journals and textbooks and testimony running thousands of pages. One of those testifying was Bustin, who explained that the finding of measles genes in autistic children rested on shoddy science. "Normally it hardly matters when a scientific paper gets it wrong," Bustin says. "But in this case, it matters a great deal."

On Feb. 12 Special Master George Hastings Jr. announced his decision in the Cedillo case. Every study conducted to test Wakefield's MMR hypothesis, he concluded, "found no evidence that the MMR vaccination is associated with autism." And the evidence "falls far short" of showing a thimerosal connection.

That is hardly the end of the legal cases. All three sets of parents in the test cases say they will take their claims against the manufacturers to civil court, hoping to convince juries— through the emotional power of tragically damaged children—of what they failed to prove to the vaccine court. And if those cases, too, absolve vaccines? In postings on antivaccine sites such as GenerationRescue.org and SafeMinds.org, parents have made clear that they think the system is rigged and that vaccines condemned their children to a lifetime of being barricaded behind the impregnable wall of autism. Perhaps it should not be a mystery why people refuse to believe science, with its tentative hypotheses, zigzag pathway to finding answers and a record of getting some things wrong before getting them right (see hormone-replacement therapy). On the day the court announced its decision, Offit pointed out that "tens of millions of dollars have been spent trying to answer these questions [about vaccines and autism]," but many people "refuse to believe the science." Perhaps, he mused, that's "because while it's very easy to scare people, it's very hard to unscare them."

And it's impossible to prove a negative such as "vaccines do not cause autism." The slim hope of finding a link—perhaps only children with specific genetic variants are at risk of developing autism as a result of vaccines; perhaps the vaccine is dangerous only in combination with other environmental triggers—keeps activists at the barricades. (They received some support in 2007, when the federal government settled the case of Hannah Poling, admitting that a vaccine had exacerbated a rare underlying cellular disorder and, as a result, brought on autistic symptoms.) Wakefield, unrepentant, slams the vaccine-court decision for "not being based on any definitive science." One powerful advocacy group, Autism Speaks, said after the decision that it will continue to support research into whether certain children with "underlying medical or genetic conditions may be more vulnerable to adverse effects of vaccines." Chief science officer Geraldine Dawson says they "owe it to the parents to listen and address their concerns. We don't want to close the door." Not even a door that,

since it was opened 11 years ago this month, has let through such demons. It is bad enough that the vaccine-autism scare has undermined one of the greatest successes of preventive medicine and terrified many new parents. Most tragic of all, it has diverted attention and millions of dollars away from finding the true causes and treatments of a cruel disease.

ARTICLE 28

Helping Students with Disabilities Transition to College

21 Tips for Students with LD and/or ADD/ADHD

Making the transition from high school to college poses challenges for most students. Moving from the secure regulated world of secondary education into an unfamiliar environment that requires greater independence, autonomy, and personal decision making can be a destabilizing experience. Managing this change can make students with disabilities feel even more anxious and overwhelmed. The 21 tips featured in this article are intended to help counselors, teachers, and parents support high school students with disabilities in preparing for this transition. By previewing these strategies, teachers and parents can increase student awareness of situations they will encounter, help them play an active role in making important decisions, and guide them toward a greater chance of success.

DAVID J. CONNOR

Increasing numbers of students with disabilities are pursuing postsecondary education. The number of students with learning disabilities (LD) attending college has more than tripled in the last 3 decades (Stodden, Conway, & Chang, 2003). An estimated 23% of students with LD enroll in a 2-year college program, with 11% attending a 4-year institution (Wagner, Newman, Cameto, Garza, & Levine, 2005). Similarly, 30% of students with attention deficit disorder/attention deficit hyperactivity disorder (ADD/ADHD) enroll in 2-year college programs, and 6% attend 4-year institutions (Wagner et al., 2005). However, the transition to a postsecondary education environment can make students with LD and/or ADD/ADHD feel anxious and overwhelmed (Cohen, 2004; Cohn, 1998; Lee & Jackson, 1992; Sandler, 2008). Only 28% of these students manage to graduate, which is approximately half of the graduation rate for students without disabilities (Gregg, 2009).

Such sobering statistics indicate the numerous difficulties that students with LD and/or ADD/ADHD face when transitioning to and negotiating the complex demands of college. College requires students to respond to an increase in the volume and complexity of academic work (Lindstrom, 2007); manage "standard" classes such as Freshman Composition (Clinton & Higbee, 2011; Hadley, 2007); learn largely via lecture format, despite the growth in technology-based options (Komarraju & Karau, 2008); meet second-language requirements (Madaus, 2003); study with professors whose support of students can be unpredictable (Ginsberg & Schulte, 2008); and maintain an acceptable grade point average (DaDeppo, 2009). Many students with LD and/or ADD/ADHD begin college unprepared to manage what might be the most significant demand placed upon them: to shift from others leading their learning to students leading their own learning. Student success is dependent on students knowing the full range of supports available to them—from technology to personnel.

Students with LD and/or ADD/ADHD need to learn to be autonomous in their decision making while they are still in high school, so they will be able to use these skills when they enter college. The need for autonomy is best described in the words of a college student with LD: "It's not like high school. Most classes are so big nobody cares about you; they don't even know who you are. Nobody will say anything until they are ready to kick you out" (Trainin & Swanson, 2005, p. 271).

To help students play an active role in making important decisions for a greater probability for success, teachers, counselors, administrators, and parents can ensure students address critical situations while they are still in high school and can make them aware of potential issues they might encounter in college and in the job market. Consider how you can use the following 21 tips to assist students with LD and/or ADD/ADHD to prepare for the transition to college.

Many students with LD and/or ADD/ADHD begin college unprepared to manage what might be the most significant demand placed upon them: to shift from others leading their learning to students leading their own learning.

---

1. Be Comfortable with the LD and/or ADD/ADHD Classification

Many students have negative associations with being labeled *disabled* and receiving special education services (Mooney, 2008). However, students who are able to shift this original disposition and "reframe" their understanding (Reiff, 2004, p. 185) come to see how LD and/or ADD/ADHD is not primarily an academic deficit, but rather an integral part of who they are and how they operate in the world (Mortimore & Crozier, 2006; Olney & Kim, 2001). To facilitate this, albeit a major undertaking, students can be part of a support group (Luna, 2003); seek an accomplished college student mentor with a similar disability through an organization such as Project Eye-to-Eye (http://www.projecteyetoeye.org/), for encouragement and support; and learn about neurodiversity as a way of accepting how normal human variation is—instead of seeing differences as abnormal (Armstrong, 2010).

2. Acknowledge Strengths and Areas of Need

Teachers and parents can help guide students with LD and/or ADD/ADHD to identify the skills in which they are proficient and the content areas where they excel. This information should be counterbalanced with self-knowledge of the skills and content areas in which they struggle (Milsom & Hartley, 2005). By using their proficient skills (e.g., organizing, asking questions, or thoroughly preparing) in classes where they might struggle with content, students can hone their abilities to self-assess, self-strategize, and problem solve—allowing them to self-manage.

For example, students who are visual learners but struggle in recalling voluminous amounts of information in a history class can make one-page concept maps with icons to help highlight the importance of and organize information, creating effective study aides. This can be done free-hand or by using technology (Mortimore & Crozier, 2006), including Internet-based programs such as https://bubbl.us/, designed to help students brainstorm, or readily available organizers such as those at http://my.hrw

Law	Ensures
Individuals with Disabilities Education Act (IDEA, 2006)[a]	K-12 school districts are required to provide a free and appropriate public education to all students with disabilities.
	Guarantees students with disabilities have the right to nondiscriminatory assessment, confidentiality, and due process.
	Individualized education programs (IEPs) can include accommodations and testing modifications.
Section 504 of the Rehabilitation Act of 1973 (2006)	Colleges are required to make their programs accessible to qualified students with disabilities.
	Colleges are required to make reasonable accommodations for students with disabilities that impact their ability to participate in college.
	If a college receives federal funds (regardless of whether it is public or private), it must be accessible to qualified students with disabilities. However, private schools are not held to the same level of requirements as public schools.
ADA Amendments Act of 2008 (ADAAA, 2009)	The 1990 Americans With Disabilities Act prohibited discrimination against individuals with disabilities in a variety of settings, including any entity that received federal funds (i.e., colleges and universities). The ADAAA expanded the spectrum of disabilities that may be eligible for accommodations; it is updated language also applied to Section 504, through a "conforming amendment."

Note. ADA = Americans with Disabilities Act.

[a]IDEA provisions terminate at high school graduation or at age 22, so students with disabilities cannot claim rights under this provision when in higher education.

TABLE 1   Laws That Ensure the Educational Rights of Students with Disabilities

.com/nsmedia/intgos/html/igo.htm. In addition, students can research their own learning styles (http://members.shaw.ca/mdde615/lrnstylsquiz7.htm) and multiple intelligence affinities (http://www.literacyworks.org/mi/assessment/findyourstrengths.html) with a view to improving their learning process.

3. Learn About the College Disability Services Office

Section 504 of the Rehabilitation Act of 1973 (2006) ensured the civil rights of people with disabilities. As part of that legislation, all colleges that receive any type of federal funding are required by law to have disability services on campus for students with disabilities (see Table 1). A student's request for accommodations and support services is verified by this office, which then approves relevant support from a range of possibilities (e.g., alternative testing arrangements, priority registration, assistive technology services, readers, note takers, sign language interpreters). The campus disability services office also prepares a document notifying professors of accommodations required by the student (without disclosing the specific disability)—although it is often the student's responsibility to give the information to the professor.

4. Practice Making Decisions

A central goal of education for all individuals, including those with LD and/or ADD/ADHD, is to develop autonomy (Hadley, 2007). Students should have opportunities to practice their decision-making skills consistently throughout high school and in different settings (i.e., home and community). Students can ponder hypothetical scenarios about commonplace problematic situations pertaining to the academic, social, and financial realms of college life. Simple decision-making strategies may include considering such things as

- The pros and cons of selecting a course load.
- Ramifications of different decisions pertaining to personal budgeting.
- Prioritizing choices in social situations.
- Learning to make a "Plan B."

In problem solving around these scenarios, students with LD and/or ADD/ADHD can come to recognize the highly personal nature of how individuals respond to the demands of college (Troiano, 2003).

5. Read "College Success Stories"

Students with LD and/or ADD/ADHD are experts on their own lives. Several have survived college and shared their experiences in the form of "how-to" books that are informative, useful, and decidedly from an "insider's" point of view (Sandler, 2008; see Table 2). This peer-to-peer approach is often written in an engaging manner and infused with the right amount of empathy, wit, and know-how, frequently focusing upon serious situations that are cast in humorous ways to help keep things in perspective (Mooney & Cole, 2000). Students with significant difficulties in reading can get these books on tape (Nelson & Lignugaris-Kraft, 1989) or use a text-to-speech program.

6. Know Student Rights before Attending College

Students who have documented accommodations throughout their earlier school years can usually receive testing accommodations

when taking college entrance exams such as the SAT or the ACT (Beale, 2005). These same accommodations can be secured in general at postsecondary institutions, through the campus disability services office. Students should be aware that rights to accommodation during any testing, however, does not mean diminution of their own responsibilities to prepare for the test.

7. Know Student Responsibilities before Attending College

With greater autonomy comes increased self-responsibility. Individuals with LD and/or ADD/ADHD intending to go to college should know about the federal regulations that affect them, including what kind of assistance they personally require (the more specific, the better)—and be able to provide documentation to substantiate their claim (Beale, 2005). The burden of proof is on the student to have his or her disability verified (Madaus & Shaw, 2006). Students should maintain information throughout high school on their school-based assessments and be prepared to share it with the campus disability services office. Once this information is shared, students will be notified of their status (i.e. "officially" recognized as having a disability), the accommodations they are entitled to, and possible optional services that exist at the college, such as access to a writing center, priority to quiet areas of the library, and so on.

8. Take a College Course While in High School

Taking a college class as part of a high school–college collaboration (Foley, 2006; see University of Pittsburgh, 2006, for example) permits students to gauge the difference between typical high school work and expected levels of college work, helping them prepare to meet increased standards. Many

Jonathan Mooney and David Cole's *Learning Outside the Lines: Two Ivy League Students with Learning Disabilities and ADHD Give You the Tools for Academic Success and Educational Revolution* (2000)	Two students who graduated top of their class from Brown University tell their tales and give advice on ways to maximize control over the educational experience and celebrate human diversity.
Michael Sandler's *College Confidence with ADD: The Ultimate Success Manual for ADD Students, from Applying to Academics, Preparation to Social Success and Everything Else You Need to Know* (2008)	A comprehensive, user-friendly book designed in "bite-size chunks" that addresses how to succeed in all aspects of college and in life.
Christopher Lee and Rosemary Jackson's *Faking It: A Look into the Mind of a Creative Learner* (1992)	The story of one boy's frustration with school experiences in which he learned to "get by," how they did not prepare him for college, and what he had to do to succeed there.
Pano Rodis, Andrew Garrod, and Lynn Boscardin's *Learning Disabilities and Life Stories* (2001)	The editors feature 13 autobiographical chapters of college students with LD and/or ADD. Each person shares their highly personal account of how they learn, how it has impacted their lives–and what they do to be successful in college.

TABLE 2   College "Success Stories"

universities extend their facilities so that high school students can take a class online or attend specific sessions on campus. A student with LD in reading comprehension who is a whiz in mathematics can find a course to his or her liking, as can an entrepreneurial-minded student with ADD/ADHD who can take a class in business. Such school-to-college links may influence high school students in their choice of selecting the college they have attended part-time, especially if they have developed personal contact with supportive staff and faculty there.

9. Participate in Precollege Academies

High school students with LD and/or ADD/ADHD who visit college campuses describe their experiences as valuable to understanding the academic differences between both settings (Kato, Nulty, Olszewski, Doolittle, & Flannery, 2006). A visit can consist of an intensive, day-long schedule including time for students with individualized education programs (IEP) to meet with personnel from the disability services office. Students should align any additional support services (e.g., vocational rehabilitation) with other key college contacts and offices. Another option is for school faculty or parents to arrange a visit for students with LD and/or ADD/ADHD to visit freshman college classrooms as early in their high school career as possible, with follow-up discussions with students and faculty on campus in areas of interest.

10. Develop Essential Skills

Study skills taught and practiced in high school help prepare students for the increased rigor of college (Connor & Lagares, 2007). Explicitly teaching students with LD and/or ADD/ADHD in high school to organize when and how to complete assignments, as well as how to manage time, can provide a strong foundation for using these skills in college (see Table 3; http://www.academictips.org; Lagares

Time Management

- Plot assignments, tests, and other commitments on paper or electronic organizer to see the long-term schedule "at a glance."

- Schedule time to study every week, and before midterms and finals. Err on the side of overbudgeting time; if you end up not needing it then it's a reward.

- Create a daily schedule based on the fluctuating demands of classes.

- Prioritize "to-do" items by placing them on an A-list, B-list, or C-list.

- "Self-check-in" at different times throughout the day (e.g., make a mental list of what needs to be done while taking a shower).

- Learn to be comfortable in saying "no" to social invitations that conflict with your study plans.

Writing Papers

- Budget plenty of time.

- Research sources, make hard copies, and write notes on them.

- Use prewriting activities to explore ideas about what you want to say.

- Write an outline, including the estimated number of pages for each section. Share this with your professor.

- Write a rough draft (or two) before a final version.

- Utilize support services available from the campus writing center and departmental peer tutors.

Test Taking

- Quickly review the entire test before answering anything; make notes on anything you may forget.

- Budget time for each section, as well as some at the end to review your work.

- Read directions carefully; circle or underline exactly what is being asked.

- Answer the easiest questions or sections first.

- Answer all questions, unless you are penalized for wrong answers.

Reducing Stress

- Use lists to keep organized, and take pleasure in crossing off completed items.

- Manage anxiety as best you can; use relaxation techniques such as deep breathing, meditation, self-affirmations, etc.

- Focus on the possible positive outcomes of a situation; do not dwell on negative thoughts.

- Cultivate healthy habits of eating and exercise.

- Use visualization techniques to temporarily imagine being in a preferable place.

- Balance study with recreational "rewards" such as meeting friends for coffee or going to the movies.

TABLE 3   Success Skills for College

& Connor, 2009). These skills should be taught explicitly across content-area classes. For example, a student can prepare for assignments by blocking out time on a calendar several days before the due date (depending upon the length of assignment) and by minimizing or eliminating social engagements. In preparing for an assignment, students can reduce distractions in their study environment by seeking an alternative environment (such as a quiet space in the library), selecting appropriate documents beforehand, and outlining the response in a bulleted format before writing a first draft.

11. Align Study Skills to Specific Classes

Although it is useful for students with LD and/or ADD/ADHD to learn a variety of strategies, it is more important for them to develop the ability of matching the best strategy to a

Strategy Acronym	Components	Use
I SWAM	I – INTEGRATE previous notes and readings S – SIT close to the teacher W – WRITE down everything A – ANALYZE verbal, nonverbal, and body language M – MONITOR for attention	To help takes notes when the instructor talks fast.
PP 123	P – PREPARE to takes notes P – PLAY the tape in small sections 1 – Listen . . . for meaning 2 – Listen . . . and takes notes 3 – Listen . . . and review	To help takes notes from a taped lecture.
TASSEL	T – TRY not to doodle while taking notes A – ARRIVE at each class prepared S – SIT near the front of the classroom S – SIT away from friends E – END daydreaming L – LOOK at the teacher	To help focus and reduce distraction when taking notes.

Note. Adapted with permission from the Learning Toolbox (http://coe.jmu.edu/LearningToolbox/notetaking.html). The Learning Toolbox has descriptions of each of these strategies, as well as other note-taking approaches.

TABLE 4   Strategies for Note-Taking in Classes with Dense Content

specific assignment. Students who are able to actively determine what they need to do and why they need to do it are inclined to develop a strong sense of autonomy (Allsopp, Minskoff, & Bolt, 2005). For example, a student who is easily distracted in classes involving a lot of note-taking can employ a variety of strategies (e.g., I SWAM, PP 123, and TASSEL; see Table 4).

12. Make Connections Among Classes

Just as strategies can be selected to match a specified task, they can also be generalized among courses. Once acclimatized to the content and format of all their classes, students with LD and/or ADD/ADHD can make connections to develop a set of preferred strategies to use with most of their classes. For example, time management and test-taking

> In learning to prepare for tests by blocking time, creating a review plan, and using memory-based strategies for all courses, students cultivate good study habits that increase the likelihood of academic success.

strategies can be used in every course (Kirby, Silvestri, Allingham, Parrila, & LaFave, 2008). In learning to prepare for tests by blocking time, creating a review plan, and using memory-based strategies for all courses, students cultivate good study habits that increase the likelihood of academic success.

13. Utilize Peer Tutor Services

The campus disability services office might offer the possibility of a peer tutor on a weekly basis for students with LD and/or ADD/ADHD, as do some academic departments. However, it is important to note that the most effective approach to peer tutoring is for students with disabilities to actively play a collaborative role in developing strategies guided by the tutor to help them strategize (Butler, Elaschuk, & Poole, 2000). For example, a student who struggles to determine what is important in assigned readings should specifically identify this area to work on with his or her tutor, actively describing what methods have been successful and unsuccessful to date.

14. Use Informal Peer Mentors

College is a place to develop friendships with diverse people. Students with LD and/or ADD/ADHD can cultivate friendships with a peer who understands their struggles in certain academic areas in high school or in the community. Informal peer mentors have often proven valuable to students with LD and/or ADD in discussing and reinforcing aspects of various classes (Kirby et al., 2008). Note that this can be a reciprocal arrangement in that students with LD and/or ADD/ADHD who excel in different areas—academics, sports, or arts—can in turn mentor their peers. In college, counselors (e.g., from the school's counseling services office, academic advisors, or disability services) can play an important role in introducing more experienced students who can serve as peer mentors.

15. Access Class Notes

Many students have difficulty taking detailed notes, and there are various ways to ameliorate this, including using a tape recorder, accessing notes from a note-taker, sharing or reviewing notes with trusted peers, or requesting a copy of the professor's notes (Hadley, 2007). The majority of universities provide ongoing information and professional development for faculty members to ensure that they know why and how to accommo-

date students with disabilities (Salzberg, Hardman, Price, & Morgan, 2002). It is worth mentioning, however, that although accommodations are legally guaranteed, some individual professors still are resistant providing them—causing students to either challenge professors or reluctantly accept the terms (Ryan, 2007). It is useful to interpret a challenging situation with a professor as an opportunity to problem solve. Despite increased awareness and professional development, some professors often do not know how to support students with disabilities. By suggesting solutions such as the professor preposting materials on the class web page one day in advance, students can help guide faculty to understand ways of working together to ensure maximum access to the curriculum. Further, explaining legal accommodations such as making an audio presentation that is the equivalent in content to written work expected in class, students help guide faculty to understand accommodations required of them. If all good-faith attempts fail, students should discuss the situation with the campus disability services office.

16. Evaluate a Professor before Taking the Class

Students with LD and/or ADD/ADHD may feel more anxious than their peers without disabilities when interacting with a professor and feel unsure of how that professor will respond to a request for accommodations. However, there are several ways to find out who are the most understanding and supportive professors. The first option is to have a direct conversation with the possible professors and ascertain the level of receptivity toward students with disabilities in their classes. Another way is to consult with the campus disability services office, as they will know which professors have been deemed particularly receptive toward students with

LD and/or ADD/ADHD and which have not (Cornett-DeVito & Worley, 2005). Another way to find out more about professors is simply being part of a student network that informs each other of allies and obstacles. Additonally, there are many web pages in public domains that share information about professors and their practices. Generally speaking, this suggestion is not meant to infer that students with disabilities seek out less rigorous courses than their peers, but rather gauge the degree of understanding particular professors may hold toward them.

17. Use the Benefits of Technology

Methods of teaching and learning within college have changed significantly due to the increased use of technology. Students with LD and/or ADD/ADHD can choose the types of classes they prefer, including online and hybrid courses that allow students to fulfill class assignments asynchronously. Utilizing assistive technology such as screen readers can help students to process large quantities of text in auditory form (Hecker, Burns, Elkind, Elkind, & Katz, 2002). Whether it is using a digital tape recorder, replaying podcasts, or maintaining a digital organizer, students with LD and/or ADD/ADHD have options to help them organize and manage their work.

18. Consider the Benefits of Self-Disclosure

It is important for students to know that their rights in college include the right not to reveal their disability to any faculty or staff member—and some students believe it beneficial to consciously shed a label that makes them uncomfortable. However, this strategy can prove to be counterproductive if students try to go it alone only to discover late in the semester that, in order to succeed in classes,

they actually do need accommodations. Individuals with LD and/or ADD/ADHD can register with the campus disability services office at any time during their college career. However, in general, there is a greater likelihood of success if students self-identify early in their college careers (Janiga & Costenbader, 2002). Students who feel they cannot cope with their workload can meet with a counselor to strategize how to better manage the demands of college (Getzel & Thoma, 2008). All students should be aware of the college student code of conduct for clear delineations of their rights and responsibilities.

19. Take Responsibility for One's Own Education

Once registered, it is vital for students with LD and/or ADD/ADHD to maintain an ongoing relationship with the campus disability services office; the advisers and counselors employed in these offices are often important advocates and allies. They can assist in many ways, including advising about courses, facilitating preferential registration, and resolving problems with professors (Durodoye, Combes, & Bryant, 2004). Students should make an appointment in person with the coordinator of the campus disability services office, and build a personal relationship with those who could be their biggest advocates as challenges arise over time (Janiga & Costenbader, 2002).

20. Cultivate Individual Talent

College is a place for students to grow in many ways, including cultivating abilities and talents (Heiman, 2006). Often, the emphasis on the "dis" in disability can overshadow what a student with LD and/or ADD/ADHD can do. It becomes imperative, therefore, that students continue to nurture their talents and gifts, and receive recognition and further encouragement. After all, it is highly likely that a student's talent will significantly influence that student's choice of job (Levine, 2002). So, whether it is becoming captain of the swim team and managing people (Lee & Jackson, 1992), cultivating empathic skills that formed the basis of a career in counseling (Schmitt, 1994), or developing advocacy skills and becoming a public speaker (Mooney, 2008), everyone should nurture and develop individual strengths.

Often, the emphasis on the "dis" in disability can overshadow what a student with LD and/or ADD/ADHD can do.

---

21. Self-Advocate

Students with LD and/or ADD/ADHD who have a greater likelihood of succeeding in college are those who exhibit a strong sense of self-acceptance—including being sufficiently comfortable in sharing their disability status with college staff and faculty. The challenge is to develop specific attributes of being proactive, assertive, and self-determined, as these will serve students well in their pursuit of autonomy and the increased likelihood of graduation (Getzel & Thoma, 2008; Janiga & Costenbader, 2002). Further, experiences in school and college can serve as the basis for general advocacy for the students with LD and/or ADD/ADHD who will "come after" (Mooney & Cole, 2000; Sandler, 2008).

Final Thoughts

This list of 21 suggestions to help students with LD and/or ADD/ADHD transition into college is far from exhaustive. It does, however, open the door to begin important discussions about the many aspects involved in this transition. In contemplating these points, students with LD and/or ADD/ADHD can

begin to strategize for their own success. Given the difference in general opportunities and the quality of life that a college education affords, it is incumbent on all of us to support college students with LD and/or ADD/ADHD to lessen their struggles and help them ultimately succeed in college (Hamblet, 2011).

Although students with LD and/or ADD/ADHD constitute a sizable proportion of all students with disabilities who attend college, these tips certainly are applicable for counseling with students on the autism spectrum, students with intellectual disability, and those with emotional or behavioral challenges. Being comfortable with one's disability, registering with the campus disability services office, utilizing resources available, being proactive in organizing a schedule of classes, and employing customized strategies that help academic success are suggestions relevant to all students with disabilities. Providing students with disabilities with these critical strategies is essential to ensuring their success in college and beyond—in life.

References

ADA Amendments Act (ADAAA) of 2008, Pub. Law No. 110-325, to be codified at 42 U.S.C. § 12101 (2009).

Allsopp, D. H., Minskoff, E. H., & Bolt, L. (2005). Individualized course-specific strategy instruction for college students with learning disabilities and ADHD: Lessons learned from a model demonstration project. *Learning Disabilities Research & Practice, 20*, 103–118. http://dx.doi.org/ 10.1111/j.1540-5826.2005.00126.x

Armstrong, T. (2010). *Neurodiversity: Discovering the extraordinary gifts of autism, ADHD, dyslexia, and other brain differences.* Cambridge, MA: Da Cappo Press.

Beale, A. (2005). Preparing students with learning disabilities for postsecondary education: Their rights and responsibilities. *Techniques: Connecting Education and Careers, 80*(3), 24-27.

Butler, D. L., Elaschuk, C. L., & Poole, S. (2000). Promoting strategic writing by postsecondary students with learning disabilities: A report of three case studies. *Learning Disability Quarterly, 23*, 196-213. http://dx.doi.org/10.2307/1511164

Clinton, L., & Higbee, J. L. (2011). The invisible hand: The power of language in creating welcoming post secondary learning experiences. *Journal of College Teaching & Learning, 8*(5), 11-16.

Cohen, A. (2004). Test anxiety and its effect on the personality of students with learning disabilities. *Learning Disability Quarterly, 27*, 176-184. http://dx.doi.org/10.2307/1593667

Cohn, P. (1998). Why does my stomach hurt? How individuals with learning disabilities can use cognitive strategies to reduce anxiety and stress at the college level. *Journal of Learning Disabilities, 31*, 514-516. http://dx.doi.org/10.1177/002221949803100509

Connor, D. J., & Lagares, C. (2007). Facing high stakes in high school: 25 successful strategies from an inclusive social studies classroom. *TEACHING Exceptional Children, 40*(2), 18-27.

Cornett-DeVito, M. M., & Worley, D. W. (2005). A front row seat: A phenomenological investigation of learning disabilities. *Communication Education, 54*, 312-333. http://dx.doi.org/10.1080/03634520500442178

DaDeppo, L. M. W. (2009). Integration factors related to the academic success and intent to persist for college students with learning disabilities. *Learning Disabilities Research & Practice, 24*, 122-131. http://dx.doi.org/10.1111/j.1540-5826.2009.00286.x

Durodoye, B. A., Combes, B., & Bryant, R. M. (2004). Counselor intervention in the post-secondary planning of African American students with learning disabilities. *Professional School Counseling, 7*, 133-141.

Foley, N. (2006). Preparing for college: Improving the odds for students with learning disabilities. *College Student Journal, 40*, 641-645.

Getzel, E. E., & Thoma, C. A. (2008). Experiences of college students with disabilities and the importance of self-determination in higher education settings. *Career Development for Exceptional Individuals, 31*, 77-84. http://dx.doi.org/10.1177/0885728808317658

Ginsberg, S. M., & Schulte, K. (2008). Instructional accommodations: Impact of conventional vs. social constructivist view of disability. *Journal of Scholarship of Teaching & Learning, 8*(2), 84-91.

Gregg, N. (2009). *Adolescents and adults with learning disabilities and ADHD: Assessment and accommodation*. New York, NY: Guilford.

Hadley, W. M. (2007, Spring). The necessity of academic accommodations for firstyear college students with learning disabilities. *Journal of College Admissions*, 9-13.

Hamblet, E. C. (2011). *7 steps for success: High school to college transition strategies for students with disabilities*. Arlington, VA: Council for Exceptional Children.

Hecker, L., Burns, L., Elkind, J., Elkind, K., & Katz, L. (2002). Benefits of assistive reading software for students with attention disorders. *Annals of Dyslexia, 52*, 243-272. http://dx.doi.org/10.1007/s11881-002-0015-8

Heiman, T. (2006). Social support networks, stress, sense of coherence and academic success of university students with learning disabilities. *Social Psychology of Education, 9*, 461-487. http://dx.doi.org/10.1007/s11218-006-9007-6

IDEA Regulations, 34 C.F.R. § 300 (2006).

Janiga, S. J., & Costenbader, V. (2002). The transition from high school to postsecondary education for students with learning disabilities: A survey of college service coordinators. *Journal of Learning Disabilities, 35*, 462-468, 479. http://dx .doi.org/10.1177/00222194020350050601

Kato, M., Nulty, B., Olszewski, B.T., Doolittle, J., & Flannery, K. B. (2006). Postsecondary academies: Helping students with disabilities transition to college. *TEACHING Exceptional Children, 39*(1), 24-27.

Kirby, J. R., Silvestri, R., Allingham, B. H., Parrila, R., & LaFave, C. B. (2008). Learning strategies and study approaches of postsecondary students with dyslexia. *Journal of Learning Disabilities, 41*, 85-96. http://dx.doi.org/ 10.1177/0022219407311040

Komarraju, M., & Karau, S. J. (2008). Relationships between the perceived value of instructional techniques and academic motivation. *Journal of Instructional Psychology, 35*(1), 70-82.

Lagares, C., & Connor, D. J. (2009). 20 ways to help students prepare for high school examinations. *Intervention in School and Clinic, 45*, 63-67. http://dx.doi.org/ 10.1177/1053451209338399

Lee, C., & Jackson, R. (1992). *Faking it: A look into the mind of a creative learner.* Portsmouth, NH: Reed.

Levine, M. (2002). *A mind at a time.* New York, NY: Simon & Schuster.

Lindstrom, J. H. (2007). Determining appropriate accommodations for postsecondary students with reading and written expression disorders. *Learning Disabilities Research & Practice, 22,* 229-236. http://dx.doi.org/10.1111/ j.1540-5826.2007.00251.x

Luna, C. (2003). (Re)writing the discourses of schooling and of "ilearning disabilities": The development of critical literacy in a student action group. *Reading & Writing Quarterly, 19,* 253-280. http://dx.doi.org/ 10.1080/10573560308211

Madaus, J. W. (2003). What high school students with learning disabilities need to know about college foreign language requirements. *TEACHING Exceptional Children, 36*(2), 62-66.

Madaus, J. W., & Shaw, S. (2006). The impact of IDEA 2004 on transition to college for students with learning disabilities. *Learning Disabilities Research & Practice, 21,* 273-281. http://dx.doi.org/ 10.1111/j.15405826.2006.00223.x

Milsom, A., & Hartley, M.T. (2005). Assisting college students with learning disabilities transitioning to college: What school counselors should know. *Professional School Counseling 8,* 436-441.

Mooney, J. (2008). *The short bus: A journey beyond normal.* New York, NY: Henry Holt.

Mooney, J., & Cole, D. (2000). *Learning outside the lines.* New York, NY: Simon & Schuster.

Mortimore, T., & Crozier, W. R. (2006). Dyslexia and difficulties with study skills in higher education. *Studies in Higher Education, 31,* 235-251. http://dx.doi.org/ 10.1080/03075070600572173

Nelson, R., & Lignugaris-Kraft, B. (1989). Postsecondary education for students with learning disabilities. *Exceptional Children, 56,* 246-265.

Olney, M. F., & Kim, A. (2001). Beyond adjustment: Integration of cognitive disability into identity. *Disability & Society, 16*(4), 563-583. http://dx.doi.org/ 10.1080/09687590120059540

Rehabilitation Act of 1973, 29 U.S.C. § 701 *et seq.* (2006).

Reiff, H. B. (2004). Reframing the learning disabilities experience redux. *Learning Disabilities Research & Practice, 19*, 185–198. http://dx.doi.org/10.1111/j.1540-5826.2004.00103.x

Rodis, P., Garrod, A., & Boscardin, M. L. (Eds.). (2001). *Learning disabilities and life stories.* Needham Heights, MA: Allyn & Bacon.

Ryan, J. (2007). Learning disabilities in Australian universities: Hidden, ignored, and unwelcome. *Journal of Learning Disabilities, 40*, 436–442. http://dx.doi.org/10.1177/00222194070400050701

Salzberg, C., Hardman, D., Price, E., & Morgan, R. (2002). *Accommodating students with disabilities in higher education, participant's handbook (2nd ed): Preparing faculty & teaching assistants to accommodate students with disabilities.* Logan, UT: Utah State University.

Sandler, M. (2008). *College confidence with ADD.* Naperville, IL: Source.

Schmitt, A. (1994). *Brilliant idiot: An autobiography of a dyslexic.* Intercourse, PA: Good Books.

Stodden, R. A., Conway, M. A., & Chang, K. B. T (2003). Findings from the study of transition, technology and post secondary supports for youth with disabilities: Implications for secondary school educators. *Journal of Special Education and Technology, 18*(4), 29–43.

Trainin, G., & Swanson, L. (2005). Cognition, metacognition and achievement of college students with learning disabilities. *Learning Disabilities Quarterly, 28,* 261–272. http://dx.doi.org/10.2307/4126965

Troiano, P. F. (2003). College students and learning disability: Elements of self-style. *Journal of College Student Development, 44,* 404–419. http://dx.doi.org/10.1353/csd.2003.0033

University of Pittsburgh. (2006). *College in high school course descriptions.* Retrieved from http://www.asundergrad.pitt.edu/offices/chsp/coursesbrief.html

Wagner, M., Newman, L., Cameto, R., Garza, N., & Levine, P. (2005). *After high school: A first look at the postschool experiences of youth with disabilities. A report from the National Longitudinal Transition Study-2 (NLTS2).* Menlo Park, CA: SRI International. Retrieved from http://www.nlts2.org/reports/2005_04/nlts2_report_2005_04_complete.pdf

DAVID J. CONNOR (New York CEC), Associate Professor of Special Education, Hunter College, City University of New York, New York.

Address correspondence concerning this article to David Connor, School of Education, 917 West, Hunter College, City University of New York, 695 Park Ave., New York, NY 10065 (e-mail: dconnor@hunter.cuny.edu).

The author would like to thank the three anonymous reviewers and the editor for their feedback and suggestions.

ARTICLE 29

Addressing Test Anxiety

"I'm OK until I get in the room. Everyone is talking about the test and what they studied and
what they think will be on the test. It makes me so nervous, and I start to freak out."

"I'm working on the test and then when I encounter something I'm not sure of,
I start to panic. My chest gets tight, my stomach starts churning, and I get sweaty,
and feel overwhelmed. I don't care about the test or how I do on it.
I just want to get it over with and get out of there."

"I start to think about what will happen if I don't do well on the test and then things
snowball and I lose my focus. Even if I know the answer, I start to blank out and
struggle to find the right words to explain it or start to think about other things.
As soon as I leave the room, I remember everything and can answer the questions."

SPENCER J. SALEND

Students take many tests throughout their school years. The results are used to make important decisions about students and educational programs, including determining levels of curriculum mastery, report card grades, gradelevel promotions, honors, and graduation (Carter et al., 2005). Educators also use testing data to monitor students' learning progress and to assess the effectiveness of their instruction and identify ways to improve it (Salend, 2009).

Many students, however, experience test anxiety. Students with test anxiety experience high levels of stress, nervousness, and apprehension during testing and evaluative situations that significantly interfere with their performance, emotional and behavioral well-being, and attitudes toward school (Cizek & Burg, 2006; Huberty, 2009). An estimate is that between 25% and 40% of students experience test anxiety (Cassady, 2010; Huberty, 2009). Furthermore, students with disabilities appear to be particularly vulnerable to test anxiety

and have higher prevalence rates (see box, "What Does the Literature Say About Test Anxiety and Students With Disabilities?").

Students from culturally and linguistically diverse backgrounds also tend to have high levels of test anxiety. Due to stereotype threat—the social and psychological pressure and beliefs that members of certain groups may feel when they are asked to perform a task (like taking a test)—they may feel that their failure may strengthen negative stereotypes about the group or themselves (Cheryan & Bodenhausen, 2000; Osborne, Tillman, & Holland, 2010).

Although test anxiety and anxiety disorders share some characteristics, and students with test anxiety often have anxiety disorders, these conditions are different (Huberty, 2009). People with anxiety disorders have *trait anxiety,* which means that their high levels of stress appear to be ongoing personal characteristics that are evident across settings and situations (Cassady, 2010; Cizek & Burg, 2006).

What Does the Literature Say about Test Anxiety and Students with Disabilities?

Students with disabilities experience test anxiety at higher rates than their peers without disabilities (Heiman & Precel, 2003; Lufi, Okasha, & Cohen, 2004; Peleg, 2009; Whitaker Sena, Lowe, & Lee, 2007; Woods, Parkinson, & Lewis, 2010). Although academic difficulties significantly increase the probability that students with disabilities may be overly anxious during testing (Peleg, 2009), cognitive interference (e.g., thoughts not related to the test); negative academic self-concepts (Peleg, 2009; Swanson & Howell, 1996); poor past performance on tests (Cizek & Burg, 2006); and attention, concentration, motivational, and organizational difficulties (Heiman & Precel, 2003) also contribute to the fact that students with disabilities report high levels of stress and frustration when taking tests. Inadequate study and test-taking skills and strategies and learned helplessness are other variables that appear to increase the likelihood that students with disabilities may encounter heightened levels of anxiety during testing (Heiman & Precel, 2003; Swanson & Howell, 1996).

Studies suggest that a collaborative, multifaceted approach—consisting of a range of effective interventions that address the many factors that trigger test anxiety in students with disabilities—is the best way to address students' test anxiety (Ergene, 2003; Peleg, 2009; Rothman, 2004; Whitaker Sena et al., 2007).

People with test anxiety, however, seem to have *state anxiety,* which means that their high levels of stress are situation specific (e.g., extreme and unwarranted tension during testing or evaluative activities; Cassady, 2010; Cizek & Burg, 2006).

This article offers strategies and guidelines that teachers can use to help students with disabilities overcome high levels of anxiety that interfere with their performance on tests. You should individually determine, based on your students' characteristics and learning strengths and challenges, what strategies to select (Elliott et al., 2010; Huberty, 2009). In addition, make sure that the strategies you use facilitate student access and performance, minimize anxiety, and provide an accurate measure of students' skills and content knowledge and do not undermine the validity of the test results (Roach, Beddow, Kurz, Kettler, & Elliott, 2010).

Helping Students Overcome Test Anxiety

Identify Students with Test Anxiety

Most people feel some level of stress when preparing for and taking tests, and moderate and appropriate levels of nervousness can foster students' motivation, memory and attention, and enhance test performance (Cizek & Burg, 2006). Identifying students who experience heightened and detrimental levels of anxiety when taking tests is one of the first steps you can take to help students (Peleg, 2009).

Possible triggers of testing anxiety vary and include factors related to individual students; family dynamics; and school, classroom, and teaching practices (see Figure 1). These triggers can lead to physical, behavioral, and affective symptoms that serve as warning signs that a student may be experiencing testing anxiety (see Table 1). Research suggests that elementary students are more likely to show the physical signs of test anxiety, and older students are more likely to experience the behavioral and affective symptoms associated with test anxiety (Whitaker Sena, Lowe, & Lee, 2007). In many cases, these triggers and symptoms interact to create a cycle that leads to escalating levels of test anxiety (Cassady, 2010). Thus, students may initially perform poorly on a test because of insufficient studying and preparation, learned helplessness, family pressures, or badly designed tests. Students may then experience increased

- Anxiety and attention disorders
- Obsessive compulsive behaviors
- Learned helplessness
- Perfectionist tendencies and unrealistic expectations
- Stereotype threat
- Poor study and test-taking skills
- Past poor test performance
- Peer comparisons and pressures including achievement levels of classmates
- Low self-esteem and confidence levels
- Negative attributions and self-statements and criticism
- Lack of motivation and procrastination

- Family-related expectations to excel
- Teacher- and school-related pressures concerning the use of high-stakes testing to assess school and teaching effectiveness
- Highly competitive classroom/school environments
- High-stakes testing and grading
- Distracting testing environments
- Poorly constructed or timed tests
- Ineffective instruction

Sources: Cassady (2010); Cizek & Burg (2006); Dorland (2009); Goetz, Preckel, Zeidner, & Schleyer (2008); Huberty (2009); Osborne, Tillman, & Holland (2010); Prevatt, Welles, Li, & Proctor (2010); Putwain & Daniels (2010); Whitaker Sena, Lowe, & Lee (2007).

FIGURE 1 Potential Triggers of Test Anxiety

Physical Symptoms	Behavioral Symptoms	Affective Symptoms
Excessive perspiration	Difficulties with concentration, attention, and memory that interfere with the following:	Making negative self-statements
Sweaty palms	• Reading and understanding test directions and items	Having pessimistic expectations (e.g., "I'm going to fail this test")
Unexplained headache or stomachache	• Retrieving words, facts, and concepts	
Nausea	• Organizing thoughts and answers	
Shaking body parts	Performing poorly on tests when the content	Being apathetic and unmotivated
Rapid heartbeat	• has been studied	
Dizziness and light-headedness	• has previously been mastered as demonstrated on nontesting performance assessment activities	Negative comparisons of self to others (e.g., "I'm not as smart as others")
Muscle tension	Off-task behaviors, such as inappropriate comments, fidgeting, squirming, pacing, staring, tapping, crying, and rapid speech during testing	Making excuses for poor test performance (e.g., "I don't do well on tests because I have test anxiety")
Tics		
Flushed skin color	Asking numerous unnecessary questions about the test	
Difficulty sleeping, eating, or using the toilet before tests	Experiencing repeated mental blocks and forgetting	
	Feeling overwhelmed during testing	Expressing avoidance and fear of testing situations
	Complaining about test items (e.g., "We didn't cover this in class")	
	Seeking unnecessary assistance from others	
	Cheating on tests	
	Feigning illness and being absent on testing days	

Sources. Cassady (2010); Cizek & Burg (2006); Dorland (2009); Heiman & Precel (2003); Huberty (2009).

TABLE 1 Possible Symptoms Associated with Test Anxiety

stress, as well as concentration, attention, self-esteem, and memory difficulties during subsequent tests (Peleg, 2009). These factors may interact and serve to hinder students' performance and increase the likelihood that they will be anxious on future tests (Goetz, Preckel, Zeidner, & Schleyer, 2008).

Teachers can assess the presence of the physical, behavioral, and affective warning signs of test anxiety in their students by observing during testing, as well as by interviewing students and their families about their reactions to testing. Also, students can complete surveys that rate the extent to which they experience the physical, behavioral, and affective symptoms associated with test anxiety (Peleg, 2009; Prevatt, Welles, Li, & Proctor, 2010; Whitaker Sena et al., 2007). Cizek and Burg (2006) offer a summary and review of surveys for assessing test anxiety. Figure 2 provides a sampling of online surveys related to test anxiety. Once you determine which students may be experiencing testing anxiety, use these assessments as a springboard to explain the condition to the students and their families and to enlist support in creating a plan.

Possible triggers of testing anxiety vary and include factors related to individual students; family dynamics; and school, classroom, and teaching practices

---

Teach Study Skills

Inadequate and inefficient studying can contribute to and intensify the test anxiety that your students may experience (Cassady, 2010; Heiman & Precel, 2003; Huberty, 2009). Because a critical foundation for studying is knowing what to study, help your students learn about the content and types of items that are most likely to appear on tests

Test Anxiety Scale
http://www.learningskills.com/test.html

A Test-Taking Inventory
http://www.uiowa.edu/~c07p075e/ClassActivities.pdf

Questionnaire on Attitudes Toward Examinations
http://www.psych.uncc.edu/pagoolka/Testanxiety.html

Test Anxiety Questionnaire
http://www.wwcc.edu/student_services/online_adv/success/test_test.cfm

Are You Test Anxious?
http://istudy.psu.edu/FirstYearModules/TestTaking/AnxietySurvey.html

Achievement Anxiety Test
http://www.wright-counseling.com/checklists/TestAnxietyAssessment.html

Westside Test Anxiety Scale
http://www.peacewithmyself.com/tests/scaleauto.htm

Test Anxiety Survey
http://www.brandeis.edu/acserv/web/worksheets/Test%20Anxiety%20survey%20web%20resource.doc

FIGURE 2   Online Test Anxiety Surveys

(Lagares & Connor, 2009). Following are several ways to support your students as they learn better study skills:

- Provide students with study guides addressing the purpose, content, and format of the test (Walker & Schmidt, 2004).
- Ask students to work in groups to predict the content and test items that are likely to appear on tests, to quiz each other, and to create study materials and memory aids (Strichart & Mangrum, 2010).

- Use educational games and simulated tests to review and practice possible test content, questions, and conditions (Conderman & Pedersen, 2010).
- Provide students with a list of items (e.g., essay questions) that may be on a test (Salend, 2009).

In addition to knowing what to study, students also need to learn how to study (Leininger, Taylor Dyches, Prater, & Allen Heath, 2010). Encourage students to create a schedule to include an early and significant study session that allows them to identify difficult material that may require them to contact their teachers for additional clarification and instruction (Salend, 2009). Once your students have developed an appropriate study schedule, they can learn to use effective study skills and strategies to implement it (Lagares & Connor, 2009). Teach students that during each study session they should (a) focus on specific goals; (b) have the necessary resources and materials available (e.g., writing instruments, highlighters, index cards, technology); and (c) create an outline, summary, or visual aid related to the session's main and secondary points or key questions and corresponding resources (e.g., textbooks, notes, quizzes, classroom and homework assignments, and handouts; Salend, 2009; Strichart & Mangrum, 2010). Moreover, encourage students to practice and review the material by playing educational games and creating flash cards and mnemonic devices related to key terminology, formulas, and lists (Lagares & Connor, 2009; Rozalski, 2007).

Teach Effective Test-Taking Skills

One way to reduce your students' anxiety during testing is by teaching them to use effective test-taking skills and strategies (Carter et al., 2005; Holzer, Madaus, Bray, & Kehle, 2009; Whitaker Sena et al., 2007). These strategies

can help students stay relaxed, focused, and motivated to succeed on tests. To lessen the fear of forgetting important information, teach your students how to perform a *memory dump* or *download* as soon as the test is handed to them, by listing key points, definitions, formulas, dates, mnemonics, and names that they are likely to use throughout the test, and jotting down memory clues and drawings to promote recall (Rozalski, 2007; Walker & Schmidt, 2004).

Teach students to work on easier test items first so they can build their confidence. Your students also can improve their test performance by learning to budget their time based on the amount of time given to them to complete the test, the specific point values and weights associated with the different questions and sections, and the levels of difficulty of the various test items (Denstaedt, Kelly, & Kryza, 2009; Strichart & Mangrum, 2010). They also can learn to strategically highlight essential aspects of test directions and items, as well as pay attention to parts of tests that have been highlighted by their teachers so that they understand (a) specific details (e.g., *answer three out of the five essay questions*); (b) types of answers they are asked to provide; (c) aids, resources, and assistance they can use; and (d) time, length, and space constraints (Rozalski, 2007; Salend, 2009).

In addition, help students learn test-taking strategies for answering specific types of questions, such as multiple-choice, matching, true-false, sentence completion, and essay questions (Carter et al., 2005; Conderman & Pedersen, 2010; Leininger et al., 2010; Salend, 2009). Students can use a range of mnemonic test-taking learning strategies that help them remember and implement a series of test-taking skills (Conderman & Pedersen, 2010; Holzer et al., 2009). These test-taking learning strategies can guide them in effectively and efficiently responding to the different types of items they will encounter on tests (Rozalski, 2007; Strichart & Mangrum, 2010; Therrien, Hughes, Kapelski, & Mokhtari, 2009; Yell & Rozalski, 2008).

Teach and Prompt the Use of Anxiety Reduction Strategies

To lessen the physical and affective symptoms associated with test anxiety, be sure to collaborate with school psychologists, school counselors, and families to teach and encourage students to use anxiety reduction strategies before, during, and after testing (Goetz et al., 2008; Rothman, 2004; Whitaker Sena et al., 2007). For example, teach your students to come to the testing environment on time, rather than early, to avoid interactions with others that can intensify their anxiety (Salend, 2009). You and your colleagues can also teach students how to handle anxiety-producing questions and comments, such as peers asking questions about what they studied, seeking the answers to questions, or spreading false rumors about tests and answers by learning how to avoid conversations politely (Rothman, 2004). Your students can learn to engage in encouraging self-statements, wear comfortable clothes, and take a few minutes to relax and focus on their goals and plans for success (Conderman & Pedersen, 2010; Denstaedt et al., 2009).

Taking cues from these researchers and others, you can teach students who experience test anxiety to use such anxiety reduction techniques as meditating, praying, taking deep breaths and breaks, engaging in positive self-talk, and focusing on past successes (Cizek & Burg, 2006).

Some of your students may find it relaxing to listen to guided imagery, affirmations and meditation recordings, or calming music; to visualize positive and relaxing images and experiences (Koch, 2010); or to sit in a non-

distracting area of the room (away from doors, windows, aisles; Conderman & Pedersen, 2010). Other students may reduce stress by engaging in motor activities like tensing and relaxing muscles (Cizek & Burg, 2006), exercising (Lytle & Todd, 2009; Mulrine, Prater, & Jenkins, 2008), or using a squeeze ball (Conderman & Pedersen, 2010). Use verbal reminders for students regarding the use of anxiety reduction techniques and embed visual reminders in tests to prompt students to use these strategies (see Figure 3).

Offer Attribution Training

Students with disabilities may experience learned helplessness and feelings of stereotype threat, which can have a negative effect on their attributions and expectations of their success and failure and contribute to the development of test anxiety (Putwain & Daniels, 2010). Thus, rather than believing they are well prepared and therefore will perform well on a test, these students often approach the testing environment with the expectation that they are unprepared or unlucky, and will fail or perform poorly (Cassady, 2010). As a result, they ascribe their poor performance to bad luck (e.g., "I got the hardest questions"), teacher mistakes (e.g., "The teacher didn't teach that"), lack of ability (e.g., "I'm not good at that"), and other factors that they view as out of their control (Rothman, 2004).

To counter students' negative thoughts, offer attribution training to teach students to understand the events and actions that contribute to their success and failure on tests (Hong, Ivy, Gonzalez, & Ehrensberger, 2007). Through attribution training, students learn to engage in positive attributions that credit their successful test performance to their effort (e.g., "I worked hard studying for this test"), ability (e.g., "I learned the material"), and other

Prompting Students to Relax

Relax, Take a deep breath.

Smile. You are halfway through the test.

Prompting Students to Engage in Self-Reinforcement

Working hard? Give yourself a high-five.

FIGURE 3 Sample visual and Text-based Prompts

factors within themselves (Merlone & Moran, 2008). To foster your students' use of positive attributions, introduce a range of learning activities that help students (a) understand how attributions and effort affect their test performance, (b) interpret poor performance as a signal of the need to work harder and to identify ways to improve, (c) acknowledge and analyze successful outcomes to identify behaviors that need to be continued and enhanced, and (d) discuss and learn from their mistakes (Dorland, 2009; Eisenman, 2007).

The role of teacher feedback is critical in attribution training. In addition to grading test items as correct or incorrect, you can provide students feedback on their effort (e.g., "You really worked hard to learn this"), and ability (e.g., "You showed you learned this") and respond to students' incorrect responses with a strategy or informational feedback (e.g., "Can you think of another way you could have answered this?"; Joseph & Konrad, 2009; Margolis & McCabe, 2006).

After testing, prompt your students to reflect on their test performance by completing statements like the following:

- I did well on this test because_____.
- I struggled on this test because_____.
- The things I can do to be successful on future tests are_____. (Salend, 2009)

Create Accessible and Student-Friendly Tests

Rather than giving surprise tests or quizzes, make the testing experience less stressful for all your students, including those with disabilities, by creating accessible and student-friendly tests that assess a reasonable amount of content and are regularly scheduled (Salend, 2009). First, when creating tests, use best practices for composing valid objective and essay questions that relate to important content taught in class. Next, be sure to provide your students with opportunities to take practice tests that use the same format as they will encounter on their upcoming exams. Taking these steps will ensure that you create accessible and student-friendly tests for your class (Brookhart & Nitko, 2008; Conderman & Pedersen, 2010).

Tests that cause confusion and distraction can make students with organizational and attention difficulties feel anxious before they begin. You can lessen confusion by providing user-friendly tests that have proper presentation, organization, spacing, and sequencing of items (Beddow, Kettler, & Elliott, 2008; Roach et al., 2010; Rotter, 2006). Presenting items in a fixed, predictable, symmetrical, and numbered sequence that guides students in making the transition from one item to another can help students avoid skipping test items (Acrey, Johnstone, & Milligan, 2005). Test questions and the directions for completing them should appear on the same page so that students do not have to turn back and forth. You can facilitate student attention to test items by limiting the number of items on a page, grouping similar question types together, and surrounding test directions and items in text boxes (Salend, 2009).

Allowing students to write on the test rather than asking them to transfer their answers to a separate page also can reduce anxiety (Walker & Schmidt, 2004). Providing enough space for responses allows students to complete an answer without continuing on another page and can structure the length of responses (Salend, 2009). Including page numbers on test pages also can help when you are giving directions to students; page numbers can also guide students in locating or asking questions about specific items (Beddow et al., 2008).

Another way to make your tests more accessible and user-friendly is by using prompts that guide students in engaging in behaviors that help them stay focused, remain calm, and succeed on tests. At the beginning of the test, include a statement and graphic icon (i.e., dump truck, computer download) that reminds students to perform a memory dump or download of important information and mnemonic devices that they may need to access as they work on the test (Salend, 2009;

Walker & Schmidt, 2004). Strategically place prompts throughout the test to remind students to pay attention, ask questions, use relaxation techniques, maintain their effort and motivation, use effective test-taking strategies, and engage in self-reinforcement (see Figure 3; Salend, 2011). Finally, at the end of the test, use text and visuals that acknowledge your students' efforts (e.g., "Way to go." "Congratulations on finishing the test"), and remind students to review each question before submitting the test.

Make the testing experience more motivating and meaningful for your students by devising test items that are related to students' lives and interests and that are appropriate for their academic abilities (Savage, Savage, & Armstrong, 2006). Where feasible and appropriate, you can personalize their tests by phrasing items using the students' and educators' names (make sure that individuals will not be embarrassed or object to having their names used in questions) and incorporating students' interests and experiences, as well as integrating popular characters, items, and trends in test items (Salend, 2009). For example, questions can be presented in the context of using problems, names, persons, places, and things associated with students' communities (David, 2008). Don't forget to create test items that incorporate humor, curiosity, and novelty (McKinley & Stormont, 2008; Mulrine et al., 2008). When tailoring test items to students and their communities, however, make sure that the items are inclusive, multicultural, and respectful. Therefore, individuals and groups should be represented in realistic, factually correct, and nonstereotypical ways; and be sure to use a variety of appropriate cultural and universal referents, terms, and experiences (Beddow et al., 2008; Salend, 2011).

Accessible and user-friendly tests contain clear and complete directions that help students understand the context and conditions associated with test questions. Good test directions are presented in language all students can understand and do not contain vague terms (e.g., *frequently*, *usually*) and irrelevant information that may confuse and frustrate students or be misinterpreted by them (Brookhart & Nitko, 2008; Elliott et al., 2010). Help your students with disabilities understand test directions by using the following supports:

- Numerals or the number words (e.g., *first, second,* and *third)* to present sequenced information in chronological order (Salend, 2011).
- Bullets to present essential information that does not have a numerical or hierarchical order (Rotter, 2006).
- Stylistic variants such as circling, underlining, boldfacing, and enlarging to highlight critical information (Acrey et al., 2005; Roach et al., 2010).
- Text boxes surrounded by white space to focus attention on important directions and to present a correct model of each type (Salend, 2009).
- Direction reminders placed at important locations throughout the test (e.g., "Remember to write clearly and in complete sentences"; Salend, 2009).
- Symbols, icons, and pictorials to prompt students to pay attention to directions (e.g., color-coded arrows pointing to directions for specific item types; Elliott et al., 2010) and to depict important content (Roach et al., 2010).

Involve Students in the Testing Process

You can make tests less threatening to your students by involving them in the testing process (Edyburn, 2009; Salend, 2011). For instance, ask students to devise possible test questions to include on tests. Allow your students to assume responsibility and control over the testing experience by structuring tests so that students have choices in responding to items. For example, students can be provided with the option of not responding to a specified number of test items. Thus, a test can consist of 20 items of varying types of questions, and students can choose to respond to the 15 of them that best match their response style and study habits. In addition, you can give students a series of open-ended questions presented in a tic-tac-toe format and ask students to select a specific number of questions to answer or to respond to three questions that give them tic-tac-toe (Edyburn, 2009). When giving students these options, you should identify the topics or types of items students avoided and find alternative ways to assess students' mastery of the content and teach them the skills they need to answer all types of questions.

Provide Appropriate Testing Accommodations

Students with disabilities who experience high levels of stress may need a range of appropriate testing accommodations (Leininger et al., 2010; Woods, Parkinson, & Lewis, 2010). In particular, students with disabilities may benefit from timing, scheduling, and setting accommodations for testing (Salend, 2009), such as the following:

- Timing accommodations are designed to lessen the stress associated with timed tests by giving students additional time to complete tests or having them take untimed or shortened versions of tests.
- Scheduling accommodations, which also can minimize time pressures, involve varying the times of the testing sessions, administering tests during shorter sessions and over several days, adjusting the order in which sections of tests are administered, and allowing students to take breaks as needed. For example, secondary teachers

can coordinate testing schedules so that tests are given at times students do not have other tests or assignments due.

- Setting accommodations include having students take tests individually or in small groups in private locations within the school and providing them with preferential seating. Setting accommodations also address specific environmental arrangements, such as having glarefree lighting, providing appropriate and comfortable furniture (e.g., lefthanded desks for left-handed students) and room temperatures, disabling intercoms and phones, eliminating auditory and visual distractions, and placing "Do Not Disturb" signs on doors (Conderman & Pedersen, 2010).

Some students with disabilities also may require the assistance of a proctor (Cox, Herner, Demczyk, & Nieberding, 2006). The proctors need to be prepared to follow professional guidelines so that they do not provide students with cues, hints, coaching, and information that may have an effect on students' answers (Clapper, Morse, Thur-low, & Thompson, 2006) and that students have had preparation to work effectively with proctors (Woods et al., 2010).

Students with disabilities may benefit from timing, scheduling, and setting accommodations for testing

---

Employ Technology-Based Testing

Taking tests by way of technology can help some students with disabilities lessen the test anxiety they experience (Stowell & Bennett, 2010). Technology-based testing allows the experience to be customized for students by offering choices regarding the format, conditions, and accommodations they want to use (Beddow et al., 2008; Russell, Hoffmann, & Higgins, 2009).

Consider Collaborative Test-Taking Arrangements

Some teachers use cooperative-group testing to minimize stress related to test completion by allowing students to work collaboratively on open-ended tasks and test items; and the group's product and cooperative behaviors are evaluated (Michaelsen & Sweet, 2008). When you use such group testing, also ask individual members of the group to respond to questions about the group's answers and product. Allow students the *choice* of collaborative testing, because keep in mind that peer pressure can heighten the anxiety that some students experience.

Consider a Range of Scoring Methods

Because some of the tension students experience can be related to the pressure associated with grades (Huberty, 2009), you might consider using a variety of scoring methods to lessen anxiety and to motivate students and encourage their efforts to succeed on tests (Brookhart & Nitko, 2008). Here are some scoring methods that you can add to your test grading strategies: (a) granting partial credit for correct aspects of answers, (b) offering extra credit options, (c) awarding bonus points for certain items, and (d) letting students earn back points by revising incorrect answers or retaking the test using different questions that assess similar content (Salend, 2011). When grammar, spelling, and punctuation are not the elements being tested, consider refraining from penalizing students for these errors, or giving students separate grades for content and mechanics. On essay questions, award your students points for an outline, web, diagram, or chart in place of a written response. Make sure, however, that students do not interpret the use of different scoring methods as a reason to slack off in preparing for tests (Salend, 2009).

Collaborate with Students' Families and Other Professionals

As mentioned earlier, your efforts to reduce test anxiety can be enhanced by collaborating with your students' families and other professionals (Conderman & Pedersen, 2010; Woods et al., 2010). Educators can strengthen the involvement of families by providing them with information about testing and assessment practices, test anxiety, and testing accommodations and alternatives available for their children. You can work with families to develop, implement, and evaluate the effectiveness of interventions to address test anxiety and incorporate effective strategies into students' individualized education programs (IEPs). Offer families guidelines, strategies, and resources for addressing test anxiety and fostering their children's use of effective study and test-taking skills and strategies. Finally, solicit feedback from families about their children's study habits and test-related stressors (Salend, 2009). For example, you and your colleagues can offer workshops and resources for families that help them work with their children to develop schedules for studying for tests.

Evaluate Strategies and Actions to Overcome Test Anxiety

Educators need to continually evaluate strategies and actions to help their students overcome test anxiety to determine if the strategies and accommodations are effective, useful, and acceptable. Obtain feedback from students, other educators, and family members regarding interventions you have used; then examine the feedback for an indication of the effectiveness, efficiency, fairness, and acceptability of your strategies (Roach et al., 2010; Woods et al., 2010). You should reflect on the effect of the strategies on *all* your students, as well as the extent to which you have the time, resources, and preparation to implement specific techniques. Students and family members can also share their perceptions of your strategies, identify successful and unsuccessful aspects, and make suggestions for improving them (Roach et al., 2010).

Final Thoughts

Many students with disabilities may experience test anxiety, which can hinder their academic and social-emotional development and the validity of the important educational decisions that are made about them based on test performance data. Providing students with helpful study skills and test-taking environments and strategies can promote student success in academic arenas and in life.

References

Acrey, C., Johnstone, C., & Milligan, C. (2005). Using universal design to unlock the potential for academic achievement of at-risk learners. *TEACHING Exceptional Children, 38*(2), 22–31.

Beddow, P. A., Kettler, R. J., & Elliott, S. N. (2008). TAMI: Test accessibility and modification inventory. Retrieved from http://peabody.vanderbilt.edu/TAMI.xml

Brookhart, S. M., & Nitko, A. J. (2008). *Assessment and grading in classrooms.* Columbus, OH: Merrill/Pearson Education.

Carter, E. W., Wehby, J., Hughes, C., Johnson, S. M., Plank, D. R., Barton-Arwood, S. M., & Lunsford, L. B. (2005). Preparing adolescents with high-incidence disabilities for high stakes testing with strategy instruction. *Preventing School Failure, 49*(2), 55–62.

Cassady, J. C. (2010). Test anxiety: Contemporary theories and implications for learning. In J. C. Cassady (Ed.), *Anxiety in schools: The causes, consequences, and solutions for academic anxieties* (pp. 7–26). New York, NY: Peter Lang.

Cheryan, S., & Bodenhausen, G.V. (2000). When positive stereotypes threaten intellectual performance: The psychological hazards of "model minority" status. *Psychological Science, 11*, 399–402. doi: 10.1111/1467-9280.00277

Cizek, G.J., & Burg, S. S. (2006). *Addressing test anxiety in a high-stakes environment: Strategies for classrooms and schools.* Thousand Oaks, CA: Corwin Press.

Clapper, A.T., Morse, A. B., Thurlow, M. L., & Thompson, S.J. (2006). *How to develop state guidelines for access assistants: Scribes, readers, and sign language interpreters.* Minneapolis, MN: University of Minnesota, National Center on Educational Outcomes.

Conderman, G., & Pedersen, T. (2010). Preparing students with mild disabilities for taking state and district tests. *Intervention in School and Clinic, 45*, 232–241. doi:10.1177/1053451209353446

Cox, M. L., Herner, J. G., Demczyk, M. J., & Nieberding, J.J. (2006). Provision of testing accommodations for students with disabilities on statewide assessments: Statistical links with participation and discipline rates. *Remedial and Special Education, 27*, 346–354. doi:10.1177/07419325060270060401

David, J. L. (2008). Project-based learning. *Educational Leadership, 65*(5), 80–84.

Denstaedt, L., Kelly, J. C., & Kryza, K. (2009). *Winning strategies for test taking, grades 3–8: A practical guide for teaching test preparation.* Thousand Oaks, CA: Corwin Press.

Dorland, S. (2009). *Exam stress? No worries!* Milton, Queensland: Wrightbooks.

Edyburn, D. (2009). RTI and UDL interventions. *Journal of Special Education Technology, 24*(2), 46–47.

Eisenman, L.T. (2007). Self-determination interventions: Building a foundation for school completion. *Remedial and Special Education, 28*(1), 2–8. doi:10.1177/07419325070280010101

Elliott, S. M., Kettler, R.J., Beddow, P.A., Kurz, A., Compton, E., McGrath, D., ... Roach, A.T. (2010). Effects of using modified items to students with persistent academic difficulties. *Exceptional Children, 76*, 475–495.

Ergene, T. (2003). Effective interventions on test anxiety reduction: A meta-analysis. *School Psychology International, 24*, 313–328. doi:10.1177/01430343030243004

Goetz, T., Preckel, F., Zeidner, M., & Schleyer, E. (2008). Big fish in big ponds: A multilevel analysis of test anxiety and achievement in special gifted classes. *Anxiety, Stress and Coping, 21*, 185–198. doi:10.1080/10615800701628827

Heiman, T., & Precel, K. (2003). Students with learning disabilities in higher education: Academic strategies profile. *Journal of Learning Disabilities, 36*, 248–258. doi: 10.1177/002221940303600304

Holzer, M. F., Madaus, J.W., Bray, M.A., & Kehle, T.J. (2009). The test-taking strategy intervention for college students with learning disabilities. *Learning Disabilities Research and Practice, 24*, 44–56. doi: 10.1111/j.1540-5826.2008.01276.x

Hong, B. S. S., Ivy, W. F., Gonzalez, H. R., & Ehrensberger, W. (2007). Preparing students for postsecondary education. *TEACHING Exceptional Children, 40*(1), 32–39.

Huberty, T. J. (2009). Test and performance anxiety. *Principal Leadership, 10*(1), 12–16.

Joseph, L. M., & Konrad, M. (2009). 20 ways to have students self-manage their academic performance. *Intervention in School and Clinic, 44*(4), 246–249. doi: 10.1177/1053451208328834

Koch, S. P. (2010). Preventing student meltdowns. *Intervention in School and Clinic, 46,* 111–117. doi:10.1177/1053451210375303

Lagares, L., & Connor, D. J. (2009). Help students prepare for high school examinations. *Intervention in School and Clinic, 45,* 63–67. doi:10.1177/1053451209338399

Leininger, M., Taylor Dyches, T., Prater, M.A., & Allen Heath, M., (2010). Teaching students with obsessive-compulsive disorders. *Intervention in School and Clinic, 45,* 221–231. doi:10.1177/1053451209353447

Lufi, D., Okasha, S., & Cohen, A. (2004). Test anxiety and its effect on the personality of students with learning disabilities. *Learning Disability Quarterly, 27,* 176–184. doi:10.2307/1593667

Lytle, R., & Todd, T. (2009). Stress and the student with autism spectrum disorders: Strategies for stress reduction and enhanced learning. *TEACHING Exceptional Children, 41*(4), 36–42.

Margolis, H., & McCabe, P. P. (2006). Improving self-efficacy and motivation: What to do, what to say. *Intervention in School and Clinic, 41,* 218–227. doi:10.1177/1053451206041004040

McKinley, L.A., & Stormont, M.A. (2008). The school supports checklist: Identifying support needs and barriers for children with ADHD. *TEACHING Exceptional Children, 41*(2), 14–21.

Merlone, L., & Moran, D. (2008). Transition works: Self-awareness and self-advocacy skills for students in the elementary learning center. *TEACHING Exceptional Children Plus, 4*(4) Article 1. Retrieved from http://escholarship.bc.edu/education/tecplus/vol4/iss4/art1.

Michaelsen, L., & Sweet, M. (2008). Teambased learning. *NEA Higher Education Advocate, 25*(6), 5–8.

Mulrine, C. F., Prater, M.A., & Jenkins, A. (2008). The active classroom: Supporting students with attention deficit hyperactivity disorder through exercise. *TEACHING Exceptional Children, 40*(5), 16–22.

Osborne, J. W., Tillman, D., & Holland A. (2010). Stereotype threat and anxiety for disadvantaged minorities and women. In J. C. Cassady (Ed.), *Anxiety in schools: The causes, consequences, and solutions for academic anxieties* (pp. 119–136). New York, NY: Peter Lang.

Peleg, O. (2009). Test anxiety, academic achievement, and self-esteem among Arab adolescents with and without learning disabilities. *Learning Disability Quarterly, 32,* 11–20.

Prevatt, F., Welles, T. L., Li, H., & Proctor, B. (2010). The contribution of memory and anxiety to the math performance of college students with learning disabilities. *Learning Disabilities Research and Practice, 25,* 39–47. doi:10.1111/j.1540-5826.2009.00299.x

Putwain, D. W., & Daniels, R. A. (2010). Is there a relationship between competence beliefs and test anxiety influenced by goal orientation? *Learning and Individual Differences, 20*(1), 8–13. doi:10.1016/j.lindif.2009.10.006

Roach, A. T., Beddow, P. A., Kurz, A., Kettler, R. J., & Elliott, S. N. (2010). Incorporating student input in developing alternate assessments based on modified academic standards. *Exceptional Children, 77,* 61–80.

Rothman, D. K. (2004). New approach to test anxiety. *Journal of College Student Psychotherapy, 18*(4), 45–60. doi:10.1300/J035v18n04_05

Rotter, K. (2006). Creating instructional materials for all pupils. Try COLA. *Intervention in School and Clinic, 41,* 273–282. doi:10.1177/1053451206041005040

Rozalski, M. E. (2007). Practice, practice, practice: How to improve students' study skills. *Beyond Behavior, 17*(1), 17–23.

Russell, M., Hoffmann, T., & Higgins, J. (2009). NimbleTools: A universally designed test delivery system. *TEACHING Exceptional Children, 42*(2), 6–12.

Salend, S. J. (2009). *Classroom testing and assessment for all: Beyond standardization.* Thousand Oaks, CA: Corwin Press.

Salend, S. J. (2011). *Creating inclusive classrooms: Effective and reflective practices* (7th ed.). Columbus, OH: Pearson Education.

Savage, T. V., Savage, K., & Armstrong, D. G. (2006). *Teaching in the secondary school* (6th ed.). Upper Saddle River, NJ: Merrill/Prentice Hall.

Stowell, J. R., & Bennett, D. (2010). Effects of online testing on student exam performance and test anxiety. *Journal of Educational Computing Research, 42,* 161–171. doi:10.2190/EC.42.2.b

Strichart, S. S., & Mangrum, C. T. (2010). *Study skills for learning disabled and struggling students* (4th ed.). Upper Saddle River, NJ: Merrill/Pearson Education.

Swanson, S., & Howell, C. (1996). Test anxiety in adolescents with learning disabilities and behavior disorders. *Exceptional Children, 62,* 389–397.

Therrien, W. J., Hughes, C., Kapelski, C., & Mokhtari, K (2009). Effectiveness of a test-taking strategy on achievement in essay tests for students with learning disabilities. *Journal of Learning Disabilities, 42*(1), 14–23. doi:10.1177/0022219408326218

Walker C., & Schmidt, E. (2004). *Smart tests: Teacher-made tests that help students learn.* Portland, ME: Stenhouse.

Whitaker Sena, J. D., Lowe, P. A., & Lee, S. W. (2007). Significant predictors of test anxiety among students with and without learning disabilities. *Journal of Learning Disabilities, 40,* 360–376. doi:10.1177/00222194070400040601

Woods, K., Parkinson, G., & Lewis, S. (2010). Investigating access to educational assessment for students with disabilities. *School Psychology International, 31*(1), 21–41. doi:10.1177/0143034310341622

Yell, M. L., & Rozalski, M. E. (2008). Academic interventions: Effective instruction. In M. Yell, N. Meadows, E. Drasgow, & J. Shriner (Eds.), *Educating students with emotional and behavioral disorders in general and special education classrooms* (pp. 282–335). Upper Saddle River, NJ: Merrill/Pearson Education.

Spencer J. Salend (New York CEC), Professor of Educational Studies, Department of Educational Studies, State University of New York at New Paltz, New York.

Address correspondence concerning this article to Spencer J. Salend, Department of Educational Studies, State University of New York at New Paltz, 1 Hawk Drive, New Paltz, NY 12561 (e-mail: salends@newpaltz.edu).